W9-CHB-834

THE LAST INNOCENT YEAR

THE LAST INNOCENT YEAR

AMERICA IN

1964

The Beginning of the "Sixties"

JON MARGOLIS

Perennial

An Imprint of HarperCollins*Publishers*

A hardcover edition of this book was published in 1999 by William Morrow and Company, Inc.

THE LAST INNOCENT YEAR. Copyright © 1999 by Jon Margolis. All rights reserved. Printed in the United States of America. No part of this book may be used or reproduced in any manner whatsoever without written permission except in the case of brief quotations embodied in critical articles and reviews. For information address HarperCollins Publishers Inc., 10 East 53rd Street, New York, NY 10022.

HarperCollins books may be purchased for educational, business, or sales promotional use. For information please write: Special Markets Department, HarperCollins Publishers Inc., 10 East 53rd Street, New York, NY 10022.

First Perennial edition published 2000.

Designed by Ann Gold

Library of Congress Cataloguing-in-Publication Data is available.

ISBN 0-688-17907-X (pbk.)

00   01   02   03   04   ❖ / RRD   10   9   8   7   6   5   4   3   2   1

For February 15

INTRODUCTION

There never was an innocent year.

No notion is more naive (which is not the same as innocent) than the one supposing America ever had an innocence to lose, a peculiar conceit in a country that began as a slave society in the process of exterminating the folks who got here first. One need not feel guilty about this history to recognize it and to acknowledge its inconsistency with innocence.

But there was a time when the delusion of innocence was easy to believe, when the myth was at least as useful as it was deceiving. That time ended when 1964 did.

If the delusion of innocence ended in 1964, something else began: the Sixties. The calendar tells us decades begin when the next-to-last number of the year changes. We know better. When Americans at century's end hear that now-clichéd term *the Sixties,* the hopeful and relatively placid years of John Kennedy's campaign and presidency do not come to mind. Their tumultuous aftermath does. If the tumult did not start in 1964, it blossomed then.

In retrospect we can see that it was in the opening days of his presidency that Lyndon Johnson took the steps that would cost him his job four years later; that the rioting in city streets first began in 1964; that the anger of middle-class working people, whom Richard Nixon would later call the "silent majority," revealed itself in the first stirrings of "white backlash" and in the distaste for cultural elites exploited by the Goldwater movement.

If there were earlier rumblings of the political sea change that transformed the South from dependably Democratic to predominantly Republican, certainly it was in 1964 that those rumblings became unmistakably audible.

However badly Barry Goldwater was beaten in 1964, without his campaign—his movement—Ronald Reagan could never have been elected in 1980. The nationwide triumph of political liberalism that occurred on November 5, 1964, was the last. Within it lay the seeds of the conservative ascendancy that began two years later and that to some extent continues.

Curiously, it was in 1964 that cultural liberalism—or perhaps "liberation"—the ascendancy of which also continues, invaded the mainstream. It did not begin then any more than did the Goldwater movement. Both had roots stretching back at least into the 1940s. But if some people had smoked marijuana, dressed exotically, embraced Eastern mysticism, written or painted erotica, and spoken openly about sex in earlier years, it was in 1964 that this kind of behavior burst out of its Bohemian ghetto; all of a sudden, more than a few middle-class suburbanites were studying Zen, puffing pot, and taking Allen Ginsberg seriously.

From every perspective except the calendar's, 1964 started forty days early, when John F. Kennedy was murdered in Dallas. The wonder is that the belief in American innocence was not murdered that day, too. In retrospect, perhaps it was, but because beliefs do not die as cleanly as people do, their deaths can escape recognition. America spent the months after John Kennedy's death in denial. A few clung to the idea of an ersatz resurrection by hoping that Kennedy's successor would choose Robert Kennedy as vice president. Almost everyone tried to tell him- or herself that the assassination, for all its horror, was an aberration, that the country and its culture remained strong, healthy, and essentially unchanged. They were wrong.

On January 1, 1964, the dourest observer of the passing scene could not foresee a country in which students would rise up against their elders, city dwellers would set fire to their neighborhoods, large numbers of privileged young people would openly flout the law, and women would begin to wonder whether the male sex was their oppressor.

By year's end, the most optimistic observer of the passing scene would have wondered about all that—if an optimistic observer could be found. For 1964 was the first year since the end of World War II, if not in the twentieth century, in which events challenged, if they did not overwhelm, America's habitual optimism. Sure, there had always been naysayers and grouches—from Thoreau to Mark Twain to Ambrose Bierce—but these had been a minority even among the intellectuals. The prevailing ethos had been that although there were problems aplenty, they could all be solved thanks to democracy, freedom, the market economy, and plain old American know-how.

That ethos was not destroyed in 1964, but it was shaken, and the shaking came from the American people themselves, who rose up—not as one, but as many diverse, disagreeing (and disagreeable) factions—against the elites who had been governing them. For the first time, some even wondered whether America's problems *should* be solved. These uprisings destroyed the consensus.

Godfrey Hodgson, in *America in Our Time,* his excellent book about the 1960s, called it the Liberal Consensus. But as Hodgson would acknowledge, it was a conservative liberalism that ruled, in culture as well as in politics, and perhaps its internal contradiction is what eventually did it in.

What few observers could (or perhaps would) recognize at the time was that the consensus was largely confined to the elites. Not that there was perfect harmony among the various elites who had dominated the country since the end of World War II; conservative corporate executives and liberal academics disagreed over a host of issues. But they shared what Doris Kearns Goodwin called "America's faith in itself as a good society."

As 1964 began, and as it progressed, these elites had good reason not simply to hold that belief, but to be pleased with themselves for the way they implemented it. In the middle of the year, the centrists of both parties forced through the Congress passage of the single most progressive and potent law in the history of the republic, the Civil Rights Act, designed to end America's own version of apartheid, to extend equal rights under law to the descendants of African slaves, and to end the shame and the isolation of the South.

It did all that and more. But despite its success, by the end of the year, the country was more Balkanized than it had been at the beginning. Black Americans were no longer excluded from the commonwealth, but the commonwealth itself—the very idea that there was or ought to be a commonwealth—was under attack.

Nor was it just in the establishment that things split asunder. The antiestablishment was similarly afflicted. The civil rights movement, which began the year united, ended it bitterly divided. The peace movement, tiny though it was, found itself already split between moderates and radicals. Even the counterculture had its countertrends.

Something else began in 1964: the personalizing of politics and culture. One of the first young men to burn his draft card explained that "the basic issue is my right of choice." In other words, he was not doing it for the Vietnamese, or for peace or social justice, but for his psyche. Before 1964, no one had spoken this way, at least not in general circulation newspapers. Later, it became commonplace.

|||

This book makes no claim to tell it all. Longer books have been written about some of the specific events contained herein: the election, the rise of

Goldwater conservatism and of the New Left, Freedom Summer and its violence, the Gulf of Tonkin incident, the coming of the Beatles. There is no point in repeating what has been amply described.

Instead, my goal has been to integrate, to place in their context, the central events of the end of 1963 and most of 1964 that remain relevant today. Events, of course, do not just happen. People make them happen. So this is also about the people who made history that year.

If I have succeeded, I owe thanks to a great many people: to Nelson Polsby at the University of California's Institute for Governmental Studies, who let me pretend to be a scholar for a month so I could use the wonderful libraries at the Berkeley campus; to David Roepke at the John Ashbrook Foundation; to Steve Fisher at Denver University's library and Carol Bowers at the American Heritage collection at the University of Wyoming; to the staffs at the Lyndon Johnson Presidential Library in Austin and the John F. Kennedy Library in Boston, the Bailey Howe Library at the University of Vermont, and the libraries at Johnson and Lyndon State Colleges.

Needless to say, I owe thanks to everyone who agreed to sit down in person or talk with me on the phone about their memories of that year. I thank them all for any wisdom contained herein; the foolishness is all mine.

I say to my colleagues of the Senate that perhaps in your lives you will be able to tell your children's children that you were here for America to make the year 1964 our freedom year. I urge my colleagues to make that dream of full freedom, full justice, and full citizenship for every American a reality by their votes on this day, and it will be remembered until the ending of the world.

—Hubert Humphrey, July 1964

There is a stir in the land. There is a mood of uneasiness. We feel adrift in an uncharted and stormy sea. We feel we have lost our way.

—Barry Goldwater, September 1964

There is a time when the operation of the machine becomes so odious, makes you so sick at heart, that you can't take part; you can't even passively take part, and you've got to put your bodies upon the gears and upon the wheels, upon the levers, upon all the apparatus and you've got to make it stop. And you've got to indicate to the people who run it, to the people that own it, that unless you're free, the machines will be prevented from working at all.

—Mario Savio, November 1964

THE LAST INNOCENT YEAR

| **1** |

NOT ENTIRELY LEGITIMATE

At the last minute, Lyndon Johnson decided to go to the Oval Office. Yes, it might be awkward, and he knew it might be misunderstood, taking the office of a man not twenty-four hours dead. But Johnson had long ago grown accustomed to being misunderstood, and anyway, it was his office now. That's what his secretaries of state and defense had told him the night before, and the national security director, too. The world had to see the seamless solidity of the American government, they told him.

He knew.

Still, he felt . . . well, not entirely legitimate. He was the president of the United States by right and duty, but not by election, and whatever else he knew that misty Saturday morning, November 23, 1963, he knew that much of the country would see him as a usurper, in spirit if not in fact or law.

All the more reason to go right to the Oval Office. It wasn't just foreign officials who had to see the orderly transfer of power; the American people needed to see it as well. And perhaps so did their new president.

So when his car came through the gate into the White House grounds, Johnson told his driver to take him to the West Wing instead of the entrance of the Old Executive Office Building, where his vice presidential office was located.

The president knew he would not be the first to arrive. Earlier that morning, from his home in northwest Washington—the one he would soon leave—he had already called Jack Kennedy's press secretary, Pierre Salinger, and urged him not to quit. "I need you more than he needed you," Johnson told Salinger. Now, just outside the Oval Office, he encountered Evelyn Lincoln, who had been Kennedy's secretary for years and who was busily packing up his belongings. Johnson asked her to step into the Oval Office. Across the room from the desk, two small sofas faced each other. The new president sat down on one. Mrs. Lincoln started toward the nearby rocking chair, then thought the better of it and took the sofa opposite Johnson.

"I need you more than you need me," he told her, "but because of overseas"—he must have meant America's image abroad—"I also need a transition. I have an appointment at nine-thirty. Can I have my girls in your office by nine-thirty?" He'd feel more comfortable with his own secretaries.

That was less than an hour away, but Mrs. Lincoln had no other choice but to agree. Shaken, she went back to the outer office—her office—where she found another visitor.

Robert Kennedy had been out walking on the South Lawn of the White House, and his eyes had been soothed by the rain, his mind refocused on his duty, which was to his dead brother. He had already made one major decision that morning, agreeing with his widowed sister-in-law that John Kennedy's coffin would remain closed. Now he wanted to make sure that his brother's personal papers were removed from the Oval Office desk and the desk itself taken away. He expected to find the office empty, the desk as his brother had left it, the papers untouched.

He certainly did not expect to be told by Evelyn Lincoln that Lyndon Johnson was already in the office, for all they knew sitting at the desk, rifling through the papers.

"Do you know he asked me to be out by nine-thirty," she told Kennedy.

"Oh, no," Kennedy said, and he must have said it loud enough for Johnson to hear, because in a moment the door to the Oval Office opened and the president said to his attorney general, "I want to talk to you."

It was an unrequited desire, and though Robert Kennedy did not refuse to speak to his president, he did refuse to enter that office for the conversation. They went into a smaller room near the presidential bathroom.

"I need you more than he needed you," Johnson said.

"I don't want to talk about that now," Kennedy said. He wanted to talk about giving Mrs. Lincoln more time. In the best of circumstances, arranging the papers of the president of the United States in an orderly manner takes a few hours. These were not the best of circumstances.

"Can't you wait?" Kennedy said.

"Well, of course," Johnson said. She could have until 11:30.[1]

| | |

It had never gone well between them, not since Bob Kennedy had come to Johnson's hotel room in Los Angeles during the 1960 Democratic Convention to try to talk him into turning down the vice presidential nomination, the offer Jack Kennedy had made assuming it would be rejected.

Johnson knew Robert Kennedy disliked him. At a White House social event one evening in 1962, he stood in the small kitchen that the Kennedys had installed in the living quarters and baited—or was it begged?—Bobby about it.

"Bobby, you do not like me," Johnson said. "Your brother likes me. Your sister-in-law likes me. Your daddy likes me. But you don't like me. Now, why? Why don't you like me?"

The two men were not alone. This was a very un-Kennedy thing to do— losing restraint, embarrassing people. Kennedy did not reply. As a good lawyer, he knew that silence implies consent. Johnson thought Kennedy held a grudge because Johnson had criticized Kennedy's father, Ambassador Joseph Kennedy, at the 1960 Democratic Convention, something Johnson denied he had done.

He had, but Kennedy barely remembered it. What he did remember was his conclusion that Johnson "lies all the time. . . . He lies even when he doesn't have to lie."[2] Another thing bothered Kennedy. At one point, he remembered, Johnson had said to him, "You know, none of the people that work for me are any good." Even without that confession, Kennedy had seen Johnson yell and swear at his associates and his staff, as though by dressing them down he could build himself up.[3] He had heard Johnson mispronounce the names of his closest associates, regularly referring to Bill D. Moyers as "Moyer."

Kennedy didn't like that. He was the rich kid who'd chosen working-class roommates at Harvard, who had decided to join the Navy as an enlisted man. He always went out of his way to be nice to the little guys. Maybe that's because he was a little guy himself.

How could they possibly get along now, after their world had been turned upside down? Yesterday morning, Robert Kennedy was the second most powerful man in America and Lyndon Johnson was in storage. Now Johnson was president and Kennedy worked for him.

"Bobby Kennedy's just another lawyer now," Jimmy Hoffa said when he heard the news from Dallas.

No, he was attorney general of the United States. But he was just another cabinet member and the president's least favorite.

It had also not gone well between them the night before, on the evening after the assassination. Kennedy, who thought it would be fitting if his fallen brother returned to Washington as president, had been offended that Johnson wanted to take the oath of office immediately, unable or unwilling to see that the stricken public needed the assurance of presidential continuity more than the symbolic homage to the dead.

Then, when the plane with Johnson and his wife, with John Kennedy's body and his bloodstained widow, returned to Andrews Air Force Base, Robert Kennedy walked immediately to Jacqueline Kennedy's side. Johnson took it as a snub, unable or unwilling to see that the first impulse of a mourning family is mutual comfort.

Now, in the White House, it wasn't just their relationship that was new. Even Robert Kennedy didn't realize it, but he had been transformed into something that had never before existed in America. He was a prince pretender.

The Kennedys weren't like the other political families—Adamses, Harrisons, Roosevelts—fathers and sons or cousins, not brothers—in which one generation had given up (or lost) power long before the other reached for it. Besides, neither John Adams, Benjamin Harrison, nor Teddy Roosevelt had been murdered.

John Kennedy had, and his murder had triggered something akin to a metamorphosis, changing his brother into something for which American politics had no name or point of reference. Even Shakespeare had not come up with a plot this complicated; no brother of Richard II retained an honored place at the court of Henry IV.

America's political vocabulary had no term for family dynasties. *Houses* were chambers of a legislative body, not tribes plotting to take power. *Restoration* referred to fixing up old houses. What other changes had Lee Harvey Oswald wrought?

| | |

A few minutes later, back across the street in his vice presidential office, President Johnson received his first official briefing from John McCone, the director of Central Intelligence. And what McCone told him—that Lee Harvey Oswald had been in contact with the Russians—came as no surprise. From the moment Secret Service Agent Emory Roberts told him that Jack Kennedy was going to die, Lyndon Johnson was certain that some malevolent conspiracy had made him president of the United States.

But whose conspiracy was it? He suspected Fidel Castro, whose communist beachhead on Cuba had withstood a Kennedy-backed invasion in 1961. But he wasn't sure and didn't want to be, which is one reason he wasn't sure he wanted some hotshot commission looking into the assassination. If Castro or the Russians had been responsible, the pressure on Johnson to retaliate would be hard to resist. He did not want to begin his presidency with a war.[4]

Besides, Johnson's years in Congress had taught him about commissions. They went on forever. A commission would have to recruit a staff, find office space, get itself organized. It might be weeks before it actually started investigating and months before it finished, with each of its meetings and announcements getting into the newspapers, prolonging the period in which the country would live in the shadow of John Kennedy's murder.

It would be ghoulish.

||

For all the extent and variety of her wardrobe, Jacqueline Kennedy owned only one black dress. She had worn it just twice—when her husband announced his presidential candidacy and when her son was christened. Saturday morning, waking from a drug-induced sleep, she put it on for the third time. She had tasks to perform.[5]

Mass had been scheduled for 10 A.M., not in the East Room but in the family dining room, on the assumption that the widow would not be able to bear being in the same room with the coffin. But when she walked into the dining room, holding her children by the hand, she said, "Why is this here?" and Robert Kennedy told the priest to move the portable altar into the East Room.

Fresh from his meeting with John McCone, Lyndon Johnson joined the mourners. Slowly, he walked past the casket in the center of the room, covered by an American flag and resting on a catafalque—the word itself was unfamiliar to most Americans until that day.

When the service ended, Johnson and his wife, Lady Bird, crossed Lafayette Square to attend a brief Episcopal service at St. John's Church. Jackie Kennedy, who had nowhere to go, found herself comforting those who had come to comfort her, greeting the guests as they filed out of the room.

The last to leave was chief White House usher J. Bernard West. "Poor Mr. West," she said, taking his hand. He was unable to reply. "Will you take a walk with me?" He nodded. "Will you walk with me over to his office?" she said. All he could do was nod again, and off they went.

||

Outside the White House, people were standing in the rain. Some held umbrellas, but most did not bother. Some came for a few minutes, then hurried off; others stayed for much of the afternoon, barely moving, getting soaked.

It wasn't that there was much to look at. Yes, some celebrities passed by: Supreme Court justices, senators, newspaper columnists. But many in the crowd couldn't see the comings and goings, and wouldn't have recognized most of the officials had they gotten a good look at them. They just wanted to stand there, in the rain, as though time were standing still that day. They didn't know it, but they were not alone. All over the country—indeed, the world—ordinary men and women poured forth from their homes to gather in city squares, though nothing had been scheduled and nothing would occur.

I I I

When the president's first cabinet meeting began at 2:30 that afternoon, only the attorney general was not in his chair when Dean Rusk announced Johnson's arrival and led an opening prayer. Robert Kennedy's first impulse had been not to attend, but McGeorge Bundy convinced him that he had to go. When he arrived, late, some of the cabinet members rose. The president did not. He assumed—he knew—that Kennedy had deliberately walked in late to spoil the meeting.

But the next day, Sunday, November 24, Johnson and Kennedy rode together to the Capitol. The Johnsons came to the White House after church, just before noon, and waited for the Kennedy family in the Green Room. When they arrived, Eunice Shriver walked up to Lady Bird Johnson. "I hear Oswald has been killed," she said, as though reporting the latest turn in the weather.

Lyndon Johnson and Jacqueline Kennedy sat in the backseat of the limousine. Lady Bird Johnson and Robert Kennedy were in the jump seats, Caroline Kennedy was next to her mother, and John junior jumped from front seat to back. "John-John," his uncle said, "be good. You be good and we'll give you a flag afterward." In front of them walked Black Jack, the frisky riderless horse, and in front of him the caisson and coffin pulled by six white horses down Pennsylvania Avenue to the Capitol.[6]

The soldiers put the casket in the center of the Capitol Rotunda. Lyndon Johnson laid a wreath at its foot. Chief Justice Earl Warren and Senate Majority Leader Mike Mansfield spoke, and so did House Speaker John McCormack, seventy-one years old and next in line for the presidency until a new vice president took office in January of 1965. Jacqueline Kennedy and her daughter knelt at the casket's side. The widow kissed it; the child put her hand on the flag. When the ceremony was over, the Kennedys and the Johnsons left the Capitol in separate cars. President Johnson had another meeting to attend.

III

This time, in addition to McCone there were the secretaries of state and defense, Dean Rusk and Robert McNamara; Undersecretary of State George Ball; McGeorge Bundy, the president's special assistant for national security affairs; and Henry Cabot Lodge, the Republican whom Kennedy had chosen as ambassador to Vietnam.

It was an impressive assembly. Except for Bundy, all of them were big men, over six feet tall. All were men of obvious accomplishment and education—four could list Harvard or Yale on their resumes. And they were impeccably, if not uniformly, dressed. McNamara, as ever, had neither a wrinkle in his suit nor an errant hair on his head; later, the president would refer to him as "lard-hair man." Lodge, the aging Ivy Leaguer, wore loafers and a white handkerchief in the pocket of his suit jacket.

Physically, the odd man out was at the head of the conference table. Lyndon Johnson was the biggest of them all. He stood six feet three inches tall, and his head needed a seven and three-eighths size hat. His suit may have been tailored in London, but he seemed to bulge out of it, not because he was fat—he was rangy, not fat—but because his long legs and big chest rebelled.

At fifty-five years old, he was not the oldest man in the room, but his elongated face with its wrinkles, its drooping earlobes, and its double chin made him seem older. Maybe it was the heart attack Johnson had suffered a decade before. Maybe it was the years of hard drinking or the late nights running the Senate. Maybe there was no reason at all, but he looked more weathered than the others. A stranger knowing nothing of any of them could walk into the room and immediately pick him out as the one who'd grown up in the country.

There was nothing about Johnson that suggested Harvard or Yale. His one degree was a bachelor of science from San Marcos College in San Marcos, Texas. Of all the men in the room, only he had not grown up in a world that took higher education for granted.

For all their similarity, these seven men were not of one mind on the subject of their meeting: what to do about the pesky little war in the far-off Southeast Asian land of Vietnam, a place few Americans knew or cared much about.

Lodge was the most optimistic. He had to be. Of all the Americans involved, he had been the most enthusiastic supporter of the Vietnamese generals who only a few weeks earlier had overthrown, and murdered, South Vietnamese president Ngo Dinh Diem. It wasn't that Lodge favored murder. He was too proper a New Englander for that and was perhaps too proper a

New Englander to have known that the generals never intended to let Diem live. But he did believe that the new government would be more effective than Diem's.

Lodge was point man for the "hearts and minds" school of the conflicts in Southeast Asia, the enlightened cold war intellectuals who saw the struggle in Vietnam as essentially political. They believed that the United States had to help the South Vietnamese government do more than simply kill guerrillas and control land; they also had to win the loyalty of the Vietnamese peasantry.

The soldiers who were already there thought they were in a war, and wars were won by fighting. Like most military men, General Paul Harkins, the top U.S. soldier in Vietnam, had been opposed to cooperating with the coup. He and Lodge were barely speaking.

Among those who thought the generals had a good case had been Vice President Lyndon Johnson. Nobody had consulted with him at the time, but if they had, he might have told them that he thought Henry Cabot Lodge was a pompous fool. He might also have told them that a photograph of Ngo Dinh Diem hung on a wall of the Elms, the Johnson home in the Spring Valley section of northwest Washington.

Now, the discussion was only about how to help the South Vietnamese government. *Whether* to help was never considered, nor was withdrawing the 15,500 American soldiers advising the South Vietnamese Army. Even to entertain such a thought would have been to challenge the consensus, which these men would never do. After all, the consensus was theirs, and it transcended politics, which is why it could survive political bickering. It was less political than intellectual and cultural, so Republicans and Democrats could assail each other at campaign time, then work together later. They disagreed only over the specifics, over means to the end, not over what that end should be.

For proof, all one had to do was go back to the last presidential election. For all the passions John Kennedy and Richard Nixon aroused, they had agreed on the basics: the primacy of foreign affairs, containment (but not isolation) of the Soviet Union, firm but indirect management of the economy, gradual expansion of equal rights for Negroes.

So similar were the candidates' views that Harvard professor and Kennedy friend Arthur Schlesinger Jr., concerned that liberal intellectuals were insufficiently committed to the Kennedy cause, felt impelled to compose a book-length polemic: *Kennedy or Nixon: Does It Make Any Difference?* Yes, the professor answered. He was right. It did make a difference, but within the parameters of the prevailing consensus.

On that November Sunday, therefore, only one man in the room would mention the possibility of leaving South Vietnam to its own devices. That was the president, who noted that some members of the Congress were wondering whether Vietnam was worth the trouble. He wondered himself, and wondered too whether anything the United States did would work.

"I have misgivings," he said. "I feel like a fish that just grabbed a worm with a big hook in the middle of it."

But he would not allow those misgivings to dominate him. "We'll stand by our word," he said.

III

This business with the telephones would not do.

National 8-1414 was the White House number. Anyone could dial it— NA 8-1414—but there didn't seem to be any *system*. Johnson would be talking with someone and then suddenly he would be interrupted by one of his secretaries because she didn't realize he was on the phone.

"Everybody just keeps coming on," he barked at them. "Now I can't work with an office like that. If the telephone system can't work, will you just tell 'em I'll have to go home?"

Go home? He had just gotten there two days earlier. It was Monday, November 25, the day of John Kennedy's funeral, officially proclaimed by his successor as a national day of mourning. Even so, the office was now Lyndon Johnson's, and it would have to be run his way.

At this moment, the confusion was especially annoying because J. Edgar Hoover was on the line, and Johnson knew he had to stay alert while talking to Hoover. Later, the president would refer to Hoover as a "sovereignty," but right now he was determined to stay on the FBI director's good side. It was no help when the phones didn't work right.

"Mr. Hoover on 2383," said one of Johnson's secretaries.

"Let me find it," he said.

He knew what Hoover wanted, or at least what Hoover didn't want. He didn't want some special commission set up to investigate the assassination, as if the Bureau couldn't do the job. Johnson wasn't sure he wanted a commission, either. Who knew what it might find out?

"We can't be checking up on every shooting scrape in the country," Johnson said, letting Hoover know that he had his president's sympathy. The assassination had taken place in Texas, so it was clearly a job for Texas state officials. With the help, of course, of the professionals at the FBI.

"You can offer them your full cooperation and vice versa," the president said.

Hoover agreed. "We'll both work together on it."

That was all well and good, but first they would have to stop this commission idea, and Johnson wasn't sure they could. The next morning's *Washington Post* was coming out with an editorial in favor of it.

Hoover had no influence with the *Post*. "I frankly don't read it," he said. "I view it like the *Daily Worker*."

| | |

Unlike Lady Bird Johnson, most Americans did not have to be told that Lee Harvey Oswald had been killed. They saw it happen. It was the most public murder in the history of the world, the first ever seen on live television, and it happened when almost everyone was watching television and when all the stations were dealing with the same subject. The television sets were turned on, not to entertain but to heal. John F. Kennedy's assassination created America's—probably the world's—first case of mass psychosis, with most people reporting the standard symptoms: sleeplessness, nervousness, disorientation, weeping.[7] With the possible exception of Japan after Hiroshima and Nagasaki, never before had any public event so shaken an entire society.

Neither Lincoln's assassination nor Roosevelt's death had had the same impact. Both men were older when they died, and their war-weary people were accustomed to violence. John Kennedy was forty-six years old, and the country was not simply at peace; it was dominated by a harmonious consensus in which ideological bickering had been replaced by rational analysis.

Or so it told itself.

Besides, those earlier presidential deaths might as well have taken place in another country. They were pretelevision, and television, by bringing the president into almost every living room almost every day, had transformed the relationship between him and the people. Thanks to television (and radio), 90 percent of the American people heard about Kennedy's death within two hours. Thanks to television, everyone who chose to could take part in the mourning. Most of them did.

The three networks quickly dropped all regular programming. *The Lawrence Welk Show* and *Gunsmoke* were not shown Saturday night; *Wagon Train, The Ed Sullivan Show,* and *My Favorite Martian* could not be seen on Sunday. The networks even decided to air no commercial advertisements until the funeral was over.

Because almost all television stations were network affiliates, the blackout of regular programming was all but universal. And television set the tone, virtually shaming theaters into closing, radio stations into altering both the tone and content of their programs. Broadway went dark, so it was impossible for a few days to see the performances of *How to Succeed in Business Without Really Trying* or *Beyond the Fringe*. It was not impossible that weekend to hear Chubby Checker sing "Hooka Tooka" or go to the movies to see Cary Grant bamboozle Audrey Hepburn in *Charade*. But it wasn't easy.

There were recalcitrants. Some complained because the movies and the college football games were canceled and because the National Football League games, which went on that Sunday as though nothing had happened, were not televised.[8]

But it was a big, varied country, with people of all political stripes and personal peculiarities. If not quite everyone was afflicted, most were, and so they mourned together, not least because they had the mechanism for it. For millions, turning on the TV had become the first, instinctive reaction, as though this machine was the comforter of first resort. It met their expectations.

Television, which the Federal Communications Commission chairman appointed by John Kennedy had labeled a "vast wasteland," demonstrated another ability. It could create a national living room. On Monday more than 100 million Americans—93 percent of the country—watched their president's funeral.[9] Never before had so many people done the same thing at the same time.

Columnist Anthony La Camera, a Boston boy, may have been overstating when he proclaimed, "In the history of all mankind there has never been anything quite like it."[10] But surely there had never been anything quite like it in the memory of any living American. Getting over it would take some doing.

|||

George Wallace did not have a ticket to the funeral Mass. Considering that not even Nikita Khrushchev had given John Kennedy more trouble over the past three years, Wallace's uncredentialed status was something less than a shock. Still, he was upset. Unlike Martin Luther King, whose feelings were also hurt at not being invited to the funeral mass, Wallace tried to get into the church. King stood with the crowds on the street watching the cortege go by. Wallace finagled his way inside. With no assigned seat, he had to improvise, but he managed. After all, improvisation was his forte.

Wallace's presence at the funeral was not devoid of political calculation, but there was nothing phony about his grief. Those were real tears seeping from his eyes. The assassination had rendered him speechless. He had been up in Haleyville, in the northwestern corner of Alabama, helping to dedicate a new high school, and the news came just as he was introduced.

He couldn't go to the podium. He sat up, then sat back down. The music director of the First Baptist Church sang "The Lord's Prayer" to give his governor time to recover, and when the song ended, Wallace finally made it to the podium. But he was almost tongue-tied. All he could do was blurt out a few words and then sit down.

When the four little Negro girls had been blown up in the Birmingham church basement just nine weeks earlier, Wallace had taken it in stride, perhaps knowing that the murderers supported him, perhaps sensing his own responsibility. But this crime shook him to his core. He ordered the state's flags flown at half-staff and wrote Mrs. Kennedy a long note. It was as though he'd lost a friend. Like so many of Kennedy's foes, Wallace had found the man appealing.

Perhaps, also, appealing to run against. In January, three days before his inauguration as governor, Wallace had met in Montgomery's Jefferson Davis Hotel with former Mississippi governor Ross Barnett, Louisiana political leader Leander Perez, and John Synon, a segregationist newspaper columnist from Virginia, along with five other men associated with the white citizens council movement throughout the South. Synon, one of the founders of Americans for Constitutional Action, was urging Southern politicians to mount an "independent elector" movement, with slates headed by popular segregationists. The idea was to keep either party's presidential candidate from winning an electoral majority.

It was a political pipe dream, and nothing came of it except to interest Wallace in extending his political reach beyond Alabama. Early in November he had gone on a Northern lecture tour and heard some of the same cheers in Connecticut, in Colorado, and in California that so often greeted him in Alabama. Perhaps the politics of race need not be confined to the South. He had always suspected as much. That was why his inaugural address had been as much national as local; he had gone out of his way to defy John Kennedy and his brother.

"We will tolerate their boot in our face no longer," he had proclaimed. Alabama's enemy was the federal government, which "encourages everything degenerate and base" and attempts to suppress white people all over the world.

"The Belgian survivors of the Congo cannot present their case," he said, "nor [can] the citizens of Oxford, Mississippi," and he repeated the slogan that had won him the election: "Segregation forever."

Wallace was not much at careful analysis; he acted by instinct, and his instinct had granted him an extraordinary insight: Attacking government was the way to export the politics of race.

It was a lesson some Republicans were learning, too.

| | |

In Dallas, an uneasy Rabbi Hillel Silverman of Congregation Shearith Israel visited the most famous member of his congregation, Jack Ruby, in the county jail.

"I did it for the Jews," Ruby told him, for the Jews and for Jacqueline Kennedy, so she would not have to testify at Oswald's trial. He had read in the Sunday paper that she might have to return to Dallas for the trial. He could not bear the thought of it.

| | |

Senator Hubert Humphrey's tears at the cathedral were at least as sincere as Wallace's; he had been a more civil opponent when he ran against Kennedy for the 1960 nomination, and it had not been difficult for him to transform himself into a supporter and something of a friend. Still, like Wallace, Humphrey calculated his political future as he mourned.

Hubert Humphrey wanted very much to be president, and after his failure in 1960 he had figured out that with his disadvantages—not much money, not much glamour—his best route was through the vice presidency, a position suddenly vacant. He was already planning to apply. Over the weekend, he had discussed his chances with old allies—Adlai Stevenson, Chester Bowles, Bill Benton. On the morning of the funeral, he'd even called his old friend Marvin Rosenberg in New York, inviting him to a strategy meeting on Thursday. "It's very important," Humphrey told him.[11]

Humphrey also had a more limited, more immediate, political task at the funeral. On Sunday night, his dinner at home with Adlai Stevenson and a few other friends had been interrupted by a phone call from Lyndon Johnson. The president wanted to know how many votes Humphrey had against an amendment to the farm bill that would come to the Senate floor on Tuesday. Humphrey didn't know.

"That's the trouble with the place up there," Johnson had said. "You fellows don't have the votes counted." That had hurt, coming from the one-time master of the Senate floor, and Humphrey vowed he'd get a count. He was not the Majority Leader, merely the deputy, but Lyndon Johnson had put him in that slot, and everybody knew it. If he had to cadge votes at St. Matthew's Cathedral or at Arlington Cemetery, so be it. This was his first assignment from President Lyndon Johnson, whom he mightily wished to please.

| | |

Richard Russell and Barry Goldwater cried while they calculated, too. Ceremonies in general had that effect on both of them, especially military ceremony. Russell's passion was Civil War history; Goldwater's was flying for the Air National Guard. Both of them were easily moved by the sight of honor guards. Besides, they were sentimental men.

Perhaps no one in Washington had shed more tears on hearing the news than Richard Russell had, though by then his support for Kennedy had all but evaporated. For a time, the president's prudence and moderation had pleased Russell, but that had disappeared the previous summer when Kennedy proposed his civil rights bill, making clear that he shared the commitment to end forever the great love of Richard Russell's life—the racially segregated society of the South.

Still, it had been hours before he had been able to stop crying about Kennedy and to think about the man who was once his protégé, now his president.

"Lyndon Johnson has all of the talents, the abilities, and the equipment to make a very good president of this country, a very good president," Russell told his staff. "And of course old Lyndon is going to enjoy being president. He'll enjoy every minute of it, every hour of it."

As much, Russell knew, as he himself would not enjoy it. He had no doubt that Johnson would push as hard as Kennedy had for civil rights. Maybe harder. And it would be so much harder for Russell to fight Johnson than it would have been to fight Jack Kennedy. He was only fond of Kennedy; he did not love him.

Barry Goldwater's political calculation also reflected his personal feelings about the two presidents. For all their political differences, Goldwater and Jack Kennedy—earthy, blunt-spoken men who enjoyed a drink and a joke—liked each other. Goldwater had looked forward to running against Kennedy; the campaign would have been a civilized discussion of the issues. The two of them had even talked about getting on a train together and debating each other around the country. There would be no such talk with Johnson. Goldwater didn't like Johnson at all, and he figured a campaign against him could get dirty. It would also be tougher. Goldwater may have been unschooled, but he was politically shrewd, and he doubted the electorate would want three presidents in fourteen months. By the day of the funeral, Goldwater, the front-running Republican in the public opinion polls, had decided not to run.[12]

|||

The mourners at the estate outside Millbrook, New York, northeast of Poughkeepsie, did not need the help of television as they held their rituals that weekend for both of their "departed guides," John Kennedy and Aldous Huxley. Huxley had died the same day, struggling to write about Shakespeare and to read Timothy Leary's manual based on the *Tibetan Book of the Dead*.[13] Huxley died after two final shots of LSD—it didn't kill him; it merely altered his final moments—administered by his wife, Laura, who whispered to him at the end that he was "going, willing and consciously, and you are doing this beautifully; you are doing this so beautifully—you are going toward the light."[14]

To most people, Huxley was best known for writing *Brave New World,* the 1932 novel that looked into the superscientific future and found it horrible. To Timothy Leary and his friends at that Dutchess County estate, the more important Huxley book was his 1954 *Doors of Perception,* which he wrote after he first took mescaline and approached "the Pure Light of the Void." It was an experience that convinced him that Westerners should "be shaken out of the ruts of ordinary perception, to be shown for a few timeless hours the outer and the inner world, not as they appear to an animal obsessed with survival or to a human being obsessed with words . . . but as they are apprehended, directly and unconditionally, by Mind at Large."

Thanks in part to Huxley's influence, Leary, a psychology professor at Harvard, tried LSD. It changed his life. "Blow the mind and you are left with God and life—and life is sex," he wrote.

At Millbrook, he could seek all three.

|||

This Monday was not Lyndon Johnson's day, and he knew it. The horse-drawn casket led the procession, followed by the dead man's widow and his two surviving brothers, all three looking straight ahead, stone-faced but dry-eyed, walking steadily up Seventeenth Street and Connecticut Avenue toward St. Matthew's Cathedral. "Romans," Murray Kempton would call them in the *New Republic.*

Behind them were other members of the family, and five yards behind them were the Johnsons, so surrounded by Secret Service agents that they were barely visible to the thousands lining the sidewalks. But no one was looking at the Johnsons, any more than they were looking at Charles de Gaulle or Haile Selassie or Queen Frederika. No one even seemed to be looking at Robert or Edward Kennedy. All eyes were on the veiled woman between them.

|||

At 231 East Forty-seventh Street in Manhattan, Andy Warhol was distressed. Not because Jack Kennedy was dead but because of "the way television and radio were programming everybody to feel so sad." It wasn't that Warhol didn't like Kennedy. He'd found it thrilling that such a young, handsome, and smart fellow should be president. But he couldn't stand this collective, somewhat manufactured, sorrow. So he got his friends together and they "all went out to one of the Berlin bars on Eighty-sixth Street for dinner."

It was easy for Andy Warhol to get his friends together. He was a nucleus around whom others orbited. He wasn't gregarious as much as he was receptive, open to . . . well, to just about anything. Although there was much he would not do, there was nothing he would not discuss and almost no one of whom he disapproved, not even the proper and conventional.

He was thirty-three then (or close to it; he was always vague about his age), and although he was hardly the best-known artist in America, he was considered one of the most outrageous, for both his paintings and his personality. The paintings were lifelike reproductions of the common: boxes of Brillo soap pads, Campbell soup cans, and, increasingly since her death in 1962, portraits of Marilyn Monroe, as though he were obsessed by her death, or perhaps by death itself.

When he wasn't painting, Warhol took delight in flaunting the unconventional, if not bizarre, tenor of his life. Though he appeared asexual and temperate himself, the men around him were, in his own words, "mostly fags," and both the men and the women used his hospitality to take whatever drugs they could find.

His midtown loft was known as the Factory, and it attracted the offbeat artists, writers, and hangers-on in New York. They had names (or he gave them names)—Rotten Rita, the Mayor, Binghamton Birdie, Stanley the Turtle—reminiscent of the names Damon Runyon gave the characters in his stories, though what real-life versions of Harry the Horse and Nicely Nicely would have made of the skinny, spaced-out homosexuals at the Factory could be a subject of interesting discussion.

These were people who lived for the moment, for art, for style, for one another. What did they care about the president?

But Warhol's plan of avoiding the ceremonies of sorrow by gorging on German hot dogs didn't work. Even he and his friends were too depressed.

"David Bourdon was sitting across from Suzi Gablik, the art critic, and John Quinn, the playwright," Warhol later wrote, "and he was moaning over and over, 'But Jackie was the most glamorous First Lady we'll ever get.' "[15]

| | |

Jack Weinberg watched the funeral with friends in Berkeley, where most of them no longer went to school. They had not been big fans of President Kennedy—he was far too timid on civil rights for their taste—but they found themselves as absorbed by the proceedings as everyone else.

Weinberg had been in Professor Charlie Sellers's office when he heard about the assassination. Sellers was a professor of history, but Weinberg was not there on academic business. His field was math, and anyway, he'd dropped out of grad school to spend his time fighting for civil rights, which was why he was visiting Sellers, the head of the Berkeley branch of the Congress of Racial Equality. Jack was active in CORE, too, and he was one of the leaders of the protest demonstration scheduled for that Sunday to protest local hiring practices. He came to show Sellers the leaflets, but when he got there Sellers was on the phone learning the news.

It took Weinberg a few minutes to figure out that his demonstration wouldn't happen, so he just wandered the campus for a few minutes, noticing how much it had grown and changed in the two short years he had been in Berkeley.

According to its own boss, the University of California at Berkeley wasn't a university anymore; it was a "multiversity," said Clark Kerr, the president of the state university system. It had an "educational outlook attuned to [the] high-tech, military, space, agribusiness and entertainment economy," from which it received millions of dollars in government and corporate grants. But it attracted "a culture that is youthful, disheveled, searching and experimental, and resolutely antivocational."

Jack Weinberg was part of the disheveled culture. He'd grown up in Buffalo, New York, and majored in mathematics at the University of Buffalo but dropped out before getting his degree. He didn't know why, exactly, but he was bored. He went to Mexico, living in semipoverty and reading a lot of math textbooks. After a while he came home, got a job, got married, moved to California, got divorced, finished his bachelor's degree at Berkeley, and decided to go to graduate school.

Meanwhile, he had discovered the world around him. Like so many of his contemporaries, he'd grown up with what he later called "an idealistic version of America." He'd known nothing about racial discrimination; he hadn't even realized that Southern Negroes had trouble voting.

In some ways, Berkeley was a perfect place to learn about society's ills. For years, the place had attracted a small army of dissidents, devoted to the causes of free speech and racial equality. For Jack Weinberg—at loose ends, lonely, increasingly angry at injustice—these folks provided not just a cause, but a home. They filled a void in his life.[16]

|||

But what did it all *mean*?

That's what Tom Hayden and Dick and Mickey Flacks tried to figure out all weekend, all through Monday, sitting in the Flackses' living room with the TV on. Hayden had been on his way to a conference in Minneapolis on Friday. Like everything else, the conference got canceled, and Hayden got himself back to Ann Arbor. It was not a good time to be alone, which is what he was at home now that his marriage had broken up, so he spent the extended weekend with Dick and Mickey in front of their television, watching and questioning.

Lee Harvey Oswald they could figure out. They invented a whole new classification for him—he was of the "lurking class"—but beyond that they could not analyze; they had come, for the first time, face-to-face with a situation that defied analysis. Considering that analysis was their strong suit, this was a disconcerting development. Later, Hayden would write that "the tragic consciousness of the sixties generation began here," but at the time, he and Dick Flacks were befuddled. The assassination did not fit.

Their hero, the late sociologist C. Wright Mills, had taught them that whatever its flaws, American society was stable. It was safely—excessively—controlled by powerful elites with shared interests. Among those interests was order. How could they have let this happen?

This confusion might have been a product of youth. Hayden and Flacks were twenty-six years old. Yet for a couple of young guys, they had done a lot. The two of them had helped start a political organization, and Hayden was already its ex-president. It didn't really matter that the organization was made up of fewer than seven hundred paid-up members. There was no doubt in their minds that Students for a Democratic Society was about to become a political force.

The new president, Todd Gitlin, was twenty.

As a functioning organization, SDS existed only at Ann Arbor, where there were 123 members. The next biggest chapter was at Vassar, where 26 young women belonged. But at Hunter and Oberlin, at Texas and Wayne State, there were a few students who considered themselves members even if they hadn't paid dues, even if they had no contact with the grandly titled national office in New York.

Still, the first effort at a national "action" had flopped. When Mme. Ngo Dinh Nhu, President Diem's sister-in-law, came to the United States in September, Gitlin invited the dwindling Student Peace Union to cooperate in a demonstration against U.S. policy in Vietnam. Only five SDS supporters picketed in Washington; students were more concerned about civil rights than foreign affairs. Vietnam didn't seem likely to become a major problem. After all, Laos hadn't become one. On top of all that, SDS was running out of money, its office workers didn't like working in offices, and it didn't have a clear idea of what it wanted to do.

So? It had energy. It had attitude. And though even Hayden and Flacks couldn't know this that November weekend, soon it would have opportunity.

| | |

President Johnson was supposed to be standing near the Kennedy family at the cemetery, but things go awry at even the best-planned events, and somehow he found himself, still surrounded by guards, somewhere in the midst of the crowd. Members of the cabinet and leaders of the Congress were where he was supposed to be. "What the hell am I doing here?" he said to no one in particular. But it didn't really matter. The world was watching the coffin, listening to the salute of the guns and to the bugle playing "Taps."

Eight white-gloved soldiers folded the flag that covered the coffin, folded it into a perfect triangle, which the man at the head of the coffin clutched to his chest, then passed to the next man and across the coffin to the next, until all eight men had held it. The last of them, Sp/4 Douglas Mayfield, handed it to Jack Metzler, the cemetery's superintendent, who then presented it to Jacqueline Kennedy.

Roman or not, she had cried at the cathedral, once when the hymns began, again when Richard Cardinal Cushing broke from the Latin of the Mass and cried, "May the angels, dear Jack, lead you into Paradise."

But now she took the flag, without words but also without tears, and then took a torch and lit the flame at her husband's grave, a flame she had determined would never go out. Lyndon Johnson walked past it on his way to his car, on his way to begin his presidency.

2

"LET US CONTINUE"

A deal was a deal. Under some pressure, Senate Majority Leader Mike Mansfield had agreed to bring Karl Mundt's farm bill amendment to the floor, and the vote would be held on schedule, on Tuesday, the twenty-sixth of November.

Life had to go on.

To Hubert Humphrey, that meant it would go forward, toward prosperity, equality, peace, the very things he and Walter Reuther had been discussing the night before with Willy Brandt and the Social Democrats from Norway and Sweden who'd come to the funeral. It had been a good session, especially when Reuther assured the Europeans that Lyndon Johnson would carry on Kennedy's policies, explaining that Johnson had called him as early as Saturday night to say how much he needed his help. Johnson was a New Dealer, Reuther said, who supported public power and a better deal for the poor. His past transgressions—supporting Taft-Hartley, weakening the civil rights laws of 1957 and 1960—were simply the acts of a man honoring his constituency. Now that his constituency was the whole country, the real—the liberal—Lyndon Johnson would emerge.

Humphrey agreed. Reporting it all to Johnson the next afternoon, he summed up their common assessment. "We're on the way," he said.

But first there was this amendment, part of the counterrevolution of the troglodytes. Like the rest of the enlightened world, Jack Kennedy had wanted better relations with the Russians, and one way to do that was to sell them wheat. The United States certainly had enough of it, and the Russians didn't. But the thinking was that selling grain would provide a lubricant for other arrangements, perhaps a disarmament deal.

That's why almost everyone in town was for it: Democratic and Republican diplomats, foreign policy scholars, even corporate executives. Dwight

Eisenhower was not complaining about selling grain to the Russians. He might have done it himself. But Senator Karl Mundt of South Dakota and his allies were against it. They weren't trying to dismantle trade; they were trying to dismantle the consensus. They didn't want disarmament. They wanted victory.

In the world beyond the Washington diplomatic corps, the foreign policy experts, and the corporate boards of the Northeast, the appeal of the consensus was something less than consensual. In Miami, a local ordinance forbade anyone who was not an official of the Soviet Union from wearing a hammer and sickle in public.[1] In Columbus, Ohio, and Birmingham, Alabama, laws restricted the sale of "communist goods." In Wyoming the state legislature had passed a resolution calling on the United States to quit the United Nations, abolish foreign aid, and forget about arms control.

In this political context, Humphrey did what he had to do all day Tuesday. He sweet-talked this senator and reasoned with that one, and after each conversation he'd take a folded-up piece of paper from the side pocket of his suit jacket and make a note to himself. He wasn't going to get caught not knowing his count. Larry O'Brien and Kenny O'Donnell from the White House staff helped him. If nothing else worked, they'd say passage of the Mundt amendment would be an affront to the new president just when he most needed support. Nine Democrats and a Republican switched. But it took all day to round up the votes, and it wasn't until 9:30 that evening that a relieved Humphrey called his chief to report the good news.

"What are you doing for dinner?" Johnson said.

Dinner? Humphrey had already eaten.

"Well, come on over anyway and have something more to eat," Johnson said. "I want to talk to you."

He did as Johnson asked. He usually did.

III

That morning, Barry Goldwater's Arizona friend Denison Kitchel called Cliff White of the Draft Goldwater Committee and told him not to do anything until further notice. White was not surprised. Just a week or two earlier, after Barry Goldwater had told White that he would announce his candidacy in late November, Goldwater told a reporter that he was "still wishing something would happen to get me out of all this." Now something had.

Nor was White surprised to get the news secondhand. Kitchel was Goldwater's old friend from Arizona, recently brought to Washington to handle several political chores, chief among them insulating Goldwater from his most capable campaign strategist, F. Clifton White.

Cliff White was a driven man, though it is hard to say what drove him more—his political vision, his pursuit of success, or simply his determination to matter. Probably the last, because he was already successful by the early sixties, and his politics had changed. He had made some money, as much as his modest tastes required, and he had forged a reputation as a skilled political operative. He had a wife, children, friends. But he could not sit still, neither literally—he was in airplanes and hotel rooms almost as often as he was home—nor internally, as though his life had been designed as a refutation of its origins in middle-class, upstate New York, as firm a bastion of stability as exists in America.

White was an apple-knocker, as native upstate New Yorkers called themselves, who disdained apples, or just about any other fruit or vegetable. He was actually allergic to tomatoes. His staples were scotch and steak.[2] He was a Northeastern Yankee who had turned against the political and cultural tradition of his forebears, and even of his own early adulthood, to make common cause with a rebellion coming out of the West and the South. It was his last chance at glory.

He still had a full head of dark hair and a rich baritone voice, but he was forty-five years old now and too firmly identified with the Republican Party's conservative wing to become anything else. He was committed to a faction, a movement, a candidate, a campaign that he led even though it did not yet formally exist. If he was ever to matter, it would be as the man who made Barry Goldwater president of the United States, or at least the Republican nominee.

Not alone, but more than anyone else, White had transformed a set of ideas into a national political movement and brought that movement to the brink of success. And now, in the waning weeks of 1963, he thought Lee Harvey Oswald might have killed his campaign, too.

By no means was White a heartless fellow who was unmoved by the assassination. In fact, he could be something of a sentimentalist. But he was a man with a mission, the mission depended on another man, and that other man was . . . well, he could be cantankerous.

They were, at the very least, an odd couple: White, the reserved Easterner of old-line Yankee stock, an intellectual with a Ph.D. in political science who came to politics from academia; Goldwater, the gruff, outgoing Westerner, the grandson of Jewish immigrants, a salesman without a college degree who had come to politics from business.

Like White, Goldwater was something of a contradiction. He could be so friendly and forthright that even his political opponents—Jack Kennedy in Washington, Stewart and Morris Udall back in Arizona—found him an engaging fellow. But he could also be grouchy. At fifty-five, he was barely old enough to be called an old curmudgeon, but that made no difference. He'd been a curmudgeon at thirty-five.

His contrariness transcended his personality. Goldwater was now the leader, willing or not, of a political revolution. To succeed, that revolution would have to overthrow the leadership of its party. But Barry Goldwater was a party regular, the chairman of the Republican Senate Campaign Committee who was devoted to electing Republicans of whatever stripe. Yes, he remained the ideologue who'd criticized the Eisenhower administration, but he was loyal to the Republican Party as an institution. He was even, to the dismay of some of his supporters, friendly with their archenemy within the party, Governor Nelson Rockefeller of New York. Once a month or so, Rockefeller would come to Washington, and he and Goldwater would have breakfast at the home Rockefeller kept for himself on Foxhall Road. They liked each other. In May 1963, Goldwater was one of the first people Rockefeller called to tell of his remarriage. Goldwater wished the couple well.

A month later, the Young Republican (YR) Convention, dominated by Cliff White's acolytes and the John Birch Society, endorsed a "Southern strategy" for victory in 1964, which stopped just short of suggesting that Republicans forget about Negro votes.

Rockefeller pounced immediately. On July 14, he issued a press release pointing out "the growing danger . . . through subversion from the right." The YR Convention, Rockefeller said, was "dominated by extremist groups, carefully organized, well-financed and operating through the tactics of ruthless, rough-shod intimidation. These are the tactics of totalitarianism." As for the "Southern strategy," Rockefeller dismissed it as an attempt "to erect political power on the outlawed and immoral basis of segregation." If Goldwater were to run in 1964 as a "captive of the radical right," Rockefeller could not support him.

That was the end of the Foxhall Road breakfasts. Goldwater got mad. He also got cracking on a real presidential campaign. Not that he'd have anything to do with White. Instead, he got Kitchel to come to Washington to open a political headquarters, ostensibly for Goldwater's reelection campaign in 1964 but actually for a presidential campaign.

. His party loyalty was one reason Goldwater kept White at arm's length. He distrusted outsiders. He distrusted political technicians and hired guns. Strictly speaking, White had not been hired; he had hired himself by creating the organization that then hired him as its chief. As any politician would, Goldwater wanted his campaign to be *his* campaign, run by men he trusted, loyal only to him. As he well knew, the Draft Goldwater Committee had evolved out of earlier, conservative organizations. Their guiding light had been their ideology, not a candidate. It might well have been called the Draft the Most Appealing Conservative Committee. Goldwater just happened to be that most appealing conservative. He was neither the founder nor the focal point of the movement. He was its instrument. He knew it.

But there was no point in moping. If Goldwater decided to run, things had to be done. If he decided against it . . . well, so much time had been spent on this effort already that wasting a little more would hardly matter. White decided to proceed as if nothing had changed.

| | |

At the White House, of course, everything had changed, and on the afternoon of Tuesday, November 26, the soon-to-be-departing lady of the house invited the woman who would succeed her to come by for tea. "Don't be afraid of this house," Jacqueline Kennedy told Lady Bird Johnson. "Some of the happiest years of my marriage have been spent here. You will be happy here."

Mrs. Kennedy then conducted a short tour of the living quarters, during which she introduced Mrs. Johnson to the staff. Just before the two women parted, Mrs. Kennedy brought up the subject of her daughter Caroline's small private school, which met in the White House. Not wanting to disrupt the children right now, Mrs. Kennedy asked if it would be all right to keep the school there until the Christmas break. Mrs. Johnson agreed.

That evening, Jacqueline Kennedy wrote to Lyndon Johnson: "Thank you for walking yesterday—behind Jack. You did not have to do that. I am sure many people forbade you to take such a risk, but you did it anyway."

Walking behind his predecessor in policy, Johnson earlier that day had issued his first executive order. Security Memorandum No. 273 ordered the Central Intelligence Agency, as well as the State and Defense departments, to plan more secret operations against North Vietnam and more military actions inside Laos.[3]

But it wouldn't just be military action. Johnson's accompanying memorandum made it clear that political, social, economic, and educational efforts were integral parts of United States strategy. "We should seek to turn the tide not only of battle, but of belief," he said.

He had converted. For now, he would accept the advice of the wise and educated men who had gathered in his office on Sunday. He would do as they asked, not only because they were wise and educated—with that polish he had never acquired—but because they were the men John Kennedy had chosen as his advisors. Johnson was going to do everything Kennedy had done, only better.

| | |

A few days after the funeral, J. Edgar Hoover came to the White House with information for his new president. The information had nothing to do with national security or criminal activity. Instead, the FBI director bore dossiers on the personal lives of several members of Congress and on both the personal lives and past political connections of John Kennedy's top appointees.[4]

For Hoover, the visit served several purposes: He had done the president a favor; he had demonstrated the kind of power he and his agency could wield; and he had done it directly. Gone were the days when the FBI director had to clear things through his nominal boss, the attorney general of the United States. The attorney general was no longer the president's brother.

Hoover wanted to make sure the president knew about all the senators who had dallied with pretty young women at the Quorum Club presided over by Johnson's old sidekick Bobby Baker, the secretary for the Senate Democrats. He wanted to make sure the president knew that some members of his cabinet and the White House staff were now having or had recently had extramarital affairs. Mainly, he wanted to make sure the president knew that his FBI director knew all this, and no doubt more.

| | |

The president called Martin Luther King Monday night, after the funeral. Johnson wanted to make sure that King knew how much his president needed him.

"I'll have to have you-all's help. I never needed it more'n I do now," he said, conveying the same message he had sent to the White House staff and cabinet members, but in a more down-home idiom. Johnson also called because he'd gotten word that King had been hurt about not being invited to the church service, and he wanted to make him feel better.

In fact, King's sorrow was deeper than that. When news of the assassination had come, his son, little Martin Luther King III, had said to his father, "President Kennedy was your best friend, wasn't he?" The elder King had to wonder if the boy knew something his father didn't. The two men had not known each other all that well, and from King's perspective, the president had not moved nearly fast enough on civil rights. But there had to be some reason why he never gave up on John Kennedy, why he always felt confident that in the final analysis the president would support his cause. The cause was the same; the situation had changed. When he had talked to President Kennedy, he talked while Kennedy listened. Now, on the phone with Lyndon Johnson, he'd barely been able to get a word in.

"It's just an impossible period," Johnson told him. "We've got a budget coming up . . . and we've got a civil rights bill." He didn't even mention the tax bill, not to King, but later that night he mulled over strategy on it with Bill Moyers and Ted Sorensen. He had two speech drafts on the budget, and he would read them late into the night.

| | |

Exhausted after the vote and not a bit hungry, Hubert Humphrey went to the Elms for his second dinner of Tuesday evening. When Humphrey arrived, he was greeted by Lady Bird Johnson and by the elder Johnson daughter, Lynda Byrd. Also there were Jack Valenti and Johnson's friend Abe Fortas, one of Washington's best-connected lawyers.

It was an enjoyable dinner, but Humphrey knew he had not been invited just for the pleasure of his company. There was work to be done. As early as Saturday, it had been assumed that the new president would have to deliver a formal address to the nation. It would mark the end of the brief and horrible interregnum, making the day after the funeral the appropriate date. Humphrey was one of those who had argued against having Johnson deliver the speech from behind the Oval Office desk and in favor of the president appearing before a joint session of Congress. He had prevailed.

Some of official Washington's best writers, including Theodore Sorensen and John Kenneth Galbraith, had worked on drafts of the speech, but their work did not impress the only critic who mattered. Lyndon Johnson wanted another perspective, a politician's perspective, and after dinner that night he asked Humphrey and Fortas to rewrite the speech.

It was a delicate assignment for a difficult, if opportune, moment. After all, this was to be no ordinary speech, and they knew it. Nobody wins as many elections as Johnson and Humphrey had won without some instinct for understanding their constituents. No president had come to office under quite these circumstances. The national trauma presented him with an unprecedented problem and with unprecedented opportunity. He had, for the moment, a nation as united behind him as most nations ever get. In their grief most people were ready to trust this new president. They were ready to be led.

Johnson was ready to lead. He never said that some destiny had decreed his presidency. But from the beginning, he had pursued political advancement as though there were no limits to his success, and now he was embracing the office as though it belonged to him by divine right.

Humphrey and Fortas worked on the speech until 2 A.M. Mostly, they cut down the earlier drafts. Humphrey thought the speech should be short and that its thrust should be to reassure the public that the new president would walk in the ways of the old. "Let us begin," Kennedy had said in his inaugural address. Humphrey penned in the words for Johnson: "Let us continue."

| | |

At noon on Wednesday, November 27, somber but strong, Lyndon Johnson stood behind the lectern of the House of Representatives, that ultimate symbol of popular government, and began by saying, "All I have I would have given gladly not to be standing here today."

Speaking slowly, keeping his eyes on his text, Johnson proclaimed that "the greatest leader of our time has been struck down by the foulest deed of our time. Now the ideas and ideals which he so nobly represented must and will be translated into effective action."

Lest anyone wonder where the century's first Southern president stood regarding his predecessor's civil rights bill, Johnson wasted little time before endorsing it:

> We have talked long enough in this country about equal rights. We have talked for a hundred years or more. It is time now to write the next chapter, and to write it in the books of law. I urge you again, as I did in 1957 and again in 1960, to enact a civil rights law so that we can move forward to eliminate from this nation every trace of discrimination and oppression that is based upon race or color. There could be no greater source of strength to this nation both at home and abroad.

He used Humphrey's slogan, all right, and used it early in the speech. It was perfect for the occasion, but Johnson had more than continuity in mind and for good reason. More than most of the more sophisticated, better (or at least fancier) educated men with whom he dealt, Johnson suspected that the consensus was a delusion. He planned to transform it into reality.

"We will serve all of the nation, not one section or one sector, or one group, but all Americans," he said. "These are the United States—a united people with a united purpose. Our American unity does not depend upon unanimity. We have differences, but now, as in the past, we can derive from these differences strength, not weakness, wisdom, not despair."

It was political boilerplate, to be sure, but he meant it. Lyndon Johnson—the Southerner who believed in civil rights, the rich man who wanted to uplift the poor, the rough-hewn pragmatist who was more of a dreamer, more of a revolutionary, than he ever let anyone know—would not simply unite his country. He would lead it to an era of unprecedented wealth, and beyond wealth to wisdom. It makes no difference whether he thought this was his destiny. It was his obsession.

As the president no doubt knew, he had a receptive audience that week. In their distress, Americans wanted more than stability; they wanted reassurance that despite the chaos of the last weekend, theirs remained a healthy, blessed land. And despite the chaos of the last weekend, it seemed to be.

One of the enduring images of those four days of mourning had been a sign posted outside a New York City newsstand that said, "Closed because of a death in the American family."[5] On both counts, the newsie had had it right. There had been a death—a murder—but for all its horror, that murder had demonstrated the reality, and the resilience, of the American family.

Even the few who would place themselves outside of the family only proved its strength. After Malcolm X all but applauded the assassination, saying "chickens will come home to roost," he was rebuked by Elijah Muhammad, the leader of his Black Muslim sect. At the University of Illinois, a classics professor named Revilo Oliver, a member of the John Birch Society, proclaimed that Kennedy's memory would always be "cherished with distaste." A few on campus called for his ouster, but officials dismissed such talk and were praised by the student editor of the *Daily Illini,* a senior named Roger Ebert, who wrote that "only a strong and free society could permit Professor Oliver his own freedom."

Strong, free, and perhaps more united than ever, Americans were just beginning to realize that over the past two decades their country had become a nation in social reality as well as in legal-political theory. That greatest of collective enterprises, World War II, fought by conscripted citizen soldiers, had helped forge a country that had so recently remained a collection of regions.

Not that it was just the war. Franklin Roosevelt's New Deal created national standards. The automobile brought people and regions together. It also inspired Dwight Eisenhower's great socialist enterprise (he didn't call it that), the $40 billion interstate highway system, with its obvious cohesive influence.

That symbiosis between the car and the highway told the tale. American unity was the combined product of business and government, both of which were growing larger and more centralized and integrating the country behind them. By now Americans, wherever they were, whoever they were, bought and used the same products and services—Cokes, Hershey bars, Vaseline, Chevies, the news, long distance calls—provided by the same corporations—GM, GE, CBS, AT&T—and watching, all at the same time on the same night, the same television programs.

Telephones were bringing people together, too. Eighty-one percent of all households had telephones, and on most of them it had just become possible to make a long distance call without going through the operator. Not long after forsaking named exchanges in favor of all-digit dialing, the Bell System had created and installed the area code. It took a little getting used to, these three new digits. The confusion was aptly satirized late in December by Danny Kaye on his variety show, with the tunes "Way Down Yonder in Five-Oh-Four" and "As I Walked Out on the Streets of Five-One-Two."[6]

So powerful was the force of centralization that even the region that had kept itself—and been kept—outside the national consensus was being drawn in, perhaps dragged in. Gradually, businesses were moving into the South, rendering it both richer and more industrial than it had been. Gradually, the federal government was moving into the South, insisting that it obey the Constitution. And now, in perhaps the strangest consequence of this strange event, one of its own was leading the charge against it.

I I I

The night after his brother's funeral, Robert Kennedy told some of his relatives and close friends that if they wanted anything from the administration, they'd better get it quickly because "in a few weeks, the Kennedys will be forgotten in this country."

No one argued with him, not necessarily because they agreed, but because they could see that he had no interest in being consoled just then. Nor would he for weeks thereafter. The only comfort he seemed to allow himself took the form of gallows humor. "Come on in," he said to one visitor. "Somebody shot my brother and we're watching his funeral on television." When New York's legendary former governor and senator Herbert Lehman died, Kennedy flew up for the funeral services, explaining, "I don't like to let too many days go by without a funeral."

It was, perhaps, not the most mature reaction, but he had just turned thirty-eight years old, and his friends recalled that he had been gloomy even before the assassination. On his birthday, November 20, Bobby had made sour fun of himself as a great asset to his brother thanks to his work on civil rights, wiretapping, and prosecuting Jimmy Hoffa. He had blamed himself for John Kennedy's political problems. What his party guests hadn't known was that the two brothers had been discussing whether Bobby ought to step down as attorney general, deciding against it only because "it would look as if we were running away" from the civil rights fight.

It was not that their political situation was unenviable. When they held their first planning meeting for the 1964 campaign on November 13, the president's job-approval rating stood at 59 to 28 in the Gallup poll. John Kennedy knew that civil rights would cost him votes, so he wasn't going to campaign on civil rights. Instead, he would campaign on peace and prosperity. The campaign planners hoped that Barry Goldwater got the nomination, not because Kennedy led him 55 to 39 percent in the latest poll, but because, as Robert Kennedy had said, they "knew he was not a very smart man."[7]

Still, Kennedy's poll numbers had been down a bit, especially in the South and the West, where some of the opposition was especially nasty, and the issues that were costing him votes were Bobby's issues, mostly civil rights. The president's brother had been well aware of this, which may have explained his birthday melancholy. But it seemed a transient gloom, because that evening, at a raucous birthday party that his wife, Ethel, threw for him at their Virginia home, he was staying up very late talking with the great dancer Gene Kelly.[8]

But that had been three days before, in another era. Now, his brother dead, Robert Kennedy sank into a despond that threatened to be bottomless. He didn't want to go back to work, and when he finally did, in mid-December, his mind wandered. Sometimes when he got a memo, he'd throw it away without looking at it. He'd leave his office early in the day. "I don't think there's much left for me in this town," he told some friends. His hair, uncut for weeks, straggled over his collar. His eyes were bloodshot.

Douglas Dillon, the Republican whom Jack had appointed as treasury secretary, loaned Bobby his house in Hobe Sound, Florida, and he and Ethel and the children went there for a few days in December. Friends visited, and as Kennedys will, Bobby organized touch football games. He had always played hard. Now he played viciously.

But even that couldn't lift his despondency. Perhaps nothing could. For all its privilege, Robert Kennedy's life had not been without its sorrows. His oldest brother, Joseph junior, had been killed in the war. His sister Kathleen had died in a plane crash. But Jack's death was different. It wasn't just that he had been so much closer to Jack, or even that they had been such an effective team. What made this different was that by the early 1960s, being John Kennedy's brother was who Robert Kennedy *was*. His sense of himself, his sense of purpose in life, was as John Kennedy's agent, advisor, protector, even the courtier who would do the unsavory work unfit for the king.

It was a subsidiary role he welcomed despite his assertive, scrappy confidence, not just out of brotherly love but also out of recognition that Jack had the qualities he lacked, qualities needed to get the job done. Jack was tall, handsome, suave, outgoing, a good performer in public. Bobby was small, thin, shy, ill at ease in crowds, uncomfortable at a podium. Whenever he made a speech, Bobby held his hands low, behind the lectern, so nobody could see how they shook. He was hardly the kind of guy who could get elected to anything, much less the presidency.

And getting elected was necessary in order to do what had to be done. Politics was not, for Robert Kennedy, just about getting power and glory. Oh, he liked the power and glory. He liked hanging around with movie stars and schmoozing with poets and novelists, but as a Kennedy, he could have had some of that without politics. The real point of politics was getting things done, bringing the bad guys to justice, winning equality for Negroes, helping the poor, stopping the communists. Robert Kennedy was a moralist and an activist. His life had a purpose that transcended himself, and for him that purpose had always depended on Jack. Without him, what purpose was there? "Why, God?" he asked in the journal he kept, and then he wondered just whom he was asking: "The innocent suffer—how can that be possible and God be just." Also: "All things are to be examined and called into question—there are no limits set to thought."

No limits. Everything would be called into question, not only whether God was just but whether He was there at all. Nothing before, not his oldest brother's death nor a Harvard education, had shaken that core belief of his upbringing, of his ancestry. This did.

3

FATHERS AND SONS

Two days after he spoke to the nation, Lyndon Johnson decided that after all he would have to name that special presidential investigating commission to look into the assassination.

It had become clear to him that he didn't have much choice. Senate Minority Leader Everett Dirksen was calling for a full investigation by the Senate Judiciary Committee, and Congressman Charles Goodell of New York proposed a joint congressional investigation. Though both were Republicans, a Democratic Congress would have had a hard time rejecting some kind of congressional probe. And Oswald's murder while in police custody had rendered Texas law enforcement a national embarrassment, so the argument that this was a Texas crime to be solved by Texas authorities was for the moment risible.

Johnson even figured out a way to assure J. Edgar Hoover that the commission would be good for the FBI. He told Hoover that it was the only way to stave off the "rash of investigations" the director feared. Hoover probably wasn't pleased—he was certain the commission would turn into "a three-ring circus"—but he knew better than to argue with a president whose mind was made up.

One thing that Johnson didn't tell Hoover was who he'd decided should chair the commission. In this situation the president wanted to go right to the top, to the Chief Justice of the United States, but Earl Warren's was a name he did not mention to Hoover, nor to Richard Russell when he called and asked him to become one of the members. In fact, one of the first things he said to Russell was, "I don't think I can get any member of the Court. I'm going to try to get Allen Dulles. I'm going to try Senator Russell and Senator Cooper from the Senate."

Russell cut him off. "Oh, no, no, no, get somebody else now. It would really save my life. I declare I don't want to serve."

"I know you don't want to do anything," Johnson said, "but I want you to. And I think this is important enough and you'll see why."

But Russell could not see what was behind Johnson's next question.

"What do you think about a justice sitting on it?" Johnson said. "You don't have a president assassinated but every fifty years."

The president did not specify which justice, though he did seem, obliquely, to rule out Chief Justice Earl Warren. "Who would be the best then if I didn't get the Chief?" he asked Russell, who apparently thought Johnson wasn't referring to a Supreme Court justice at all. Get a good judge from a state supreme court, Russell said, or "some outstanding circuit court judge," not knowing that Johnson had already asked Earl Warren to come to the White House, and that the Chief Justice was due to arrive there within half an hour.

Warren was no more enthusiastic about serving on the commission than was Russell, not because he disliked any of the other members but because he considered it an unconstitutional violation of the separation of powers for the leader of the judicial branch to serve on a presidential commission. In fact, before arriving at the White House, he had sent word to the president that he would not even consider serving.

Whereupon Earl Warren became the first recipient of what was soon to be known as the "Johnson treatment." The president presented Warren with his own worst fears, that if the public believed rumors that the Russians or the Cubans were behind the assassination, he would have to go to war in revenge, a war that could quickly turn nuclear.

"When he talked about nuclear war, I could not turn him down," Warren later said.[1]

After his meeting with Warren, the president again called Russell, this time to tell him, "I made that announcement."

"Announcement of what?"

"Of this special commission."

"Oh, you have already?"

He had, and he read him the announcement. Russell was horrified.

"I couldn't serve on it with Chief Justice Warren," Russell said. "I don't like that man. I don't have any confidence in him at all."

"Dick," the president said, "it has already been announced. And you can serve with anybody for the good of America. . . . You've never turned your country down. This is not me. This is your country. . . . You're my man on that commission and you're going to do it. And don't tell me what you can do and what you can't because I can't arrest you and I'm not going to put the FBI on you. But you're goddamn sure going to serve."

"Mr. President," said Russell, almost sobbing, "you ought to have told me you were going to name me."

"I told you!" Johnson barked. "I told you today I was going to name the Chief Justice when I called you."

"You did not," Russell said. "You talked to me about getting somebody from the Supreme Court. You didn't tell me you were going to name *him*."

"I told you," Johnson insisted.

"Oh, no," said Russell, and a few minutes later he plaintively told Johnson, "You're taking advantage of me."

"No. No. No. I'm not taking advantage of you," Johnson said. "I'm *going to* take a hell of a lot of advantage of you, my friend, 'cause you made me, and I know it, and I don't ever forget."

"I'm at your command," said Russell, his devotion to the president, any president, finally overpowering his distaste for Earl Warren. "I'll do anything you want me to do."

Having prevailed, Johnson comforted. "Nobody ever has been more to me than you have, Dick, except my mother," he said, and when Russell laughed, the president insisted: "No. No. That's true. I've bothered you more and made you spend more hours with me telling me what's right and wrong than anybody except my mother. . . . I just want to counsel with you and I just want your judgment and your wisdom 'cause I haven't got any daddy and you're going to be it."[2]

This expression of devotion must have pleased Russell but could not have surprised him, because when Lyndon Johnson got to the Senate fifteen years earlier he began a courtship of Richard Russell, the lifelong bachelor whose only real home was the Senate. With no one to cook for him or join him for meals at home, Russell ate breakfast at the Capitol and enjoyed his bourbon and dinner at a Capitol Hill restaurant. Soon enough, young Senator Johnson started to join him.

On Sundays, Johnson often asked Russell over for breakfast, after which the senators and Lady Bird lolled about with the Sunday papers. Should Russell drop over in the middle of the week, Lady Bird would prepare a good Southern dinner. Russell was around the Johnson home so much that the Johnson daughters began referring to him as "Uncle Dick."

What Russell probably did not know was that he was not the first daddy Lyndon Johnson chose. At San Marcos, he ingratiated himself with the college president. On arriving at the House of Representatives, he walked up to Sam

Rayburn, who had served with Johnson's father in the Texas legislature, and said, "I'm Sam Johnson's boy." Rayburn quickly became the younger Johnson's Washington patron. Sam Johnson's boy, as someone noted, was "a born apple-polisher."

| | |

On the morning of Wednesday, December 4, twenty of the twenty-nine presidents of the unions in the AFL-CIO came to the White House, where the president told them he needed their help.

"George, give me the first names. I want this on a first-name basis," Johnson said to the federation president, George Meany, as the meeting began. Johnson wanted more than their help and support; he wanted their friendship. But then again, he wanted that from everyone. "We're Americans first and trade unionists second," proclaimed Meany, on behalf of the entire assemblage. This was music to Johnson's ears.

That same afternoon, Johnson spoke to the men who managed the companies that employed the union workers. He brought eighty-nine leaders of America's largest corporations into the cabinet room for an hour-long "exchange of thoughts" with the secretaries of commerce, the treasury, agriculture, and labor. The cabinet room isn't big enough for all those folks, so it must have been a tight fit, but Johnson didn't care. "We have much work to do together," the president declared.

This was the more important of the two meetings. Few of the executives had voted for the Kennedy-Johnson ticket in 1960, and most of them had been angry at the administration since the steel price squabble of 1962, when Kennedy had been quoted as agreeing with his father, Joe Kennedy, who had said that businessmen were sons of bitches.

Now just two weeks into his own presidency, Johnson made his first, unstated but unmistakable, break with his predecessor. It was not a change of policy but of attitude. LBJ would have no sons of bitches. He wanted only friends.

"I'm not going to be going around telling you how to run your business," he told them. "I think that you know better than I do how to do that, and I believe that I know how to run the government." But he made sure to remind them, "I am the only president you have," knowing that for all their rhetorical disdain of government, they needed a president more than most. Just as he knew, better than they did, that just thirty years before it was his political faction, the New Deal Democrats, who had saved corporate America despite itself. Fools that they were, the leaders of the country's biggest businesses couldn't see that they would be better off being Democrats.

But Johnson would show them, and in doing so he would remake the political map. His party might be about to lose much of the white South, but if he had his way, it would more than make up for that loss by taking corporate America from the Republicans.

This was profound political strategy, perhaps so natural to this president that he would not recognize its profundity. What Johnson was planning was nothing less than the completion of the New Deal, the historic transformation that had brought him to politics. Johnson understood the significance of the New Deal better than most of its intellectual champions. For them, it involved a redistribution of power and wealth to workers, farmers, and intellectuals such as themselves. It was that for Johnson, too; he had worked to bring electricity to the farmers of west Texas, to expand educational opportunities and credit to lower-income folks. But his was not the New Deal of elite campuses, of sit-down strikes and the urban working class. It was the Southern and Western New Deal of cooperation between government and large businesses. Johnson's New Deal hero was not labor leader Sidney Hillman but Houston businessman Jesse H. Jones, who headed the Reconstruction Finance Corporation, which poured so many billions into industrializing the West. Johnson was not opposed to government helping businesses grow rich; he had grown rich himself that way.

At the very top of the business pyramid, some agreed. "Whether we like it or not, the federal government is a partner in every business in the country," Lamont duPont Copeland, the president of the huge chemical company, would tell the New York Chamber of Commerce a few weeks later. "We are confronted with a condition and not a theory. . . . As businessmen we need the understanding and cooperation of government in our effort to throw the economic machine into high gear."

Despite being "inherently averse to government's financial entry into the private sector of the economy," Eugene Black, president of the World Bank, and Stanley deJ. Osborne, former chairman of the Olin Mathieson Corporation, were about to issue a report urging the government to subsidize development of a supersonic commercial jet aircraft.[3]

The Federal Aviation Administration had suggested that the government kick in 75 percent of the estimated billion dollars the supersonic transport (SST) would cost. Black and Osborne were proposing 90 percent. That they wouldn't get it did not negate the point: The corporate world needed government help.

It was getting that help for developing another product that was just beginning to attract attention. At the inspiration (and with the money) of the Defense Department, public and private technicians had been improving the calculating machine, transforming it into a device whose thousands of switches and vacuum tubes could actually remember information as well as perform calculations. Devices such as the Control Data Company's 6600 could perform a million calculations a second. By the early 1960s, these machines were being called *computers*, and some firms were using them for clerical tasks. In a few cases, computers were even being used in the manufacturing process, where they had the potential to save billions of dollars. The machines were expensive, but they could replace employees, who in the long run cost much more.

Lyndon Johnson encouraged cooperation between government and business, between labor and business, indeed between and among everyone, and in those first days of his presidency, he reached out to all factions. He called Negro leaders to pledge his support for the civil rights bill, and he called segregationist politicians to tell them he understood how wrenching it would be for them to grant equality to Negroes. In these conversations, he pronounced the word "nigruhs."

It was as though he was trying to wrap all of America in his long arms, as though his design was not simply to be all things to all people but to gather all the diverse, quarreling factions of the nation around him in community. He kept quoting Isaiah: "Come, let us reason together." It was hard to argue with that. Who could resist the appeal of the Prophet Lyndon, who had come to heal the nation's wounds?

For the conservatives, he ordered his cabinet secretaries to cut their budgets so that the total would be less than $100 billion. He ordered the lights turned off at the White House to save on the electric bill. He preached frugality. To make the liberals happier, he not only stood firm on civil rights but also told senior White House aides to go ahead with the planning begun under Kennedy to launch a major assault on poverty. "I'm interested," he told Walter Heller, who had been putting together the plans for Kennedy. "Go ahead. Give it the highest priority. Push ahead full tilt."

He even reached out to Bobby Kennedy. He called and left a message that he'd like to see the attorney general, anytime. The message made clear that this was not a command, nor was it about any pressing business, so Bobby didn't have to call back. He didn't. He didn't feel like seeing him.[4]

| | |

On Monday, December 2, President Johnson presided over a healing ceremony that John Kennedy had planned, presenting the prestigious Fermi Prize for science to J. Robert Oppenheimer, the brilliant physicist who had helped create the atomic bomb and whose security clearance had later been revoked on the basis of the kind of spurious evidence and sloppy reasoning that afflicted so many of these decisions in the 1950s. The ceremony was a remarkable display of harmony. Edward Teller, the onetime Oppenheimer friend whose testimony later had helped get his clearance revoked, had urged the prize committee to make this award, and he was there for the presentation. "I am so very glad that you came," Oppenheimer said to Teller. Another guest, the great physicist I. I. Rabi, called the award "a righting of a great wrong done to him and to the American people."

There was a political point to this gesture, as there was to everything Johnson did. Presidents have a vested interest in national unity. They alone represent the nation as a whole, so the more harmonious the electorate, the more electable the president. But Johnson's motives transcended politics. The first weeks of the Johnson presidency showed the extraordinary confluence of a man and his era. As he preached rationality, harmony, and cooperation, Johnson was not just seeking votes. He was trying to create national community, as if he, as the embodiment of the consensus, could make it real by the sheer force of his personality. In an increasingly centralized era, he wanted to centralize more than policy. He wanted to centralize national goodwill around himself, creating a new Era of Good Feeling.

And more. The president spoke not just of power and prosperity, of reason and harmony, but also of wisdom, compassion, and even love. Not a common topic for a politician, love, but this big, droopy-faced country boy from Texas, this man's man who shot deer, drove fast, drank copious amounts of Cutty Sark scotch, and ate great hunks of beef—he could mention the word without seeming like some pantywaist professor.

And that's what he was asking of all those civil rights leaders and segregationists, all those labor leaders and corporate bosses, all the liberals and as many conservatives as he could reach. He didn't just want their votes. He wanted their admiration, their friendship, their love. It was as though he didn't have enough of it without them.

| | |

Jesus Christ, do I have to fuck every girl that comes into this place?"

Everybody has troubles, and in late 1963 this was one of Timothy Leary's. When not meeting that obligation, he would be riding on a horse painted pink on one side, blue on the other. Sometimes psychiatrist R. D. Laing would perform a mystical ballet in the kitchen.

There were less than a dozen of them, reading, talking, and writing the second issue of the *Psychedelic Review*. They'd converted one of the tower rooms into an experimental lab, painted the ceiling gold, and installed speakers so music could be piped in from below. Next to a bed were statues of Shiva and Buddha.

They were in a house owned by William Mellon Hitchcock,[5] a stockbroker in his twenties and the grandson of Gulf Oil founder William Larimer Hitchcock. From his inheritance, young Hitchcock had $15,000 a week in spending money, and he was more than happy to rent his 4,000-acre estate in Dutchess County for $500 a month.

Hitchcock had been introduced to psychedelics by his sister Peggy, the director of the New York branch of the International Federation for Internal Freedom, which Leary and Richard Alpert had established after they were kicked out of Harvard. At the center of the estate was a turreted sixty-four-room mansion called Millbrook, surrounded by polo fields, a stable, pine forests, tennis courts, a lake, a gatehouse, and a fountain.

By then IFIF had a new name, the Castalia Foundation, after a colony in Hermann Hesse's *The Glass Bead Game,* so named because Leary was "concerned about the relationship between the mystic community and the rest of society." He did not want his retreat to become a haven for isolated intellectuals.

But it was Tim who needed the haven. In the past several months he had been fired by Harvard and kicked out of Mexico. What could he expect? He pursued controversy more ardently than he pursued women. In 1962, in a speech to the Harvard Humanists, he proposed a level of individual freedom that would have blown the mind of Barry Goldwater's biggest booster—the "Fifth Freedom"—in behalf of which he proposed a constitutional amendment: "Congress shall make no law abridging the individual's right to seek an expanded consciousness."

On his way to Millbrook from Boston, he had taken a detour to speak to a group of Lutheran psychologists at the American Psychological Association convention in Philadelphia. In an effort to blend science and theology, he outlined what he called "the Eight Technologies of God," based on "eight basic questions about human destiny [which] correspond to the eight states of evolution and to eight circuits of the human brain."

But he grew more animated when he addressed the politics of the situation. "You are witnessing a good old-fashioned, traditional religious controversy," he told them. "On the one side the psychedelic visionaries, somewhat uncertain about the validity of their revelations . . . and on the other side the establishment. . . . The issue of chemical expansion of consciousness is hard upon us. You can hardly escape it. . . . Internal freedom is becoming a major religious and civil rights controversy."

He got a standing ovation. Undoubtedly, the Lutheran psychologists had read about how he had been fired, about the dangers posed by the drugs he advocated. No matter. Freedom was its own justification.

||| |

Ever alert to threats to national security, the New York office of the Federal Bureau of Investigation on Wednesday, December 4, forwarded a confidential memorandum to Washington concerning the "Negro question, Communist Influence in Racial Matters, Internal Security."

It reported that "a confidential source who has furnished reliable information in the past"—meaning a wiretap—had revealed that on the previous Saturday Clarence Jones, Martin Luther King's lawyer, had called King, who said he was to meet with President Johnson on Tuesday, December 3, and who also proclaimed himself "horrified" about a column he had read in the "Long Island Express."

The column, in the *Long Island Press,* was by Robert S. Allen and Paul Scott, who said that Attorney General Robert Kennedy faced the "politically explosive" decision of whether to permit Democratic Party officials to continue working with an unnamed Negro leader "known" by the FBI to be linked with a Soviet agent. Kennedy, said the column, was "on the spot since the Negro leader has been in close contact with both the White House and the Justice Department in the past."

The unnamed Negro leader was King, whose phones the FBI had been tapping since October, on the grounds that his friend Stanley Levison was a communist. Allen and Scott had gotten their information from the FBI as part of its campaign to discredit King, to stop the civil rights bill, and perhaps to embarrass Bobby Kennedy in the process.

It was no accident that Martin Luther King was the object of so much attention, helpful and harmful, from the most powerful men in America. By accident of history and force of personality, he had become one of them. Without being elected or appointed to office, without personal wealth, without the support of any formal institution, he had become a force to be reckoned with, a force welcome to some, anathema to others.

He did not look powerful. He was a dapper, rather mischievous little fellow—five feet seven inches tall—who, like so many other extraordinary men, was something of a contradiction. He was not quite thirty-five, which is pretty young to be the head of a national political movement, much less about to become *Time* magazine's Man of the Year.

He didn't seem that young. Such were his accomplishments, so easily did he move among the powerful, so somber was the face he turned to the general world, the white world, that he gave the impression of being well into middle age. No wonder the *Time* cover story about its Man of the Year would describe him as a man with "very little sense of humor."

If they only knew. Earnestness was King's pose for the white folks, something he had cultivated in his student days so that whites wouldn't confuse him with the shuffling, grinning Negroes of the movies. Relaxed, in the company of other Negroes or the few whites with whom he felt comfortable, King acted . . . well, he acted his age. He loved spicy Southern food, spicy jokes, good scotch whiskey, a good belly laugh. He liked to party. He may have worn sober dark suits in public, but in high school M. L. King was known by the nickname "Tweed," thanks to his snappy clothing.

Were his somberness nothing but an act, he couldn't have pulled it off so well. Underneath the private gaiety was an even more private sobriety, one that manifested itself in serious scholarship. More than any other public figure of his day, more than John or Robert Kennedy or Adlai Stevenson or William Buckley, Martin Luther King Jr. was a serious intellectual, a stern student of philosophy and theology.

It wasn't that he himself was a philosopher; his mind, for all its depth, lacked the spunk of originality. Nor was there much breadth to his intellectual pursuits, which embraced the social sciences as well as philosophy but neither the physical sciences nor the arts. He was conversant with Tillich and Niebuhr, Berkeley and Kierkegaard, but indifferent to, if not ignorant of, Eliot and Yeats, Joyce and Hemingway.

But he did hold a Ph.D. in philosophy from Boston University, as well as a divinity degree from the Crozer Seminary in Pennsylvania, and one of his professors at B.U., suggesting an academic career for him, had called him a "scholar's scholar."

The professor had been wrong. Martin Luther King was a seeker's scholar. His pursuit of philosophy was no abstract academic exercise. It was part of a political process, a search for both the ethical foundation and the effective mechanism needed for the liberation of his people. It was, he later wrote, "a serious intellectual quest for a method to eliminate social evil."

It was also a troubled young man's search for personal truth, a constant reexamination of belief and behavior by someone who could never be sure that his own measured up.

Years earlier, his quest had led him to the ideas of Mohandas K. Gandhi, and though he didn't know it at the time, he was not the only Negro intellectual-politician looking to Gandhi for guidance. James Lawson, a Vanderbilt University divinity student from Massillon, Ohio, who had studied in India, had established an unofficial but potent program in Gandhian studies in Nashville. Energetic young Negroes such as John Lewis from rural Alabama and Marion Barry from Mississippi flocked to Lawson's lessons in the basement of a Baptist church in Nashville's Negro section. Bayard Rustin had also discovered Gandhi through his pacifism. All these Negro scholars found in Gandhi's teachings a possible model for American Negroes to follow.

That model was not just passive resistance or civil disobedience but *satyagraha,* an active "noncooperation" with evil through boycotts and protest marches, all done in the spirit of love for the oppressor. It was a foreign and apparently naive strategy. It was working.

| | |

The new presidential commission to investigate the assassination held its first meeting the next day, Thursday, December 5, at the National Archives Building. John McCloy, the former president of the World Bank, was the first to arrive, showing up at room 105 twenty minutes early. Congressman Hale Boggs got there with but a minute to spare. The others were Representative Gerald Ford, Republican of Michigan; two senators, Richard Russell and Republican John Sherman Cooper of Kentucky; former CIA director Allen Dulles; and Chief Justice Earl Warren.

There was some nervousness on everyone's part. Police from the General Services Administration searched the room for bombs and microphones three times before the meeting began. But the men on this commission were not easily distracted, and they quickly got about their business. At that first meeting, they decided to conduct their own investigation rather than relying on the FBI. They named former solicitor general J. Lee Rankin as the committee's general counsel, and they formally asked Texas attorney general Waggoner Carr to hold off on his planned "Court of Inquiry" until the commission had finished its work.

Sensible though that request was—competing investigations might interfere with each other—by closing off competing probes, the commission inadvertently reinforced what was already a growing popular distrust of the official, established version of the events of November 22. The innate distrust so many Americans hold toward the proper and the official was further stimulated by the news that Oswald had lived in the Soviet Union, the apparent difficulty one man would have had firing three shots accurately from a window more than a hundred feet from his target, the confusion surrounding the first hours following the shooting, and the incomprehensible murder of the murderer while in police custody.

A few days before the first commission meeting, a Gallup poll revealed that only 29 percent of the American people thought that Oswald had acted alone. For the first time, some skeptics began to hint that perhaps there had been two gunmen. One of John Kennedy's wounds seemed to have been in the throat. Oswald had fired from behind the presidential motorcade. If there was an entrance wound in the throat, someone must have fired from the other direction, from a grassy knoll near the underpass just ahead of the presidential motorcade.

But when the FBI submitted its report to the commission in early December, it seemed to answer those questions. According to the Bureau's five-volume report, neatly packaged in flexible blue plastic with white spiral bindings, it had indeed been that peculiar little man, Lee Harvey Oswald, who had acted alone, killing the president with the mail-order rifle he had bought under an assumed name nine months earlier. Oswald's fingerprints were found on that rifle. The Bureau concluded that there was no entrance wound in Kennedy's throat.

The evidence for the FBI conclusions seemed overwhelming. Oswald had been in the book depository building from which the shots were fired. He had been near the window where eyewitnesses had seen someone firing a rifle. The murder weapon was his. And he had shot and killed a police officer later in the day.

Still, almost immediately doubts were being raised about the events surrounding the assassination. At year's end, even the sober magazine *Commentary* inquired about "the possibility of a treasonous political conspiracy."[6] It made sense that the commission planned to do more than rely on the FBI's evidence.

In a talk with J. Edgar Hoover, even the president wondered about some past link between Oswald and his murderer, Jack Ruby. "Was he ever in his bar and stuff like that?" Johnson asked Hoover.

"There was a story that this fellow [Oswald] had been in this nightclub [the Carousel Club, owned by Ruby] that is a striptease joint. . . . But that has not been able to be confirmed," Hoover told the president, assuring him that no connection had been found.

Hoover, ever conscious of ethnicity, always referred to Ruby by his original name, Rubenstein.

|||

On Saturday, December 7, J. B. West, the White House steward, called the Johnsons to say that Jacqueline Kennedy and her children had moved out of the East Wing and into the fawn-colored brick house that Mrs. Kennedy had bought at 3017 N St., Northwest, for $175,000. It was a Kennedyesque choice, an understated Federal-style brick home with an elevator. The former First Lady did not depart before calling the White House switchboard operators to say good-bye. And she left a bouquet of flowers for Mrs. Johnson, along with this brief note: "I wish you a happy arrival in your new house, Lady Bird. Remember—you will be happy here. Love, Jackie."

From the Elms, daughter Lucy Baines Johnson (only later would she change the spelling of her first name to "Luci") took the two beagles, "Him" and "Her," and drove to the White House in her new convertible. Lady Bird rode in another car carrying the framed photograph of Sam Rayburn, the only photograph of a person that the Johnsons kept in their living room, wherever they were.

One of the president's first calls that day was to Dick Russell, who was not feeling well.

"I've got this short-winded business," said Russell, who apparently did not like to use the word *emphysema,* which described his condition. "I can't breathe."

"Why don't you just come and sit then in the warm weather? Have a little sherry with me and eat lunch and go back. Now I'll have a car pick you up in fifteen minutes and you can go on back after your lunch, and we'll get you a good hamburger. You're going to have to eat something anyway, and I want to talk to you about reducing forces in Korea."

So the president sent a car to bring Russell over to the White House, where the two of them, in the buff, paddled around the swimming pool. But Johnson had more than Korea on his mind. This time, he brought up the subject they tried to avoid, civil rights.

"I'm not going to cavil and I'm not going to compromise," Johnson told his old mentor. "I'm going to pass it just as it is, Dick, and if you get in my way I'm going to run you down. I just want you to know that, because I care about you."

"Mr. President, you may be right," Russell answered. "But if you do run over me, it will not only cost you the South, it will cost you the election."

For Johnson, this was legislative strategy. The president knew he could not change Russell's mind about civil rights, but he hoped to use their personal friendship to make it more likely that Russell would support him on other matters. As long as the two of them could take their clothes off and paddle around in the pool, perhaps they could work together.

Besides, Johnson really did care about him.

Later that afternoon, Johnson invited the reduced Saturday White House press corps into the Oval Office for coffee. Some thirty reporters sat on the couches or stood against the walls while the president sat in his new rocking chair.

"This will be your first night here?" one reporter asked.

"Yes."

"How do you feel about it?"

"I feel like I have already been here a year."

What, asked another reporter, was the biggest problem?

The man in the rocker did not hesitate. "Being president," he said.

Later that afternoon, the president called Mrs. Kennedy himself, just because, he told her, "I wanted to flirt with you a little bit." He had flirted with her by telephone just five days earlier, calling her "sweetie" and "darling" and urging her to "come over and put your arm around me."

Now he wanted to tell her that he was afraid to sleep in the White House. She understood. "It's the worst on your first night," she said.

"Darling, you know what I said to the Congress," he told her. "I'd give anything in the world if I wasn't here today."

She laughed. "Oh, it's going to be funny, because the rooms are all so big, you'll all get lost."

He wanted her to come visit him in the White House. Her first response was a throaty giggle, and then she said, "Someday, I will."

"Someday?"

"But anyway, take a big sleeping pill," Mrs. Kennedy said.

Sleeping pills would not suffice, said Lyndon Johnson, who seemed to ask about another kind of pill, as though the Kennedys had given him some of the amphetamine pills prescribed for them by Dr. Max Jacobson of New York. The pills, legal at the time though considered dangerous by many physicians, had perked up both John and Jacqueline Kennedy when their energies flagged. They seemed to have done the same for Johnson.

"Aren't you going to bring, aren't you going to bring . . ." he said. "You know what they do to me? They're just like taking a hypo. They just stimulate me, and I just get every idea I'd ever had in my life comes back and I start thinking new things and new roads to conquer."

"Great," she said in her breathy voice.

"So, I can't take . . . a sleeping pill won't put me to sleep. It just wakes me up. But if I know that you're going to come back to see me some morning, when you bring the kid to school, and the first time you do, please come and walk, and let me walk down to the seesaw with you, like old times."

"I will, Mister President."

"OK, darling. Give Caroline and John-John a hug for me. Tell them I'd like to be their daddy."

On Sunday, December 8, Barry Goldwater summoned his top advisors to a meeting in his Washington apartment to tell them he had decided not to run for president. Kitchel was there, along with Senators Norris Cotton of New Hampshire, John Tower of Texas, former senator William Knowland of California, Peter O'Donnell from Cliff White's Draft Goldwater Committee, and conservative analyst Bill Baroody.

Cotton tried to talk him out of the decision, saying that Johnson would never be able to stand up to the leftist intellectuals and the labor unions on foreign policy or on what all of them considered a drift to socialism. If Goldwater didn't run, Cotton said, he would be betraying the conservative cause.

Cotton knew what he was doing. Goldwater's personal ambitions were limited; his devotion to conservatism was not. Still, the most he would do was promise to think it over for a while. Most of his friends left his apartment thinking they'd have to find another candidate.

Two days after that meeting in Goldwater's apartment, Cotton, Senator Carl Curtis of Nebraska, Kitchel, and Goldwater assistant Dean Burch went to the senator's office. He was still noncommittal, but he did concede that he had ordered a private poll to be taken to see how the assassination had affected his political standing.

Only politicians who are running commission polls. Cliff White's confidence had been well placed. Now he would see whether all the work he'd done would pay off.

| | |

That next Saturday, the phone in Cartha DeLoach's house rang as soon as his teenage daughter hung up from talking to one of her friends. This time it was one of his friends, the president of the United States, who complained about "the real talkers" tying up the phone. DeLoach was now the president's liaison with the FBI, and he told Johnson he would work on the problem.

The next day, as he and his family were about to go to church, two men arrived bearing tools and "instructions from the White House to run a direct telephone line into your house." DeLoach was somewhat surprised but also pleased about his newfound importance. He showed them into the kitchen, pointed to his existing telephone, and said, "You can put it right over there, beside the other phone."

"Sorry," said the man with the toolbox. "We've got orders to locate it in your bedroom."[7]

| | |

The first sign that Robert Kennedy had begun to snap out of his despair came at a Christmas party that columnist Mary McGrory hosted every year at an orphanage. A child stopped in front of Kennedy and said, "Your brother's dead! Your brother's dead!"

Everyone froze in silence. The little boy started to cry, but Kennedy picked him up, held him close, and said, "That's all right. I have another brother."

In recent weeks, Kennedy had been doing a lot of reading, English poetry and Greek drama, mostly, some of it recommended by his widowed sister-in-law, whom he visited often at her Georgetown home. He'd read, and while reading he would write his thoughts in the journal he kept, and sometime in December he returned not just to his job but to the world of the living.

But he was not the same man, nor did he return to the same place. For the first time in his life, he was nobody's kid brother. That's what he'd been for thirty-eight years: Joe Kennedy's son, John Kennedy's younger brother. Now Joe, who suffered a stroke late in 1961, sat silent and crippled in a wheelchair; Jack was dead; and Robert was the oldest living son of a disabled father. He was the man of the family.

Whether he liked it or not, he was the leader of a political faction. Already there was talk that he should try to get Johnson to choose him as his running mate. It was impossible to know where such talk began, but one day it was just there, bubbling up from the body politic rather than organized by an officeholder or a columnist.

Some of it sprang from raw emotion, from an absurd effort to deny that John Kennedy was really dead. Without quite knowing it or in any way planning it, the country was in the process of creating a myth—with a bit of orchestration. Four days after the funeral, Jacqueline Kennedy went to Hyannis Port. First, she told her father-in-law all that had happened, everything from the plane ride to Dallas the previous Friday, to Monday afternoon's folding of the flag, the flag she was giving to him. A few days later, she called journalist Theodore White and implored him to come to Hyannis Port to see her. Now.

White had written *The Making of the President, 1960*, which revolutionized political journalism by presenting a presidential campaign as process and personality, and placing it in the context of the social and economic trends changing the country. The book had hardly been without some criticism of John Kennedy, but there was little doubt that he was the author's favorite, and not only because he won. Mrs. Kennedy believed she could trust White, and in him she had made a wise choice of confidant.

White drove up from New York in the rain and arrived to find a widow who was pale and shaken but possessing a firm agenda. She wanted him to write an article for *Life,* the magazine for which he was a regular contributor, an article that would show her husband as he had really been, not the way the historians—"those bitter old men," she said—would write about him.

"I want to say this one thing," she told White. "It's been almost an obsession with me. All I keep thinking of is this line from a musical comedy. It's been an obsession with me."

The musical was *Camelot,* with lyrics by Kennedy's old friend Alan Jay Lerner. At night before they'd go to sleep, she said, they would play the music on an old Victrola, "and the song he loved most came at the very end of this record, the last side of *Camelot,* sad *Camelot . . .* 'Don't let it be forgot, that once there was a spot, for one brief shining moment that was known as Camelot.' "[8]

No magazine was going to turn down an article based on an exclusive interview with Jacqueline Kennedy that week. White's article, which appeared in the December 6 issue of *Life,* was heavily promoted, widely read, and all but universally discussed. It did more than strike a chord. It named an era. From then on, the thousand days of John F. Kennedy's presidency would be known as "Camelot," an epoch and a style always to be longed for, never to be recaptured.

Nor did the article do any harm to the political prospects of the dead president's brothers. Talk of restoration had started before White's article appeared, but the interview surely provided that talk with emotional ballast and gave it a slogan. There is no reason to think that either Robert or Edward Kennedy or any of the family's semiofficial political strategists played any role in convincing Mrs. Kennedy to arrange that interview. There was barely time, and there was no need; she had her own agenda, and it had far more to do with her husband's place in history than with whatever future office his brothers might hold.

At any rate, however orchestrated the myth, however overblown, it could not have succeeded were there not more truth than fantasy to it. Despite its setbacks, the Kennedy presidency was successful according to the standards by which presidents are measured (peace and prosperity, mostly) and then some. There was something exciting, perhaps dangerous, about those three years, a feeling that has never been recaptured and probably never will be.

Jacqueline Kennedy was no political analyst, but in her loss she understood the country's better than most of the professionals. She was no political strategist, either, but she knew precisely how to lay the foundation for establishing her husband's place in history and her own image in the present.

4

CONSERVATION

Interior Secretary Stewart Udall was the last of the Kennedy cabinet members to meet with President Johnson. This was no accident. Aside from Robert Kennedy himself, Udall was the cabinet secretary Johnson trusted the least and for a similar reason. Udall wasn't a Kennedy, but he was thoroughly a Kennedy man.

So on Monday, December 9, Udall went into his meeting with his new boss figuring he'd be fired, a fear not eased when Johnson kept referring to him as "a Kennedy man." Udall remembered being "sort of terrified" as he reminded Johnson that they were from the same part of the country and that "I thought I understood his convictions and desires and that we could work together." The president took this in but kept repeating, after almost every sentence, Udall's Kennedy connection.

Finally, the president said, "We'll give you a try," and issued an order. "I'm from an oil state," Johnson said. "Oil's a very controversial subject. I want to have a relationship that Roosevelt and [Interior Secretary Harold] Ickes had. I want you to make all the oil decisions. You run the oil program. I want oil out of the White House. I want you to walk out and tell the reporters this."

Udall did. "I went in like a lamb and came out like a lion," he said.

He needn't have worried. There was no way Lyndon Johnson was going to fire Stew Udall that day, and not just because it would have been politically stupid to single him out. Johnson had at least two other reasons for retaining Udall. One of them was that Lady Bird Johnson liked Udall, his wife, and his book, *The Quiet Crisis*. The book was about the increasing threats human activity posed to the natural world. Mrs. Johnson cared about the natural world.

So, in his own way, did Mr. Johnson, which was the final reason he was going to keep Udall in his job. That reference to Harold Ickes was not limited to petroleum decisions. As a Westerner, Johnson understood the importance of natural resource issues. Although they rarely got onto the front pages of the Eastern newspapers, they often determined the future: how, where, and to whose benefit the nation would grow.

He knew, for instance, that there was neither enough water nor enough electricity in the fastest growing region in America—Southern California—to allow it to keep growing, just as he knew that there were too many powerful people making too much money from that growth to allow it to stop or even to decelerate. Soon enough, that problem would end up in the federal government's lap, meaning in his.

And as a Western politician, Johnson knew all too well the ability of the developers, miners, power companies, construction companies, and ranchers, as well as the banks that finance them, to pressure the government. Some of them were his friends and patrons. It wouldn't hurt to have an interior secretary who was known as a friend of public power, of consumers, and of conservationists. Johnson wanted that countervailing pressure on himself, perhaps as much as he wanted someone else for his friends and his patrons to get mad at.

Johnson's construction contractor friends and Udall's conservationist friends differed largely over who would benefit from government projects and hardly at all over whether such projects should go forward. They fought over whether new dams would be built by public agencies or private utilities, whether the price of new natural gas wells would be high or low, but not over whether dams should be built and gas fields should be tapped.

This, too, was part of the consensus. Conservatives and liberals agreed that bigger is better, that growth is progress, and that nature had to be altered for human convenience. American history proved it; without dams much of the West would be uninhabitable and unarable, without government-subsidized pesticide spraying there wouldn't be as much food. At the time, the prevailing view was that nature was all but indestructible, that there was plenty of everything, and if it wasn't all in the right places, that was okay because American ingenuity would fix that.

Was the West running out of water? The solution was simply to dam it up and pipe it in, or sift the salt out of the seawater. That's what President Kennedy had wanted to do, and even though Wayne Aspinall, the crotchety Democratic congressman from western Colorado, had cut Kennedy's Office of Saline Water proposal to a mere $75 million for a six-year program, desalination was "already a practical fact and is only a cost problem."[1] The Bureau of Reclamation had established the Office of Atmospheric Water Research in Denver, and research was proceeding.

As for warnings that the country might soon run out of coal and oil, a solution was at hand. Nuclear power plants "may be safely operated under all normal conditions," according to the Atomic Energy Commission. Meanwhile there were billions of barrels of oil in tons of shale in Colorado and Utah. All Americans were grandchildren of the frontier, and hadn't Jack Kennedy recently proclaimed a new one? On the frontier, there was always fresh grass across the next hill and always a way for a strong and determined person to get to it.

It was even within our power to alter the weather. On Wednesday, December 11, Floyd Dominy, the head of the Bureau of Reclamation, announced grants to two Western universities to study "snowpack augmentation," in which snow fences would be erected on the prairies, in the hope that deeper drifts would reduce evaporation.

|||

The same day Dominy made that announcement, the Steering Committee of the Draft Goldwater Committee held its final meeting at Washington's Mayflower Hotel. Peter O'Donnell, presiding, said he thought Lyndon Johnson could be beaten. The latest polls gave Johnson a 2:1 lead over anyone the Republicans might name, but there were some hopeful signs for the Goldwaterites. Finance director Frank Kovac reported on the "large number of checks that had been written after November 22."

Furthermore, the usual Republican constituencies were standing firm. That very day, in Chicago, the American Farm Bureau Federation was passing resolutions opposing most government action, especially federal government action—except, of course, for the necessity of "support prices for feed grains," as well as the peanut, rice, and tobacco programs; higher cotton price supports; the present sugar quota system; and more federal aid for "eradicating diseases and pests."

Cliff White understood, if the Farm Bureau did not, the inconsistency here. He knew the difference between the conservative intellectuals, whose hostility to government was ideological, and the business communities, who were hostile to government only when it was not in their interest.

But White knew better than to discuss this publicly. There were both observations and sentiments White kept to himself. In fact, there were sentiments he kept *from* himself. He had been so relieved when Goldwater finally decided to run for president after all that he was hardly even insulted about hearing the news secondhand. He was by now accustomed to being mistreated by the people he was trying to help, even by the man he was trying to put into the White House. So committed was he to his cause that occasional humiliation was a small price to pay. He had already agreed to give the official title of chairman of the Draft Committee to his friend Peter O'Donnell of Texas. Goldwater liked O'Donnell. White, who was really running the committee, took the title of national director.

Titles didn't really matter to him, and by now he had figured out that there was a difference between the Goldwater campaign and the Goldwater movement that had created it. There was even a difference between the Goldwater movement and the conservative movement that had created *it*.

Despite its apparent hostility to intellect and the higher culture, the latter was a movement founded by serious intellectuals such as Friedrich A. Hayek, Russell Kirk, and Richard Weaver. Hayek was the hero of the free-marketeers, who longed to restore the near-absolute freedom of individuals to do as they chose, especially in the economic realm. Kirk and Weaver inspired the moralists who wanted to restore the ethical (and usually religious) values of the past. That there were real questions about whether economic life had ever been as unfettered or personal behavior as saintly as they believed did not deter them or their devotees.

Ultimately, the two factions united behind a fear of communism and hostility to government, which had the power to redistribute wealth and to replace what Kirk called "custom, convention, and old prescription" as the guardians of progress and virtue.

Interesting ideas, but as White well knew ideas alone do not a political movement make. Money must be added, and organization, and a hook to appeal to the millions who do not read economic tomes or philosophical essays.

And a candidate. Every political movement needs a candidate.

All this White kept to himself. He was, he knew, something of a conduit among the several realms of Republican conservatism. As founder of the Draft Goldwater Committee, he was part of the Goldwater movement, but he was also the senior political strategist in the embryonic Goldwater campaign. And because he was friends with Bill Rusher, he was the link between the practical pols and the theorists who read and wrote for the *National Review,* the conservative magazine founded by William Buckley and his brother-in-law Brent Bozell. Rusher was the editor.

| | |

Late in the afternoon of Friday, December 13, Robert Kennedy sat in his office with Richard Goodwin and Arthur Schlesinger. They were not pleased. Schlesinger had just been informed by Averell Harriman that President Johnson was about to appoint Thomas Mann to coordinate Latin American policy.

It may not have been what Johnson intended, but Kennedy and his friends interpreted the appointment as the first open break with John Kennedy's policies. To them, Mann was a hard-liner, something of a colonialist with condescending attitudes toward Latin Americans and devotion to the American companies who did business South of the Border.

In the fading winter afternoon, Robert Kennedy spoke as though he, as though all of them, were exiles in the government they served.

"Our power will last for just eleven months," he said. "It will disappear the day of the election. After November fifth we'll all be dead."

Kennedy wasn't speaking out of self-pity. Or at least it was more than self-pity (and minor confusion—Election Day would be November 3). "Sure, I've lost a brother," he said. "Other people lose wives . . . but that's not what's important. What's important is what we were trying to do for this country. We worked hard to get where we are, and we can't let it all go to waste. My brother barely had a chance to get started—and there is so much now to be done—for the Negroes and the unemployed and the schoolkids and everyone else who is not getting a decent break in our society. This is what counts. The new fellow doesn't get this. He knows all about politics and nothing about human beings."

But how would he know? By his own testimony, he would not talk to the new fellow. When Schlesinger and Goodwin asked him about this, he replied, "I don't feel mentally or physically prepared to do so yet. When I talk to him, I am ready to be tough about what we must have."

The next day, Johnson announced the appointment of Thomas Mann, and Schlesinger wrote to Kennedy, "We are weaker—a good deal weaker—than we had supposed." Kennedy thought Schlesinger was being too pessimistic, but which of them was right was less important than that both of them considered themselves at war with the leader of their own party and administration. Within that party and administration were two factions. Each assumed the worst of the other, and in those assumptions, each faction was following its leader.

But if Johnson was subtly signaling a shift in Latin American policy, he openly proclaimed his adherence to his predecessor's centrist views about the Soviet Union, disarmament, and the United Nations. On Tuesday, December 17, he went to the United Nations to announce that "the United States of America wants to see the cold war end. We want to see it end once and for all. The United States wants to prevent the dissemination of nuclear weapons to the nations not now possessing them. . . . We support the United Nations as the best instrument yet designed to promote the peace of the world and to promote the well-being of mankind."

While Johnson was away, Jacqueline Kennedy returned to the White House to see the Christmas play put on by her daughter Caroline's class, which would continue to meet in the White House until the start of the new year. She had hoped to see President Johnson, she wrote him, until the morning newspapers reminded her that he would be in New York. She felt, she said, "so stupid" and promised to accept the invitation he'd extended earlier to visit soon after the Christmas holidays.

But she never did. If she thought she could bear to return to the White House, that visit to see the Christmas play apparently convinced her otherwise. She did not go back there until 1971.

| | |

A week before the president spoke to the United Nations, the fight against grain credits to the Soviets had resurfaced, this time in the House of Representatives, where the president's nemesis was not a vapid Republican from the Great Plains but Otto Passman, an ostentatious Louisiana Democrat whose white suits and courtly manner masked his harsh stubbornness and his quasi-medieval worldview.

Though he was chairman (indeed, dictator) of the Foreign Relations Appropriations Subcommittee, Passman was genuinely opposed to foreign aid and, in fact, to almost any foreign dealings except perhaps those related to the extortion of ship contracts from foreign governments, for which he would be indicted twelve years later. A week earlier, he had reported out a bill authorizing only $2.8 billion in foreign aid, instead of the $3.6 billion minimum Johnson wanted, and with the House version of the Mundt amendment.

"It's a shame that a caveman like Passman does like he does," Johnson told Speaker John McCormack. "Mr. Eisenhower told me that he wasn't a dependable man, and Mr. Kennedy told me he wasn't a dependable man. . . . And I don't think this man knows much about our country, and notwithstanding his great facility with figures I think he's got a real mental problem."

Showing his petulant side, Johnson told McCormack that they might as well bring the bill to the floor and let Passman beat them.

"Just fight him," he said. "We've got an expression down in my country that just says, 'Fight him till he's shitty as a bear.' "

But it wasn't just Passman. As McCormack and Carl Albert tried to tell the president, the American people didn't like foreign aid, and too many members had promised their constituents that they would oppose trade with communist countries.

This was obviously a position with some political resonance. In fact, it was one of the driving forces behind the movement that created Barry Gold-water's candidacy. Less than eighteen months earlier, a conservative organization called Young Americans for Freedom had held a rally at Madison Square Garden where Brent Bozell's speech brought the crowd to its feet.

Bozell was living in Spain. He had by then become a Roman Catholic "integrist," an opponent of church-state separation. He would no longer celebrate the Fourth of July. Franco's Spain was more to his liking. But he had come back to help rally the troops, and he was succeeding.

Bozell's speech was recorded, and years later young conservatives were still playing the record to inspire each other and convert their friends. The most persuasive part of the speech came when Bozell recounted what he said were the words of President Kennedy: "Will you not understand, he said, why I cannot lead you to victory? Can't you see that we no longer live in the kind of world in which the good side can hope to have its way? That in the very nature of the battle, this can only be a 'twilight struggle'?"[2]

John Kennedy never said any such thing. At best, it was a bizarre misinterpretation of Kennedy's November 16, 1961, speech in Seattle in which he concisely outlined the bipartisan cold war consensus. But Bozell was as prescient as he was unscrupulous. He knew that there were people out there who were seeking moral absolutes, who were seeking assurance that there still *were* moral absolutes, and who therefore were in rebellion against the apparent relativism of the centrist establishment. They wanted America to be a force for virtue, not just prudence.

Part of that relativism was reflected in negotiations with the Soviets. If communism was evil—objectively evil—why could it not be defeated rather than simply neutralized? Or as Bozell put it in the title of the book he published that year under Barry Goldwater's name, *Why Not Victory?*

That was the second book Bozell had ghostwritten for Goldwater. The first, *Conscience of a Conservative,* had been inspired (and published) by Clarence Manion, dean of the Notre Dame Law School and a leader of the John Birch Society. It was the Birchers who created the nucleus of the political organization that Cliff White was heading, and it was Senator Joseph McCarthy of Wisconsin, America's other self-proclaimed scourge of communism, who created the candidate.

McCarthy went into Illinois in 1950 to campaign against Senate Majority Leader Scott Lucas, who had dared to criticize McCarthy's reckless accusations. Lucas lost to Everett Dirksen. Shaken, Senate Democrats named as their new leader a man with a safe seat, Ernest McFarland of Arizona, one of the authors of the G.I. Bill of Rights.

But McFarland had also criticized McCarthy, and in 1952 McCarthy made two trips to Arizona, questioning McFarland's loyalty. McFarland lost by only 6,725 of almost 200,000 votes cast, and it was probably McCarthy who made the difference. The surprise winner was city councilman Barry Goldwater, who was now the front-runner, said the polls, for the Republican presidential nomination. True, that nomination didn't seem to be worth much, and Goldwater may have been the front-runner because the Republican Party was weak, its candidate pool shallow. But no candidacy so removed from the political mainstream, or what seemed to be the mainstream, could have gotten this far were there not forces behind it.

Those forces were moralism and nationalism, which have endurance. Liberal intellectuals such as I. F. Stone may have disparaged conservative fear as "the need for a devil being as deep as the need for a God." But for many people that need was part of their sense of dismay at the flouting of traditional standards and at the apparent inability of their nation to assert itself.

To the growing evidence that such sentiments were on the rise—indeed, that they were held by a majority of the people—champions of the consensus had a simple, common reaction: If evidence is discomforting, it should be ignored. Aside from an occasional editorial or column dismissing anticommunist nationalism as unenlightened, the consensus proceeded as though it was an annoyance, not a threat.

Indeed, such was the confidence of the consensus that it did not shrink from considering the implications of the assassination. Was it just an aberration, or was social critic Irving Howe onto something when he said that it had revealed a "social pathology"? Whatever the country's troubles, Americans had retained a faith in themselves as essentially a good people inhabiting a good society. Now that conclusion had to be reconsidered.

It was reconsidered most prominently by *The New York Times Magazine* just before the turn of the year in an unsigned article entitled "What Sort of Nation Are We?"

Not a bad one, came the answer. "We are, first and foremost, a democracy," the article said, but a special kind of democracy. Noting that popular majorities no doubt opposed many of the country's political institutions—free speech, the presumption of innocence—the article concluded, without using the offending word, that this was something of an elitist democracy, in which only a select minority upheld liberal values.

Instead, American democracy was "a social rather than a political phenomenon," based on the fact that more Americans "have been able to ascend to a level of material security and a consciousness of personal worth" than the people of other lands, to such an extent that "social classes play . . . a small role in our national life."

Even members of racial minorities could attain this wealth and consciousness, the article said, for the real division in the country was based on neither race nor class; it was . . . well, it wasn't education, exactly. It was more like degrees of enlightenment, or what would later be called "lifestyle."

The division was between a "provincial America," mired in the past but well represented in Congress and in local government, and the future-oriented "metropolitan America," whose voice was heard in the big corporations, the universities, the new suburban developments, the communications industry, and the presidency.

What distinguished these two Americas, said the author, was "our [there was no doubt about which side he was on] commitment to a democratic society and to technological innovation." Nor was there much doubt that "we" would prevail. After all, suburbia, the corporate economy, and the power of the presidency could only grow, and as more people got college educations, there would be more of "us," fewer of "them."

So not to worry. The Dallas fourth graders who cheered the assassination were remnants of the fading "provincial America." The murders in Dallas were "unpredictable and unpreventable." To be sure, America has its problems, the article said, but "our problems are those of success."

Though the snobbery of this article was unusually blatant, the essential content of the piece accurately reflected both the conservative and the liberal realities of the consensus, which embraced the centralized corporation as well as centralized government. The consensus was internationalist, integrationist, sophisticated, cosmopolitan. Above all, it was rational. Like John Kennedy and Richard Nixon, like corporate executives and respected academics, the consensus honored restraint and careful analysis. It knew that the modern world had to be managed and that to manage it well one had to think clearly. This was an age of objectivity.

| | |

Late Friday night, Passman agreed to a flat $3 billion aid bill that would allow wheat sales to the Soviets on the condition that the president declare them to be in the national interest. The president was furious. Every time he made such a declaration, he told his old friend Albert Thomas, "they write a story that you're pro-Russian."

Nor was the president mollified when Thomas suggested putting the declaration in the mail, rather than announcing it in person.

"Then they say that you're yielding to the Soviet Union, and H. L. Hunt puts out a news release," Johnson said. "You know goddamn well when I ask them not to make me notify them publicly so it wouldn't be in the papers—you know I know what I'm doing . . . and we screwed it up. This damn fool Humphrey put that paragraph on."

Thomas, who held Johnson's old congressional seat, tried to convince LBJ that the requirement wouldn't be damaging, but the president was having none of it. "Don't try to shit me because I know better," he told him, and then railed again about Passman. "I think it's awful that a goddam Cajun from the hills of Louisiana has got more power than all of us. . . . If I ever woke up in the cold of the night and a rattlesnake's out there about ready to get him, I ain't gonna pull him off."

| | |

On Saturday, December 21, Defense Secretary McNamara and General Maxwell Taylor returned from a two-day trip to Saigon. "The situation is very disturbing," McNamara announced, "but I am optimistic as to the progress that can be made in the following year."

The next day, bypassing the joint chiefs of staff, the president ordered an interdepartmental group under Marine Lieutenant General Victor Krulak to select targets to be bombed in North Vietnam.

To protect his political flank, Johnson invited Cartha DeLoach over for an Oval Office chat and asked him, as chairman of the American Legion's Public Relations Commission, to arrange for the president to "get some letters and telegrams into the White House supporting our handling of the war in Vietnam."

DeLoach said that could be arranged.[3]

| | |

On Monday, December 23, as snow fell in huge flakes all day long, the official mourning period for President Kennedy came to an end. The black crepe came down from the White House, and Lady Bird Johnson put her black dresses in the rear of her closet.

By the middle of the afternoon, many government workers had gone home to avoid getting stranded downtown by the snowfall. Among those ordered to stay were the public information officers of the cabinet departments and independent agencies, who were herded into the White House Fish Room to be greeted by press secretary Pierre Salinger. Salinger proceeded to give them a standard pep talk about the importance of the work they do and to ask them to produce story ideas for the White House for the next day, Christmas Eve, so he could take them to Texas and work on getting favorable stories out during the holiday break.

At that moment, Lyndon Johnson entered the room and told the public information officials that even though Salinger had told him what hard workers they all were, in his opinion they were doing hardly anything at all. They were not amused.

The foreign aid bill had not passed the House, and opponents of the wheat sales were still making trouble. Besides, it was almost Christmas, and most of the representatives had gone home. In the middle of the afternoon, Larry O'Brien told the president that seventy Republicans and fifty-six Democrats were absent.

To keep the others from leaving and lure a few back to town, Johnson held a Christmas reception at the White House that evening. The president's aides followed his advice to attend the reception, "smile and shake hands and thank everybody," to convince them to vote for the foreign aid bill. The president himself stood atop a gold velvet chair in the middle of the state dining room and told the partying congresspeople that "the eyes of the world are upon the United States tonight."

As for those who voted the wrong way or who did not return, Johnson urged O'Brien to "just cut their peter off and put it in your pocket."

The president did not let the occasion pass without calling Mrs. Kennedy. It was their second conversation in two days. He had called her on Saturday evening to tell her, again, that he loved her and that he wished he could make her Christmas happier. The Johnsons' daughter Lucy had brought some Christmas presents for the Kennedy children to the Georgetown house, and Mrs. Kennedy had given the president a book.

Briefly, Johnson handed the telephone to his wife to wish Mrs. Kennedy a nice Christmas. When he came back on the line he scolded her again for not coming to visit him, and she assured him that as soon as he got back after Christmas, "I'll come and get a vitamin B shot from Dr. [Janet] Travell, and see you."

"Won't you do that? Thank you, honey," the president said.

Now, on Monday evening, they continued their flirtatious banter, and he continued his mock anger at her for not visiting.

"If you ever come back here again and don't come to see me, why there's going to be trouble," he said. "You don't realize I have the FBI at my disposal, do you? I'm going to send for you if you don't come by."

She laughed. She promised she would visit. He called her honey. She called him Mister President.

|||

The next day, for the first time in its history, the House of Representatives met on the day before Christmas and passed the bill, without the restrictions on U.S. credit for Soviet wheat sales, in a vote of 189 to 158. Somehow, the president had convinced thirty-eight members to come back from wherever they were.

On other substantive matters of state, top officials of the Federal Bureau of Investigation met all day Monday in the office of F. J. Baumgartner to discuss their campaign for "neutralizing Martin Luther King Jr. as an effective Negro leader."

This was considered to be a vital task because even if King himself was not a communist, he was the most dangerous kind of security threat precisely because he did not believe that internal communism was a dangerous security threat. Besides, FBI probing had left little doubt that King "pretty much agreed with Hegel" on the central role of dialectics in history, and since Hegel had influenced Marx . . . well, one needn't go on. The official agenda of the meeting proclaimed that "we are most interested in exposing him in some manner or other in order to discredit him."

William C. Sullivan, the chief of Domestic Intelligence, asked his colleagues for nominees for the "right kind" of Negro to replace King as the nation's preeminent civil rights leader.[4] John Malone, the top agent in New York, was one of several who proposed Roy Wilkins, the director of the NAACP. Sullivan overruled them. His choice was a little-known attorney named Samuel Pierce.

|||

That evening, the president of the United States tried to place a call to Geraldine Whittington, a secretary who worked in the office of presidential aide Ralph Dungan. Johnson did not know Whittington—he would later refer to her as "this Wilkinson girl"—but he was going to move her to his office. She was efficient, she was good-looking, and she was a Negro.

The phone system was still annoying him. By now he had enough lines—eighteen of them—but the system was not running smoothly. "How long does it take me to get her?" he barked at someone in the Oval Office. . . . "Gerri? Where are you?"

"I'm at home. Who's this?"

"This is the president."

"Oh, I think someone's playing with me," said the confused young woman.

But that really was the president of the United States who sent a car for her, and when she got to the White House, he informed her about her new job. Two days later, she was celebrating Christmas at the LBJ ranch.

It was a working vacation. A few days after Christmas, some of the top White House aides were working in the "guest house," a small green frame house some two hundred yards from the main ranch house. Herefords grazed outside while the educated technicians within plotted what would soon become known as a war on poverty. The setting did not suit everyone. Budget director Kermit Gordon wore a khaki Western shirt he had borrowed from the president, but he was still wearing the pants from an expensive suit.

Gordon, Bill Moyers, Horace Busby, Ted Sorensen, and economist Walter Heller sat and brainstormed for hours, crumpling up pieces of notepaper, swilling endless cups of coffee. One of the ideas put forth was to create a convenient poverty service center at Washington's Union Station. Busby was confused, asking how poor people would get there and where they would park. The president immediately summoned him outside.

"Why did you say that?" he asked his longtime friend. "Don't you realize these are Kennedy people?" At almost any cost, he did not want to feel humiliated before Kennedy people.

To honor Busby, a University of Texas graduate and active alumnus, and to welcome in the new year, the powers who ruled the White House and Austin society prepared a party at the Forty Acres Club, the University of Texas faculty club from which many professors had resigned to protest its policy of racial segregation.

The president arrived with a guest on his arm, Gerri Whittington. She was a little nervous at first and asked him, "Mr. President, do you know what you're doing?"

"I sure do," he said. "Half of them are going to think you're my wife, and that's just fine with me."

From that moment on, the Forty Acres Club was integrated.

5

HAPPY NEW YEAR

New Year's Eve is a bittersweet time, but Tuesday night, December 31, 1963, was more bittersweet than usual. The wounds of November had not entirely healed. Life went on, all right. Men and women went to work, kids went to school, people went shopping. Old habits were easily resumed. Once radio and television stations went back to their regular programming and the movie theaters reopened, audiences returned willingly, if not avidly. The radio played Lesley Gore telling her boyfriend, "You Don't Own Me." At the movies, Debbie Reynolds starred as a recently divorced beauty in *Mary, Mary,* Jackie Gleason taught Steve McQueen the meaning of life in *Soldier in the Rain,* and James Garner and Lee Remick spoofed Texas millionaires in *The Wheeler Dealers.*

On Broadway, Paddy Chayefsky directed his own play, *The Passion of Josef D,* and bookstores were full of copies of *Caravans,* James Michener's epic of the Asian desert.

There were also weightier cultural pursuits. Artur Schnabel had recently recorded all the Beethoven piano sonatas for Angel Records, and there were new poetry collections by May Swenson, James Merrill, and Edward Field, whose *Stand Up, Friend, with Me* was the Lamont poetry selection for the year. For devotees of serious expository prose, the second volume of Shelby Foote's history of the Civil War had recently been published. Serious intellectuals were still arguing about whether Hannah Arendt had "blamed the victim" and somehow excused the coordinator of the Holocaust in her 1963 book, *Eichmann in Jerusalem.* Other scholars, and some parents, were debating the impact on children of an unusual new kids' book called *Where the Wild Things Are.*

But none of these diversions entirely obliterated the ache. For most Americans, at the beginning and end of each day, or during quiet moments in between, it came back, a feeling of emptiness, a feeling that things were not right. It wasn't just the loss of Jack Kennedy, though that was part of it. It was also the loss of security, of the assumption that such things simply did not happen here. It was not the loss of optimism, exactly, but the loss of the certainty that optimism was the American norm. It was as though Lee Harvey Oswald had killed two men that November day and unleashed a million demons.

Even some of the New Year's joys were haunted. The big game on New Year's Day—Navy versus Texas for the national championship—was being held in the Cotton Bowl, in Dallas, which meant the Midshipmen and the Longhorn fans were partying less than a mile away from the jail where Jack Ruby was being held for trial and only blocks from the Dealey Plaza, where Oswald had fired the fatal shots.

With all that unease, there were predictions that this year's celebrations would be less spirited, especially in New York, where the weather guys were predicting a cold, snowy evening and where truculent Mike Quill, the union boss with the charming Irish brogue (which he could turn on and off at will), was threatening to take his United Transportation Workers off the job at the stroke of 1964, shutting down the buses and subways.

The predictions were wrong. In the judgment of New York's Finest, the New Year's Eve crowd at Times Square was "the biggest and noisiest in many years." Those wondering why might have found a clue to the crowd's size in its behavior. Decorously, *The New York Times* reported that the throng "tooted and toasted in traditional revelry." Somewhat more bluntly, the cops said it was the drunkest New Year's Eve they could remember. Maybe this was a year when you had to try harder to have fun.

In and out of town, there was plenty of fun to be had. After two years, little Robert Morse was still breathlessly energetic every night in *How to Succeed in Business Without Really Trying*, on Broadway. For a slightly more sophisticated evening, theatergoers could choose Zero Mostel in *A Funny Thing Happened on the Way to the Forum* or Anthony Newley in *Stop the World—I Want to Get Off*.

The hottest new play—it had opened in late October—was the Neil Simon comedy *Barefoot in the Park*, starring Elizabeth Ashley and Robert Redford. But Broadway was not entirely devoted to froth. At the Billy Rose Theater, Uta Hagen and Arthur Hill were the symbolically named Martha and George in *Who's Afraid of Virginia Woolf?*, Edward Albee's pitiless portrait of marriage and intellect. For a few more days, the dramatization of the poignant Carson McCullers story *The Ballad of the Sad Café* would still be at the Martin Beck, and Tennessee Williams's *The Milk Train Doesn't Stop Here*

Anymore would open New Year's night at the Brooks Atkinson, with Tallulah Bankhead and Tab Hunter in the starring roles.

Not everything put forth by the culture was so comforting. That's because there was more than one culture. There were many, and if most of them were usually dismissed by the mainstream, they persisted nonetheless. On New Year's Day hundreds of thousands of Americans had in their homes the latest issue of *Esquire* magazine, with the first installment of Norman Mailer's new novel, *An American Dream,* mingling the themes of politics and crime, sex and murder, with John F. Kennedy as both hero and rogue.

It was no accident that Mailer's novel was serialized in *Esquire.* His non-fiction was a regular feature of the magazine, where he regularly held forth with his skeptical view of the arms race, technological "progress," and respectable thinking. The respectable thinkers honored him for it. "No one," wrote Midge Decter in *Commentary,* "is currently telling us more about the United States of America." She might not have been so effusive a few months later, when Mailer became a regular contributor for an irregular little journal called *Fuck You.*

Under the leadership of Arnold Gingrich, *Esquire* had become the leading (though not the only) conduit between the offbeat adversary culture and the intellectual mainstream. Dwight Macdonald, Gore Vidal, Terry Southern, and Gay Talese also wrote for it. Its last issue of 1963 had sold 883,000 copies, helped by a sprightly cover photograph of heavyweight champion Sonny Liston dressed as Santa Claus. Negroes had been on covers of national magazines before, but not as Santa Claus, and there were a few subscription cancellations.

People all over the country seemed to be reassuring themselves by immersing themselves in the familiar. In Pasadena, California, there was a good crowd at the seventy-fifth Tournament of Roses parade. The grand marshal was former president Dwight Eisenhower, who was fresh from telling the Kiwanis Club kickoff luncheon that football helped mold the American character and that every game "means something to the United States."[1]

Football was even prescribed as a partial cure for the nation's most pressing problem. At the post–bowl games meeting of the American Football Coaches Association, the renowned social critic Wayne W. Hayes was unable to resist explaining that if only everyone played football, racial antagonisms would dissolve. "Play with a Negro and you get to know him for what he is, and you will never have a great bias toward him," said the Ohio State coach. "If you block for him and he blocks for you, through teamwork and close association with him, you get to know him."

Perhaps mercifully, his advice was largely ignored. More attention was paid to Princeton coach Dick Colman's speech on "advancing the ball along the ground" and to the inspirational address by Ohio State's Glenn C. "Tiger" Ellison, who lamented the poor character, and subsequent sad fate, of a major league baseball player named Jerry Simmons, who never existed.

In Pasadena and Dallas, in Miami and New Orleans, the alumni hit the good restaurants and the student fans partied outdoors, singing one song about a girl who seemed to be named "Tra La La La Suzy," another about a guy who loved Popsicles, icicles, and baseball, and yet a third about someone whose name seemed to be "Dominique, ni-que, ni-que, bum-bum-bum-bum-bum-bum-bum." The "bum-bum-bum" part was because the words were French, which few Americans could understand, but that made no difference. It was the number one song, sung by a nun. She was going to be on *The Ed Sullivan Show* the very next Sunday. Sullivan himself had flown to Belgium to supervise the eighteen-minute taped session in a monastery near Waterloo. He'd even paid a . . . well, you'd have to call it a bribe: a heavy-duty jeep with rain curtains for missions in the Congo, as demanded by the Mother Prioress.[2]

And—how fitting—loyal fans of the Huskies or the Huskers, the Tide or the Illini, could dance through the night proclaiming the message "Be True to Your School." The bouncy Beach Boys hit hadn't been number one for a few weeks now, but it was certainly appropriate for the night before a big game. A few college revelers, seniors no doubt, ended the night by crooning "September Song," the haunting ballad of lost youth, recently revived by the great Jimmy Durante, who had made many of their grandparents laugh back in the days of vaudeville.

Parents must have been reassured to find that their children were engaged in such traditional rituals: college educations, football games, fraternity parties, sweet songs, the continuity of popular entertainment. Just as well that the parents were less familiar with another tune played that night where college students and younger teenagers gathered: a foot-stomping number called "Louie Louie," with a beat that was almost as Latin as it was erotic.

At the Cotton Bowl, Navy was the favorite in the big game. Texas was ranked number one to Navy's number two, and most of the 75,504 fans in the Cotton Bowl, including Lyndon Johnson's daughters, would be rooting for the Longhorns.

But the Midshipmen had Roger Staubach—"a legend before his time," his coach called him—the best quarterback in what the sportswriters called "the year of the quarterback." Texas had a quarterback named Emmet Augustus Carlisle II, who had thrown one touchdown pass all year. Darrell Royal was a Texas coach who didn't believe in throwing many passes or even running wide of the line. "They call me the Barry Goldwater of college football because I'm so conservative," Royal said.

But on Texas's first possession, Carlisle threw long to wingback Phil Harris for a touchdown, and in the second quarter he did it again. As for Staubach, he spent most of the game running away from tackle Scott Appleton and guard Tommy Nobis. On one of his scrambles away from the pesky defenders, Staubach bumped into the referee. Such humiliation. By the time it ended, Texas was on top 28 to 6 and in firm possession of the unofficial but much-sought national championship.

| | |

The most celebrated Longhorn fan didn't much care that his team had won. Lyndon Johnson occasionally went to a football game, but he'd spend all his time talking politics. He followed sports only because other politicians liked to talk about them. Dick Russell loved baseball, and so did Hubert Humphrey. Johnson scanned the sports pages just enough to be able to make small talk with these colleagues. Lyndon Johnson did not engage in recreation. He ate and drank. He hunted, but from the comfort of his car, where he could work between shots. When the game ended, he called both coaches, but that, too, was politics. He had more important things to do.

He saw in the new year at his ranch, where he felt at home. He had been living in the White House for three weeks, and Lady Bird had proclaimed, "When I wake up in the morning, I feel at home." But most of the pictures hanging in the West Wing were of Jack Kennedy. Whoever was supposed to take them down had not yet done so, and it was enough to make Johnson feel like an interloper in his own office. The ranch was his domain and work was his recreation, so he spent the holiday thinking, planning, organizing, telephoning.

Between phone calls, Johnson also took time out to write a letter and two telegrams. The letter was posted to Saigon, to Duong Van Minh, chairman of the South Vietnamese Military Revolutionary Council. The letter made clear that the South Vietnamese themselves would have to win their war, but it also pledged to "maintain in Vietnam whatever American personnel and materiel are needed to assist you in achieving victory."

It was an optimistic letter. "As the forces of your government become increasingly capable of dealing with this aggression," Johnson wrote, "American military personnel can be progressively withdrawn."

It was his fondest hope.

As for the telegrams, the first went to Moscow, in response to the New Year's message from Premier Nikita Khrushchev and President Leonid Brezhnev of the Soviet Union. "In our hands have been placed the fortunes of peace and the hope of millions," Johnson wrote. "It is my fervent hope that we are good stewards of that trust."

Having written to an ally and an adversary, Johnson sent his second telegram to someone who was both an ally and an adversary. It went to Aspen, Colorado, where Attorney General Robert F. Kennedy and his family observed—they did not celebrate—the coming of the new year. He wrote:

I KNOW HOW HARD THE PAST SIX WEEKS HAVE BEEN FOR YOU. UNDER THE MOST TRYING CIRCUMSTANCES YOUR FIRST THOUGHTS HAVE BEEN FOR YOUR COUNTRY. YOUR BROTHER WOULD HAVE BEEN VERY PROUD OF THE STRENGTH YOU HAVE SHOWN. AS THE NEW YEAR BEGINS, I RESOLVE TO DO MY BEST TO FULFILL HIS TRUST IN ME. I WILL NEED YOUR COUNSEL AND SUPPORT.
LYNDON B. JOHNSON.

Two days later, Robert Kennedy replied:

GREATLY APPRECIATE THE THOUGHTFULNESS OF YOUR TELEGRAM. I AM LOOKING FORWARD TO VISITING YOU IN WASHINGTON AT YOUR CONVENIENCE. RESPECTFULLY.
ROBERT F. KENNEDY

Over in Brooklyn Heights on New Year's Eve, Todd Gitlin, Tom Hayden, and Paul Potter were having a wonderful time. They were dancing, flirting, and getting good and drunk. The party was at the high-ceilinged old apartment of Sarah Murphy, another member of the Students for a Democratic Society, and though they'd all just been to their national council meeting, where they'd elected a new president and engaged in the usual endless debates, this evening was devoted to old-fashioned fun, pursued with enough intensity to make one wonder whether drinking and wooing were political acts.

Despite their determination to avoid nit-picking (and to have a riproaring good time), the SDS leaders were concerned about a letter they'd recently gotten from one of their own, Dickie Flacks, who had pronounced himself "disturbed (but not alarmed) by certain problems concerning the internal quality of SDS."[3]

It was hard to see how anyone could be discouraged after the national council meeting. Allard Lowenstein had dropped by, and so, more amazingly, had Bob Dylan, a new kind of show business star, their kind, a young man who sang folk songs in a raspy voice and did not shy from mingling political protest with entertainment. Dylan's second album, *The Freewheelin' Bob Dylan,* had been released the previous May. Among its songs was "Blowin' in the Wind," which had been a top popular hit in its sanitized version by Peter, Paul and Mary. The SDS members were far more likely to buy Dylan's original.

At the meeting, Dylan had sat in the back, listening to talk about local organizing, and then, during a recess, he had offered to help.[4] "Ah don't know what you all are talking about, but it sounds like you want something to happen, and if that's what you want, that's what ah want," he'd said.[5] What more proof did they need that the world was changing and that they were in the vanguard of the change?

They had felt this way, really, since their last convention, back in the summer of 1963. President Kennedy was talking about détente with the Soviets, segregation was crumbling in the South, and the ranks of the SDS were growing. But they were also splintering. SDS's first president, Al Haber, ever the intellectual theorist, didn't think much of ERAP, the Economic Research and Action Project, which was Tom Hayden's idea for going into the city slums, helping the truly downtrodden, and not incidentally earning their loyalty. "Is radicalism subsisting in a slum for a year or two, or is it developing your individual talents so you can function as a radical?" Haber had written, deploring the "unfortunate anti-intellectualism" in SDS, the "fascination with the novelty and excitement of the new insurgencies."[6]

Some of this was personal. After all, if any one person could claim to be the founder of SDS, it was Haber, who had dropped out of the University of Michigan before Hayden got there. But Haber, who was still in his twenties, was already losing his hair. He spoke slowly, methodically. He had no pizzazz. Tom Hayden did, and by late 1963 Hayden had become the real leader of the organization.

But now Dickie Flacks was worrying that they were simply going to "repeat the whole tragic, tired, futile history of the American left's sects" in conflicts over personalities and ideology. Was his nose out of joint, too?

Oh, well. You probably needed somebody like Flacks around, just to protect you from complacency. But they weren't going to let his dissent throw them off course. Dick was their friend, but they had work to do. Chapters were forming at Swarthmore, Oberlin, the Universities of Texas and Oklahoma. There were community organizations to form in Newark, Cleveland, Baltimore, and Chicago. They were not about to be discouraged.

The real Barry Goldwater, whom no one called the Darrell Royal of Republican politics, was at home in Paradise Valley just north of Phoenix, in the shadow of Camelback Mountain, where he was recovering from a minor operation that removed a calcium deposit from his right heel. He spent much of his time looking over drafts of a speech he would give in a few days.

The speech was not without significance. In it he would declare himself a candidate for the Republican nomination for president of the United States. But on the last day of 1963, he and his wife made the time to make another formal announcement, that their daughter Margaret would marry Richard Arlen Holt of Northridge, California, on June 27 in Phoenix.

Though he had been something of a remote father—writing letters to his children had always been easier for him than talking to them—Goldwater must have welcomed this personal diversion. It allowed him to think about something other than running for president, about which he was always ambivalent. His passion for politics was genuine, but for him politics was a means to an end, and that end was not power for its own sake. There were times when he wondered how he had gotten himself into this pickle, and considering his origins, his bewilderment was reasonable.

Barry Goldwater was the grandson of Michel Goldwasser, a Jew from Konin, Poland, who immigrated to America with his brother in 1852 and soon thereafter made his way to the Arizona territory, then dependent on the federal government, where he prospered as a merchant. Mike Goldwater retired in the late 1880s and spent the rest of his life in San Francisco, where he remained active in synagogue and Zionist causes until he died in 1903, the year the National Reclamation Act appropriated $10 million to build a dam on the Salt River, the project that made modern Phoenix possible.

His son, Baron, took over the family store in Phoenix. He was a slight, serious young man with ambitions to become part of Phoenix society. In those days, that was hard to do as a Jew, and neither religion nor ethnic tradition meant much to Baron. Even before he fell in love with Josephine Williams, he had stopped going to the synagogue, had not even bothered closing his store on the High Holy Days. He and JoJo were married in the Episcopal Church, and he subsequently converted.

Whatever Baron Goldwater's motives, his ambitions were fulfilled. His store made a lot of money, and he and his wife were among Phoenix's leading citizens. Wealth and status were important to him and to the family he and JoJo raised—Barry, Robert, and Carolyn. Theirs was a world of frontier commerce. It was business-centered. Creativity was commercial or mechanical: designing a new store, learning to fly a plane, tinkering with a ham radio. The purpose of public service was to make life easier for business.

By all appearances, Barry Goldwater was a typical son of this milieu. He was never much of a student. After his second year at Phoenix Union High School, his father and the headmaster decided he'd be better off at the Stanton Military Academy in Virginia.[7] It was there that he learned to fly and acquired his enduring interest in matters military. It was from there he went into the Air Force.

Full grown, he cut an impressive figure. He was an even six feet tall and muscular, with a square face and friendly blue eyes. He enjoyed the out-of-doors and tinkering with devices. He tried college briefly before deciding it was not for him. He didn't need it. He had a family business to run.

He ran it pretty well, and he liked running it his way. Patriotically, he displayed the Blue Eagle of the National Industrial Recovery Act in his store. But only for a while. Goldwater loved his country, and all the business the New Deal brought into his store. He didn't like those NIRA "codes" prescribing wages and hours.

By then he was already a Republican, one of the few in Arizona or in his family. Later, he called his choice of party "an act of defiance," but he never explained what he was defying. It may have been the Democratic Party itself, often arrogant in its statewide dominance. But he was neither very sophisticated about nor very interested in politics in the early 1930s, and his choice of party may have been an assertion of self, the act of a young man saying "Here I am, a bit unlike the rest of you."

And so he was. By the mid-1930s, Barry Goldwater was a wealthy man with a lively wife, two children (another, Barry junior, would be born in 1938), a successful business, a big house, lots of friendly acquaintances, and a terrible sense of emptiness within. Whether or not he ever technically suffered clinical depression or a nervous breakdown, he often displayed their symptoms: sleeplessness, anxiety, bursts of ill temper. Among his remedies: copious amounts of bourbon and tequila.

He suffered, no doubt, from that common malady of men who inherit their father's business and never know whether they could have succeeded on their own. Later he would acknowledge, "You might say I was a success by being born into a successful family."[8]

His success was in business, his friends were in business, but business bored him. As soon as they could, he and his brother Bob hired someone else to handle most of the day-to-day management of Goldwater's. Thereafter, Bob spent most of his time at the Phoenix Country Club playing golf; Barry spent most of his on his hobbies: flying his plane, operating his ham radio, hiking the desert, photography.

He became quite a good amateur photographer, especially of two subjects that had become increasingly fascinating to him—Arizona's natural wonders and its Indians—and it's hard to think of a combination of interests more defiant of frontier business culture. Barry Goldwater was happiest as an artist honoring unspoiled nature and a traditional, communal society.

But if he came into public life in large part because he was bored with business, his political attitudes were squarely that of the businessman, and that anger at the NIRA wage and hour codes set the pattern. No one influenced him more than his friend Denison Kitchel, who had married into the Phelps Dodge mining family and who headed the corporation's labor relations division. His job was union-busting. Goldwater became increasingly hostile to organized labor and to the federal government.

There was a connection there. Under the New Deal, Washington openly supported unions. "The president wants you to join a union" was one of the slogans labor organizers used in the 1930s. To Goldwater, unions were dangerous, almost un-American. By all appearances, he was a relatively generous employer; wages and benefits at his stores were at least comparable with those of his competitors, so his antipathy to labor was based on ideology rather than greed. Perhaps he had a touch of the neo-Nietzschean—the conviction that the rich and powerful deserved their wealth and power—that became part of the conservative movement that later adopted him.

Unlike some of his supporters, Goldwater never became an avowed devotee of novelist Ayn Rand, who proclaimed that life was "a constant, fierce undefined struggle between the genius and the parasite . . . in which the genius must have his independence." But as a young businessman he did seem convinced that the "better people"—he and his fellow employers—knew what was best for their workers.

Like so many of his friends, he practiced the denial common to businessmen in areas dependent on the federal government. That dependence offends their sense of themselves as rugged individualists who "made it on their own," so they pretend that they did. In the 1930s Arizona was essentially a federal protectorate. Its farmers and city dwellers lived on government-generated electricity and government-supplied water. Goldwater formed his antigovernment attitudes as the government was building Boulder (now Hoover) Dam at the edge of his state.

With time on his hands, anxiety in his soul, and a firm set of beliefs, Goldwater began dabbling in local politics in the early 1940s. He had become known around town thanks to his lectures, complete with slides from his photographs, about nature and Native Americans, and the film he had made of his trip down the Colorado River in 1940.

Then the war intervened. In his midthirties with three children and poor eyesight, he could have stayed out of it. He didn't want to. In fact, he wanted to see combat, and though he never saw an enemy aircraft, he participated in the long and potentially dangerous duty of ferrying supplies, first across the Atlantic and then in C47s across the "Hump," over the Himalayas to airfields in China.

He returned unchanged. In 1946 he supported the successful Arizona initiative that passed a "right to work" law prohibiting the union shop. He was appointed to the Colorado River Commission and became a champion of the Central Arizona Project, designed to bring more water to Phoenix. If he saw any inconsistency in promoting this huge federal project, he never mentioned it.

A year later, he was appointed to a committee designed to change Phoenix's form of government and ended up running for the new, nonpartisan city council established under a new charter. He was now a full-time politician.

As it happens, Nelson Rockefeller, the only declared candidate for president, also made a personal announcement on the last evening of the year, and like the news of Margaret Goldwater's impending marriage, the Rockefeller announcement concerned an event scheduled to occur in June. With as little elaboration as possible, the office of the governor of New York issued a one-sentence statement: "Governor and Mrs. Rockefeller today announced the expected arrival of a child in early June of 1964." It would be her fifth child and his sixth, but their first together. Rockefeller and his wife would host a New Year's Day reception at the mansion in Albany, and on Friday he would head to New Hampshire for a full day of campaigning in the state that would hold the first presidential primary.

| | |

Time magazine's Man of the Year spent New Year's Day in between telephone calls and children-catching sessions. When Martin Luther King Jr. was home, which was rare enough these days, his children were fond of climbing up to the top of the refrigerator and jumping down into his arms. All three of them loved it, and Coretta was happy just to have Martin home for a few days, even if the phone did keep ringing.

Most of the calls had to do with the internal troubles of the Southern Christian Leadership Conference. Direct-mail fund-raising was not going well, partly because there was no director in the New York office. King's inclination was to give the job to Bayard Rustin, an experienced political operative whose energy was almost as extensive as his knowledge. But King knew that Rustin was a homosexual and had once been a communist. Neither of these facts bothered King very much. He considered Rustin's personal life his own business, and his communism had not been much more than a youthful fling. But the political risks were obvious. One thing King did not want to do was give J. Edgar Hoover any more ammunition.

New Year's Day was J. Edgar Hoover's sixty-ninth birthday, and although Martin Luther King was ignorant of that coincidence, Robert Kennedy was not. The attorney general sent a gift of "beautiful gold cuff links," as Hoover described them in his thank-you note, adding that he would wear them "as a constant reminder of the friendship I shall always treasure." In the same gracious tone, he expressed his hope that the new year would bring the attorney general "good health and solace of mind."

But a few days later, when the telephone at his end of the direct line from the attorney general rang, Hoover ignored it. When it stopped, he said, "Put that damned thing back on Miss Gandy's desk where it belongs."[9]

6

THE BUSINESS OF AMERICA

The 46,102,000 men and 22,707,000 women who went back to work on Thursday morning, January 2, 1964, did not look much different than they had looked a year earlier, or ten years earlier. Perhaps 15 million of the employed men were white-collar workers, and for most of them that description could be taken literally; men who worked in offices tended to wear plain white shirts. Adorning them, in many cases, was a tie, either dark and solid colored or striped in muted tones and no more than two inches across at its widest point. If the man wore glasses, they were more likely to have thick rims, black or tortoiseshell, than they would have been just a few years earlier.

The man of 1964, whether he was a factory worker or business executive, farmer or student, carpenter or cop, was almost certain to have a clean-shaven face and, if he was not bald, a close-cropped head of hair. The origin of the bristly crew cut was the college campus, but now many a middle-aged man wore his hair that way, perhaps thinking it made him look younger. Men who wore their hair slightly longer tended to part it on the left and to keep it slicked down in place with a cream or oily tonic.

Chin whiskers, long hair, or even a mustache was extremely rare and vaguely improper unless it belonged to a European, an artist, a college professor, or a very old man. When a young or middle-aged man wore his hair long or affected a beard, it was assumed that he was making some kind of political statement.

The man who could afford to dress well might have a Brooks Brothers shirt that cost him $6.50, a $2.50 tie, and a suit that set him back some $60. For the truly fashionable and truly affluent, J. Press was advertising Italian silk suits on sale for $120.

When women worked in offices or went out for the evening, they also favored solid-colored suits or dresses, but these colors tended to be gayer: pink, light-to-medium green, light brown. A woman's hair was also likely to be short, just down to the collar, where it would turn up. It would be an exaggeration to say that every woman was trying to look like Jackie Kennedy, but it would not be a gross exaggeration.

Almost 14 million married women worked, but more than twice as many did not, and most who did were childless or women whose children had grown up. Or they were the wives of men at the very bottom of the wage scale, where a second salary was needed to support a family. Otherwise, if they could possibly afford it, mothers stayed home to raise their children. Especially in the growing suburbs, the married mother was most likely to be a housewife, devoted to home and family and content to live on her husband's income. If she was careful, her husband's income was enough to meet the necessities and then some. She shopped in one of the newer supermarkets, where a loaf of bread might cost twenty-one cents, a dozen eggs fifty-seven cents, and round steak $1.07 a pound.

The newer supermarkets were replacing not only the old-fashioned mom-and-pop stores, some of which were recombining into "voluntary chains" to save money and share expertise, but also the older chains such as A&P, which now had but forty-five hundred stores, a decline of more than 2 percent in just one year. With money saved at the grocery store, the typical man's paycheck was enough to pay the mortgage, the car loan payments, and the monthly charges on whatever loans had been taken out to buy a washing machine, dryer, dishwasher, or lawn mower (10 million Americans had Sears credit cards),[1] as well as to buy clothing and put gas in the car (at 30.3 cents a gallon), with a little left over for an occasional evening out and a vacation at least every other year. No wonder his wife was content.

Or was she? As 1964 dawned, thousands of women were reading and discussing a book that had been published a few months earlier. It was called *The Feminine Mystique,* and in it author Betty Friedan challenged the assumption that American women found marriage and motherhood fulfilling. Her contention had not yet gelled into organized opinion, much less political activity. But women were telling each other about it.

Still, it was that wife and mother, especially in her role as consumer, to whom American business was devoted. Whether it was the slender, skirted young housewife standing before one of the "flameless" stoves being promoted by the utility industry in its campaign for "total electric living," or the reddish-blonde with curl bent behind her ear who managed to look both chaste and sexy and who either did or did not use Miss Clairol ("Is it true blondes have more fun?"), the middle-income suburban stay-at-home mother was the principal object of corporate affection.

In that tension between sexiness and chastity there had been an unmistakable, if unacknowledged, tilt toward the former. The skirt worn by that young woman so delighted by flamelessness was plain and came down well below her knees; in real kitchens, skirts were as likely to be pleated and were getting shorter—midknee by day, slightly higher for evening wear—thanks to fashion designer Mary Quant, who had raised hemlines a few years earlier. The boyish look of the recent past was now "out" (which, as a word for "unfashionable," had recently become "in"), replaced by a more form-fitting style. Her clothing, all of a sudden, was proclaiming the woman qua woman.[2]

If the woman's womanliness was beginning to outstrip her motherliness, it may have been because she was beginning to be less of a mother. All of a sudden, women of childbearing age were having fewer babies. As recently as March 1963, more than 107 babies were born for every thousand women between the ages of fifteen and forty-five. By March 1964, a thousand women had only 104 babies, and the 337,000 born that month would be fewer than in any single month since 1955.

If the utility and hair coloring ads were ambiguous about the erotic in their appeal to those women, the same could not be said for the producers of the movie Sunday in New York, a film "dedicated to the proposition that every girl gets . . . sooner or later." Gets what? Well, a proposition, to be sure, but there was some ambiguity there.

The demographic reality may have been more complex than either the advertising copywriters or Ms. Friedan realized. Only half of all households met the husband-wife-children-at-home model.[3] There were many young single people and an even larger and faster growing number of married couples whose children had grown up and left the house.

The casual observer would not have known it, but there was one important change in the American workforce that went back on the job that day: Less of it went to factories. Factory workers were earning slightly more than $2.50 an hour, more than ever, but there weren't as many of them. In the mid-1950s, almost a third of employed Americans worked in factories. By the beginning of 1964, only 25 percent did.

Instead of being in factories, most of the new jobs were in education or in the service industries. The fastest growing sector was medical services, which wasn't just doctors anymore. By midyear, medical researcher Seymour Harris figured out that Americans would spend $33 billion on health care in

1964, more than double the $14 billion spent in 1950. A quarter of that $33 billion would come from the government.

The other businesses that were adding jobs at a rapid pace were hotels, motels, and private educational organizations.[4] They were the jobs of a society that had become more affluent than it knew.

Affluence, however, does not always produce satisfaction. Among the dissatisfied at the beginning of 1964 were the commanders of the automobile companies, America's most prominent industry, if not its largest. In their dissatisfaction, these titans sought help from their president, who was always willing to help corporate executives, even though they were Republicans, the better to convert them.

In this case Johnson could work on converting them while giving aid and comfort to one of his least favorite political allies. For a decade or more, Walter Reuther had been trying to convince the automobile executives to design smaller, cheaper cars that would burn less fuel and burn it without spewing as much pollution into the air. In this endeavor, Reuther was not just being a social visionary; he had noticed that most of the members of his United Auto Workers Union were driving used cars. In other words, the best-paid industrial workers in the world couldn't afford to buy the product they made.

But Reuther was not afraid of being a social visionary either. More than most people, he could see that oil might not always be plentiful and that the air was getting dirtier. These views did not impress the auto execs. Their reaction, as blunt as it was predictable, was to tell Reuther to represent his workers and to let them run their companies.

This, of course, was before the Beetle, the little German-made Volkswagen that was just the kind of car Doctor Reuther had ordered: small, fuel efficient, clean burning, cheap. The engine was in the back, "over the rear wheels, the ones that drive the car," as a VW advertisement put it, "for firm traction when the going gets sloppy."

By early 1964, VW sales were going well enough to be making a perceptible dent in auto company sales and profits. The auto executives were upset, but they were devoid of ideas. Reuther wasn't. He had suggested to President Johnson that the government help create a new auto company, either a joint venture or a subsidiary of one of the existing companies. Either way, they'd need the government to wink at possible antitrust violations.

Johnson was ready. He thought Reuther was an egotistical pain in the neck, but he did not think he was a fool. "I think it ought to be done," he told Defense Secretary McNamara, whose auto industry connections and expertise Johnson was exploiting. "If we could get some company to . . . put this little car on the market," Johnson said, "it'd be real novel." As to antitrust, he'd leave it to McNamara to talk to the attorney general. "I want to see how much influence you've got with Bobby," he told him.

But Johnson didn't leave it there. Suppose, he said, the Defense Department helped this new company out by ordering a bunch of small cars. "Why don't you give 'em a contract," he told McNamara. "Why couldn't you, instead of running around in those damn big old water boats you gotta haul? Why couldn't you buy a hundred thousand?"

"We couldn't buy this small a car," said McNamara. "I really believe it's not right for the military."

McNamara ought to have known; he had been president of Ford Motor Company. But Johnson would have none of it. "Well, I see these sergeants come down here every day from Andrews Base, all these White House drivers and everything else and they're whirling around in Mercurys. I don't know why you got a sergeant that's delivering a message for the general down to the chamber of commerce why he's got to have a Mercury or a Chevrolet."

Poor McNamara tried to explain that military procurers "mostly buy what's known as the [Ford] Fairlane size" that the Pentagon gets at bargain prices, but LBJ wasn't letting him off the hook. "I dunno why you don't buy a few of them," he said.[5]

If the president and his defense secretary thought there was anything unusual, much less improper, about the government helping big companies and big unions, they made no mention of it. Nor were they likely to have thought so, or even to let the question enter their minds. They were part of—indeed, they were at the apex of—an interdependent industrial system in which large corporations and the strong central government had intertwining, if sometimes contradictory, interests. Only the official rhetoric of both corporations and government denied this relationship. Reality disproved that denial every day.

| | |

Be-Nun-I-Kin is Navaho for "house on the hill," and Barry Goldwater, devotee of Indian artifacts and history, had given the Navaho name to his own house on the hill north of Phoenix.

Still using one crutch, he hobbled out to its flagstone patio on the morning of Friday, January 3, to make an announcement. As usual, he did not waste words. "I want to tell you that I will seek the Republican presidential nomination," he said, leaning against the lectern to favor his right heel. As usual, he did not temporize. "I will not change my beliefs to win votes," he proclaimed, and he proceeded to enumerate some of the beliefs likely to lose votes: distaste for the United Nations and for negotiating or trading with the Soviet Union; opposition to federal aid to education; even a suspicion about the wisdom of Social Security.

"I will offer a choice, not an echo," he said.

Already, those were fighting words. They became the title of a book by a young lawyer in Illinois named Phyllis Schlafly. The book would not appear for a few months, but advance publicity had made the phrase a motto of sorts. The book argued that the Republican Party should stop trying to accommodate Franklin Roosevelt's New Deal and start trying to reverse it.

To most political commentators—to most Americans—this did not seem to be a winning strategy. Eisenhower, the only Republican president of the last thirty years, had succeeded precisely because he accepted the New Deal. He may have trimmed it around the edges a bit, but he also extended it. Ike had been a soldier, a government official. He believed in government—prudent, probusiness government, but government all the same.

Goldwater didn't. Well, he *said* he didn't, but his stance was confusing. He was a big fan of the FBI and an advocate of a bigger and more expensive military establishment. And he'd once proposed a national law requiring schools to teach how evil communism was. Otherwise, he kept saying that there were too many government programs, benefiting too many people who didn't deserve the benefits, bothering too many businessmen who didn't deserve the trouble.

That was why, according to those in the know, Goldwater had no chance. He was unelectable and therefore unnominatable. Vermont's Republican senator George Aiken called on him to "disassociate himself from his weird and vulgar supporters." In New Hampshire, Nelson Rockefeller challenged Goldwater to a series of debates. "How can there be solvency when Senator Goldwater is against the graduated income tax?" asked Rockefeller. "How can there be security when he wants to take the United States out of the United Nations?" Rockefeller knew where he was; he was in the East, among Yankee internationalists who abhorred government red ink.

In Washington, James Reston, the nation's most influential columnist, wrote in *The New York Times* that "the Republicans who really want the Presidential nomination—Rockefeller, Goldwater and Nixon—probably can't get it, and the man who really doesn't want it—Gov. William Scranton of Pennsylvania—is probably going to have it forced on him."

| | |

A few hours before Barry Goldwater announced his candidacy, a crew of moving men began carting equipment out of the Polo Grounds, making it ready for demolition. To New Yorkers, to baseball fans everywhere, the old ballpark was holy ground. There Fred Merkle forgot to touch second base, Bobby Thompson hit mankind's most fabled home run, and Willie Mays ran farther than any man could possibly run to catch the line drive Vic Wertz hit into that alley in dead center field in the first game of the 1954 World Series, not a decade ago.

But the stadium was dilapidated, it was odd-shaped, and it was in Harlem. It was part of the past, so in the words of the Brook Benton song heard regularly on the radio, it was "Going, Going, Gone." The New York Giants, victims or victors of those historic events, had been in California for seven seasons, and their replacements, the hapless but cuddly New York Mets, were moving into a new stadium that the city had prepared for them. It would be ready by opening day in April.

Shea Stadium was to be the new ballpark's name, in honor of the real estate lawyer and political deal-maker who had helped convince the National League to expand to ten clubs, adding one for fast-growing Houston, the other to fill the void left when the Giants and the Brooklyn Dodgers left for the West Coast after the 1956 season.

The new park was to be circular and symmetrical, fit for football as well as baseball so that the American Football League's New York Jets could play there, too. And it was nowhere near Harlem. It wasn't even in Manhattan, but five miles across the East River in the borough of Queens, in the part of the city where many people lived in single-family houses lined up along quiet streets.

It was a little piece of suburbia, which seemed to be the future. As recently as the last census, taken just three and a half years earlier, a plurality of Americans had lived in cities. No longer. Now more people lived in the suburban subdivisions that had been sprouting up since the end of World War II despite the best efforts of some of the nation's best minds. To the renowned architect Edward Durell Stone, suburban houses were "little boxes set on handkerchief lawns," inappropriately imitating the British model.

Though he was hardly the first observer to note the diminutive ugliness of suburban subdivisions (a year earlier folksinger Pete Seeger had made a hit record of Malvina Reynolds's song about "little boxes made of ticky-tacky and they all look just the same"), Stone didn't just complain. He proposed an alternative: single-family homes surrounding a common atrium, enabling families to live closer together, hence saving open space without surrendering privacy.[6] It may have been a good idea, but he got few takers. In 1963, more than half the new movie theaters were built in suburban shopping malls. The theaters were only chasing the audiences. Suburbia had become the American middle-class norm.

Specifically, it had become the norm for white, middle-income (and higher) families with children. For a family with the median income for the time, a tract home would cost $17,999, and to buy it with a conventional mortgage, a family needed to be able to afford a $3,600 down payment and then to pay $81.76 a month on a thirty-year mortgage. But several other payment plans required lower down payments, especially if the family bread-winner was a war veteran.

Nor was suburbia simply white-collar. By now, so many factory workers had moved to the suburbs, so many roads had been built to them, that the factories themselves were going up there. A decade earlier, most manufac-turing jobs in metropolitan areas were in the central city; now, most were in the suburbs.

Like Shea Stadium, like the Verrazano Bridge being completed across the narrows between Brooklyn and Staten Island, like the Bay Area Rapid Transit System nearing completion in San Francisco, suburbia was the product of cooperation between government and business. The interstate highways made suburbia accessible, the G.I. Bill made it affordable, and the tax deduction for mortgage interest kept it that way.

Although these government subsidies were necessary for the growth of suburbia, they were not sufficient. Suburbia had something else going for it: Its residents weren't just buying a house, they were buying "a way of life," in the words of William Levitt. And he should know. Levitt did not exactly create the suburban explosion—it was coming one way or another—but he was the first to see it coming and to exploit it. He bought up some Long Island potato fields and put up small, nondescript tract houses that returning World War II veterans bought as soon as they were built.

This burgeoning suburbia was a way of life that enhanced conformity, self-interest, homogenization, and separateness. Until the postwar growth of suburbia, most Americans lived either in small or midsize towns or in city neighborhoods, where they regularly rubbed shoulders with all kinds of peo-ple, or at least all kinds of white people. Sure, there was the rich side of town and the fancy city neighborhood; country club members rarely drank at the corner saloon. But in the small towns all the kids went to the same school, meaning all the parents joined the same PTA and went to the same football and basketball games. In the cities, the rich and the not-so-rich walked along the same shopping streets, went to the same neighborhood movie theaters, perhaps attended the same church.

Levittown and its imitations introduced something new: the preplanned neighborhood in which all the houses were built at the same time and sold at just about the same price. All the buyers were in the same income bracket, roughly of the same age, and with children of roughly the same ages. And almost all of them were white. Levittown was not the only development in which the sales contracts contained a clause prohibiting resale to anyone who was not Caucasian, and though the New York State courts invalidated those provisions as early as 1948, even the Negroes who could afford a suburban home had a hard time buying one.

People had started living under this corporate, planned homogeneity in the late 1940s, and by the mid-1950s, most young, middle-income, white families were living in suburban subdivisions. By 1964, a majority of America's white middle-income teenagers had grown up in a neat, orderly, well-maintained artificial setting.

Some of them were bored out of their minds.

| | |

And ready for something new.

Later that evening, a few hours after the moving men at the Polo Grounds knocked off for the day, *The Jack Paar Show* on NBC featured a filmed performance of a musical quartet that was quite the rage in Britain. In fact, they were already something of a rage on this side of the Atlantic, too, ever since December 10, when *The CBS Evening News* had broadcast a report about them. Someone who liked their sound called a Washington, D.C., disk jockey named Carroll James, who arranged for a stewardess on BOAC to sneak a copy of the record on a flight back from London. James paid her for the record and played it on his program, days before it was to be released in the United States. The song was called "It's a Hard Day's Night," and for some reason American teenagers went ga-ga over it.

Their elders did not. The morning after the group's appearance on the Paar show, *New York Times* television critic Jack Gould casually dismissed the English quartet known as the Beatles as the most passing of fads:

"With a love like that, you know they should be bad," Gould began, taking off on a line from one of the group's songs. He went on:

> They aurally suggested a Presley multiplied by four. Visually, their calisthenics were wilder, and upon somewhat fuller examination, might prove infinitely more amusing.
>
> From a nation where the best-selling record is now The Singing Nun's delicate and charming "Dominique," there can be extended to the British the comforting assurance that an occasional cultural purgative can have a beneficial effect.[7]

Gould had a point. American entertainment did not seem to be in need of transfusions. The Singing Nun was Belgian, but her song and her tone were very much inside the mainstream of America's popular arts. Sweet melodies, not quite as sweet as "Dominique" but not harsh either, were being rehearsed for a new Broadway show called *Hello, Dolly,* which would open midmonth.

Show tunes had of late become the only pop songs for grown-ups, their record sales enhanced by development of the long-playing album in the 1950s. That left the single-record, 45-rpm market mostly to the teenagers, who gobbled them up and who provided a market—the only market—for rock and roll, which had come along less than a decade earlier, dominating popular music for a while, thanks to Elvis Presley.

But lately not everything Elvis was singing was rock and roll; his current hit, "Kissin' Cousins," was pretty bland stuff. Looking at the charts, you'd think that perhaps even the teens were getting tired of rock music. At least half of January's hit songs were decidedly unrock: Brenda Lee's countryish "As Usual," Andy Williams's ballad "A Fool Never Learns," and the sappily sentimental "See the Funny Little Clown" by Bobby Goldsboro.

So it wasn't such a bold suggestion that this new rock group from England would be a passing fancy. Besides, for American taste, they wore their hair too long.

| | |

Revolutions, it is said, eat their young, but Barry Goldwater's may have been the first to eat its father. Perhaps F. Clifton White was merely its godfather, but either way, the humiliations he suffered before Goldwater officially became a candidate were trifles compared to those visited on him afterward.

Again he bore them, as though his psyche were beyond pain. He had no choice, because every penny of his emotional capital was now invested in the Goldwater movement. To cash in now would be to lose all. Besides, he was no naïf. He knew that while he was using Goldwater, Goldwater had been using him, so he was hardly surprised that when the campaign became official, the candidate took command.

That much had been expected. But White had also expected, not unreasonably, that he would remain the chief political strategist. Goldwater had other ideas. He wanted his own people in there, and White was not one of his people.

There was more involved here than the natural desire of any man to be surrounded by underlings he could trust. Goldwater had never lost the insecurities that bedeviled him long before he entered politics. He felt ill at ease in the company of Eastern college professors such as White or sophisticated jet-setters such as Buckley. He preferred to spend time with the plain-spoken Western businessmen he knew from the country club locker room.

He had never really felt comfortable in Washington or in the Senate. He wasn't all that interested in legislation ("My aim was not to pass laws, but to repeal them," he said), and he didn't have to be. Democrat Carl Hayden took care of Arizona's interests in the Senate. Bored and powerless, Goldwater had plenty of time to wander around the country making speeches to conservative groups.

Goldwater was so determined to demote White that he was not deterred by the reality that his homegrown political operation was inadequate to the task of a national campaign. He had no choice but to turn to his old union-busting buddy, Denison Kitchel. It was a disastrous decision. Kitchel knew nothing of politics outside Arizona. He didn't understand the delegate-selection process. He had few contacts with Republican leaders around the country. His qualifications were that he was a smart lawyer who was Barry Goldwater's friend.

He and Goldwater didn't even keep Cliff White in charge of the field operation. Instead, Goldwater chose another old friend, a Phoenix lawyer named Richard Kleindienst. He did have some political smarts; he had run Richard Nixon's delegate-hunting operation in 1960. But that wasn't much of a challenge; as the sitting vice president, Nixon had that nomination wrapped up from the start.

White was crushed. He and Kleindienst met for the first time in Kleindienst's room at the Mayflower Hotel in Washington. Kleindienst found White "on the verge of deserved tears." In the Hollywood version, the two would end up the best of friends. In the real world, they ended up disliking each other. Kleindienst, though, was not without kindness, nor was he without shrewdness; White was too valuable a resource simply to cast aside. Kleindienst asked him to stay on as codirector of field operations. White, who had given the last three years of his life to this campaign, the last decade to this movement, couldn't let go now. He accepted. And he consoled himself with the knowledge that he was one of the few people in politics, in the whole country, who understood what was really going on.

It was the common self-delusion of the defeated, but in this case it was no delusion. Along with his handful of allies, Cliff White saw what was happening in the Republican Party and in America. It was being infiltrated from the grass roots.

On Monday, January 6, one day after the San Diego Chargers demolished the Boston Patriots, 51 to 10, to win the American Football League championship, Martin Luther King took his seat in the visitors' gallery of the United States Supreme Court. He was there to hear arguments in the case known as *New York Times* v. *Sullivan.* Before the official proceeding began, a court messenger came by with Justice Arthur Goldberg's copy of King's book, *Stride Toward Freedom,* along with a note asking him to autograph it.

New York Times v. *Sullivan* was a bizarre case, stemming from a 1960 advertisement placed by such prominent Negroes as Harry Belafonte and Bayard Rustin. They were appealing for money to defend King against an Alabama indictment described, correctly, as an obvious effort by "Southern violators of the Constitution" to suppress opposition to segregation.

The text of the ad did not name any of these violators of the Constitution, including Montgomery police commissioner L. B. Sullivan, who nonetheless sued the *Times* and several public supporters of the advertisement, including Eleanor Roosevelt, claiming that he had somehow been defamed by inference.

Because the advertisement did make a few trivial mistakes (it said, for instance, that at one point the demonstrators sang "America" when they'd actually sung the national anthem) and because Alabama law allowed juries to decide whether any factual error was defamatory, a jury had awarded Sullivan half a million dollars in damages.

After the testimony that day, King went back to the Willard Hotel. FBI agents placed a bug in the room and learned that King and a few of his colleagues got good and drunk with two women from Philadelphia.[8] When J. Edgar Hoover heard the results the next day he exulted, "This will destroy the burrhead." He also made the decision not to inform Attorney General Robert Kennedy about the tapes. A week later, though, Cartha DeLoach took excerpts to the White House, where he played them for the president and his chief of staff, Walter Jenkins.

Hoover did not get the reaction he'd expected when Johnson announced that he would meet at the White House just a few days later with most of the nation's leading civil rights leaders, including Martin Luther King. Disappointment, however, only intensified Hoover's determination. When efforts to monitor King in Milwaukee failed to turn up evidence of similar behavior, Hoover was furious. His agents in Milwaukee had an excuse; the local cops had been protecting King, which restrained his activities. Hoover didn't buy it. "I don't share the conjecture," he said. "King is a 'tomcat' with obsessive degenerate sexual urges."

Clearly, the local agents were doing their best. It wasn't their fault that four different threats to blow up the auditorium where King would be speaking had been telephoned to the *Milwaukee Journal,* prompting the Milwaukee police to enhance their protection of King and his rally. Why, the Milwaukee police even alerted demolition experts from . . . the FBI.

The Bureau, then, was working against itself. The additional security, including FBI bomb squad guys, displeased the FBI agents who had planted microphones in King's room. They worried that the extra scrutiny would either weaken his sex drive or enhance his prudence.

Perhaps they were right. Their account of the hotel surveillance in the next morning's report to headquarters in Washington was "No activities of interest developed."

|7|

ROT IN THE STRUCTURE

On the same morning that the Supreme Court heard the *Sullivan* case argument, there was a story in the business section of *The New York Times* that had nothing to do with Sullivan, civil rights, or for that matter anything that had happened the previous day, indicating that it was the result of enterprising reporting or carefully planted information, or both.

The gist of the story was that the future development of the southwestern corner of the country, including southern California, was at risk unless sufficient sources of clean water and electric power could be found. Already, some 20 million people lived in southern California and Arizona. Another 20 million or so could be expected in the coming decades, but not without water to drink and power at the flick of a switch.

In the West, as the story pointed out, providing these services was beyond the reach of the individual family or community: "In the East, individual settlers could dig wells and harness streams almost everywhere. But the settlement of the West is premised on the collective exploitation of resources."

In this case there were two collectives—the federal government and the private utility industry—sometimes cooperating, sometimes competing over who would exploit the coal, oil, and water power of the region. Both of them wanted to build a direct current transmission system to bring to Los Angeles electricity generated by dams on the Columbia River 650 miles away. The power was created by cooperation between nature and the government-owned Bonneville Power Administration, but the private companies wanted to sell it.

That transmission line was only a small part of private industry's grand plan, however—indeed, it was dubbed the grand plan by James Mulloy of the Los Angeles Department of Water and Power—to transform the West.

In what was the closest approximation to national economic planning for private profit in American history, ten companies were planning to cover the Colorado plateau with mines, power plants and coal-gasification facilities, coordinated with new nuclear power plants on the California coast.

Almost all of this development would take place on public land, some of it ecologically delicate and some of it under the nominal control of Indian tribes. For the private companies, which included the California and Arizona utility firms as well as engineering giants such as Bechtel, Morrison-Knudson, and Kaiser, one obvious advantage was that they wouldn't have to pay for the land. The power companies involved in this grand plan were calling their combined entity the Western Energy Supply and Transmission Associates, or WEST.

There was nothing new about this, for in the West, public and private enterprise had long been as intimately intertwined as the supply of water and the supply of electricity. The biggest interconnection was the Colorado River Storage Project, approved in 1956 over the strenuous objections of Senator Paul Douglas of Illinois, who pointed out, correctly, that the project's ten dams and their 48.5-million aggregate acre-feet would produce expensive electricity to finance the irrigation needed to produce crops and livestock, which were already in oversupply.

They were and it did, but this socialism for the resource-producing capitalist was the foundation of Western prosperity, and the region's leaders were alert to anything that threatened it.

| | |

Barry Goldwater made his maiden campaign trip to New Hampshire on Tuesday, January 7, pleased to find a small crowd awaiting his 3 A.M. arrival. At his very first press conference in Concord, he was asked about Social Security. His response was that he would suggest "one change," and that would be to make the program voluntary. "If a person can provide better for himself, let him do it," he said. He also proposed a more belligerent policy toward Cuba.

That afternoon the headline of the Concord *Monitor* read: "Goldwater Sets Goals: End Social Security, Hit Castro."

End Social Security? Well, making it voluntary would probably be the end of it. Still, it was something of an interpretative headline, and the Goldwater forces believed then and ever after that the editor who wrote it was on Rockefeller's payroll. He was not. Charley Shenton, the *Monitor*'s managing editor, who loved to write headlines, was convinced that making Social Security voluntary would destroy it.[1]

Two days later, Goldwater said the Johnson administration was pursuing a "no win" foreign policy. For instance, he said, the military depended too much on these new intercontinental ballistic missiles rather than good old B-52 bombers. "I don't feel safe at all about our missiles," he told a press conference in Portsmouth. "I wish the Defense Department would tell the American people how undependable the missiles in our silos actually are."

He provided no evidence for this assertion, but he did underscore the suspicion that his real enemy was neither communism nor liberalism but the modern world. It was becoming clear that for all its intellectual provenance, the conservatism behind the Goldwater movement rested also on a visceral grouchiness, a disdain for "new-fangled contraptions" such as missiles. The movement held even greater scorn for new-fangled ideas such as disarmament or reducing poverty and outright hatred of new-fangled culture; conservative theorist Richard Weaver hated jazz and modern art as much as he hated the welfare state.

Conservatism rested also, though perhaps no more than its liberal opposition, on an "us against them" mentality. Any idea that came from a fellow conservative was deemed to be wise; one from a liberal or moderate was suspect at best. For instance, had a conservative administration begun to replace B-52s with missiles, gadget-loving Barry Goldwater might have been its biggest supporter.

Furthermore, Goldwater felt that supporting your friends despite their failings was a true test of loyalty. That explains why he never attacked the John Birch Society or Joe McCarthy. He knew how much he owed them.

A Goldwater-for-president boomlet got under way in 1960. It was a gesture, not a campaign, a minirebellion inspired by Clarence Manion and Roger Milliken, chairman of the board of South Carolina's Deering Milliken textile empire, known for his antipathy to labor unions and his commitment to racial segregation.

Under the leadership of the Birch Society, four hundred Americans for Goldwater clubs were formed, as were Youth for Goldwater chapters on sixty-four college campuses. Clubs do not vote at the Republican National Convention that was going to nominate Richard Nixon, however, and Goldwater, who could count, had no interest in being a spoiler. He planned to withdraw on the opening day of the 1960 convention. Accompanied by his one campaign aide, conservative speechwriter Steve Shadegg, Goldwater went to Milliken's hotel suite to let him know he was pulling out.

Milliken knew when he was licked, but he also knew opportunity when he saw it, and he insisted that Goldwater and Shadegg follow him into the privacy of his bedroom. There, Milliken told Goldwater not to quit just yet.

Better to quit at the convention, he said, on television, with a gracious but feisty speech that the whole country would see. All right, Goldwater said, I'll do it. Shadegg was horrified.

"You aren't going to let these country bumpkins push you into this, are you?" he asked Goldwater.

"Write the speech," Goldwater said. Shadegg did. Milliken was right. Much of the country saw Goldwater ascend to the podium that night to tell his fellow conservatives to "grow up" and work to take back the party. Here was a conservative with the common touch. Conservatism had its candidate.[2]

In September 1960, a hundred or so young conservatives who had been in those Youth for Goldwater clubs gathered on the front lawn of the Buckley estate in Sharon, Connecticut, to form the Young Americans for Freedom. Being young, energetic, and flush with conviction, they gave themselves a birth certificate, the "Sharon Statement," modeled without humility on the Declaration of Independence and declaring that "in this time of moral and political crisis, it is the responsibility of the youth of America to affirm certain eternal truths."

Among them were that "political freedom cannot long exist without economic freedom," that "the market economy . . . is the single economic system compatible with the requirements of personal freedom and constitutional government," that "the United States should stress victory over, rather than coexistence with," communism, but that otherwise the federal government should do less.

At no level, said the Sharon Statement, should government attempt to work toward economic equality, for "when it takes from one man to bestow on another, it dominates the incentive of the first, the integrity of the second, and the moral autonomy of both." If there was any sense of irony in expressing such concern for the moral autonomy of poor bestowees by the children of wealthy parents gathered on the lawn of a multimillionaire whose wealth was based on extraction of a publicly owned natural resource at a preferred tax rate, it was not evident.[3]

But neither was it important at the moment. Cliff White, Bill Rusher, and their allies had taken control of the Young Republicans. So now there were two grassroots political organizations dedicated to Barry Goldwater's candidacy.

| | |

On Wednesday, January 8, President Johnson delivered his first State of the Union message. It was by any measure a masterful performance, not just because of what he said but because of the way that he said it. For all forty-one minutes (including eighty interruptions for applause, almost none of it from Southerners), Johnson appeared to be in command of the House chamber, if not of all humanity. His big head, his weathered face, and his somber but confident voice combined to create the image of a man fully in control.

He was. His weeks of cost cutting had been so successful that he could declare a billion-dollar "unconditional war on poverty" while *cutting* the budget. "By insisting on a dollar's worth for a dollar spent," the president said, "I am able to recommend in this budget the most federal support in history for education, for health, for retraining the unemployed, and for helping the economically and physically handicapped."

In fact, all that insisting was not the only reason he could propose new spending. Another reason was that the money was flooding in. A few days earlier, his economic advisors had flown to his ranch to tell him how great things looked. The gross national product had risen $30 billion in a year; both workers and corporations were profiting.

Among the many statistics his advisors threw at him, the big one was "six point five." That was the rate of growth the economists predicted. For Johnson, growth was the holy grail. At that rate, there would be enough tax revenue to finance his programs without going deeper into debt, without touching anybody's tax rate.

Johnson knew that beneath the happy statistics, there was a dark side to the economy, to the society. He had read the new manpower report from the Pentagon that showed that one-third of all draftees flunked their exams, half for physical reasons and half for mental. For all the prosperity, not everyone was getting in on the action. Most Negro children and almost one of every four white kids had never been to the dentist. If all those young men were too sick or too ignorant to get into the Army, that meant some people weren't eating right, and their schools were no good. And it wasn't just the Negroes, either. There weren't that many Negroes.

There was, then, rot in the structure, if not in the foundation. Johnson wasn't going to say that, of course; it would be bad politics. It would challenge the centrist consensus. He didn't want to challenge it; he wanted to embody it.

As soon as the speech was over, Robert Kennedy told a reporter that he'd certainly stay on as attorney general until after the election. This may have been less an expression of loyalty than an admission that he needed time. The Prince Pretender was considering his options.

He could always go back to Massachusetts to run for governor, but that could get awkward with his brother as U.S. senator from the state. Some of his friends and relatives, including Edward Kennedy and Stephen Smith, had suggested he move to New York, either to run for governor or to purchase the *New York Post,* the liberal tabloid rumored to be for sale.

Unfortunately, New York had a five-year residency requirement for its governors, but he could run for the U.S. Senate from there, or from anywhere; the only requirements for election to Congress were that a person "when elected, be an inhabitant of that state for which he shall be chosen." The incumbent, a centrist Republican named Kenneth Keating, would be no push-over but was beatable. A memorandum to that effect was sent to Kennedy while he was skiing in Aspen. He showed little interest.[4]

Sometime in January, it came to Kennedy that his best course was to try to get—or to force—Lyndon Johnson to select him as his 1964 running mate. He knew that Johnson didn't want him. Like most other top Democrats, Johnson wanted Hubert Humphrey, and Humphrey had something like a campaign going, with friends calling labor leaders, governors, and senators, urging them to tell the president that they preferred Hubert.

Kennedy couldn't do that. All he could do was hope that Johnson would keep reading the polls showing that most rank-and-file Democrats preferred him for the second spot. It was the longest of shots, but he took it. He thought he could help the ticket. He knew that the office would make him the favorite for the presidential nomination in 1968 or 1972. It was part of the Restoration. He didn't know what else to do.

Still, if Johnson's running mate wasn't going to be Robert Kennedy, who would it be? Humphrey was the most obvious choice, but Johnson was cau-tious. His old buddy John Connally thought Humphrey would be a mistake because he would hurt in the South. Connally's choice was the other senator from Minnesota, Eugene McCarthy, who may also have been Lady Bird John-son's choice. She liked McCarthy. She socialized with his wife, Abigail.

McCarthy had a couple of advantages. He was a liberal, but not nearly as bubbly about it as Humphrey. He was urbane and sophisticated, a nice balance to Johnson's tendency to be blunt, if not crude. And he was a Catholic. Some polls and some politicians were telling Johnson it would be good politics to have a Catholic running mate. That's why he briefly considered R. Sargent Shriver. He wasn't just a Catholic; he was a Kennedy, the husband of Robert Kennedy's sister Eunice. That choice, however, would have done more than simply avoid Robert Kennedy; it would have enraged him. Kennedy and Shriver were friendly because they were brothers-in-law, but they were hardly each other's favorite person.

Early in the year, Johnson deputized Jim Rowe to make an initial overture to Humphrey. Rowe, once a law clerk to Oliver Wendell Holmes, later the White House aide who would usher young Lyndon Johnson into the presence of Franklin D. Roosevelt, invited Humphrey for a personal visit, and the two of them sat on Rowe's front porch in Washington's Cleveland Park section, where Rowe told Humphrey that—no commitment, mind you—he was being "very seriously considered" for the job.

Then Rowe asked a bunch of questions. What did Humphrey think of Johnson? Would he be loyal? Did he have any basic disagreements with LBJ's policies?[5]

And, of course, the personal stuff. Any skeletons in the closet?

Skeletons? Hubert didn't even have a closet.

But Johnson was also playing a game. At one White House dinner, the president leaned over to Humphrey, who was a few place settings away, and said loud enough for several others to hear, "I think I'm going to drop Mike Mansfield's name into the hopper. He'll like it and it will give a lot of people something to talk about."

People did, until Mansfield declared his lack of interest. So other names got thrown into the hat: Governor Edmund Brown of California, Mayor Robert Wagner of New York. Johnson was engaging in his small cruelties; the bigger ones would come later.

I I I

On Wednesday, January 22, Interior Secretary Udall fired the government's first volley in the war over who would control the future of the American West. Udall's proposal was hardly hostile to the interests of the large corporations doing business as WEST. But in an indication that the government would not cede total control to them, Udall proposed authorizing $3.2 billion to create the dams and aqueducts needed to make 7.5 million acre-feet of water available for Arizona and southern California.

Well, that's how it was described at least. The reality was more complicated. Even its name was complicated. The official name was the Pacific Southwest Water Plan, but within that plan was another, that Central Arizona Project long so dear to Barry Goldwater's heart, and to his state's thirst.

In fact, the Central Arizona Project wouldn't get much water into Arizona and none at all to California. Instead, it would make money. Two huge dams on the Colorado River, in Marble Gorge and Bridge Canyon at opposite ends of Grand Canyon National Park, would be built, and each of them would produce hydroelectric power, 2.1 kilowatts of "peaking power," to be sold at premium prices.

With that money, the Interior Department could pay for . . . more dams: two on the Trinity River in northern California to supply water for southern California, one in New Mexico, and one or two in Utah. These projects were necessary, according to Udall. In a letter to the president a few weeks later, he wrote: "The Pacific Southwest is at once the driest and the fastest growing area in the United States." Indeed, the whole West was growing, along with the rest of the country. Experts consulted by a Senate select committee had just concluded that by 1980, there would be 260,578,000 Americans, 46,500,000 of them in the West. By the year 2000, there would be 383,072,000 Americans, with 73,947,000 in the West. Without more dams, there wouldn't be enough water.

The Central Arizona Project was designed to finesse a Supreme Court decision of 1963 that reduced California's share of Colorado River water. Under this plan, southern California would get Trinity River water instead, leaving the Colorado River water for Arizona.

The only problem was that there wasn't any more Colorado River water, at least none that wasn't legally spoken for upstream. As the plan acknowledged, it "did not provide an overall solution for the region's water needs."

Details, details. Whatever it lacked in hydrological justification, the Pacific Southwest Water Plan made up for in political balance. Public power and reclamation projects were ideological liberalism that benefited powerful conservatives, including all those "antigovernment" Western ranchers and developers.

The same day Udall made his proposal, the president talked to Richard Russell. They were talking about the nationalistic flare-up over the canal in Panama, not Johnson's political future, but in recounting a conversation he'd had the previous night, Johnson said, "As long as I'm President, which is going to be for eleven months." Sticking to the subject of Panama, Russell did not respond to this apparent declaration of noncandidacy. Neither did Johnson's old Texas friend Frank Erwin a few days later when the president said, "I wish I didn't have to run for this job. I may *not* run for it. I don't know how to get out of it."

Although it must have seemed to them like nothing more than idle chitchat, it was a good deal more. As early as January, Johnson could see that Lady Bird was worried about his staying up so late. He'd had a heart attack. His father and grandfather had both died young. However breezily Johnson may have mentioned to others the possibility that he would not be a candidate, he was discussing it at length with his wife. She knew enough to take him seriously. She had been through this before. She remembered that when Senate candidate Lyndon Johnson was hospitalized with kidney stones three weeks before the 1948 Texas primary, he tried to hide his condition from the public, telling his doctors not to operate and ordering his campaign staff to keep mum. It was an absurd order, and after three days, campaign manager John Connally told the truth.

Furious that he had been disobeyed, the candidate dictated a statement of withdrawal: "If I can't control my own campaign, I certainly can't control the Senate, and if I'm not in control, I'm much better off in Johnson City where no one can hurt me."

Even his closest aides and his wife would not tell him that he wasn't going to control much as a freshman senator, anyway. But they did disobey him again. With the encouragement of Lady Bird Johnson, the campaign aide to whom Johnson dictated the statement never released it. That night, without benefit of surgery, Johnson passed his kidney stones, and when morning came he resumed campaigning without mentioning the hours in which he must have assumed that he was no longer a candidate.[6]

That was not the first time Johnson had gotten sick just before an election. He was in the hospital recovering from an appendectomy the day he was first elected to the House of Representatives. The appendicitis was real, as were the kidney stones, but the timing was interesting. In both cases, there would have been an explanation for failure, if not an excuse; in both cases, he would have been the object of pity more than scorn.

| | |

The day after the State of the Union speech, Matt Saurez sat in his new office at 2505 1/2 Fifth Street, above Fiedler's Pharmacy in Meridian, Mississippi, and drafted a memorandum to Dave Dennis at the national office of the Congress of Racial Equality, requesting a budget.

All of east-central Mississippi was "virgin territory . . . open for organizing," he wrote. In Meridian alone there were ten thousand Negroes who were not registered to vote. Already he had an eight-member staff including his newest recruit, a local young man named James Chaney. With $444 a month for three months, plus an initial $300 to set up the office, he could buy office supplies, get another phone, pay the electric bill, put gas in their vehicles, and pay each employee a salary—ten dollars a month.

What Saurez was planning was nothing less than an invasion, the seeds of which had been planted in 1963. The plotters were two whites and two Negroes, two Mississippians and two New Yorkers. Aaron Henry was a Negro druggist from Greenville. Edwin King was a white minister at Tougaloo University. Robert Moses was a Harlem-born Negro with a graduate degree from Harvard and a mystical aura about him. Allard K. Lowenstein was a short, serious-faced, bespectacled Jewish liberal from New York.

Henry and King got the basic, simple idea: Because Mississippi effectively prohibited Negroes from voting, how about creating a separate system, holding a parallel election. It wouldn't count, of course, but it would disprove the lie that Negroes weren't voting because they didn't want to; it would teach people how to organize, to campaign, and to vote; it would reveal the state's corruption—its tyranny—to the world.

Aaron and King would be the "candidates" for governor and lieutenant governor in 1963. Any Mississippian, white or Negro, could go to a cooperating church, business, or community center and cast a vote. Moses would handle organizing the impoverished Negro communities of the state.

Most civil rights leaders thought little of this plan and of its creators. The Gandhians of Martin Luther King's SCLC found the Student Nonviolent Coordinating Committee (SNCC) leaders too eager for trouble. Were it not for Aaron Henry, the NAACP would not have been involved at all. Roy Wilkins had little use for Martin Luther King or for James Farmer of CORE. He thought they were communists or at least influenced by communists. As for this pseudoelection, the NAACP thought the idea wildly impractical.

But it worked. The turnout was extraordinary; on election day in November of 1963, some ninety-three thousand Mississippi Negroes who were effectively barred from their state's official polling places went to their unofficial polling places and voted for Aaron Henry and Edwin King, thanks in part to the efforts of some Northern college students, most of them white, who had been driven by conscience and commitment. There were perhaps a hundred of them, and mostly they worked in the offices, freeing up the local Negro SNCC workers to go out into the field. It was Lowenstein who got the kids to come.

| | |

Until Saturday, January 11, few Americans knew that Luther Terry was the surgeon general of the United States. Indeed, not many knew that there *was* a surgeon general of the United States. But on that day more than a hundred reporters gathered in the new State Department auditorium to hear him and ten members of his Advisory Committee on Smoking and Health deliver some shocking news: Cigarettes were unhealthy.

So unhealthy, the committee's 150,000-word report concluded, that smoking presented "a health hazard of sufficient importance in the United States to warrant appropriate remedial action."

Considering that almost 80 million Americans over the age of seventeen (and who knows how many below it) had smoked 523 *billion* cigarettes in the year just past, this was sobering news. The tobacco companies pointed out that no one had really proved a physiological link between smoking and any disease. They seemed calm.

So did singer Eddie Fisher, even though his wife, actress Elizabeth Taylor, had been conducting a sizzling, and most public, love affair with Richard Burton, her on-screen lover in the movie *Cleopatra,* a four-hour spectacle, or bore, depending on the taste of the viewer.

There was a certain rough justice to Fisher's plight; only a few years earlier, he and Taylor had been the adulterous lovers while the previous Mrs. Fisher, dancer-actress Debbie Reynolds, stayed home alone. Now he was not only the cuckold, but (relatively speaking) the low-income cuckold. He hadn't had many hit records lately, and his income paled beside Taylor's. Nonetheless, he ridiculed reports that he would not grant her a divorce without some kind of cash settlement. "I wouldn't stand in the way of this earth-shattering, world-shaking romance for anything in the world," he said. Taylor may not have been convinced. Without waiting for Fisher's permission, she filed for a Mexican divorce on Tuesday, January 14.

| | |

The next day, Willie Mays signed a $105,000, one-year contract with the San Francisco Giants, jazz trombonist Jack Teagarden died in New Orleans at the age of fifty-eight, and Mickey and Rita Schwerner left New York in their Volkswagen Beetle, headed for Mississippi. They would have left New York even earlier, but they couldn't take the dog, and it took them a few days to find someone they trusted to take good care of the pup, whose name was Gandhi.

They got to Jackson the next day. They were pioneers, the first white, full-time civil rights workers in the state, and Robert Moses thought they'd be well advised not to venture beyond Jackson. But Mickey was irresistible. There was something about him—his warmth, his flexibility—that made it hard to turn him down when he said he'd rather be in the field. Rita was something else; she had a harder edge. But they were young lovers. They were a team. After a few days, Moses thought it would be all right if they took over the community center in Meridian.

They got there on Tuesday, January 21. In a laughable effort to blend in, Mickey had shaved off his beard. By the end of February, the Meridian Community Center was going strong. It had a library of ten thousand volumes, most of them donations from New York publishers responding to Rita's pleas. On Sunday, young kids came for story hour, and twice a week Mickey taught an evening class in voter registration.

The Schwerners stood out. Nobody else in Meridian looked quite like them, with their long dark hair, their sharp features, their piercing eyes. Nobody dressed quite the way they did, either. Mickey's must have been the only Mets cap in town. So it wasn't long before all sorts of folks began to notice them: the Negroes, the shopkeepers, the Klan.

SOBER, RESPONSIBLE MEN

On Friday, January 17, Tom McCabe, the chairman of the board of Scott Paper Company, hosted a lunch for Pennsylvania governor William Scranton at Scott's corporate headquarters in Philadelphia. On the guest list were Ike's onetime press secretary, Jim Hagerty; former defense secretaries Neil McElroy, who was now head of Proctor & Gamble, and Thomas Gates, who was now president of Morgan Guaranty Trust; David Kendall of Chrysler; New York Stock Exchange president Keith Funston; and George Leness of Merrill, Lynch.

Scranton had served but one term in Congress and was just in his first term as governor, but Eisenhower had put him on a "short list" of potential Republican candidates, so he had credibility. And he had ... well, breeding. He'd gone to Hotchkiss and to Yale. His brother-in-law, James Linen, was president of Time Incorporated Publications. Henry Luce himself was a friend of the family.

The day before the luncheon, the new edition of the *Saturday Evening Post* had hit the newsstand with a column by Stewart Alsop calling Scranton "more nearly a Republican Stevenson—a reflective man, oddly reserved, highly intelligent, but seemingly without ambition or deep political passion."

For those who considered Scranton too bland, other moderate Republicans were proposing an alternative: Ambassador Henry Cabot Lodge. In his hometown of Boston, some of Lodge's acquaintances announced plans to urge New Hampshire Republicans to write in his name in their primary. In the *New York Herald-Tribune*, the semiauthoritative voice of Eastern Republicanism, columnist Roscoe Drummond declared that "the unresolved question is not whether Mr. Lodge is going to resign his ambassadorship and become an open, active and campaigning candidate for the nomination, but when."

The counterrevolution of the Republican Establishment was beginning. For months, the men who ruled the Republican Party had held their peace. They could afford to. They had heard that Cliff White had signed up delegates in all these Podunks around the country. But they knew Podunk didn't run the Republican Party. They did.

They had been controlling its presidential nomination for a quarter of a century. Wendell Willkie had been their candidate, as had Thomas Dewey, Dwight Eisenhower, and Richard Nixon. Reasonable men all, moderate men with no intention of disturbing the social order. The men who ran the Republican Party did not want the social order disturbed. They were atop it.

They were the senior executives of the biggest financial, manufacturing, and communications companies in America. They were not politicians; they had more important work to do, and most of the time they were content to leave politics to the politicians. But every four years, they used the tools at their disposal—campaign contributions, the "responsible" positions taken by the editorialists at *Time, Life,* the *New York Herald-Tribune,* a few well-placed phone calls—to determine the party's presidential nominee.

They could do this because power flowed from the top down. Convention delegates in most states were chosen by the governor (or the state chairmen if the governor was a Democrat) in consultation with county chairmen, such congressmen and mayors as were interested, and a few big contributors.

It wasn't that the Republican rulers were éminences grises exercising improper influence over elected officials. They were responsible men. They were sober men, even when, as was not uncommon, they had too much to drink. They exercised their influence quietly and for the good of the country as they saw it.

They were New Yorkers, most of them, because that's where the corporate offices were. As leading citizens of America's most cultured city, they gave money to symphony orchestras and art galleries, and if they only attended the openings, and in some cases just to please their wives . . . well, they were there all the same. Like most men of culture, the Establishment Republicans were devotees of personal gentility and political moderation. They served the federal government as ambassadors, cabinet members, and commissioners. They were opposed to economic liberalism, but they knew how to distinguish it from socialism.

They may have spoken to no Negroes save the ones who carried their golf clubs or shined their shoes, but they associated bigotry with the crudeness of uneducated, rural (and Democratic) Southerners. Some of them, proud that theirs was the party of Lincoln, were genuinely committed to racial equality. All of them regarded blatant bigotry as déclassé.

For all their prudence and power, the Establishment Republicans had a problem. That problem—the reason they were flirting with Scranton and Lodge—was the front-running moderate, the deeply flawed political whirlwind that was Nelson Rockefeller.

He was fifty-five years old when the year began, and he had been governor of New York since 1959. He was of average height and just a little chunky. His head was almost as big as Johnson's, but where Johnson's head was long, Rockefeller's was square, with a touch of jut to the chin. His voice was gravelly, his stride was brisk, his ambition was consuming, and his energy was exceeded only by his confidence.

That confidence forbade him to fail. He would not allow it. His will would overcome all obstacles. He spoke French and Spanish fluently, and he spoke English with brisk intelligence, if without eloquence. He was what would later be called a "policy wonk." Rockefeller loved the intricacies of government. He was interested in . . . well, everything: modern art and bridge construction, street crime and Latin America, the state of the public schools, and the state of the armed services.

As a candidate, he had obvious strengths. He was a magnificent campaigner. He had beaten the incumbent governor, Averell Harriman, in 1958 by walking the streets of New York, saying "Hiya, fella" to voters and munching blintzes to prove that he was a regular guy. He loved to campaign and seemed to like people. They liked him back.

As the grandson of John D. Rockefeller, he was one of the richest people in the world, and for all his pursuit of the common touch, he acted it. When he stepped out of a doorway or off an airplane, he'd automatically hold his hands behind him, knowing someone would be holding his coat. Someone always was.

But among the things money cannot buy is a new image, and Nelson Rockefeller had badly damaged his political reputation in 1963 when he married Margaretta Murphy, known to her friends as "Happy." The marriage took place only eighteen months after Rockefeller divorced his first wife and less than a year after Mrs. Murphy divorced her husband, Dr. James Murphy, who won custody of the couple's four young children. Nelson Rockefeller and Happy Murphy were married in May of 1963, in a ceremony that was held at the home of Nelson's favorite brother, Laurance, but boycotted by brothers John, David, and Winthrop.

The groom was fifty-four. The bride was thirty-six. The reaction was tumultuous. Even a political ally from the Eastern wing of the GOP, Senator Prescott Bush of Connecticut, called Rockefeller a "destroyer of American homes." From pulpits around the country, especially (but by no means only) in the South, Nelson and Happy Rockefeller were portrayed as sinners.

Many men, probably most, would have made the prudent judgment that such a marriage meant an end to political ambition, and like Edward VIII would have given up public office for the woman they loved. Not Nelson Rockefeller. Then, as always, he wanted it all, and he saw no reason why he could not have it all. Here was a man who had succeeded in everything he had ever done—in business and government, with the electorate, and with women. And he desperately wanted to be president.

That was one of the big differences between him and Goldwater. Both men had been brought up in wealth, but their backgrounds were strikingly different, and not only because the Rockefellers could have bought out the Goldwater holdings with a day's income.

To Nelson Rockefeller's parents, business was irrelevant. John D. Rockefeller Jr. had so much money that it, and the making of it, were a trifle. When he spoke to his children, usually at breakfast, "his constant refrain was duty, responsibility, the purposeful existence."[1] John D. Jr. was a firm believer in capitalism, but his own passions were for the arts and for public service for its own sake.[2]

Rockefeller's political ambitions were personal. He led a faction of the Republican Party, but his candidacy was self-generated, a product of his boundless energy and ambition. Goldwater was less a candidate than the somewhat reluctant leader of a movement. Rockefeller needed no movement; he was part of the Republican Establishment, the structure that the movement behind Goldwater was determined to topple. Few political observers thought that the movement could do that. Certainly, Nelson Rockefeller didn't. He found it difficult even to take the movement seriously.

|||

On Saturday, January 18, civil rights leaders Martin Luther King, Roy Wilkins, James Farmer, and Whitney Young met with the president in the White House. It was an extraordinary meeting, both for what was said and what was not. The Negro leaders had feared that Johnson would urge them to accept a weaker civil rights bill. To their pleasant surprise, he pledged to press for passage of the bill "without a word or a comma changed," and he predicted success in the House of Representatives within a month.

He did not predict success in the Senate, nor repeat to them his private doubts about breaking the inevitable Southern filibuster. Nor did he drop the gentlest hint to Martin Luther King that just five days earlier he had read transcripts of the tapes secretly recorded in King's hotel room. Perhaps he was saving that ammunition should he ever need it. Perhaps he simply recalled that when he was thirty-five, his behavior had not always been that different from King's.

After the meeting, King told reporters that even if the civil rights bill passed, millions of Negroes would still face economic deprivation. But so, he said, would millions of whites. "Some kind of compensatory crash program" for the poor of both races was the answer, he said. If this was little more than a hint, it was the first public hint that King was beginning to see himself as something more than a leader of Negroes. Like Lyndon Johnson, he could see that the country's social and economic injustices did not apply only to members of one race.

To consider the details of such a program and to work out some of their other problems, King's Southern Christian Leadership Conference held a retreat at Black Mountain, North Carolina, starting Monday, January 20. King tried to relax; he played Ping-Pong and softball, but when it came time for business, it was hard to get his mind off SCLC's problems long enough to focus on national policy.

King preached love and conciliation, but his own organization was riven with personal rivalries and policy disagreements. At the moment, the most troubling challenges came from his left, from those who wanted more marches and civil disobedience, less patience and compromise with established authority. Some of King's followers were not impressed that he had just met with the president, the apotheosis of established authority.

Chief among them was Ella Baker, who had in effect become the mother hen for the young Negroes who had formed the Student Nonviolent Coordinating Committee after the 1960 lunch counter sit-ins. Baker seemed to think of herself more as SNCC's emissary to King than as King's liaison with SNCC. She and the students were not simply tired of waiting for their civil rights. They were tired of being told what to do. In their view, more than just politics was at stake.

The Black Mountain retreat didn't solve anything. When it ended, King, his wife, and colleague Dorothy Cotton boarded a flight back to Atlanta from Asheville. The plane pulled back from its gate but got no farther than the runway when the pilot ordered all passengers to evacuate immediately and walk back to the terminal. Someone had called in a bomb threat.

"I've told you all that I don't expect to survive this revolution," King told his wife and Cotton. "This society's too sick."

"Oh, Martin, don't say that," Cotton said.

"Well, I'm just being realistic," King said.

Coretta said nothing. She had heard him talk like this before.

| | |

In the middle of the month, CBS presented in prime time Ernest Kinoy's play *The Blacklist,* starring Jack Klugman. It was an indictment of hate groups, and not too subtly of the McCarthyite hysteria about communism that had polluted so much of the previous decade.

On NBC a few days earlier, Dr. John Rock, the Roman Catholic physician who had helped develop the oral contraceptive, sat and discussed its implications with David Brinkley. Dr. Rock acknowledged the religious complexity of his work—with the pill, more people would have sex, in or out of marriage—but he didn't seem upset about it. The nation, he pointed out, had entered a new era. Modern people resisted being bossed about.

As if designed to prove his point, a few days later the Federal Communications Commission renounced the right to censor sexually or politically "provocative" radio or television programs. Censorship, the commission said, would mean that "only the inoffensive, the bland, could gain access to the radio microphone or television camera."

A few days later, NBC unveiled a new television program called *That Was the Week That Was,* which did something new and daring: It made fun of politics and politicians. In the past, Steve Allen, Jack Paar, and Ernie Kovacs had sneaked in a political joke now and then, but never before had political satire been the raison d'être of a regular, prime-time American television program. *TW3,* as it soon became known, was mildly liberal, as was most mainstream entertainment that had any political content at all. For example, on Thursday nights, CBS had a show called *The Defenders,* in which father and son lawyers, the Prestons, appeared in court on behalf of draft dodgers, birth control operatives, and atheists.

This liberalism was cultural, not economic. Television's two most popular doctor shows, NBC's *Dr. Kildare* and ABC's *Ben Casey,* displayed the American Medical Association's seal at the end of each episode, but only because the AMA had been assured that physicians would be portrayed as hardworking and not too rich. It was part of the association's fight against Medicare.[3] On *TW3,* however, a rich doctor would be more likely to be satirized than, say, a Medicare advocate. The show made fun of everyone, but the attitudes of small-town Republicans, the traditionally religious, the bigoted, and the wealthy were on the receiving end of the sharpest barbs. Dr. Rock and Ernest Kinoy were more likely to be amused than, say, Billy Graham or William Buckley. George Wallace would not have been tickled at all, nor

would Huntington Hartford, who was plotting to subvert the artistic establishment right in its own neighborhood. On a choice plot of land on the
southwest corner of Central Park, the heir to the A&P fortune was erecting
a museum that would house modern art as he defined it, instead of the way
the guys across town at the Museum of Modern Art defined it. Back in 1951,
Hartford had written a book called *Has God Been Insulted Here?*, a diatribe
against modernism. Among God's insulters, in Hartford's view, were Pablo
Picasso, William Faulkner, and Tennessee Williams. Four years later, he took
out a full-page advertisement in several New York newspapers assailing abstract and impressionistic art. Now he had hired Edward Durell Stone to
design a museum on a small and oddly shaped chunk of Columbus Circle to
serve as a redoubt of the cultural counterrevolution.

All this liberalization was hardly universal. In his apartment in the Bronx,
Ralph Ginzburg wondered whether he'd soon have to go to jail for the crime
of publishing works that were too spicy and offensive for some tastes, including that of Attorney General Robert F. Kennedy, who had personally
decided to prosecute Ginzburg for violating the obscenity laws by publishing
a magazine called *Eros*.

Fittingly erotic but hardly pornographic, *Eros* had published only four
issues. Among its contributors were Salvador Dali and Norman Mailer. But
one of its photo-essays showed two nude dancers, a Negro man and a white
woman. This offended Kennedy, who called it an effort to undermine support
for civil rights by raising the specter of miscegenation. On orders of its boss,
the Justice Department prosecuted. Ginzburg had been found guilty and late
in 1963 had been fined $28,000 and sentenced to five years in prison.

The conservative counterculture was not limited to Huntington Hartford.
Being in New York, he was noticeable, but far from Broadway and Madison
Avenue a right-wing communications world thrived, especially on the radio.
Radio programs featuring Texas oil billionaire H. L. Hunt, the Reverend Carl
McIntire, evangelist Billy James Hargis, and John Birch Society bigwig Clar-
ence Manion reached millions of listeners via hundreds of radio stations.
These programs were government-subsidized thanks to tax-exempt founda-
tions.

Most of these stations were heard in rural areas and smaller cities in the
middle of the country. All the programs preached opposition to accommodation with the Soviet Union, conspiracy theories about the government,
antipathy to civil rights laws, and disagreement with the 1962 Supreme Court
decision on school prayer. Most of them also made fun of Darwin's theory
of evolution. Like their listeners, these broadcasters were not devoted to the
scientific method.

Thanks to the zaps created by the new electron accelerator owned by Harvard University and the Massachusetts Institute of Technology, researchers were able to announce on Wednesday, January 22, that protons do not have cores and that electrons are even smaller than everyone thought.

Dr. Roy Weinstein of Northeastern University told the opening session of the American Physical Society at New York's Statler-Hilton Hotel that the new machine enabled scientists to generate mu-mesons, or muons, particles that are much heavier than electrons but are still too small for even the Cambridge accelerator to see. The electron, the scientists speculated, must be so light that it barely exists. The universe seemed to be fading away before mankind's very eyes. No wonder those religious broadcasters found an audience.

| | |

On Thursday, January 23, the New York Repertory Theater at the Lincoln Center for the Performing Arts opened its doors for the first time. In the modern, white, filigreed performing arts center designed by Max Abramovitz, the company presented the debut performance of *After the Fall*, the new play by Arthur Miller.

It hardly mattered that most of the critics didn't like the play. What was important was the new theater, and it wasn't the only one. Across the country, workers were completing the white granite and glass Dorothy Chandler Pavilion, a theater designed to bring the finest of arts to Los Angeles. As designed by Welton Becket, none of the 3,250 seats was more than 130 feet from the stage. At Tempe, Arizona, the Grady Gammage Auditorium at Arizona State University got the backseats even closer; all 3,000 seats were within 115 feet of the action.[4]

By the time the 1963–64 season ended, more plays were produced on Broadway than in any season in the past twelve years. As usual, most of them were flighty; for example, *Nobody Loves an Albatross*, which opened at the Lyceum on Thursday, December 19, was not written for the ages. Nor did "serious" drama always succeed; Tennessee Williams's *The Milk Train Doesn't Stop Here Anymore* opened on New Year's night and closed three days later, despite the presence of Tallulah Bankhead and Tab Hunter in the cast.

But *Hamlet*, which would open in April, was still going strong by year's end, only in part because Richard Burton played the title role. And audiences didn't have to go to New York to absorb the higher culture. In fact, no one had to leave his or her living room. The weekend before the New York Rep opened, NBC presented a one-hour program about some of the country's greatest private collections of fine art, especially Nelson Rockefeller's. That evening, the network devoted two hours to a performance, in English translation, of Gaetano Donizetti's *Lucia di Lammermoor*.

Television hadn't suddenly ceased to be the "vast wasteland" former FCC chairman Newton Minow had complained about. Early in the year, ABC announced it would drop *The Sid Caesar Show*. The great comic was as funny as ever, but the network had decided that his brand of humor simply didn't have the mass appeal needed to attract the big audience the network needed during prime time. By now almost every household—92 percent of them, or more than 51 million families—had television sets. Gone were the days when programs could succeed by appealing only to a relatively affluent and educated elite.

Most of those television sets received black-and-white pictures only, but color TV was on the way. Its big breakthrough would not come until 1965, but the television manufacturers and their advertising agencies were already letting everyone know how superior it was. Leafing through a popular magazine, one was bound to come upon a full-page advertisement showing Shirley Booth as "Hazel," the bottom half of her in grayer-than-usual black and white, her smiling face and a green telephone receiver in "living color" from RCA.

Color was not the only innovation planned for television. Out in California, former network executive Sylvester L. (Pat) Weaver was preparing to charge viewers a fee for watching certain programs. Weaver was the president of a new company called Subscription Television, Inc., and he told shareholders at the company's first annual meeting that the company would begin transmitting baseball games as early as July 1.

"In addition to sports events," Weaver said, "we will bring to subscribers such programming as Broadway and off-Broadway plays, first-run motion pictures, instructional self-improvement, and other programs. Those will be brought into the homes of subscribers at a modest fee."

The very idea of a fee, determined by a meter attached to a subscriber's television set, enraged some Californians, including owners of the television networks, who were planning to scuttle Weaver's plan by hook, crook, or politics. They were circulating petitions to put on the November ballot a proposition to outlaw TV for a fee.

As the reaction to the Kennedy assassination demonstrated, television could be a potent source of information, and there was little doubt that many Americans wanted information. In fact, there was so much curiosity about public affairs that in September 1963 two of the three television networks had expanded their evening news programs from fifteen to thirty minutes. So momentous was this step that President Kennedy had agreed to be interviewed for the first half-hour editions of *The CBS Evening News* with Walter Cronkite and *The Huntley-Brinkley Report* on NBC.

In fact, the audiences for these news shows were modest. According to a poll by the Roper organization, even the "regular" viewers tuned in fewer than four times a week, and at least a third of the people hardly watched at all. More people still got their news from newspapers than from television, and more of them watched the local news. Because the news programs were nationwide, however, the audiences of the network news shows dwarfed the circulation of any one newspaper or magazine. Furthermore, the opinion elites were much taken by the expanded newscasts, which seemed to confirm their sense of their own importance.

This expansion of news reflected both the appeal of the technology— news on television was more immediate than in the newspapers, more dramatic than on the radio—and the fact that there was a good deal of interesting news. The networks doubled the number of newscast minutes when there was a telegenic president and when Negro Americans began using public demonstrations to win their full rights as citizens. Demonstrations were both morally compelling and visually fascinating.

For the most part, though, television provided entertainment. On Sunday nights, families gathered together to watch Ed Sullivan introduce singers, comedians, ventriloquists, and trained animal acts on CBS. Then many switched to NBC for *Bonanza,* an all-male Western series about a widowed rancher and his four grown (though not always grown-up) sons. After the kids went to bed, parents often stayed up to switch back to CBS for *What's My Line,* where John Daly, Dorothy Kilgallen, Arlene Francis, and publisher Bennett Cerf tried to guess what ordinary people did for a living and then, blindfolded, guess the identity of a celebrity "secret guest."

On Saturday nights, teenagers and young couples went out. Parents and grandparents watched Jackie Gleason and then Lawrence Welk, and if they could stay up late enough, they watched Marshal Matt Dillon track down another villain on *Gunsmoke.*

But no program was more popular than the one that took up just a half hour every Wednesday evening. At 9 P.M. (8 in the central and mountain time zones), millions of Americans dropped whatever else they were doing to see what was happening with the Clampetts, the poor family from the Ozarks who struck oil and relocated to southern California.

They were *The Beverly Hillbillies,* and they were so inane that a reviewer for *Variety,* hardly a guardian of the higher culture, complained that "at no time does [the show] give the viewer credit for even a smattering of intelligence."[5] The critic's complaints—that "the lines were as cliché-ridden as the situations were obvious"—were the show's strengths as far as its adoring audience was concerned. Every week, the crude Clampetts—blustering but shrewd Jed, ditzy Granny, and goofy (but well-built) Ellie May—would run afoul of the local sophisticates. Every week, the Clampetts would outfox them. It was the oldest formula in the American book of comedy.

It was also mildly subversive. What was charming about the Clampetts was not that they had money but that they valued their origins and traditions more than the gadgets they could buy or the appearance they presented to the proper world. The program, like all programs, was designed to sell products; its message seemed to be that buying products was not as important as remembering who you were.

And it was probably no accident that the show's popularity coincided with the continuing decline in the rural population and an accelerating erosion of economic opportunity in rural areas, especially in the South, whence the fictional Clampetts emigrated. The millions of former farmhands now in suburban subdivisions had not struck oil. But they had found good factory or office work, and though it had not taken them to Beverly Hills, it had gotten them off the farm and into a life more luxurious than any they had known. No doubt it had also gotten them into embarrassing situations as they rubbed shoulders with veteran urbanites. The Clampetts provided a nice antidote.

And maybe a little expiation. So many of the new suburbanites had left kinfolk or old buddies behind in the Ozarks, the Appalachians, the Texas Panhandle, or one of the hundreds of other places where many people still lacked indoor plumbing. American prosperity was spreading itself around, but slowly.

| | |

The ninth and final issue of Wallace Berman's magazine, *Semina*, which came out early in 1964, contained one poem, "Dallas Poem," by Michael McClure, and one photograph, Berman's, of Jack Ruby killing Lee Harvey Oswald on the television screen. The poem:

> DOUBLE MURDER! VAHROOOOOOOHR!
> Varshnohteeembreth nahrooohr PAIN STAR.
>   nrah paws blayge bullets eem air.
> BANG! BANG! BANG! BANG! BANG!
>   BANG! BANG! BANG! BANG!
> BANG! BANG! BANG! BANG! BANG!
> BANG! BANG! BANG! BANG! BANG!

BANG! BANG! BANG! BANG!
Yahh oon FLAME held prisoner.
DALLAS!

Like a lot of the art coming out of California, this was not easy to understand. One critic later called it a "primal scream against American insanity." The flame was the one at JFK's grave, yes, but wasn't it something more? Together, the poem and the picture seemed to be saying that violence for its own sake was deeply ingrained in American culture, thanks in part to psychological repression, especially sexual repression.

It was part of the subjective rebellion against the rational. Like the Goldwaterites, these young artists finessed a basic contradiction. Berman and his fellow avant-gardists in California were able to become artists thanks to . . . the government. The G.I. Bill created more artists than did the discovery of perspective. So many veterans flocked to art schools in California that there wasn't enough room; new schools opened to provide slots for would-be veteran artists. The artistic rebels owed more to the consensus than they liked to admit.

But it was impossible to dismiss either the power of their appeal or the quality of some of their work. The seeds of the middle-class youth rebellion of 1964 had been sown by the irrepressible poets and writers of the "beat generation," which arose in the 1950s and which rebelled not against specific elements of organized society but against the very need for organization. Against the structure of organized society, they upheld the sanctity of the self.

Unlike the individualists campaigning for Barry Goldwater, however, these rebels claimed to be less interested in the material part of the self than in its aesthetic and spiritual aspects. Their heroes were novelist Jack Kerouac and poet Allen Ginsberg. Their intellectual leader, though many were unaware of him, was psychotherapist Norman Brown, who would replace the rational with instinctual freedom—"Dionysian ecstasy," he called it.

For more than a few of them, lubricating this ecstasy with the aid of mind-altering drugs was acceptable, perhaps necessary. For some, drugs were an escape from the reality of their lack of talent. For others, they became an indispensable (or so they thought) accompaniment of enormous talent.

| | |

At its first meeting of the year on Tuesday, January 21, the Warren Commission decided not to open its sessions to the public. This seemed to be a reasonable decision because public sessions might jeopardize the fairness of Jack Ruby's trial. Besides, a wild accusation made in January might not be refuted until March. So it would be better to hold information in check until it could be presented in context. It would be better to trust the unimpeachable reputations of the commissioners than to risk spreading panic about plots that had never been plotted.

In fact, the first wild accusation came, in private, even before the second meeting took place January 27. "We have a dirty rumor," chief counsel J. Lee Rankin told the commissioners, that Lee Harvey Oswald had once been on the payroll of the FBI, as informant number 179.[6]

The commission could ask J. Edgar Hoover if it was true, or look into it independently. Justice Warren decided to pursue both courses. To no one's surprise, Hoover immediately told Rankin that "Oswald had never been an informant of the FBI."

But on January 24, three days before the commission met, the Secret Service had told the Warren staff that the source of this rumor, a Texas newspaperman named Alonzo Hudkins, had gotten his information from Allan Sweatt, who was the chief of the criminal division of the Dallas sheriff's office. Neither Hudkins nor Sweatt was ever questioned by the commission.

To give the commission the excuse it needed not to pursue this line of investigation, Gerald Ford wrote that the commissioners "would not be justified in plunging into this matter in some irresponsible manner that might jeopardize the effectiveness of an important agency's future operations." The option of plunging in in a responsible manner seemed not to have occurred to anyone.

| | |

On Thursday, January 30, Judge Howard Smith admitted defeat. For months, the eighty-year-old Virginia segregationist had kept H.R. 7152, the civil rights bill, from even being considered by the Rules Committee he chaired. "You'll have to run over us," he smugly told civil rights supporters. They may have been in the majority, but he was in the chairman's seat, and to Lyndon Johnson's dismay, even the Republican members of the House were reluctant to challenge the chairman's authority and sign a discharge petition to dislodge the bill from committee.

What protocol forbade, simple politics ultimately achieved. The polls showed that 60 percent of the public supported the bill, perhaps because the new president had proclaimed it the most fitting monument to his predecessor. It was now time for Smith to acknowledge that he had been run over, and he brought the bill before his committee. By an 11 to 4 vote, the measure was sent to the House floor under an "open rule." Every line was open to amendment.

In Saigon that day, Major General Duong Van Minh, the head of the coup that had ousted and killed General Ngo Dinh Diem, was himself ousted in a coup headed by Major General Nguyen Kanh. Minh, who preferred playing tennis and tending his orchids to presiding over meetings, was not killed. He was merely replaced, because, according to Kanh, Minh had been conspiring with the French to create a neutral South Vietnam.[7]

Kanh may have been right about Minh's behind-the-scenes activities. The next day, President Charles de Gaulle of France called for the "neutralization" of all Southeast Asia.

| | |

On the evening of the last day of the month, a Friday, Lewis Allen, a forty-four-year-old Negro logger, was driving back to his country home outside McComb, Mississippi. A few months earlier, Allen had seen a state legislator named E. H. Hurst shoot and kill Herbert Lee, a Negro who was trying to register to vote. In fear of his own life, Allen had backed up Hurst's fraudulent claim of self-defense, ending whatever slim chance may have existed that the lawmaker would be brought to justice by the state of Mississippi. But he was still worried. Since the charges against Hurst had been dropped, Allen had talked to federal authorities. The local whites did not know what he had told them, but they knew he had met with them.

He was going to run away. He had a brother in Milwaukee, and though he despaired of his chances of making a living up North, he had a train ticket for the next day, Saturday, February 1.

Hoping he could get some kind of job, he had driven over to see a former employer to ask for a letter of recommendation. He drove home, got out of his pickup, and was about to open his gate when he saw the gunman. He dived under the truck, but the man with the shotgun merely crouched low enough for his first shot to rip off Allen's forehead. The second shot tore through his neck and blew out the left front tire.

The sheriff arrived quickly and almost as quickly announced that the murder had nothing whatever to do with whether Negroes should vote. Only a little more subtly, J. Edgar Hoover agreed, making sure that his agents knew that the Bureau was involved only because of the "specific request of A. A. G. Burke Marshall," the head of the Justice Department's Civil Rights Division. Before the day ended, the FBI had concluded that the matter of voting rights, which would have triggered federal activity, could not have been relevant to the murder because "the victim is not a registered voter, has never been active in voter registration activities, and there has been no voter registration activity in Amite County in the past two or three years."

In rural Mississippi, at least, political murder had been granted the imprimatur of the federal government.

|9|

ONE GOOD WAR DESERVES ANOTHER

On Saturday, February 1, Lyndon Johnson surreptitiously escalated both of his wars. The previous afternoon, a few hours before Lewis Allen was shot in Mississippi, the president welcomed Sargent Shriver to the White House and offered him the position of commanding general of the new war on poverty.

Shriver barely knew what Johnson was talking about. He'd been out of the country for a month. Yes, in Pakistan or somewhere he'd read that Johnson had talked about poverty. But a war? Besides, Shriver was running the Peace Corps. That was enough. Shriver asked for some time to think things over.

The next morning, Johnson called him at home.

"I'm gonna announce your appointment at the press conference," he said.

"What press conference?"

"This afternoon."

"Oh, God," said Shriver, protesting that he knew little about the subject. "Could you just say that you've asked me to study this?"

"No, hell no," Johnson said. "You're Mister Poverty. You got the responsibility. You've got the authority. You got the power. You got the money. Now, you may not have the glands."

"The glands?"

"Yeah," Johnson said.

"I've got plenty of glands," said Sargent Shriver, firmly. That afternoon, Johnson announced Shriver's appointment.

That same day, Operation Plan 34A began. The Plan, under the control of the Office of the Special Assistant for Counterinsurgency and Special Activities, was to increase espionage and sabotage, including commando raids against North Vietnam's transportation system and bombardment and coastal facilities by PT boats.

Then there would be air raids by American pilots flying American planes with Laotian Air Force markings against North Vietnamese troops in Laos. Finally, there would be patrols, code-named DeSoto, by U.S. destroyers in the Gulf of Tonkin.[1]

These were policies created by men who didn't like the idea of having American forces in Vietnam. They were the liberals in the argument. On the other side, the military brass didn't think any of this would work. The liberal foreign policy intellectuals assumed that "progressively escalating pressure," as Secretary McNamara called it, would force the North Vietnamese government to order the guerrillas in the South to cool it. With its economy "wobbly," Hanoi would have to call off its support for the insurrection in the South.[2]

The foreign policy intellectuals apparently didn't ask themselves several obvious questions: Could North Vietnam tell the guerrillas in the South what to do? Was there a North Vietnamese transportation system worth sabotaging? What were the potential consequences of sailing U.S. destroyers close to North Vietnamese waters in the Gulf?

These questions went unasked because they would have complicated the grand strategic thinking, which is what the foreign policy intellectuals preferred to do. They were, in their own minds, saving the world, because in their own minds there was no doubt whatsoever that Vietnam was just a small part of a larger problem. Liberal or conservative, American policymakers carried in their unconscious the text of Nikita Khrushchev's 1960 speech on the three kinds of war: nuclear, conventional, and "wars of national liberation." According to Khrushchev, the first was unthinkable and the second was to be avoided. But as for the third, the Soviet Union would continue to help the "socialist camp" in any internal conflict.

All these supposedly indigenous uprisings, then, were simply—or at least were *also*—part of the Soviet Union's plan to increase its influence at the expense of ours and perhaps to dominate the world. For this reason, any "wars of national liberation" could not be allowed to succeed. Vietnam was another in a series of challenges that would test the resolve of the United States to stop communist encroachment. If we failed there, we'd only face a similar threat soon somewhere else, probably somewhere closer. A loss in Vietnam would lead to pressure on Cambodia, and then on Malaysia and

Indonesia; they could fall one by one, like a row of dominoes. It was a meta-phor the president could appreciate; like his father before him, he played dominoes.

Within the political mainstream, there was almost no opposition to this conclusion. If anything, liberals were more convinced than conservatives that the Soviet star was in ascendance. After all, the Russians had been first in space, with *Sputnik* in 1957. Most Americans believed the CIA reports that the Russian economy was growing faster than ours, and at the time the fact that these reports were untrue was less important than that they were widely believed. Many of the poor nations of Asia and Africa were looking to the Soviet system and to Soviet economic aid. It was no wonder that Khrushchev could bluster so aggressively wherever he went.

Liberals worried that the United States was letting itself be overtaken in every field: politics, economics, even nuclear missiles. John Kennedy had claimed that the United States faced a "missile gap" vis-à-vis the Soviets. This was an incorrect claim as it turned out, but it had seemed plausible to him and his supporters.

Almost the only visible dissent came from the political right, and it dis-sented only about prudence. The underlying assumption of some hard-line conservatives was that we were already in a war and that the only way to win it was through more vigorous military action. In Vietnam, that meant bomb-ing all over Southeast Asia if necessary. Farther east, it meant "unleashing" the armed forces of Chiang Kai-shek's Taiwanese to harass mainland China if they could not retake it. In Europe, it meant liberating the "captive nations," whose plight was honored each year by a week devoted to them.

The conservative strategists never seemed to consider that the Taiwanese army had no intention of letting itself be "unleashed" on what would be suicide missions or that any effort to push the Soviets out of Poland or the Baltics would mean war. The conservatives didn't want to complicate their thinking, or at least their rhetoric, which often stopped just short of welcom-ing nuclear war. "We need victory even at the risk and fear of annihilation and death," said a conservative strategist identified only as a "senior aide" to Senator Goldwater, "for death itself is not the end of everything for men and women of the Judeo-Christian tradition."[3]

The dissent from the left was less potent. A few leftists actually had some sympathy for communism. Others—devotees of British philosopher Bertrand Russell and his slogan "Better Red than dead"—were so concerned about the dangers of nuclear war that they considered communism the lesser evil. And of course there are always among the intelligentsia contrarians for whom being out of the mainstream is the whole point of existence.

These dissenters from both the left and the right would have been out-numbered even if they were united. Even as enlightened a foreign policy intellectual as Senator J. William Fulbright reinforced Johnson's determination to stop communist encroachment in Vietnam. In a telephone conversation with Fulbright in early March, Johnson laid out his analysis of the Vietnamese situation and his decision "to continue our present policy."

"I think that's right," Fulbright said. "That's exactly what I'd arrive at under these circumstances at least for the foreseeable future."[4]

Contrary to his own instincts, then, or at least some of them, the president soldiered on, fortified by the advice of the smartest folks around, comforting himself that, if nothing else, he was doing what John Kennedy would have done.

| | |

In Atlanta on the first of February, Robert Moses called a meeting to consider plans to bring more young people into Mississippi that summer. By now he and his allies had a name for their idea. They were calling it Freedom Summer. In Washington a few weeks later, Moses explained his plans to Joseph Rauh, the general counsel for the United Auto Workers, a pal of Hubert Humphrey and a vice president of the Americans for Democratic Action. Rauh was a tall, bushy-haired man with enormous eyebrows, enormous energy, and a devotion to civil rights that approached the demonic.

"If there's a challenge," he said, "if there's anybody at the Democratic Convention challenging the seating of the outlaw Mississippi Democrats [he meant the party regulars], I'll help make sure that the challengers are seated."

The rebels now had their friend in the establishment.

There was no Ku Klux Klan in Cleveland, Ohio, but when some Negroes walked in front of a school carrying "separate is not equal" signs, whites ripped up the signs, knocked the demonstrators to the sidewalk, and roughed up two of them. The civil rights revolution was coming North, and the North was not happy about it.

In New York Bayard Rustin organized a one-day boycott of the public schools, directing his anger not at segregationists or conservatives but at white suburbanites. "By running to the suburbs, the whites are leaving to the Negro the total burden of improving schools," Rustin said. "Whites must learn to share this burden. We will force them to learn—and I say *force*."[5]

In California, support was growing for a voter initiative to repeal the Rumford Act, which banned discrimination in housing. The initiative procedure had been on the books since the Progressive Era, but it had never been used to overturn a law passed by the legislature, especially not a liberal law. Initiative was a liberal invention.

Almost all the state's influential Republicans, including Senator Thomas Kuchel, opposed the initiative. So did Republican State Chairman Caspar Weinberger. But the California Real Estate Association was spending one hundred fifty thousand dollars to gather enough signatures, and the repeal effort was endorsed by the California Young Republicans.

| | |

For a few days in early February, Sargent Shriver wondered whether every liberal policy intellectual in America was in his living room. Shriver called some of them, Shriver's friends called others, and still others just heard that folks they knew were gathering there and came uninvited.

Adam Yarmolinsky, an assistant to Defense Secretary McNamara, was one of the first ones Shriver approached. "You've got to come to a meeting Sunday evening," Shriver told him, which was a great relief to Yarmolinsky because it gave him an excuse not to go to an embassy dinner he'd been dreading. What he didn't expect was that he wouldn't go back to the Pentagon for six months.

It was, as one participant later said, "a typical Shriver meeting," or series of meetings, during which Shriver spent much of his time on the phone consulting out-of-town experts while his guests tossed ideas around over sandwiches, cigarettes, and copious amounts of coffee. All this was necessary because of a little lie Lyndon Johnson had told when he announced his War on Poverty. "We know what must be done," he had said.

In fact, nobody had the foggiest idea what to do. When all those experts gathered at Shriver's Maryland estate, they realized that they couldn't even agree on a definition of poverty, much less on what caused it. "Do you concentrate on finding jobs for people or preparing people for jobs?" one of the participants later asked. Should the "war" be run by the existing cabinet departments or a brand-new agency? Should poor people play a role in designing the programs intended to help them?

Shriver's brain trust disagreed about all these questions and more during those first days of February. Despite their disagreements, the participants had much in common. To begin with, almost all of them were white. They supported civil rights, but they were not part of the civil rights movement. And though they knew that Negroes made up a disproportionate share of the poor, they did not envision Negroes as the main beneficiaries of the fight against poverty. If they had a stereotype of poverty in mind, it was white Appalachia, not Negro Harlem.

They had their statistics right. As the year began, some 9.3 million, or about 19 percent, of the 47 million families in the country earned less than $3,000 annually.[6] Almost half of these very-low-income families lived in the South, and most of them were white. Negroes made up 22 percent of the poor, more than twice their share of the population but still less than a quarter of the poverty population. A third of the poor were elderly.

Except for these elderly, few of the poor voted; however, this was not a factor for the antipoverty planners, who were not politicians. If they had been, none of them would have been there at all. The War on Poverty was politically counterproductive. Even a less ambitious program to alleviate poverty would have been bad politics. That's what John Kennedy's advisors had told him in 1963. He believed them, but he told them to go ahead with their planning for it anyway.

Shriver's guests were creating a program, but they were not creating it out of context or designing it on a blank page. This was an effort that had already been on the minds of a few people in academia, the foundations, and the government for a few years, and its origins were as significant as they were peculiar.

For years, poverty was a subject most Americans, including liberals, simply tried to avoid. That's why it took a nonliberal to remind them of it. The reminder came in 1962 in a book called *The Other America,* in which Michael Harrington, one of America's few avowed socialists, laid bare the realities in sparse and understated terms. President Kennedy had read the book and been moved by it. He gave copies to some of his policy advisors, and though he did not specifically direct them to devise a program, why else do presidents hand out copies of such a book?

Separately, and inspired largely by Robert Kennedy, the administration tried to do something about the one consequence of poverty that was part of the political agenda: the tendency of low-income young people to get into trouble. This was viewed as a problem not of income but of behavior. It was known as juvenile delinquency.

With the help of a few academics and both expertise and money from the Ford Foundation, the administration funded a few small pilot programs among low-income youth. It was social work with one new twist: The professionals sought the suggestions of the troubled young people themselves. At some point, this idea got a name: *community action.*

By late 1963, the policy experts planning John Kennedy's approach to poverty had adopted that idea. Somehow—nobody ever figured out quite how—the government would help the poor help themselves. In a sense, these young policy planners were subversives, undercutting their own liberal allies.

They realized that traditional social services were perpetuating poverty as much as they were dealing with it. So they would organize the poor as a counterweight to traditional social service agencies.

It was a new idea, and in the view of some experienced politicians, a very bad one, "like telling the fellow who cleans up [the newsroom] to be the city editor," Mayor Richard J. Daley told a group of Chicago reporters.

Lyndon Johnson did not know any of this, and when it came to the matter of poverty, he didn't need the impetus of following, and bettering, his predecessor. Johnson had a big advantage over Kennedy; the new president had grown up surrounded by poverty, if not quite in it. Johnson was a pragmatist, but if he had any ideology, it was that of a New Dealer. Now that he had become president, doing something about poverty would have come to him naturally.

But Kennedy had already started the process in motion, even if only as a vague idea, so there was no doubt that Johnson would keep it going, would expand it, and would embrace it. To Kennedy, it had been an idea. Johnson would forge it into an institution and then turn it into a war.

| | |

On Sunday, February 2, Florida conservation agents aboard a U.S. Coast Guard cutter, alerted by Navy planes, intercepted four Cuban fishing boats and arrested their crews for violation of the Florida Territorial Waters Act, which had been passed the previous year precisely to prevent Cubans from fishing near Florida. For reasons never explained and in defiance of reason, the Coast Guard did not order them back to international waters but brought them to Key West, where they could be arrested.

Back in Washington, Thomas Mann, the new, hard-line Latin American honcho, told the president that Castro had sent the fishing boats as some kind of provocation. Robert Kennedy wondered whether Mann had any evidence for this assertion. Kennedy, inclined to believe the fishermen's explanation that they had been blown off course by a storm near the Dry Tortugas, thought it would be wise to treat the incident as a mistake, not a provocation.

Rather than provoke a confrontation, Kennedy said, why not treat the incident "like a speeding, parking ticket. Why don't you just tell them to get out of there and go home?"

Senator Barry Goldwater suggested sending in the Marines. Senator Humphrey did not go that far but insisted that the United States would have "to be firm." The president sent no Marines. For the moment, he did nothing.

The next day Lee Harvey Oswald's widow, Marina, began four days of testimony before the Warren Commission. Two of the commission lawyers, Albert Jenner and Wesley Liebeler, had spent the last several weeks becoming experts in the life of Lee Harvey Oswald, but they did not interrogate Mrs. Oswald. Their boss, J. Lee Rankin, did. When she finished, Chief Justice Warren emerged from the closed hearing to tell reporters that she had been moderately helpful. Without telling reporters, the commission staff disagreed. Some of the lawyers thought Rankin hadn't challenged anything Mrs. Oswald said. One of the lawyers threatened to quit unless she was brought back for a tougher grilling. Tempers flared. That was the last formal staff meeting.

| | |

On Wednesday morning, February 5, President Johnson spoke at the annual presidential prayer breakfast at the Mayflower Hotel. While upholding the principle of church-state separation, he told a thousand clergy and lay religious leaders that "in these last seventy days, prayer has helped me to bear the burdens of this first office, which are too great to be borne by anyone alone."

This is the kind of thing presidents say at these breakfasts. Most voters, after all, have a religious affiliation. There were 66,854,200 Protestants (more than a third of them Baptists), 44,874,371 Roman Catholics, and 5,500,000 Jews, 3 million of whom described themselves as Orthodox. In all, the 253 separate religious sects contained 120,965,235 members, or 64 percent of the population.

As usual, a closer look reveals a more complex reality. More than a third of the people were unaffiliated with any faith; the smaller, less cerebral, and more emotional sects within Christianity were growing faster than the mainline churches; and "a small but discernible movement toward Buddhism" was under way,[7] inspired both by the Buddhist monks who immolated themselves in protest in South Vietnam and by the interest in Eastern religions displayed by writers such as Jack Kerouac and Allen Ginsberg.

Still, a presidential display of Christian piety was good politics. In this case, though, Johnson may have been engaged in something other than pleasing rhetoric. Mrs. Johnson had noticed that her husband, not the most pious fellow in the world or even in his family, had been praying rather regularly since the previous November 22.

| | |

Later that day, the utility industry resumed its battle against public power. In a letter to Jack Valenti at the White House, Frank Snell of the

Phoenix law firm Snell and Wilmer complained about the "advantages granted public power distributors," especially "the preference right given to public power agencies to purchase government generated power at low rates."

Snell did not mention all the government's assistance to the private power companies, such as that resulting from the Atomic Energy Act of 1954, which gave private utilities primacy in building nuclear power plants. This was quite a good deal for the private companies, considering that the fuel was on public land and the government had already absorbed most of the research and development costs. Showing no signs of gratitude, the companies were ever on the alert for any sign of vigor in the public power world. In February, when Assistant Reclamation Commissioner N. B. Bennett suggested placing a steam-generating power plant at the government facility on Lake Mead, the private companies moved to quash the idea as quickly as possible.

They sensed a plot. Already, Secretary Udall had declared southern Idaho within the marketing area of the Bonneville Power Authority. Private utility executives did not look kindly at the prospect of all that cheap hydropower coming into their area. Governor Love of Colorado, a Republican, wrote to Wayne Aspinall that no more transmission lines were needed from the BPA generators into the Inter-Mountain West because "adequate power has been available . . . at a rate less than five mills per kilowatt hour from the private power supplier."

BPA power would be cheaper, and there was the Western concern with any threat to the Colorado River Storage Project, the principal means by which the United States government subsidized the Rocky Mountain West. "If the BPA transmission line . . . is extended to interconnect with the CRSP system," Love wrote, the result "might seriously affect marketability of CRSP power and jeopardize the financial feasibility of the CRSP project and potential irrigation assistance available from this project."

In other words, Love's (and Barry Goldwater's) backers—ranchers and developers who didn't want the federal government to do anything except nurture them—would be in a pickle if lower-cost power came into the area.

The very day Snell wrote his letter, and perhaps not coincidentally, the Senate gave the private utility industry a gift, preserving a law prohibiting federal agencies from requiring the companies to pass on to their consumers the money they would save from the accelerated depreciation provision of the new tax code. The purpose of accelerated depreciation was to encourage business to make new, job-creating investments. As regulated companies with guaranteed profit margins, utilities needed no such incentive; their tax cuts would be pure profit, a $300 million windfall.[8]

And the next day, the Federal Power Commission, over the strenuous objections of its chairman, issued a license to the privately owned Pacific Northwest Power Company to build the High Mountain Sheep Dam on the Snake River between Oregon and Idaho. Chairman Joseph Swidler and Commissioner David Black dissented, arguing that if any dam were needed, the publicly owned Washington Public Power System ought to build it. Interior Secretary Udall went further, contending that the Northwest already had more electric-generating capacity than it would need for several years. The company's real goal, Udall indicated, was to "create additional financial problems for the Bonneville Power Administration," which under the law had to eat the losses from regional power surpluses. The commission decision, the secretary said, allowed private firms "to preempt now a great public resource site for a speculative future need."[9] This was, of course, precisely what the private utility companies wanted to do.

I I I

The day of the FPC's decision, the Cuban government, in reprisal for the seizure of the fishing boats, cut off the water supply to the U.S. naval base in Guantánamo Bay. The president, who was in New York City for lunch with the editorial board of *The New York Times* and for the annual dinner of the Chaim Weizmann Institute, proclaimed that "our troops in Cuba and their families will have the water they need," and he sent water-laden Navy tankers steaming toward Guantánamo.

At a meeting of the National Security Council, Thomas Mann argued that the United States should take a hard line as "a sign to the rest of the countries of Latin America that this was a new administration that was going to stand up to them."

Favorably comparing this "new administration" to its predecessor did not please Security Council member Robert Kennedy, who observed dryly that Mann "sounded like Barry Goldwater making a speech at the economic club." When Mann, Johnson, and McNamara suggested firing all three thousand Cuban workers at the base as security risks, Kennedy asked why they had not all been fired after the 1962 missile crisis.

"If they're security risks," he said, "can you tell me why we kept security risks on our base for all this period of time?"

It must have seemed strange to his listeners—this brash young man who had once been so eager to provoke a crisis was now eager only to defuse one. Like Goldwater, Robert Kennedy was challenging the consensus but from within the very government he served.

The workers were all fired.

| | |

On Friday, February 7, the White House finally got its new phone number. All-digit dialing had come to the District of Columbia, so NA 8-1414 was out, and 202-456-1414 was in. It wasn't the first time the White House's number had been changed. It was actually the fifth change since the first phone was installed in President Rutherford B. Hayes's office in 1878. His number had been just plain 1.

Also on February 7, 1964, Judge Leon F. Hendrick declared a mistrial in the murder case against Byron De La Beckwith, accused of killing civil rights leader Medgar Evers the previous summer. The jurors were reportedly split 7 to 5 in favor of acquittal, and more than a few observers reported themselves shocked that five white men in Mississippi voted to convict one of their own for killing a Negro.

But Mississippi and its neighbors were not the only places where some folks were feeling they were out of step with the rest of the country. That day in Albuquerque, Interior Secretary Udall warned that the West was experiencing a growth in the number of people who "fear Washington more than Moscow." This Western "antifederalism," Udall said at the John Field Simms Memorial Lecture at the University of New Mexico, could end up being as dangerous as Southern resistance to federal authority, though it was not rooted in racism but in what historian Joseph Franz of the University of Texas employing an all-but-lost piece of Texas slang for rubbish, called the consequences of "swallow[ing] whole a whole hunk of home-manufactured, self-illuminated halwo without chewing it first."

| | |

The following day, the U.S. House of Representatives met in a rare Saturday session to consider amendments to the civil rights bill. One after another, each Southern effort to weaken the legislation was defeated, until finally, toward day's end, Judge Howard Smith arose with a very simple proposed change: If the country was going to ban job discrimination by race, it would also have to outlaw it on the basis of sex.

"Now, I am very serious about this amendment," assured the crusty old segregationist, and he read a letter from a Nebraska woman who insisted that Congress make sure that the country's population be equally divided between the sexes instead of sending so many eligible young fellows off to their death in war.

Despite his protestations, Judge Smith was not taken seriously, except by pro–civil rights forces who saw it as a ploy to kill the bill with ridicule. Emanuel Celler of Brooklyn, the liberal chairman of the Judiciary Committee, opposed the amendment on the basis of his own fifty years of domestic bliss, an arrangement, he said, in which he usually had the last words. "And those words are 'yes, dear,' " he explained.

The members of Congress were just about beside themselves with laughter. The Southerners were especially delighted; how could any Southern gentleman not vote to grant white women at least as much privilege as Negro men? After all, with this little attachment, the whole bill might be disgraced. Everybody was having quite a jolly time.

With twelve exceptions: the women of the House. Martha Griffiths of Michigan said all the laughter only proved that "women were a second-class sex." She was a liberal Democrat whose devotion to civil rights could not be questioned. Nonetheless, she challenged her fellows: "A vote against this amendment today by a white man is a vote against his wife, or his widow, or his sister."

Katherine St. George, a Republican from upstate New York, was not kidding, either. "We do not want special privilege," she told her colleagues. "We do not need special privilege. We outlast you. We outlive you. We nag you to death. So why should we want special privileges? I believe that we can hold our own. We are entitled to this little crumb of equality. The addition of that little, terrifying word, 's-e-x,' will not hurt this legislation in any way."

All of a sudden it wasn't funny. The administration's operatives on Capitol Hill were worried that any amendment to the bill could lead to troubles for it down the road. But now that the ladies had put it that way . . . well, not many men wanted to vote against it. Of the twelve women, only Edith Green of Oregon, who acknowledged that she would "be branded an Aunt Jane," the female version of an Uncle Tom, opposed the amendment, fearing that it would endanger the bill. Over her objections and the administration's, it was adopted 168 to 133.

Even then, not everyone took it seriously. *Newsweek* dubbed it the May Craig amendment after the "frilly-bonneted Maine reporter seen so often on television." Ironically, the final retroactive joke was that Howard Smith really had been serious all along; his belief in equality of the sexes was almost as deep as his belief in the inequality of the races.

Two days later, after ten hours of debate, the House passed the civil rights bill by a vote of 290 to 130. Mike Mansfield said he would keep the measure away from the Senate Judiciary Committee, which would not prevent a filibuster but would save it from the ministrations of Committee Chairman James Eastland of Mississippi.

Then Mansfield made another, less obvious, decision. In defiance of the conventional wisdom, he refused even to discuss the idea of keeping the Senate in session around the clock in an effort to exhaust the Southerners. "This is not a circus or a sideshow," he said. "We are not operating in a pit with spectators coming into the galleries late at night to see senators of the republic come out in bedroom slippers, without neckties, with their hair uncombed, and pajama tops sticking out of their necks."

Not only that, he was worried that one of those old Southern senators might croak. How would that look?[10]

The president, almost jolly after the House vote, told Robert Kennedy and Deputy Attorney General Nicholas Katzenbach to get the bill through the Senate any way they could. "Whatever you want I'll be for," he said.

This was most generous of the president. On the other hand, should the whole thing blow up in their faces, his face would be a few feet away.

| | |

Johnson's jolliness over the bill's passage was not his norm those days. Young Americans were singing "Fun, Fun, Fun" with the Beach Boys, but their president wasn't having much. Had he adopted one of the currently popular songs as his theme, it would have been "Have You Ever Been Lonely?" He seemed almost constantly annoyed—at the Republicans, at other Democrats, and at the press, which knew things he didn't want it to know. At one point he was so angry about a story in the *Washington Star* that he asked J. Edgar Hoover to find out who the newspaper's source was. Hoover told him it was Sargent Shriver.

But nothing continued to upset the president more than his attorney general, who, Johnson was convinced, was plotting against him, angling at least for the vice presidency and perhaps even trying to damage the president so badly that the Democratic Convention would dump Johnson and nominate Kennedy in his stead.

If a newspaper had a story embarrassing to the administration, the president assumed that Robert Kennedy or someone loyal to him had leaked the information. "Who is leaking this poverty stuff that's making such a damned mess?" he complained early in March. "You read the *Baltimore Sun* story? Well, it must be the attorney general."

Who, in Johnson's view, also started the whole Bobby Baker investigation. Johnson "found that out pretty definite," as he told his close friend Edwin Weisl. He didn't say how he had found it out or why he would assume that another Democrat would be the secret source of an issue the Republicans were raising in public every day. Like any true believer, he did not need evidence; he had revelation.

|10|

A CIVIL WAR

Just before the House passed the civil rights bill, but after there was no doubt that it would do so, the president told Hubert Humphrey to come to the White House. The easy part was over. The House represents the people, so getting it to pass a law most people want wasn't too difficult. The Senate represents states, the small getting as many votes as the large, and under its rules any thirty-four senators could hold up legislation forever or for as long as they could keep talking.

The filibuster, first used in 1841, was a revered Senate tradition. Not until 1917 had the Senate even adopted a cloture rule empowering two thirds of its members to end a filibuster, and cloture had never been invoked on a civil rights bill. There were eleven states in the deep South. Getting sixty-seven senators to vote to close debate on the bill would not be easy; it would require far more than simply arguing the merits of the case.

"You bomb throwers make good speeches," Johnson told Humphrey. "You have big hearts, you believe in what you say you stand for, but you're never on the job when you need to be there. You spread yourself too thin making speeches to the faithful."

This was blunt talk, but these two had been speaking bluntly with each other almost since they arrived together as rookie senators in 1949, from opposite wings of the Democratic Party but with much in common. They were both the sons of populist fathers who'd served in their state legislatures, dreamt of running for governor, and died hoping their sons might achieve the political success that escaped them. They were about the same age— Johnson just over forty, Humphrey just shy of it. They both wanted to be president of the United States one day.

So they entered into a mutually beneficial friendship. Humphrey made Johnson acceptable to Northern liberals; Johnson made Humphrey acceptable to the Southern Bourbons of the Senate, who at first ostracized the brash young idealist from Minnesota.

If their friendship was mutually beneficial, however, it was never equal. Humphrey owed more; Johnson was the stronger personality, and as he became Humphrey's friend, he became his dominator.[1] Once in 1963, Johnson invited Humphrey to his ranch, and the two of them got into Johnson's Lincoln, the vice president driving fast across the hill country. When they saw a deer, Johnson screeched to a stop. "Hubert," he said. "There's one for you. Get it."

Humphrey grew up in South Dakota, where almost every man shot birds, and he was no exception. A good shot, he'd brought down many a duck and pheasant. But he'd never killed a deer, and he didn't want to now. He did, though, climbing out of the car and bringing down the animal with one shot.

That wasn't good enough for Johnson.

"Bobby Kennedy got two of them," he told Humphrey. "You're not going to let Bobby get the best of you, are you?"

Repelled but obedient, Humphrey got his second deer, probably unaware that Johnson was either confused or lying. Bobby Kennedy never killed a deer in his life, not even on Lyndon Johnson's ranch.

Johnson could speak as bluntly as he chose to Humphrey. Besides, by now Humphrey agreed with Johnson's assessment of some of the more intense liberals, and he knew exactly what his friend, the president, was doing: He was trying to get Humphrey's back up so that he'd work harder to pass the bill, just to show Johnson. Because he knew this, and knew that Johnson knew he knew it, it worked.

Then the president got down to the only strategic point that mattered.

"Now you know that this bill can't pass unless you get Ev Dirksen. You and I are going to get him. You make up your mind now that you've got to spend time with Ev Dirksen. You've got to let him have a piece of the action. He's got to look good all the time."

But even as he plotted for success, the president feared failure. He kept telling his closest allies in private that the votes for cloture were not there. He might even have said it in public were it not for the earnest appeals of Nicholas Katzenbach. "Mr. President," Katzenbach told him, "if you ever indicate any doubt about getting cloture, we can't get it."[2] This was at the end of a conversation in which Johnson insisted that getting cloture was next to impossible, and Katzenbach insisted that it was not.

Katzenbach, the assistant attorney general, was the bill's chief lobbyist. Robert Kennedy did some of the Capitol Hill negotiating, but most of the responsibility was delegated to Katzenbach and to Burke Marshall, the head of the Civil Rights Division. Together, they came up with an audacious strategy of allowing no compromises, at least not with the bill's opponents. They'd make deals with the centrist Republicans who might provide the votes for cloture, but they were determined not to weaken the bill in an effort to get the Southerners to quit talking. They had decided that this filibuster would prevail or be beaten. This time, Lyndon Johnson, the Southerner and deal-maker, decided he would be neither.

Besides, with whom could he deal? He had told Richard Russell he would not deal with him, only run over him, and if Johnson would not deal with Russell he would hardly deal with any of his less impressive Southern allies.

Russell and Johnson still socialized, and they still talked on the phone almost every day. Russell still came now and again to the White House to dine with the Johnsons. They sat around and talked about . . . almost everything, except civil rights.

This issue would have been painful to discuss, because here the student had not simply defied his teacher but had defied him on the very matter dearest to his teacher's heart, a heart that still could not turn away from the one who had betrayed it. And they both knew what the eventual outcome would be. Johnson doubted only that he'd win this time. Russell knew he would lose eventually.

The prospect had to pain Russell. He was not old; he would turn sixty-seven in November. But his years of heavy smoking had taken their toll. Emphysema hampered his breathing and forced him to quit smoking, which he enjoyed almost as much as his evening Jack Daniel's. Fortunately, he didn't have to quit that. He had a lady friend, but he lived alone, with his many books. He had always been a reader, mostly of history, military affairs, biography, and baseball. For all the comfort his books provided, he was a sick, solitary man who was facing the end of his days knowing that the social structure to which he had devoted his life was about to be eradicated.

And he knew, down deep, that it should be. Russell's belief in segregation was absolute, but he could see that his version of a racial utopia—in which Negroes would be separate, not quite equal but able to provide decent lives for themselves—was a chimera.

| | |

Michael Hollingshead, who had first visited Timothy Leary on the advice of Aldous Huxley, came to Millbrook from New York, where everything in his Fifth Avenue apartment had been covered with LSD—the food, the furnishings, even the doorknobs. Hollingshead was the Englishman who, with Dr. John Beresford, had years ago mixed LSD with powdered sugar and distilled water and "experienced . . . the equivalent of death's absolution of the body . . . an ecstatic nirvana."

Now he was joining Tim Leary and the others for their regular trips with high doses of LSD-25 that would allow them "to break through to the other side without losing the love and radiance of the acid high during the crucial reentry period."

Their routine was regular, rather like that of a suburban household, that is, if the suburbanites could afford a baronial fireplace, Persian carpets, and crystal chandeliers. The bell would ring four times an hour starting at 9 A.M., a signal that it was time to stop and record what they were doing. They composed scorecards and "rapped endlessly about how LSD was affecting them." Dogs, cats, and goats wandered freely about. It was, Leary said, a party with a purpose.

They converted one of the tower rooms into a laboratory, with a gold ceiling and a sound system to pipe in spiritual music. Once a week each person would enter the lab for an "ontological adventure," designed to map the Other World with the help of a psychedelic drug. The aim was to try to figure out how psychedelics changed behavior. The Millbrook residents were both the scientists and the guinea pigs.

Here was the problem: Drugs neutralized the mind's "reducing valves," opening up the cortex (and therefore the consciousness). But these "doors" stayed open only for a little while; soon, one begins to slide back into one's "normal" behavior patterns. The group wanted to find out if there was some way to keep the doors open longer.

For a while, they tried music and meditation to see if they could prolong the effect. When this didn't work, they realized they also had to change the conditions of their lives when they weren't using a drug. They called this "breaking set," and it included communal child rearing (that didn't last long), spending five days with one other person in the adjoining coach house, and then "the third floor experiment," in which anyone could copulate with any-one else. There was one "bisexually promiscuous lesbian" who enjoyed that, but the rest of them found it difficult. "We did a lot of sitting in bed and talking about how it felt," one of them later wrote. "It was unsettling."

Gradually, more people arrived. Art Kleps, a school psychologist in up-state New York who had taken mescaline, read a *New York Times* story about Castalia, came for a visit in January, and found life there "better, more lively, more meaningful, funnier, happier" than anything he'd experienced.

Still, watching one man return from a first session in the tower to report that he "left part of myself up in the tower," Kleps realized that the idea of taking LSD was beginning to "scare the living piss" out of him.

| | |

Paul Corbin was a short, square, blunt, brazen, gravelly-voiced political operative from Wisconsin whose values were sufficiently flexible that he had been an advocate, at one time or another, of both the Communist Party and Joe McCarthy. In 1960, Corbin had worked the Wisconsin primary for Jack Kennedy, and thereafter his devotion grew more stable. He was a Kennedy man, mostly a Robert Kennedy man. He even converted to Catholicism so that Bobby could be his godfather. Corbin's deference to propriety, indeed to the law, was tenuous; his commitment to Kennedy was absolute. He would do anything for Robert Kennedy, whether Kennedy wanted him to or not.

A few weeks before the New Hampshire primary, Corbin, who was working for the Democratic National Committee (DNC), went up there on his own and started schmoozing with Democratic leaders about a Kennedy-for-vice-president write-in campaign. But Corbin didn't start this campaign, and neither did Robert Kennedy. Robert Shaine and Joseph Myers did. Shaine was a public relations man in Manchester, and Myers was the Democratic city chairman there. For them and their neighbors—Catholic Democrats from New England—the effort involved both momentum and denial. They had spent the last few years looking forward to working in Jack Kennedy's reelection campaign. Deprived of that opportunity, they would create one on their own. It was also part of the denial, as if making Robert Kennedy vice president would erase his brother's death or at least make sense of it.

Shaine and Myers genuinely longed for a Johnson-Kennedy ticket, but they probably didn't mind the publicity for themselves, either. They got plenty of it, even before Corbin made his little trip. The state was crawling with national political reporters, and anything with the name Kennedy in it was a story.

Besides, the conditions were ripe for embarrassing the president, whose name would not be on the ballot either. Officially, the only candidates in either party were those for delegates to the national conventions. The Republicans were also holding a personal preference, or "beauty contest," vote, with the names of their presidential candidates on the ballot. The Democrats were not. No Democrat, after all, had formally announced his candidacy.

So New Hampshire Democrats who wanted to express their support for Lyndon Johnson would have to write his name on their ballots. But why bother? Everyone knew Johnson would be the party's nominee. Nobody knew who his running mate would be. So it would be no great shock if Robert

Kennedy ended up with more write-in votes for vice president than Lyndon Johnson got for president. No great shock, but nothing Johnson wanted to read in the papers the morning after the primary.

Kennedy's friends in New Hampshire, led by Bill Dunfey, who owned the Sheraton Carpenter Hotel in Manchester where the reporters slept and drank, sent Corbin home, but not before Johnson found out what he'd been up to. At the end of a cabinet meeting on Wednesday, February 11, President Johnson invited, all but ordered, his attorney general into the Oval Office. He'd heard about Corbin, Johnson said, and he wanted Corbin out of New Hampshire and off the DNC payroll. "If he is such a good fellow, you pay him," the president said. "He's around town knocking my head off . . . and has been for three years, and I never met the bum in my life. Why should I have him on my payroll?"

Kennedy insisted that he had not sent Corbin north and added, "He was loyal to President Kennedy. He'll be loyal to you."

"I know who he's loyal to," Johnson said. "Get him out of there.³ President Kennedy isn't president anymore. I am."

"I know you're president, and don't you ever talk to me like that again," Kennedy said.

Then Johnson told Kennedy he had done him a "favor" by sending him to the Far East. It was a bizarre thing to say because it was partly true; in the immediate postassassination period, Johnson had felt pity for Kennedy, had thought that giving him something, anything, to do would take his mind off his troubles.

But then why say so? This was precisely the sort of gesture that is robbed of its kindness by disclosure, and Kennedy was not mollified; he was enraged.

"A favor!" he said. "I don't want you to do any more favors for me. Ever."

Kennedy got up and walked out of the Oval Office without looking back or saying good-bye. At his Justice Department office, he stood at the window staring into the night for a few minutes. "I'll tell you one thing," he said to Ed Guthman. "This relationship can't last much longer."

What Kennedy did not know at the time was that this was a two-man relationship with a third-man complication. The president was angry at Kennedy because he was convinced his attorney general was leaking negative information about him to favored reporters, and the reason he thought this was that J. Edgar Hoover kept telling him so. Or if not Hoover himself, his cupbearer Cartha DeLoach, who also prowled the corridors of the Capitol seeking out political intelligence for the president. Johnson wanted all the information he could get, and he was ready to believe the worst about Robert

Kennedy. Hoover and DeLoach wanted to please the president, to damage Kennedy politically, and to make trouble. Making trouble was an old Hoover tactic, and in this case he clung to some hope that trouble between Johnson and Kennedy could complicate passage of the civil rights bill.

| | |

Less than two weeks after moving into her new home in Washington, Jacqueline Kennedy was house hunting in New York. She spent the middle weekend of February—its Friday was Valentine's Day—inspecting a vacant apartment at 810 Fifth Avenue, near the corner of Sixty-third Street.

| | |

On Friday, February 14, President Johnson, observing that "Americans are seeking the out-of-doors as never before," urged Congress to provide for more outdoor recreation facilities on public land. The next day, at an outdoor gathering in Brookhaven, Mississippi, some fifty miles south of Jackson, two hundred young white men created their own independent version of an old organization revered in those parts. They called their new group the White Knights of the Ku Klux Klan, pledging "violent, physical resistance" to preserve racial segregation. The leader of the new organization was a man named Sam Bowers from Laurel, a small city farther east, between Hattiesburg and Meridian.

Though the White Knights were an unofficial, private organization, their existence was known to, and approved by, state authorities, who were making similar plans. The legislature authorized adding two hundred more troopers to the state police, and in Jackson, Mayor Allen Thompson had created a police riot squad, arming it with two hundred shotguns and a new, custom-built armored wagon.

Mississippi was preparing to defend itself against an invasion. But not all its preparations were defensive. The State Sovereignty Commission, Mississippi's secret police force, was contemplating the wisdom of bringing bribery charges against a woman named Fannie Lou Hamer, a sharecropper's wife in the Delta town of Ruleville who was trying to vote and urging others to do the same. It seems that she had been distributing free food and clothing to poor Negroes in the Delta on condition that they try to register to vote. That could be termed bribery.

The commission was also moving against Tougaloo College in Jackson, the Negro college whose white chaplain, the Reverend Edwin King, was active in the civil rights movement. Erle Johnston, the director of the Sovereignty Commission, got a list of the college's trustees and contributors, and he hinted that unless King and President Daniel Beittel resigned, the college might lose its accreditation. In that case its graduates would not be allowed to teach in Mississippi's public schools, which was about as good a job as Mississippi Negro college graduates could hope to get.

The Sovereignty Commission may have been unique to Mississippi, but it had allies elsewhere. Through an organization known as the Coordinating Committee for Fundamental American Freedoms, Inc., it cooperated with William Loeb, the publisher of the *Manchester Union-Leader,* the only state-wide newspaper in the state that would hold the first presidential primary. Loeb's newspaper was squarely behind Barry Goldwater.

| | |

On the evening of Monday, February 17, Cartha DeLoach went to the White House to meet with the president, Walter Jenkins, and Bill Moyers about a package that had been delivered earlier that day. The package had been sent by Burke Marshall at the Justice Department, with a cover letter saying that the FBI's file on Martin Luther King was inside and explaining that Marshall had sent it because he wanted the president to know that the FBI was using the information in an effort to kill the civil rights bill.

Being conspiratorialists, they analyzed the delivery for hidden motives. Jenkins suspected that Kennedy wanted to be known as the guy who alerted the president "about King's communistic background." Moyers suspected that Kennedy planned to leak the derogatory information about King in an effort to spread the impression that Johnson had continued cooperating with King even after learning the awful truth about him.

Such, at least, is how DeLoach later described it, and he brought his own perspectives to the situation. But it does seem that the president and his top aides were at least as interested in working with the FBI to discredit Kennedy as they were in protecting the civil rights bill. At any rate, they took DeLoach's advice to reject the file, returning the unopened package to the Justice Department.

| | |

The next day, Sargent Shriver presented his antipoverty plan to the cabinet. Central to it was a job-creation program, to be financed by a $1.25 per pack tax on cigarettes.

When Shriver finished that part of his presentation, the president of the United States stared at him. He did not speak. He did not open his mouth. He stared some more. The unspoken response was obvious: The president wanted to move on to the next proposal. Shriver got it, but Labor Secretary Willard Wirtz did not take the hint. Instead, he spoke with some passion in favor of the cigarette tax. The president ignored him, too.

Johnson was neither politically nor psychologically prepared to risk proposing either a new tax or a public jobs program. First of all, how could he ask Congress to raise some taxes while he was trying to get it to cut others? Besides, his economic philosophy was anti–Robin Hood. "This government," he said, "will not set one group against another. We will build a creative partnership between business and labor, between farm areas and urban centers, between consumers and producers."[4]

He knew that ending poverty was largely a concern of the elites. The Rockefeller Brothers Fund report of 1958 had endorsed an antipoverty policy. The Democratic Party platform of 1960 had proclaimed that "the final eradication in America of the age-old evil of poverty" was "within reach." But a Gallup poll early in 1964 found that 83 percent of the populace doubted that a war on poverty could be won.[5]

Beyond the elites, a substantial percentage of the electorate was not simply skeptical about whether the poor could be helped; it was resentful about all the attention being lavished on them and on the Negroes, too.

Horace Busby, who despite his gaffe over poor people's parking problems was one of Johnson's most politically astute associates, told him that "America's real majority is suffering a minority complex of neglect. They have become the real foes of Negro rights, foreign aid, etc., because, as much as anything, they feel forgotten, at the second table behind the tightly organized, smaller groups at either end of the U.S. spectrum."

But opposition to the job-creation approach was hardly confined to conservatives. Every idea that anything should or could be done about poverty was considered liberal, so hardly anybody noticed how quickly the administration—and most of the liberal antipoverty experts—rejected the one left-of-center option: real redistribution of income by creating public-sector jobs for the poor.

To endorse this approach would have been to acknowledge that American capitalism was not working, at least not for everyone. No one seemed ready to consider that an economic system that provided decent employment for more than 90 percent of its potential workers was working pretty well, but that something else would be required to provide for the rest.

The second possible approach was simply to give poor people money. As the Council of Economic Advisers had recently reported, the "conquest of poverty is well within our power. The majority of the nation could simply tax themselves enough to provide the necessary income supplements to their less fortunate citizens."

It may have been within the people's power, but it was far beyond their inclination. On this, liberals and conservatives agreed: Simply giving people money neither trains them nor motivates them.

So the antipoverty planners went with the third option, the one designed by social welfare intellectuals who operated on the assumption that what the poor lacked was not jobs, money, or even services. They lacked ability: skills, responsible attitudes, political smarts. The War on Poverty would provide them with all three.

In choosing this approach, the policymakers were not devoid of self-interest because they would be the ones transmitting these values to the poor. This was not greed. Neither public policy intellectuals nor social welfare professionals make enough money to be motivated by greed; if they were greedy, they'd have gone into the oil or advertising dodges. But it was belief, and it was conviction.

And it was the most conservative choice, not only because it would cost less—social workers really do come cheap—but also because it was based on an analysis that never seriously considered whether the essential problem might be an unfair distribution of power and wealth in society, as opposed to a failure to cope on the part of some people. Had the analysis seriously considered that there was a problem with the distribution of wealth, it might have proposed redistributing it. The immediate rejection of the income-redistribution option showed how devoted even liberal Americans were to denying the possibility.

This group was devoted to the consensus, and their president was devoted to enticing the wealthiest Americans, the most powerful people in the private sector, into that consensus. He knew that challenging the present distribution of private wealth and power was no way to do that.

So the Opportunity Act, as introduced, declared that its goal would be to open "to everyone the opportunity to live in decency and dignity," not by changing the economy but by helping those now unable to get in on the decency and dignity gig. The goal, said Shriver, would be to change "indifference to interest, ignorance to awareness, resignation to ambition, and an attitude of withdrawal to one of participation."

The centerpiece of this approach was community action. The government would help poor people form their own organizations. Decisions would be made with "maximum feasible participation" of poor people themselves. It was an innovative and inherently noble idea; however, nobody had any idea how it would reduce poverty, except for providing a government job for the executive director of the community action organization. In and of itself, community action would create neither wealth nor economic opportunity. It was a social worker's theory.

| | |

Like Timothy Leary, Murray Gell-Mann had postulated an Eightfold Way for understanding the world. Like Leary, Gell-Mann had read of the eight ways of right living taught in Buddhism to avoid pain. But there the similarity ceased. It was the physical world that Gell-Mann sought to understand, and his Eightfold Way was a pattern for explaining the nature of hadrons (protons and neutrons).

His design was graceful, but it postulated a subatomic particle that no one had observed and that by its nature—if nature it had—would be bizarre because it would have a "strangeness number" (the rate at which particles decay into other particles) of minus two, which no known particle had.

Until now. On Wednesday, February 19, Professor Paul T. Matthews of Imperial College, London, announced the discovery of the omega-minus, surviving for but a fraction of a second and taking up less than a millionth of a millionth of a centimeter of space, but with a strangeness number of minus two.

"Order has been made out of nuclear chaos," proclaimed the journal *New Scientist,* and if the average person found this order chaotic to the understanding, scientists found the world a touch more explicable.

| | |

On Thursday, February 20, the Cuban fishermen, their $500 fines having been paid by the Czechoslovakian embassy, went home aboard their own fishing boats. Sending the Marines had not been necessary. Nothing had been necessary. They were just fishing boats, no doubt blown off course by strong winds in the Dry Tortugas. Even Johnson must have realized that Bobby Kennedy had been right all along. Needless to say, he never said as much.

| 11 |

INVASIONS NORTH AND SOUTH

Oscar Harper, part of George Wallace's traveling party, was enjoying a local beer in a hotel on the shores of Lake Mendota in Madison, Wisconsin, when the phone rang. Harper picked it up and listened for a moment. Then he put his hand over the receiver and told Ralph Adams, "This is some damn fool wanting George to run for president in Wisconsin. You talk to him."

The caller was a right-wing businessman and political organizer named Lloyd Herbstreith. He and his wife, Dolores, had been active supporters of Senator Joe McCarthy and of the "liberty amendment" to abolish the federal income tax. Now they were telling Adams, an old friend and law partner of Wallace's, that they could set up a primary campaign for the governor, a presidential primary campaign. Adams agreed to talk to them the next morning.

Overnight, some University of Wisconsin students, armed with Kool-Aid and anger, walked out onto the lake ice and painted FUCK WALLACE in big red letters. But the gesture did not faze the Herbstreiths. They told Adams that Governor John Reynolds, who would be President Johnson's surrogate in the primary, was unpopular because of his support for open housing legislation and higher taxes.

Not only that, they said, but Wisconsin had an open primary system; anybody could vote in any party's contest. With the Republican presidential candidates bypassing the state this time, conservative Republicans could play Democrat-for-a-day and vote for Wallace.

Adams was still skeptical. Wallace, he said, had no organization in the state, much less a headquarters. The Herbstreiths volunteered to run the whole thing out of their kitchen in Oshkosh.

|||

One of the locals most helpful to Mickey and Rita Schwerner was a young construction worker named James Chaney. He was only twenty-one, he was single, and he still lived at home with his mother. Chaney went off to Canton for a few weeks, but when he came back he started spending so much time at the community center that by April the Schwerners put him on the staff.

CORE had given the Meridian center a blue Ford station wagon, and J.E., as Chaney's friends called him, would drive that wagon all over the area, just chatting up field hands, housewives, and hangers-on about how they ought to come down to the community center, maybe learn to read, maybe learn to vote. Before long, he and Mickey had set up what would have been a little political organization if its members had not been barred from political activity, with contacts in four counties.

One spot that caught Mickey's fancy was a little community called Long-dale, in rural Neshoba County just east of Philadelphia, some sixty miles north of Meridian. It was a pretty spot, with a few farms scattered among rolling hills. At the top of a rise along the single clay road that went through the settlement was the Mt. Zion Church, a small frame building with a tin roof. Mickey and J.E. went up there often, maybe thirty times between February and June.

They knew Neshoba could be dangerous. It was a county of 20,927 people, 5,901 of whom, or 28 percent, were Negroes. Ten of them voted. The sheriff was Lawrence Rainey, a six-foot two-inch, 250-pound forty-one-year-old who enjoyed chewing tobacco and prided himself on being tough. He'd been elected the previous fall, promising to be especially tough on any civil rights workers who might come to Neshoba County. His slogan had been that he was "the man who can cope with the situations that may arise." He claimed, without producing any evidence, to have shot and killed two Negroes.

His deputy was twenty-six-year-old Cecil Price, an easygoing, well-liked man who loved to go bowling. They both wore cowboy boots and big Stetson hats and carried six-shooters. The rule was that every time Mickey and J.E. went up there they would call in if they were going to be late. It was as if they thought they might be being watched.

By the end of February, when Mickey and Rita joined other CORE workers from around the South at a conference in New Orleans, they had plenty of progress to report. They may have been turned away from every club in the French Quarter—interracial parties were not allowed—but what did that matter? They were the vanguard of a new day.

In fact, Mickey felt so good, so secure, that when they returned he started to let his beard grow back. So what if he was noticed?

He had been. A state legislator from Meridian had asked the State Sovereignty Commission to investigate Schwerner's activities.[1] Sam Bowers and his Klan underlings, Edgar Ray "Preacher" Killen and Frank Herndon, were also profiting from Mickey and Rita's presence. All they had to do was drive an interested fellow down Fifth Street, past the community center, to see one of the Schwerners in the company of Negroes, and they would pretty much guarantee themselves a new recruit. They had their own nickname for Mickey even before his beard grew back, proving that they'd been aware of him for a while. They called him "goatee."

| | |

Thanks to his engaging manner, his eagerness to please, and his velvety voice, radio host William B. Williams was master of most that he surveyed. He was the host of *The Make-Believe Ballroom,* the radio program created by Martin Block, the onetime shoe salesman who had become the world's first disk jockey.

That position made William B., as he called himself, first among equals of the disk jockey world. His program on WNEW, 1130 on the AM dial, could be heard all over the New York area, but its impact spread farther. William B. was unique among DJs because he didn't just spin platters. His show was so popular that the stars actually came into the studio to chat with him. Frank Sinatra came—later on Williams was the guy who first called Sinatra "Chairman of the Board"—and so did Ella Fitzgerald, Judy Garland, and even Louis Armstrong.

William B. would never have invited the Beatles. He referred to "I Want to Hold Your Hand" as "I Want to Hold My Nose" and played only a few bars of it before telling his engineer to switch over to some real music. Other disk jockeys, who were less restrained and sophisticated, were shamelessly promoting themselves and their stations as the most Beatle-crazy in anticipation of the group's imminent first visit to the United States. This wasn't William B.'s style. He promoted himself—calling himself "William B." was part of the promotion—but he did it quietly. His vanity, like his music, was tasteful, and although he knew enough to cozy up to whichever entertainer was hot at the moment, he would never slavishly link his entire persona to one singer, or even four of them.

On the other extreme, Murray Kaufman had no such inhibitions. He labeled himself "Murray the K," a hot rod sort of a nickname. His show on WINS, 1010 on the dial, was "Murray the K and his Swinging Soiree," and he had glommed onto the Beatles fad quicker than anyone, promoting himself as their biggest fan, their biggest booster, even—audacious as it was—"the Fifth Beatle." That was the new way of doing things.

By then, even Jack Gould might have been wondering whether this British rock group had more staying power than he thought. It wasn't just that the first two single releases of the Beatles—"I Want to Hold Your Hand" and "I Saw Her Standing There"—immediately sold more than a million records and had been number one all over the country for almost a month. Nor was it simply that teenage girls sat enraptured next to radio or record player as the songs played. It was that the teenage *boys* were sitting there, too, and if the look in their eyes was not quite the same, it was nonetheless the look of an addiction.

It got even worse when American boys started trying to look like the Beatles. The barber business suffered throughout much of the country as teenage boys began to let their hair grow, the better to look like John, Paul, George, or Ringo. Family harmony suffered, too. In thousands of living rooms, kitchens, and dens, parents pleaded, urged, cajoled, bribed, and finally commanded their sons to get a haircut.

Most complied because they didn't have much choice. In 1964, fifteen-year-olds did as they were told . . . or else. But compliance was only scalp-deep; beneath millions of skulls, a rebellion brewed. Not that there was anything new about rebellious, long-haired youths. That's who the Students for a Democratic Society was composed of, as well as the group of University of Wisconsin students who sponsored an "antimilitary ball" to compete with the annual dance of the Reserve Officers Training Corps chapter. "Swords optional" was the motto of the rebels, who seemed to be having some impact. All over the country, ROTC enrollment was down.

The kids who were trying to look like the Beatles weren't longhairs. They weren't even in college. Most of them were high school students who weren't active in politics. The few teenagers who belonged to political groups were more likely to be folk song fans; their group was the Weavers, not the Beatles. The Beatles fans were white middle-class suburbanites.

Some of this "Beatlemania," as it was already known, sprang from teenage boys who were trying to make themselves attractive to teenage girls. But that explained only part of it. The Beatles had tapped into something, and if nobody was quite sure what it was, a great many people were sure that they didn't like it. Even at the beginning, there was the sense that this wasn't just a fad. It was an uprising. It was as though millions of well-bred, well-groomed suburban teenagers were rejecting, implicitly but unmistakably, everything their parents held dear.

Some of these parents reacted. Anti-Beatles groups sprang up around the country. One, in Detroit, asserted that its purpose was to "stamp out the Beatles." The more popular the group got with the teenage set—four of February's top hits were Beatles tunes—the more upset their elders got.

Even so, there weren't very many of these anti-Beatles organizations, and they weren't very big. Furthermore, they were moderate compared to the parents who had tried to ban performances or broadcasts of "Louie, Louie." Nobody was trying to get a law passed against the Beatles.

But it was definitely an unprecedented phenomenon. Older folks had ridiculed the early "bobby-soxers" who swooned over Sinatra in the 1940s, and more than a few observers feared the raw sexuality of Elvis Presley's country rock songs in the 1950s. But organizing in opposition to a few pop singers was bizarre, as though people thought differences in taste were political.

It turned out that they were. The fervor gripping so many teenagers over the Beatles did have social, and therefore political, ramifications, though exactly what they were did not become clear until the Beatles actually got here. And they got here in pandemonium. When Pan American Flight 101 landed at the recently renamed John F. Kennedy International Airport on the morning of Friday, February 7, Paul, George, John, and Ringo were greeted by several thousand school-skipping teenagers and scores of reporters and disk jockeys.

Murray the K was the most successful, or the most shameless. Somehow he managed to get right down in front of the low platform where the singers stood. He was wearing a crumpled porkpie hat. He shouted questions, talking to the Beatles, who'd never seen him before, as though he were an old buddy.

Finally, John Lennon shouted, "Everybody shut up!" and the questioning began:

REPORTER: Why do you sing like Americans but speak with an English accent?

LENNON: It sells better.

REPORTER: Are you in favor of lunacy?

MCCARTNEY: It's healthy.

REPORTER: Do you ever have haircuts?

HARRISON: I had one yesterday.

STARR: It's no lie; you should have seen him the day before.

REPORTER: How do you account for your great success?

LENNON: If we knew, we'd form another group and be managers.

REPORTER: How about the Detroit campaign to stamp out the Beatles?
MCCARTNEY: First of all, we have a campaign of our own to stamp out
Detroit.

Poor William B. It must have been the fondest hope of all the Beatle-
phobics that the singers would reveal themselves as semiliterate dunderheads,
easily dismissed as mere beneficiaries of a shrewd publicity campaign. They
were that, but they were also witty and irreverent. These four young men
represented an affront to authority, which was all the more dangerous because
it seemed so benign. They were mildly iconoclastic without being contentious,
so suburban teenagers who didn't give a hoot about politics could express
the unease they felt about school, neighborhood, and parental control simply
through their taste in music.

As if to rub in the undeniable reality of Beatlemania, on Sunday, February 9, two days after the Beatles arrived, 73 million people watched them
open and close *The Ed Sullivan Show*. World Series games and the Kennedy
funeral had attracted more viewers, but this was the biggest audience for any
entertainment program.

Just how many people found all this upsetting was never very clear. Even
at the time, some observers found it easy to ridicule grown men and women
who let themselves be bothered by nothing but the popularity of a few young
singers. But it was more than that. The Beatles phenomenon did not occur
in a vacuum. To the traditional-minded, the late winter and early spring of
1964 were full of vexing events in politics, entertainment, the arts, and even
sports.

| | |

By late February there was the tax cut which was on its way toward
passage. Most people wanted lower tax bills, but there was something dis-
quieting about this whole idea of deliberately reducing government revenue
without reducing government spending. It amounted to a conscious decision
to embrace a deficit.

To economic traditionalists, this was anathema. It was one thing to have
deficits in wartime or other emergencies, but a *planned* deficit in peacetime
was unheard of. Nor did the essential probusiness character of this tax cut
assuage their anger. It was the principle involved that upset conservatives such
as Harry Byrd, the crusty chairman of the Senate Finance Committee, who
was dead set against the tax cut.

Lyndon Johnson, who knew Byrd, knew better than to try to convince
him of the merits of the case. The president tried another tack. After one of

those Saturday night white-tie dinners in a hotel ballroom, Johnson invited Hubert Humphrey and Byrd to the White House for a nightcap. The three old friends assembled in the upstairs living room, where Johnson told Humphrey to "step out there in that Kennedy kitchen and fix us all a drink. Just bring me a little scotch with some water and just fix Harry up with about two fingers of bourbon." The president held up his big hands. Humphrey got the hint. They were fat fingers.

When Byrd was on his second bourbon, Johnson said, "Harry, before you go home I think you ought to visit with your girlfriend."

Johnson walked over to the bedroom door.

"Lady Bird," he shouted through the door. "Your boyfriend Harry is out here."

A few minutes later, a sleepy Mrs. Johnson appeared in her bathrobe. She knew what to do. She sat next to Byrd, and after they'd chatted awhile, Johnson said, "Well, Lady Bird, we can't keep Harry up much longer. You better go back to bed now. He's had his chance to see you."

Mrs. Johnson rose, and the president turned to Byrd. "Harry," he said, "Every time I can't find Lady Bird I know she's either with you or Laurance Rockefeller or Hubert. That's why I don't dare leave town too much and leave her here."

Entranced by the mix of bourbon and flattery, the old senator from Virginia laughed gently, and he was still laughing when Johnson leaned toward him, looked right into his eyes, and said, "Harry, I know you're opposed to any tax reduction. But frankly, I've just got to have that bill out of committee. You know I'm trying to pass the Kennedy program and I feel I owe it to the late president.

"Now, I know you can't vote for it and I don't expect you to. In fact, I would expect you to oppose it. But I don't want you to bottle it up. Will you give me your word that you'll just report the bill out as soon as possible?"

Byrd was overwhelmed. This was the president of the United States, crowding him and almost begging him. Byrd was flattered and slightly drunk, and who knew what had been the effect of the flirtation?

Probably Lyndon Johnson did.

Byrd looked at his former colleague and saved the one dignity left to him by virtue of age and seniority. He called the president by name.

"Lyndon," he said, "if you want that bill out, I'll do nothing to stop it. If there are the votes in that committee to report it out, I'll let it come out. You can be sure of that."

The president stood up. "Harry, it's time to go to bed," he said. "I've kept you up late. Good night."

On the Senate floor a few days later, Byrd announced in almost inaudible tones that his committee had reported out the tax cut. Then he turned to Humphrey, who sat next to him in the front row of the Senate chamber, and said, "Now, you tell the president that I kept my word—that I've reported out that bill, that I've made my speech, and now I'm leaving."[2]

But the tax cut was about more than just taxes. The whole idea of having the government manipulate the economy troubled many people. In fact, Eisenhower had followed a similar policy—reality dictated it—but he hadn't been nearly as open about it. Kennedy and now Johnson made no effort to disguise their intention to guide the economy through public policy. That was the essence of Johnson's push for economic growth. He was not only going to allow it; he was going to inspire it through government action. In doing so, he was accepting the assumptions of the nation's public policy elites. In March, Walter Lippmann, that most prestigious of columnists, wrote that the country was now in "the post-Marxian age," in which helping the poor did not mean "taxing money away from the haves and turning it over to the have nots."

Until recently, Lippmann wrote, "it was assumed that there was only so much pie and the social question was how to divide it. But in this generation, a revolutionary idea has taken hold. The size of the pie can be increased by intention, by organized fiscal policy and then a whole society, not just one part of it, will grow richer."[3]

In the context of 1964, this was not economic conservatism. Like the idea of planned deficits, the notion that prosperity depended on "intention [and] organized fiscal policy," rather than the autonomous workings of the market, came from John Maynard Keynes, the economic saint of the liberals.

This was precisely what enraged the conservatives, who thought the government was taking over. They had a point. Government had become a larger factor in the nation's life. America was now a "mixed economy," a government-guided capitalism, and in retrospect it had been since 1946, when the Employment Act committed government to promoting "maximum" employment through tax and budget policies. That law also required the president to submit an annual economic report to Congress, and it created the three-person Council of Economic Advisers.

Whatever its intent, the Employment Act represented a qualitative change. Back in the nineteenth century, government had promoted business. Later, it began to regulate parts of the economy. The Employment Act was a quantum leap. It said the government would *guarantee* prosperity.

There had been government programs during the Depression, and World War II *was* a government program, but those had been emergencies. The

Employment Act declared the "continuing policy and responsibility of the federal government . . . to promote maximum employment, production and purchasing power."

It was succeeding. One reason the economy was in good shape was that the federal government had spent almost $900 million under Jack Kennedy's accelerated public works program passed in 1962. According to the Commerce Department, that money had financed 7,762 projects, producing 1 million man-months of employment.[4]

By itself, the Employment Act was distant and abstract, but it wasn't by itself. The same attitude was evident in the increasing array of forms that had to be filled out and in the regulations that had to be satisfied before a builder could turn over a shovelful of earth or an entrepreneur could start a new company. Everything, it seemed, had to be in triplicate. And what already existed was nothing compared to what some folks in Washington were proposing: locking away thousands of acres of productive mining and timber resources in some kind of "wilderness system," giving money to old people so they could go to the doctor, telling a fellow he had to hire Negroes. Where would it all end?

| | |

Where, indeed, would defiance of all tradition end? On Wednesday, February 26, a few days after the Beatles returned to England, a play called *The Deputy* opened at the Brooks Atkinson Theater in New York over the protests of a hundred and fifty pickets, most of them religious Catholics. Their objection was to the portrayal of Pope Pius XII as indifferent to the Holocaust or at least unwilling to complicate the Church's relations with the Nazis by doing much about it.

But the real villain in the play was not the pope so much as the Church, not because it was a religious institution but simply because it was an institution, committed to its own preservation and enhancement. The hero was an idealistic priest, naive but decent, and willing to challenge an institution. Here was a clear case of the elites—the writer, the theater—portraying themselves as virtuous, in contrast to the corruption of established authority.

The Deputy had a limited run in a single theater. But in movie theaters all over the country Americans could see one of their most honored traditional institutions, the military, pitilessly lampooned in the film *Dr. Strangelove or: How I Learned to Stop Worrying and Love the Bomb.*

Directed by Stanley Kubrick, it was technically a British movie starring English actor Peter Sellers. But most of the rest of the cast—George C. Scott, Slim Pickens, Keenan Wynn, Sterling Hayden, James Earl Jones—was as

American as could be, and the object of the film's satire was the U.S. military and the arms race as run by American policy. If it was just a joke, it was a joke that treated most of the top brass as either crypto-Nazis or dunderheads, and the film's popularity challenged the assumption that this was the same country in which moviegoers had flocked to *The Sands of Iwo Jima* or even to *Battle Cry*.

Adding to the injury, one of the movie's cowriters, Terry Southern, also had a novel on the best-seller list. And such a novel. *Candy* was a brilliant, outrageous, hilarious celebration (and satire) of sex, especially as practiced by a beautiful young woman.

"Sick sex," sniffed *Publishers Weekly*, but Nelson Algren, who wrote better, responded that "sex in this country has been sick for so long . . . that by restoring the comedy of it Southern has done something we should be grateful for." Some were grateful; some outraged. Perhaps in reaction, prosecutors took to suppression. On Long Island, the Nassau County district attorney, William Cahn, confiscated all the copies of a literary magazine, *Evergreen Review,* on the grounds that it contained "a dirty story."

Cahn was a busy fellow that winter. In mid-February, his office announced the arrest of fifteen suburban housewives—suburban housewives!—who had been earning a second family income as call girls. There was a certain downscale aspect to the case; many of their customers, bettors who frequented Roosevelt Raceway, were city dwellers. But there was no denying that the oldest profession had infiltrated the inner precincts of suburbia.

Another affront to tradition that winter came not from the culture but from the United States Supreme Court. On Monday, February 17, the Court ruled that congressional districts had to be roughly equal in population. "We do not believe," Justice Hugo Black wrote for the 6 to 3 majority, "that the framers of the Constitution intended to permit . . . vote-diluting discrimination to be accomplished through the device of districts containing widely varied numbers of inhabitants."

The ruling shocked rural politicians, especially in the South. Many a rural congressman owed his job to his district's small population, made possible by apportionment based on county and town lines as well as on folks. Georgia's Fifth Congressional District, in Atlanta and suburban DeKalb County, contained 823,000 people. Only 272,154 lived in the Ninth, around Gainesville. Even getting the population differences down to a 2:1 ratio would require redrawing lines in thirteen states affecting 132 seats, most of them in the South.

Justice Harlan, obviously distressed, read his dissent from the bench, calling the occasion "certainly the most solemn since I have been on this Court." In Harlan's view, the Constitution said nothing about granting the

Court the power to meddle in congressional apportionment. It never had. William Buckley's *National Review* called it a "brazen usurpation" and neologized that the one man–one vote concept was a "democraticist . . . axiom of orthodox liberalism."

On March 9, the Court struck again, reversing the libel judgment in that *New York Times* v. *Sullivan* case that had brought Martin Luther King to the visitors' gallery weeks earlier. But the Court did not simply disallow the award to Police Commissioner Sullivan. It ruled broadly that a public official could never successfully sue for libel unless he could prove "malicious intent" or "reckless disregard for the truth" on the part of the writer or news organization. Just proving that a news article had an error would no longer suffice.

Like the Employment Act or the redistricting decision, this case had little direct impact on the lives of ordinary citizens. But it was another example of one national, elite, unelected institution—the Court—expanding the power of another—the press—at the expense of local officials. Nor was it lost on Southerners that the *Sullivan* case involved Alabama officials defending racial segregation.

The national elites had little to do with the other disturbing midwinter surprise; professors and pundits rarely pontificate about pugilism. But for sheer drama, for the triumph of the young and brazen, and for spreading the sense that nothing could be taken for granted, no event of 1964 was as shocking as the one that took place on Tuesday, February 25, at the Miami Beach Convention Center.

For months, nothing had been as certain as the belief that the heavyweight champion of the world, Charles "Sonny" Liston, would demolish his young challenger, Cassius Clay. As fight night approached, the bout loomed less as a boxing match—what kind of sporting event is it when everyone knows who's going to win?—than as a morality play with an ironic twist.

The reason for this was that today's hero, Sonny Liston, had so recently been the villain. Less than two years earlier, Liston, an ex-con who retained the sullenness of the outcast, had taken the championship from Floyd Patterson with a first-round knockout. It had not been the preferred outcome. Patterson even had the blessings of the NAACP and President Kennedy. For many Americans, he was the "good Negro," a handsome, soft-spoken man who smiled often. Liston scowled. He was the kind of Negro that liberal whites tried to pretend did not exist. He had lived for a time in the Philadelphia home of Blinky Palermo, the mob's man in the fight game. He conjured images of the big, bad black man lurking in dark alleys. "We have," wrote the great columnist Murray Kempton, "at last a heavyweight champion on the moral level of the men who own him."

But for this fight the challenger was Cassius Clay, and he was another kind of Negro altogether, a loudmouth. Whatever Liston's flaws, he didn't talk much, and he never said anything about racial or political matters. He was just a boxer. Not Clay. He talked all the time, mostly about himself. "I am the greatest" was his theme. Clay made up rhymes: "Liston's fate is to fall in eight." He was handsome, a heavyweight who looked lithe as he pranced around the ring. He was the color of dark honey-butter. He was charming, even though he was far too full of himself for a twenty-two-year-old. What's more, he had political opinions, or at least sentiments, and on occasion he would mention them. Among the men around him were disciples of the Black Muslim leader Malcolm X, and there were rumors that Clay himself had become a Muslim. It was as though he were telling the rest of the country that he had no stake in its traditions.

A few other people were expressing this kind of defiance, but they were political radicals, rendering them easy to ignore. Besides, they were white. No Negro had ever before been so outrageous, so ornery—certainly no Negro athlete. Jackie Robinson was outspoken, proud, and independent, and had bothered people, too, but he was a college-educated gentleman, a former lieutenant in the Army. And he'd been a racial pioneer. He had credentials, and his politics were in the mainstream: He was working for Nelson Rockefeller.

All of this made Sonny Liston look pretty good by comparison. Thanks to skilled press-agentry, his sullenness was transformed into dignity, his menacing demeanor simply a reflection of his genuineness. Here was a quiet man who did his job and didn't have to brag.

Besides, he was going to win. "I'm goin' kill 'im in the first roun'," Liston said, laughing as he skipped rope to "Night Train" by James Brown at his training center at the American Legion Post in Denver's Five Points area.

Few argued with that prediction. Clay's bravado was a pitiful, doomed attempt to mask his fear, to psych himself so that he dared get into the ring against the bigger, stronger champion. He may have had show business connections—fittingly, the Beatles visited his training camp, but they could not protect his chin. "Clay has no chance at all," said the greatest of all the living ex-champs, Joe Louis, who was part of Liston's entourage. "I give him about three or four rounds." Outside of Clay's circle, no one disagreed. Liston was a 5 to 1 favorite a week before the fight, 8 to 1 by fight night.[5]

But Clay was unhittable. Liston charged out at the opening bell, seemingly trying for a first-round knockout. But he couldn't connect. Dancing around the ring, gliding in to pop a jab at Liston's head, Clay would skitter away before Liston could hit him. Steve Ellis, the blow-by-blow announcer, speculated that Clay was so fast because he was so scared. But he won the first round.

He didn't win the second, which he fought in a more conventional manner, hands held high. Liston hit him hard in the body. In living rooms and bars all over America, even the most casual fight fan dredged up Joe Louis's immortal line about Billy Conn: "He can run, but he can't hide."

As the third round began, it was Liston who appeared sluggish, and by midround a cut opened over his eye. Then, at the end of the fourth round, Clay seemed ready to quit, just as everyone had anticipated. He clutched his eyes. "I can't see," he said. "Cut off my gloves. Call off the fight." Something was stinging his eyes.

His trainer, Angelo Dundee, bathed his eyes with a sponge, then pushed Clay to his feet. "This is for the heavyweight championship," he said. "No one walks away from that. Get in there and run until your eyes clear up."

He did, and Liston tired himself even more by flailing the air with wild punches. Clay's eyes weren't yet clear. Still, he managed to stave off Liston. For part of the fifth round, he rested his left glove on the champion's nose. Liston didn't know what to do. Toward the end of the round, Clay's vision cleared, and by the next round, he was controlling the fight.

Then, just before the seventh round was to begin, Sonny Liston sat on his stool, spit out his mouthpiece, and quit. Most people didn't realize what had happened. Cassius Clay did. He leaped to his feet, thrust his arms to the sky, and shouted, "I'm the greatest. I'm king."

He was more than that. Two days later, the new champion declared his new faith: "I believe in Islam. I'm not a Christian. But why's everybody so shook up when I say that? I don't wanta marry no white woman, don't wanta break down no school doors where I'm not wanted."

If that was meant to reassure, it failed, especially after he added this almost chilling defiance: "I don't have to be who you want me to be. I'm free to be who I want."

| | |

The next morning, President Johnson signed the tax cut bill, the one originally proposed by President Kennedy. Then he escorted his wife and the members of his cabinet to Jacqueline Kennedy's home in Georgetown. The president gave her one of the many pens he had used to sign the legislation, and on behalf of the cabinet, Secretary Rusk presented her with a gold tray and coffee service. She seemed so pleased.

12

LOCAL POLITICS

On Sunday, March 1, Bobby Darin was singing "I Wonder Who's Kissing Her Now," and the Serendipity Singers were pleading "Don't Let the Rain Come Down." *The Spy Who Came in from the Cold* was in its second week atop the *New York Times* best-seller list. New York was awaiting the opening of new plays by Eugene Ionesco (*Pedestrians in the Air*) and Luigi Pirandello (*Right You Are [If You Think You Are]*), and McGeorge Bundy sent the president a new set of recommendations designed to diminish "the sovereignty of North Vietnam."

First, Bundy suggested, the United States should blockade the big harbor at Haiphong and, at the same time, "warn we would go further" to bomb railways, factories, and training camps.

Yes, Bundy said, that would "normally require" a declaration of war. Under the circumstances, seeking such a declaration would not be wise, but some lesser legislative authorization might be in order. It should be carefully worded, Bundy warned, concerned that Congress would reject a "blunt instrument."

Three days later, the president told Bundy not to rush matters. "I've got to win the election," he said. "In the meantime let's see if we can't find enough things to do . . . to keep them off base . . . without getting another Korean operation started."

On that same day Jimmy Hoffa was found guilty of jury tampering, and Marina Oswald's lawyer, Mark Lane, told the Warren Commission that he understood that Lee Harvey Oswald had once visited Jack Ruby's nightclub, where the two men had talked. Lane acknowledged that his information was hearsay.

Wednesday, March 4, was ninety days before the California primary and therefore the first day to gather signatures to qualify for the ballot. Under the auspices of the political consulting firm of Spencer-Roberts, paid canvassers began circulating petitions for Nelson Rockefeller.

The Goldwater campaign didn't have to pay anyone a dime. Its volunteers got more than fifty thousand signatures before noon. Goldwater's counterpoint to Spencer-Roberts was the California Young Republicans, headed by a slender thirty-four-year-old man named Robert Gaston. It was Gaston who had commanded the troops that overran the previous year's YR convention in Denver that so offended Nelson Rockefeller.

The division of southern California into six areas was accomplished by the official Goldwater campaign, but five of the "area commanders," supervising some eight thousand volunteers, reported to Gaston. And though Gaston's conservatism was such that he found Goldwater too moderate, there was work being done off to his right, also, as the John Birch Society geared up its own members to walk the suburban precincts for Goldwater.

At the time, none of this seemed to matter. The political press was too preoccupied with the New Hampshire primary just six days away to pay attention to California canvassing. In New Hampshire, Barry Goldwater's grouchiness was becoming a bigger problem than his gaffes. He seemed bored, preoccupied. He came to the state, made a speech or two, answered a few questions from reporters, and made little effort to please. At times it seemed as though he would rather have been flying his plane, or playing cards, or doing almost anything but trying to win votes. It was as though he didn't care whether or not he won the New Hampshire primary or even the nomination.

"I'm not one of those baby-kissing, hand-shaking, blintz-eating candidates," Goldwater acknowledged. This was a dig at Rockefeller—blintzes were not part of the typical New Hampshireman's diet—but also an acknowledgment of his own failings as a campaigner—especially in comparison with the other candidates. It wasn't just Rockefeller now. At the end of January, Senator Margaret Chase Smith of Maine had joined the contest. No one took her seriously as a candidate, but she did offer another choice.

Harold Stassen was running, too—again—and though his endless attempts had already become a joke, his proposals were attracting a few supporters. One of those proposals was a "mothers Social Security plan" to pay mothers of two or more children $115 a month as an incentive to stay home with the kids rather than get a job. Stassen said that this would leave more jobs available for men and, by holding down the labor supply, exert an upward pull on wages. In a low-wage state, this idea had some appeal.

Then there were the two whose names weren't on the ballot. One was Richard Nixon. Wesley Powell, the colorful, unpredictable former governor, was organizing a Nixon write-in campaign. Powell was an old buddy of Nixon's, and his effort was authorized. A month earlier, Nixon had rented a suite at New York's Waldorf-Astoria Hotel and invited his closest political advisors to consider the question of his candidacy.[1] What they came up with was a wait-in-the-weeds strategy; Nixon would not run, but neither would he remove himself from consideration. "If the opportunity should come again, I would accept it," he finally said.

Henry Cabot Lodge wasn't on the ballot, either. He was in Saigon. But he hadn't objected to the improvised efforts of a couple of young professionals from Boston, a couple of wise guys, really, named David Goldberg and Paul Grindle, who had rented a Concord storefront and sent out sample ballots showing voters how to write in Lodge's name. At the end of February, the wise guys sent letters to ninety-five thousand registered Republicans in the state asking them to sign cards pledging their support for Lodge. To everyone's surprise, seven thousand Republicans signed the cards and sent them back.

Only Cliff White, it seemed, realized how unimportant all this was.

| | |

The relationship between Lyndon Johnson and Robert Kennedy could not last much longer, but it wouldn't simply disappear, either. For a while, both men tried to behave. In March, the president used Arthur Schlesinger and New York Liberal Party leader Alex Rose to send friendly signals to Kennedy. At the time, Kennedy was on a trip. When he got back, he asked McGeorge Bundy to find out whether Johnson wanted him to call. No, came back the response, not now. Maybe later. Later never came.

There was more going on here than a clash of personalities. Kennedy and Johnson were both Democrats, and for all the differences imposed by geography—Texans simply could not take certain positions Northeasterners had to take—they shared a political outlook best described as moderately liberal. They were growing apart in the first quarter of 1964, not simply because they didn't like each other but also because moderate liberalism was splitting in two, if not into smithereens.

Like the Kennedy-Johnson conflict, the deeper divisions reflected differences in attitude as well as in policy. John Kennedy had attracted two distinct breeds of liberals. Both factions believed in the prudent use of government to better the lot of working people and the poor. Both were committed to racial equality. Both were devoted to opposing communist expansion but also to dealing with the Soviet Union.

But one faction prided itself on its tough-mindedness and its appreciation of limits. The other was more adventuresome, less reluctant to offend, more likely to moralize. While John Kennedy lived, these differences could be contained. The managerial realists such as Robert McNamara and Dean Rusk were as loyal to Kennedy as were the romantic idealists such as Arthur Schlesinger and John Kenneth Galbraith.

The lines between the two factions were drawn in both domestic and foreign policy. When it came to the economy, the standard New Frontier outlook, held firmly by economic advisor Walter Heller, was that it would be enough to keep growth, output, and income levels high. This was the technical Keynesianism that Kennedy had accepted when he proposed his tax cuts, embracing a moderate budget deficit in the interest of economic growth. Keep the economy humming and everything else would take care of itself.

No, it wouldn't, argued the other faction, its position argued most persuasively by Galbraith. He and his allies contended that public spending, carefully targeted and "very much increased," was needed to alleviate the problems of the cities and poverty and to support the arts and culture. They were Keynesians, too, but they preferred a deficit caused by higher government output to lowered taxes, with spending targeted where it was needed most.

Probably because the essential cleavage was as much of attitude as of analysis, the two sides split similarly on what was becoming the dominant foreign policy question, Vietnam. Rostow, Rusk, McNamara, and their followers favored a military solution. Averell Harriman, his disciple Roger Hilsman, Michael Forrestal, and Galbraith were convinced that the problem was essentially political and that the South Vietnamese would have to establish a government efficient enough, and popular enough, to fend off the communists themselves.[2]

There was no doubt where President Johnson stood. He was with the tough guys. Not long after he took over, Harriman was demoted to a new roving ambassadorship, and Roger Hilsman was eased out in February. Forrestal stayed for a while and was even included in the strategy briefings that Johnson held almost every Tuesday. But it soon enough became clear that the president was listening to the advisors who were leaning toward a military solution.

The question was why Robert Kennedy, who may have coined the term *counterinsurgency*, didn't agree. But when he first used it, that word had been designed mainly to refer to events in Latin America, and it never involved the use of U.S. troops, even as advisors. The mission was to help civilian governments. Counterinsurgency meant sending enough communications equipment to Caracas to allow the police to contain terrorists trying to meddle with free elections after President Rómulo Betancourt's term expired. It meant extending rail lines to the isolated northeastern regions of Thailand. Robert Kennedy didn't even start worrying about Vietnam until the summer of 1963.[3]

Besides, he was becoming more comfortable with the people on the other side of this divide. Kennedy had always been interested in almost everything, but he had also been rooted in established opinions on almost everything. Now, he seemed open to consider any point of view, no matter how unconventional—maybe, the more unconventional, the better.

| | |

It wasn't that Cliff White didn't want Goldwater to win the New Hampshire primary. Winning was better than losing, and at some point Goldwater would probably have to win at least one contested primary, preferably the last one in California.

But New Hampshire? Let the reporters pump up its importance. They loved the New Hampshire primary. It was like a fraternity party for them: a bunch of guys on generous expense accounts, away from home, talking to one another and ogling the comelier campaign aides.

All for fourteen delegates.

That was why White didn't much care. On the calendar on the wall of his office at 1025 Connecticut Avenue, the first dates marked in red were in early February. That was when Republicans in North Carolina would be meeting in district conventions that would choose delegates, some to the state convention, which would meet on February 29 and 30, but twenty-two delegates would go right to the Republican National Convention in San Francisco.[4]

They were in the bag for Barry. White had them wired, twenty-five of the twenty-six North Carolina delegates, not to mention all twenty-two from Oklahoma's convention, or sixteen from South Carolina, who would be chosen just a few days after the New Hampshire primary.

Not that the Goldwater campaign was ignoring traditional, boost-your-guy, tear-down-the-other-guy politics. A week before the New Hampshire vote, the Goldwater high command was in search of "photographs of Rockefeller's first wife" and children to contrast with pictures of Goldwater with his one (and only) wife and kids.[5]

| | |

The *Manchester Union-Leader* editorial page of Wednesday, March 4, offered something out of the ordinary: a bit of political philosophy by a man not heretofore known for that expertise. Movie actor Ronald Reagan, introduced in boldface type as "the Gipper," referring to his role as football player George Gipp in the film about Knute Rockne, had found (or been shown) the words of "a famous historian, Alexander Fraser Tydler," who was obscure enough to be absent from most standard reference works.

Tydler, Reagan reported, warned that "a democracy cannot exist as a permanent form of government," at least not after voters discover that they can "vote themselves favors out of the public treasury." Once they figure that out, he said, "the majority always votes for the candidate promising the most benefits from the public treasury, with the result, the democracy always collapses over a loose fiscal policy, always to be followed by a dictatorship."

Whether this meant anything at all, it was music to the ears of Loeb, as long as it preceded, as it did, a plea to vote for Goldwater. Loeb was also supporting Reagan's other pet project of the year, the voter initiative to repeal the new California law banning racial discrimination in the sale and rental of housing.

The next day, the spot Reagan had taken on the editorial page was filled by a letter from John Wayne, also in support of Goldwater. That evening two other actors, Walter Brennan and Efrem Zimbalist Jr., joined some thirty-five hundred Republicans in the Manchester Armory to hear Goldwater deliver his now-standard speech in favor of "traditional virtues" and against expanding government, without mentioning that his most important New Hampshire supporter, Senator Norris Cotton, had just proudly announced that the very same government had approved plans for a $4 million watershed project on the Beebe River northeast of Concord.

"ROAR APPROVAL OF BARRY," the *Union-Leader* proclaimed the next day, apparently oblivious that the polls showed support for Goldwater dropping by the day. Loeb was not going to let reality dissuade him from his cause, though in fact his real cause was not Goldwater so much as opposition to civil rights.

And taxes. With the possible exceptions of white supremacy and the pistol he kept in his desk drawer, nothing was dearer to Loeb than New Hampshire's status as the state with neither a general sales nor an income tax, a devotion undiminished by the inconvenient fact that Loeb did not live in the state. He was a Massachusetts resident.

Alas, even in New Hampshire, public schools were getting more expensive, creating pressure for new revenue sources. So determined was Loeb to avoid a general tax that he embraced an idea imported from Europe and Latin America—a state lottery, its profits earmarked for public schools. His efforts had persuaded the legislature to let the public vote on a lottery, and for weeks the *Union-Leader* had been urging one and all to approve it. That very day Loeb's daily front-page, signed editorial had excoriated the "small, determined, sanctimonious, self-righteous group of sales taxers" in the opposition.

No one could be sure, though, just how small the opposition really was. After all, there were no public lotteries anywhere in the United States of America.

| | |

The next day, the filing deadline for the Wisconsin primary, Governor George Wallace returned to that state. At the suggestion of Lloyd and Dolores Herbstreith, he opened his campaign in Joe McCarthy's hometown of Appleton, praising McCarthy as a man "just a little ahead of his time" and reading a speech someone had written for him alleging treason in the State Department.

By the afternoon, Wallace was speaking his own piece, assailing the civil rights bill as a move toward the "destruction of property rights" and the "unnatural and unhealthy accumulation of power in the hands of an all-powerful central bureaucracy."

| | |

On Friday, March 6, Jack Weinberg and more than a thousand of his friends and allies picketed the Sheraton-Palace Hotel in San Francisco, demanding that the hotel hire Negroes for jobs other than sweeping the floors. Officials of the hotel, one of San Francisco's fanciest since 1875, denied that it discriminated but agreed to meet with a committee of civil rights leaders to see what could be worked out.

The hotel managers had little choice. They were overwhelmed. They'd been expecting a demonstration, but not this huge throng. This crowd had come from Berkeley, which was bulging at its seams. Over the past five years, the number of students had gone from 18,728 to 25,454. Already, almost 40 percent of the students were living in apartments because there wasn't enough dorm space. Classes were getting larger and were more and more likely to be taught by graduate assistants.

It took no genius to explain why the campus was so crowded. A kid who turned eighteen in 1963 had been born in 1946. Lots of babies were born in

1946 and even more the following year. In fact, more people were seventeen years old than were any other age. And more seventeen-year-olds were still in school than ever before; the postwar economy needed technicians and analysts more than farmers and mechanics, and society, as societies do, had responded to economic reality.

So in the early 1960s, for the first time in the history of the human race, a nation, this one, had more college students than farmers. And it wasn't only the numbers that were different; the kids were different. The very fact that so many of them stayed in school made them different. Adulthood was coming later than ever. So much later that Weinberg was but one of hundreds of student-age nonstudents at Berkeley alone. To be a student, enrollment was no longer necessary; self-assertion sufficed.

When nothing at the hotel was worked out by 4 A.M., the protest leaders reached the reasonable conclusion that the negotiating session was a stall, and they proceeded to sit down in front of the hotel doors, blocking them. A few hundred demonstrators went inside, defiling the ornate lobby with their dishabille and chanting, "Jim Crow must go."

Jack was among those in the lobby and among the one hundred fifty or so who were arrested and carted off to the San Francisco jail. He didn't mind. While there, he and the others learned that they had won. Not only had the Sheraton-Palace agreed that at least 15 percent of its future hires would be Negroes, but so had the entire San Francisco Hotel Employer Association.

Cheering the good news, he was introduced to one of his fellow prisoners, like him a refugee from the East, a transfer from Queens College named Mario Savio.[6]

| | |

On the afternoon of Sunday, March 8, Malcolm X announced the formation of an all-Negro political party and urged Negroes to form "rifle clubs that can be used to defend our lives and our property in times of emergency."

Earlier that day, Hubert Humphrey was the guest on NBC's *Meet the Press*. The reporters wanted to talk about all kinds of things. Humphrey only wanted to talk about Ev Dirksen and the civil rights bill.

"He is a man who thinks of his country before he thinks of his party," Humphrey said. "He is one who understands the legislative process intimately and fully, and I sincerely believe that when Senator Dirksen has to face that moment of decision where his influence and where his leadership will be required in order to give us the votes that are necessary to pass this bill, he will not be found wanting."

Johnson was delighted. "Boy that was right," he told Humphrey. "You're

doing just right now. You just keep at that. Don't you let those bomb throwers, now, talk you out of seeing Dirksen. You get in there to see Dirksen. You
drink with Dirksen. You talk to Dirksen. You listen to Dirksen."

Dirksen was delighted, too. And he always loved to have a drink with his
friend Hubert, who didn't drink as much as Dirksen or talk as much, either.
But he was a good listener, and the only thing Dirksen loved more than praise
was a good listener.

| | |

Under the watchful eye of federal agents, Stanley Levison met with Martin Luther King in Atlanta on March 9, the day King recorded his oral history
for the proposed John F. Kennedy presidential library. Thanks to a wiretap
on King's home phone, the Bureau realized that Levison spent the night as
King's guest.

That same day, the president invited J. Edgar Hoover and Cartha De-
Loach for a swim in the White House pool. Walter Jenkins joined them to
hear the FBI leaders provide the juiciest details from the Martin Luther King
tapes.

| | |

By now the political press had discovered the Henry Cabot Lodge campaign. It was fun, it was lively, and two members of its tiny staff were good-
looking twenty-three-year-old women. It would be wrong to suggest that
political reporters regularly fantasize about liaisons with such campaign aides;
it would be naive to suggest that they never do. By now, Goldwater's gaffes
and Rockefeller's flailing had become stale. Even the Kennedy write-in effort
was more interesting.

What made this worth reporting was that the New Hampshire Republican
voter had discovered Lodge, too. He was one of them, a New Englander. He
hadn't dumped his wife, he didn't say anything scary, and even if he wasn't
really running, he was a safe port, an easy way to vote against the other
candidates. Besides, they may have heard too much talk from the political
pros and reporters about how they, the voters, weren't smart enough to learn
how to cast a write-in.

On Tuesday, March 10, almost a hundred thousand New Hampshire
Republicans braved a blizzard to cast their paper ballots. Lodge got slightly
more than thirty-three thousand of them, 34 percent of the total. Goldwater
was far behind with 20,692 (21.3 percent) and Rockefeller close behind him
with 19,504 (20.1 percent).

A few days before the primary, Robert Kennedy issued a statement:

The Attorney General has said that the choice of the Democratic nominee for Vice President will be made, and should be made, by the Democratic Convention in August, guided by the wishes of President Johnson, and that President Johnson should be free to select his own running mate. The Attorney General, therefore, wishes to discourage any efforts on his behalf in New Hampshire, or elsewhere.

But 25,094 New Hampshire Democrats wrote in his name as their choice for vice president, just 3,769 fewer than the number who wrote in Johnson's name as their choice for president. It wasn't long before the Gallup poll showed that, nationwide, 47 percent of the Democrats wanted Kennedy on the ticket, more than twice the 18 percent for Adlai Stevenson and 10 percent for Hubert Humphrey. The president was not pleased, but neither was he moved. With the Republicans in such disarray, Johnson had no need of Kennedy.

"I don't need that little runt to win," he told his brother Sam. "I can take anybody I damn please."

As for Kennedy, his vote total may not have been the most memorable event of the day for him. Earlier that day, J. Edgar Hoover had Courtney Evans, Robert Kennedy's friend in the FBI, bring the attorney general excerpts from the Martin Luther King file, including a recording from a bug in King's hotel room made while he watched a taped replay of the Capitol Rotunda services for John Kennedy. At the moment when Jacqueline Kennedy and her daughter knelt in prayer at the president's coffin, King, for some reason, barked out, "Look at her. Sucking him off one last time."

Hoover wanted Robert Kennedy to hear that.

| | |

The morning after the New Hampshire primary, the only candidate who worried about Henry Cabot Lodge was Lyndon Johnson. Nelson Rockefeller knew better than to worry. He woke up in his Fifth Avenue apartment at 5 A.M., still confident that he could win the Republican nomination, and even if he was the only politically sophisticated American who clung to that conclusion, it was not irrational.

Rockefeller knew Henry Cabot Lodge, and to know him was not to fear him. Lodge was the only Republican senator who'd managed to lose in the first Eisenhower landslide, hardly an indication of political strength, even if the guy who'd beaten him was young Jack Kennedy. If a late-starting outsider was to win this race, he'd have to quit whatever else he was doing and start campaigning.

As Rockefeller knew, Lodge was more likely to vacillate than to act. The race, then, was still between Goldwater and himself. Rockefeller was constitutionally incapable of believing that any man alive could beat him one-on-one. And certainly not Barry Goldwater.

Johnson knew Lodge, too, but the president was constitutionally incapable of *not* fearing the most remote political threat. Later that day, he asked Dean Rusk to ask McNamara "to get you anything you've got on him without making it public, without letting him know it." He was even less capable of dealing with his only political problem, the one represented by all those write-in votes for Robert Kennedy. They were officially meaningless; they required nothing of New Hampshire's convention delegates, who would accept any running mate their president chose. This was a decision entirely at Lyndon Johnson's discretion, a fact he either could not recognize or would not act on. It was as though the very thought of Robert Kennedy brought on an attack of political paralysis.

13

A MATTER OF CHOICE

If I just had my choice," the president told Hubert Humphrey over the phone a few days after the primary, "I'd like to have you as the vice president."

Johnson was walking around the White House with polls in his pocket telling him he could beat any Republican challenger by 20 percentage points or more. To be sure, there were pressures on him. There were political considerations. Choosing his running mate was not necessarily an easy task, but neither, considering the political situation, was it all that difficult. And the choice was certainly his.

He didn't even have to make his selection yet. He just had to figure out a way *not* to choose Bobby Kennedy, even if those 25,094 New Hampshire Democrats and countless others around the country wanted him to. This shouldn't have been very hard for him either, but it was.

| | |

On Friday, March 13, McNamara and General Maxwell Taylor returned from their five-day jaunt to Vietnam. It had been a big triumph. "We shall stay for as long as it takes," McNamara had said on Sunday, as soon as he got off the plane in Saigon. He said Kanh was a man of "leadership and ability," who had "the full and complete support of President Johnson and our whole government and I want to let his people know this."

In fact, things were a bit more circular than that. What McNamara really wanted to do was to let Lyndon Johnson know that he (McNamara) was announcing his (Johnson's) support to Kanh. The theory was that if the Vietnamese leaders were confident that the U.S. government was behind them, they'd get their act together and do what had to be done. Just where the

Vietnamese people fit in was unclear. McNamara only had to make sure that the president was sure that the Vietnamese were sure of our devotion.

If only the president were that sure of his own policy. In a telephone conversation on Monday, February 3, two days after Operation 34-A began, Johnson had to agree with newspaper publisher John S. Knight's observation that "long-range over there, the odds are certainly against us."

"Yes," Johnson replied, "there is no question about that. Anytime you got that many people against you that far from your home base, it's bad."

But unavoidable. As Johnson reminded Knight, he had been one of those who resisted coming to the aid of the French in Vietnam ten years earlier. Johnson had never wanted to get involved in Southeast Asia.

"But we're there now," he said, "and there's one of three things you can do. One is run and let the dominoes start falling over. And God Almighty, what they said about us leaving China would just be warming up, compared to what they'd say now."

| | |

Jack Ruby was convicted of murdering Lee Harvey Oswald on Saturday, March 14, the same day a tall, self-assured, cantankerous loner named David Brower told a meeting of the Izaak Walton League that his organization, the Sierra Club, would fight Stew Udall's proposed dams at either end of Grand Canyon National Park.

Not too many people took this threat seriously, even the few who remembered that a decade ago Brower was one of the small band of conservationists who surprisingly defeated the established powers of the West—the state officials, the ranchers, the Bureau of Reclamation—and blocked construction of the Echo Park Dam near the confluence of the Green and Yampa Rivers in western Colorado.

Since then, Brower, a political conservative like most conservationists, had gone to work for the Sierra Club, which had but recently started to pay attention to the world east of California, and smart politicians had taken notice of this new constituency. One of them was Hubert Humphrey, who a few years earlier had gotten to know Howard Zahniser, a gentle, fifty-eight-year-old conservationist whose determination was as strong as his health was frail and who was leading a crusade that only a few years earlier had been considered quixotic: He wanted the federal government to set aside millions of acres of land for . . . well, for doing *nothing* on it.

Zahniser had not actually invented the idea of a national wilderness system. Aldo Leopold, Arthur Carhart, and Robert Marshall had done that decades earlier, even though they worked for the U.S. Forest Service, which saw itself, accurately, as an arm of the forest products industry.

But if Zahniser had not come up with the idea, he was peculiarly situated to advance it. He was a religious man, the son of an evangelical Christian minister. He became a bird-lover as a young man in western Pennsylvania and came to Washington in 1930 to work with the Bureau of Biological Survey, predecessor to the Fish and Wildlife Service.

The naturalists in the bureau—Leopold, Rachel Carson, and Ding Darling—influenced him, especially in their contention that protecting bits and pieces of wildlife habitat was useless. Unless large chunks of land were preserved, they had concluded, something would be irretrievably lost. In 1935, some of these naturalists helped Bob Marshall form the Wilderness Society. Zahniser attended the first Washington meeting later that year.

When the bomb went off over Hiroshima, something went off inside Howard Zahniser. He cashed in his government savings bond and quit the Fish and Wildlife Service, and in September 1945 he went to work for the Wilderness Society.[1] Four years later, when Zahniser unveiled the idea of a wilderness system at the Sierra Club's First Biennial Wilderness Conference, hardly anybody noticed. But then came the controversy over the Echo Park Dam, and when he revived his proposal in 1955 he got some coverage. Less than a week later, Humphrey had the speech reproduced in the *Congressional Record*, and a year later he and Representative John Saylor, a Pennsylvania Republican, introduced legislation to create a wilderness system.

It had no chance. To the mining, logging, and ranching industries, the whole idea was absurd. It meant "locking up" the land. It was an infringement on "property rights" to people who had somehow convinced themselves that some of the public land was their property because they'd been using it. Furthermore, it was a snobbish intrusion into the West by a small coterie of Eastern (and Californian) nature lovers. Many businessmen and workers, proclaimed W. Howard Gray of the American Mining Congress, would be "deprived of economic sustenance so as to provide a very limited number of individuals with wilderness pleasures."

But the resource extractors were not the only opponents. The Forest Service was also against the idea, not just because the service was in thrall to the timber cutters, but also because most foresters believed in "managing" forests, not just leaving them alone. The foresters were being true to the ethic of their founder, Gifford Pinchot, who had coined the word *conservation,* by which he meant prudent exploitation.

Their antagonist was John Muir, who founded the Sierra Club in 1892 and for whom exploitation of nature was akin to sacrilege. Now the split had reemerged with sufficient force that by early 1964 Brower and some of his allies were considering a new label; why not, they said, call themselves "preservationists," to distinguish themselves from the "multiple-use" Pinchotists. Fine, sniffed N. B. Livermore Jr. in the June issue of *American Forests* magazine. "In recent years there has evolved entirely too much 'con' in conservation," Livermore said, decrying the "over-emphasis on preservation." He and the real conservationists would henceforth call themselves "PROservationists."

Meanwhile, for at least two reasons, support for Zahniser's idea had slowly grown. One reason was Zahnny, as almost everyone called him. Unlike most crusaders, Zahniser argued gently, always on the issue, never against the person. He had never been a healthy man, so even more than most believing Christians, he had cause to remember that this life was fleeting. It helped him keep his bearings.

The other reason was that the public was for the idea. Official Washington tried not to notice this change. The Forest Service convinced itself that nothing more was going on than an increase in the number of "recreationists," as their bureaucratese called them, who wanted more lean-tos in the national forests. More were built, but that did not satisfy the conservationists, who were joining old organizations such as the Sierra Club and starting new ones such as the Federation of Western Outdoor Clubs. Back in Maine, plans to dam up the Allagash River had inspired creation of the Maine Natural Resources Council. Now it was on the offensive, pushing plans to protect the Allagash River forever, from dams or any other kind of development.

In 1961, a wilderness bill passed the Senate. As soon as the new Congress convened in 1963, Senator Clinton Anderson of New Mexico, chairman of the Interior Committee, introduced the same bill, setting aside 14,675,358 acres of national forest as protected wilderness. Three months later, it passed by a vote of 73 to 12. The problem was going to be in the House, and as an indication of how popular the idea had become, President Kennedy called Wayne Aspinall to the White House for a discussion, after which Aspinall promised he would try to work out an acceptable compromise.

Aspinall was a proper man. He stood five feet seven inches tall. At sixty-eight, his hair had turned gray, and though he still had a chunky chest, his back was slightly stooped. He was one of the most powerful, if least recognized, men of the decade. He had been in the House since 1949 and became chairman of the Interior and Insular Affairs Committee ten years later. All chairmen had broad discretion over what their committees would or would not consider. Thanks to his peculiar political situation and his determination, Aspinall had more than most.

Politically, on most issues Aspinall was a loyal liberal Democrat, committed to civil rights and to helping the poor. The liberals from the big cities thought he was just fine; he voted their way on what they cared about. They didn't know much about what he cared about, however, which was protecting the rights and the abilities of Western entrepreneurs to make a living by logging, mining, and ranching on the public lands.

He didn't put it that way. He called the conservationists who wanted to create a wilderness system "purists." Like a true Pinchotist, he explained that "conservation means the maximum good for the maximum number. If we stop mining and grazing and water development and timber harvest in any area, we have stopped maximum use."

His view of an acceptable compromise, therefore, was to cut in half the amount of land designated as wilderness, and keep all of it open for mineral exploration and grazing rights. Toward that end, he ordained that the House committee would consider Michigan representative John Dingell's stingy wilderness bill rather than the more generous version by Saylor. He had an obvious excuse; Saylor was a Republican. But Aspinall's real goal was to produce a weak bill, maybe one so weak that the Senate wouldn't accept it and nothing would pass at all.

| | |

Elizabeth Taylor was late to her wedding in a Montreal hotel suite on the afternoon of Sunday, March 15. "Isn't that fat little tart here yet?" griped the groom, Richard Burton, who had begun drinking in the morning. "She'll be late for the last bloody judgment."[2]

It was not the most auspicious beginning for a marriage, but the couple's fans didn't know about this, and probably wouldn't have cared. A week later, when Burton opened the American tour of *Hamlet* in Boston, a thousand fans mobbed the newlyweds at the Sheraton Plaza Hotel.

| | |

As the Senate reconvened on Monday, March 16, Richard Russell made his second speech of the civil rights debate, proposing an amendment that would resettle millions of American families until each state had the same proportion of white and Negro citizens. Holding up a large map, he demonstrated how the South would export Negroes to the rest of the country.

"I favor inflicting on New York City, the city of Chicago, and other cities the same condition proposed to be inflicted by this bill on the people of the community of Winder, Georgia, where I live," he said.

It was a completely unrealistic proposal, but a clever way of making a political point. And it served his principal purpose—delay. The civil rights bill was before the Senate, but it was not yet the order of business. Until that happened, the Southerners wouldn't even have to start their real filibustering. This was the phony filibuster.

| | |

One late March morning, the president summoned Richard Goodwin to meet him, not in the Oval Office but at the other end of the White House, the residential East Wing. A guard directed Goodwin right into the presidential bedroom, but no one was there. The room was not exactly empty; three television sets, one tuned to each network, were blaring forth. But aside from Goodwin, there was no living flesh in the room.

"That you, Dick? Come on in."

The voice came from the bathroom. Goodwin did as he was told and went in, where he found the president of the United States taking a shit.

Johnson kept silent for a moment, obviously waiting to see whether his guest would show any signs if discomfort. Goodwin knew he was being tested. Besides, he'd been in the Army; he'd seen guys on toilet seats before. He didn't blink. He did have to stand; the only seat in the room was occupied. And he had to listen as Johnson talked:

"I wanted you to work for me. Some folks around here, some of your *Kennedy* friends, were against it. They said you were too controversial. . . . Well, I'm controversial, too. Someone who isn't controversial, well, that usually means he's satisfied to sit around on his ass and get nothing done."

Under the circumstances, an interesting turn of phrase.

"You're going to be my voice, my alter ego, like Harry Hopkins," Johnson went on. "What the man on the street wants is not a big debate on fundamental issues. He wants a little medical care, a rug on the floor, a picture on the wall, a little music in the house, and a place to take Molly and the grandchildren when he retires.

"I'm going to get my War on Poverty. Of course, we can't have it all in one gulp. We'll have to make some concessions, make a few compromises—that's the only way to get anything. But that's this year. I have to get elected, and I don't want to scare people off. Next year we'll do even more, and the year after, until we have all the programs. But no compromises on civil rights. I'm not going to bend an inch, this year or next. Those civil rightsers are going to have to wear sneakers to keep up with me.

"Those Harvards think that a politician from Texas doesn't care about Negroes. In the Senate I did the best I could. But I had to be careful. I couldn't get too far ahead of my voters. Now I represent the whole country, and I have the power. I always vowed that if I ever had the power I'd make sure every Negro had the same chance as every white man. Now I have it. And I'm going to use it. But I can't if people like you go running off. Why, I never had any bigotry in me. My daddy wouldn't let me. He was a strong anti-Klansman. He wouldn't join the Methodists. The Klan controlled the state when I was a boy. They threatened to kill him several times."

Johnson paused and reached for the toilet paper. Goodwin went back into the bedroom. He had passed his test. Only later did he learn how badly McGeorge Bundy had flunked it. Bundy kept his back to Johnson during his ordeal by defecation.

It may or may not have been coincidental that both Bundy and Goodwin were Ivy Leaguers.

| | |

On Wednesday, March 25, J. William Fulbright, chairman of the Senate Foreign Relations Committee, got up to make a speech to a nearly empty Senate chamber. Fulbright was an optimist that spring, but a troubled optimist. He knew he'd have to vote against civil rights in a few months, and he knew what that would do to his reputation. Even so, he was an optimist, and what he had to say was based on an optimistic view of the world, one in which both the United States and the Soviet Union had moved away from thinking about "total victory" and toward accommodation.

"It is within our ability," Fulbright said, "and unquestionably our interest, to cut loose from established myths and to start thinking some 'unthinkable thoughts' about the cold war and East-West relations, about the underdeveloped countries and particularly those in Latin America, about the changing nature of the Chinese communist threat in Asia and about the festering war in Vietnam."

Among the myths Fulbright disdained were that the Soviet Union was "totally and implacably hostile to the West," that all communist nations always acted together, and that the regime of Fidel Castro was anything worse than "a distasteful nuisance."

On Vietnam, he supported the Johnson administration, but with a warning: No nation can "achieve by diplomacy objectives which it has conspicuously failed to win by warfare [and] our bargaining position is a weak one." In other words, we weren't winning the war.

The chamber may have been almost empty. But the press galleries must have been full because the next day Fulbright was all over page one. His remarks were received coolly by the White House but warmly indeed in much of the country, and ten days later, when Fulbright spoke at the University of North Carolina in Chapel Hill, the auditorium was full and the joint was jumping.

This time he spoke less of foreign affairs and more of this country, which had "grown rather attached to the cold war" for the intellectual torpor it had imposed. "It occupies us with a stirring and seemingly clear and simple challenge from outside and diverts us from problems here at home, which many Americans would rather not try to solve." Those problems included not just the usual ones—schools, poverty, segregation, health care—but some matters no one else in public life mentioned: "the blight of ugliness that is spreading over the cities and highways of America . . . the mindless trivia of television . . . the gaudy and chaotic architecture that clutters the central areas of our great cities."

Lyndon Johnson found this annoying, perhaps because Fulbright was horning in on his act. The president spent the Easter weekend at his ranch. He went to church Sunday morning, March 29, but spent much of the rest of the weekend in his car. Graciously, he invited some reporters to accompany him. He drove. He drove fast. When one reporter, a woman, complained that he was driving too fast, he held his big Stetson in front of the speedometer. Then he sipped some Pearl beer from a paper cup, drove fast, and sipped some more.

The reporters, as reporters are wont to do (it being their job), put all this in their newspapers and magazines. The president was furious. Were they not his guests?[3]

| | |

Robert Kennedy and his family spent Easter weekend at their favorite recreation—skiing, this time in Stowe, Vermont, and this time joined by Jacqueline Kennedy and her children, and by Senator Edward Kennedy and his family. On Monday, March 30, Jacqueline and Robert Kennedy left Stowe and flew to Antigua to stay at the home there of their friends Paul and Bunny Mellon.

The widow and her brother-in-law were functioning, but they were by no means healed, and each tried to strengthen the other. Holidays were especially hard, and when Robert Kennedy's mood darkened on those evenings in Antigua, Jacqueline gave him a book that had meant a lot to her. It was *The Greek Way*, Edith Hamilton's classic short study of how Western civilization began in a culture that honored human persistence against the incomprehensible cruelties of existence.

He read it avidly then and later, underlining the passages he found most appealing, especially those that spoke about the inevitability of suffering and the strength to deal with it. One of those passages was from Aeschylus: "Even in our sleep pain that cannot forget falls drop by drop upon the heart, and in our own despite, against our will, comes wisdom through the awful grace of God."

| | |

On the last day of the month, as a U.S. Navy carrier floated on "maneuvers" nearby, the United States helped overthrow the arguably incompetent but undeniably elected government of Brazil. A few days later, Lyndon Johnson sent his "warmest good wishes" to the new, unelected government, expressing his pleasure that the change had been accomplished "within the framework of constitutional democracy."

The president was, at the very least, misinformed. Outside the framework of both Brazilian and American democracy, Thomas Mann, Johnson's viceroy for Latin American affairs, had been working with the CIA, Americans with business interests in Brazil, and unhappy members of the Brazilian elite to plot the coup. The possibility of overt U.S. military intervention had even been discussed.

It was not the first time the United States had overthrown a democratically elected government; the CIA had arranged earlier coups in Iran and Guatemala. It was, however, the first time Lyndon Johnson's administration had overthrown a democratically elected government. It would not be the last, and it provided at least an indication that the American Empire, like the Athenian Empire Robert Kennedy had been reading about, assumed that nothing was forbidden it.

That's what Pericles had believed about Athens, that "a city which rules an empire holds nothing which is to its own interest as contrary to right and reason." So Robert Kennedy had been reading. *The Greek Way* had a political bias. Athenian imperialism, Mrs. Hamilton was convinced, destroyed Athenian democracy. Perhaps his dissent over the Cuban fishing boats indicated that her most famous new fan was starting to apply that lesson to the present.

| | |

On Monday, March 30, at a few minutes after noon, and a few hours before a new television program named *Jeopardy!* debuted on NBC, Hubert

Humphrey stood at his desk in the front row of the Senate chamber and began to talk. Four days earlier, Richard Russell had figured out that his delaying tactics had become counterproductive; the Senate was more likely to invoke cloture to shut off the minifilibuster against the motion to consider the bill than on the bill itself. He permitted a vote, and Mike Mansfield's motion to take up the bill passed, 67 to 17.

Humphrey did not finish for three and a half hours. It was a long speech even by his standards. "We are participants in one of the most crucial eras in the long and proud history of the United States and, yes, in mankind's struggle for justice and freedom," he began. As rhetoric, it was portentous but not inappropriate. The longest debate in the history of the United States Senate had begun.

| 14 |

DEMOCRATIC SOCIETIES

On Wednesday, April 1, David Henry Mitchell III of New Haven, Connecticut, was ordered to report for his draft physical.

He didn't.

Three years earlier, Mitchell, a student at Brown University, helped found the End the Draft Committee, whose Initial Statement declared that "in the tradition of Thoreau and the principles of Individual Guilt and Individual Responsibility established in the Nuremberg Trials and in the first session of the United Nations, we assert the right and obligation of the individual to protest and dissociate himself from these criminal preparations."

The committee members spoke for a small but growing minority, and early in 1964 the American Friends Service Committee helped organize the Committee to End the Draft, which proclaimed that "under the draft, our ultimate moral decision making power, that is, to be able to decide in our own minds whether or not we want to kill other people, has been denied us."

To the surprise of many, this uncompromising assertion of individual sovereignty was endorsed by the legal system. In January, the Second Circuit Court of Appeals in New York reversed the conviction of Daniel Seeger, who had refused induction into the Army on the grounds that he was a conscientious objector, even though he did not believe in God. Writing for a unanimous court, Judge Irving Kaufman declared that "the stern and moral voice of conscience occupies that hallowed place in the hearts and minds of men which was traditionally reserved for the commandments of God."

It was an extraordinary ruling. The court was saying that the individual's conscience was equal, if not superior, to any force in the universe. At the time, no one seems to have noticed that although the foreign policy of these young pacifists was as far as it could be from that of the Young Americans for Freedom, their insistence on individual autonomy was similar. The political wind buffeting America's young split at some point into two opposing flows, but both emanated from the same source, and it was no accident that at the same time that the new conservatism was evolving into the Goldwater campaign, the left was being reborn.

Like conservatism, radicalism had been all but obliterated by the New Deal, which rendered socialism politically irrelevant. Unlike the right, the left was also tarnished by association, sometimes justified and sometimes not, with the perverse socialism of the Soviet Union. As was the case with conservatism, radicalism's rebirth began with intellectuals.

In 1954, a year before William Buckley started the *National Review,* Irving Howe, Michael Harrington, and a few others founded *Dissent,* a democratic-socialist quarterly. It was not the left's version of the *National Review,* nor did it ever seek to be. Its circulation was always smaller, its content more scholarly. But it served a similar purpose by letting anticommunist radical intellectuals know they were not alone. Not all of its contributors were political, at least by the narrow definition. Psychologist Erich Fromm wrote for *Dissent.* So did Norman Mailer.

It was by not confining politics to its narrow definition that radicalism was revived. The Old Left was a European import. It rested on a complex critique of capitalism and an intricate philosophical-economic system full of esoteric terms: synthesis, labor theory of value, objects of utility. The New Left was individualist, existential, American at its roots. To the extent that its members had a common worldview, it owed as much to aesthetics and to a common folklore as to economics or historical analysis. For example, SDS president Todd Gitlin came to political involvement after reading J. D. Salinger and Albert Camus, not Karl Marx.

And this left was specific. Its purpose was not to transform society in general but to right certain wrongs. Its impetus was not theory but the individual conscience, individuals' sense of themselves as making a difference. Despite themselves, they got this from John Kennedy, as they took from him the sense of excitement of a new, intellectually vigorous generation replacing a tired and boring one. In their own minds, they personified the existential angst that always lay just under the suburban surface of 1950s torpor, now emerging to invigorate everyone around them.

Still, such is the political mind that at some point somebody was going to try to coalesce these specific impulses into an all-purpose movement. Perhaps because nobody else even thought of taking on this burden, it fell to the kids, to the Students for a Democratic Society. Or perhaps it was precisely because they were young, full of energy, and more than a little pleased with themselves and therefore intent on explaining themselves.

The explanation came at the SDS 1962 national conference at Port Huron, Michigan. Like their conservative contemporaries at Bill Buckley's estate, these young radicals were determined to create a statement of principles and had gone so far as to ask one of their number, the editor of the student newspaper at the University of Michigan, to draft it.

The *Port Huron Statement,* as it came to be known, was a most unusual political document, for much of it was not political at all. Largely created by that Michigan editor, Tom Hayden, it spoke of a politics that provided, among other things, a way "of finding meaning in personal life."

Before it even got to political issues, the *Statement* dealt with "human relationships," proclaiming that they "should involve fraternity and honesty." Like the *Sharon Statement,* the one from Port Huron insisted that there were values that transcended the material: "Loneliness, estrangement, isolation describe the vast distance between man and man today. These dominant tendencies cannot be overcome by better personnel management, nor by improved gadgets, but only when a love of man overcomes the idolatrous worship of things by man."

The young radical leftists were no less committed to individualism than the young radical rightists. "The goal of men and society should be human independence," the *Statement* said, and like their conservative contemporaries, the young leftists shunned bureaucracies and centralization.

So both the New Left and the New Right were reactions against being "managed" by outside, remote (and adult) authorities. For the signers of the *Sharon Statement,* the only objectionable management came from government. Their contemporaries at Port Huron agreed, but protested also management by corporation, foundation, university, and a vaguely defined "establishment," which set the standards of acceptability.

In common, right-wing and left-wing youth delivered this message: Don't tell us what to do. In common, having absorbed the individualizing tendencies of suburbia, they were rebelling against its prefabricated conformity. In common, they had been enabled, or "empowered" as some of them were learning to say, by affluence. These young people had more cash in their pockets than young people had ever had, both because there was more money to be had and because their cooperative (indulgent?) parents were giving it to them. The consumer economy had created a consumer culture, which to no small extent is a culture of self-indulgence. No wonder individualism bloomed on both the right and the left.

There the commonality ended. The young right-wingers would replace management by public government with management by the private collectives of corporations, with the hegemony of the wealthy, and with the authority of religion, or at least of virtue as religion defined it. The solution proposed by the young left-wingers was more complex and therefore perhaps less attainable. In place of an elitist democracy that imposed regulations from the top, they called for "participatory democracy," in which decisions that affected people's lives would be made by "public groups," locally organized and open to all, in a context that would see that politics "has the function of bringing people out of isolation and into community."

Community had not been on the agenda at Sharon.

This is not to say that the student leftists were less self-absorbed than the young conservatives. It was just a different kind of absorption. They were the suburban kids who had identified with Marlon Brando in *The Wild One*, with James Dean in *Rebel Without a Cause* (young Robert Zimmerman, later Dylan, was an especially avid James Dean fan). Their sense of themselves as a group apart did not diminish the sense of each one as a person apart, a loner confronting an uncaring world. They may have disagreed with much of American policy, but theirs were American temperaments, formed by Western movies as much as by left-wing analysts. As much as their opposing contemporaries who had gathered at Sharon (and who would have been much happier about this analogy), the members of SDS had a touch of John Wayne in them.

Alas for the SDS, the anti-anticommunism by which it distinguished itself from the older socialists did not protect it from the scorn of the unabashed procommunists. The rise of the New Left exemplified by SDS did not preclude a revival, inconsequential in number but visible, of the Old Left. For some reason, probably just because it was more outrageous, old-fashioned communism retained its appeal for a few young people. In April, a tiny leftist band called the Progressive Labor Movement held a conference, renamed itself the Progressive Labor Party, and made no effort to conceal its communist sympathies. Neither did the W. E. B. Du Bois Clubs, named for the Negro leader who had declared himself a communist shortly before his death in 1963.

On Sunday, May 2, about a thousand people, most of them young, marched to the United Nations headquarters in New York to hear speeches assailing the United States as an imperialistic power. A few weeks later, the march leaders used the date as the name for a new radical peace group headed by a Haverford student, Russell Stetler, a former SDS member who now found his old organization too academic and theoretical for his tastes.

In the two years since Port Huron, SDS had moved both ways. As it became more impatient, it grew more radical. But as it became more hostile to central authority, it grew more conservative. Thus the university, which at first had been viewed as a potential "agency for changes" (one of many oft-recited, if ill-defined, radical slogans), was now seen as too bureaucratic and too programmed.

No wonder. Among the many realities ignored by the founders of SDS was that students rarely remain students for very long; all too soon, even graduate study ends, and that long-awaited (if dreaded) "real world" looms.

And in that world, disaster loomed. In early 1964, not only SDS but much of the left-of-center intellectual world was convinced that an economic collapse was just ahead—another depression—which, for all the pain it would cause, would also present an enormous opportunity: It would create a working-class army of change, eager to take radical action against the status quo.

This scenario had been suggested in a book published in 1963 called *Free Men and Free Markets* by a maverick British-bred economist named Robert Theobald. Among those who were impressed by it was W. H. "Ping" Ferry ("This game ain't Ping-Pong," he'd said after being hurt in a Dartmouth football practice; the nickname stuck) of the Center for the Study of Democratic Institutions in Santa Barbara. A dapper, energetic, twinkly-eyed fellow who had once played piano in a whorehouse, Ferry took to the telephone, at which he was a master, and arranged a meeting.

In October 1963, he and Theobald, joined by two presidents, Ralph Helstein of the United Packinghouse, Food and Allied Workers and Todd Gitlin of SDS, met in Princeton, in J. Robert Oppenheimer's office (Oppenheimer had nothing to do with the meeting; his office just happened to be available that morning) at the Institute for Advanced Studies. The four of them adjourned to the nearby Nassau Inn for the afternoon, and by day's end they had created—what else?—an "ad hoc committee" and agreed to draft a manifesto warning of the crisis to come.

By the time they went public, in May of 1964, they had attracted the support of an impressive collection of liberal intellectuals, including Nobel laureate Linus Pauling, economist Robert Heilbroner, Michael Harrington, Gunnar Myrdal, and literary critics Dwight Macdonald and Maxwell Geismar.

According to the Ad Hoc Committee on the Triple Revolution, the root of impending evil was the computer, which was about to create a new economy requiring "progressively less human labor." The consequences of the impending "cybernation revolution," said the committee, will be "potentially unlimited output . . . achieved by systems of machines which will require little cooperation from human beings."

This could usher in a golden age in which society would no longer need "to impose repetitive and meaningless (because unnecessary) toil upon the individual," who would be "free to make his own choice of occupation and vocation from a wide range of activities not now fostered by our value system and our accepted modes of 'work.' " The alternative? Mass unemployment and spreading social dislocation.

These left-of-liberal thinkers were not alone in worrying about the impacts of automation. Back in January Hubert Humphrey had proposed creation of a thirty-two-member commission to study the problem, and in March the president had asked Congress to create such a commission, albeit smaller. Even some Republicans were getting concerned. Governor Scranton would later tell his convention's platform committee that the federal government was responsible for helping workers whose jobs were lost to machinery.

But the Ad Hoc Committee's proposed solution, inspired by Theobald's book, would not be embraced by either party. It was a guaranteed annual income, "an unqualified commitment to provide every individual and every family with an adequate income as a matter of right." Forthrightly, the committee acknowledged that such a policy would require an expanded role for central economic planning.

The Ad Hoc Committee's report got a respectable hearing, starting with a page-one story in *The New York Times* on Saturday, May 23. Then, as is common with such policy statements, it mostly faded from view—mostly but not entirely. Both Gitlin and Hayden had signed the statement, making it almost official SDS policy, and even young radicals who had their doubts about its proposed solutions accepted the wisdom of its analysis.

This conclusion, combined with growing disillusionment with academia, had two consequences for the expanding left, one theoretical and one practical. It exacerbated the young radicals' impatience with established authority, however enlightened and liberal it was. In place of the "top-down" paternalism of liberals, they would seek change from below, from the more "authentic" power of ordinary people, especially poor people.

Consistent with this attitude, SDS leaders started to spend less time and energy writing papers and more on organizing low-income people in several cities as part of a program called the Economic Research and Action Project (ERAP), designed, in Hayden's words, to create "an interracial movement of the poor."

They used $5,000 from the United Auto Workers Union and sent an organizer named Joe Chabot to Chicago, to the working-class white neighborhood on the North Side known as Uptown. Chabot got an office at 4800 N. Kedzie and began to distribute leaflets warning about the danger that automation posed to young working-class men.

Who were unimpressed. To them, Chabot seemed just another social worker.[1] ERAP wasn't a complete failure; it helped a few poor people improve their lives. But it never created an "interracial movement of the poor."

Remarkably, SDS acknowledged the failure. Here, at least, they were more adult than the supposedly grown-up policy experts in Washington. One of the great advantages SDS had was that its leaders were still thinkers as well as actors, and as thinkers they had two qualities rarely found among the politically active: They could see what was really important and they were more ambitious for their cause than for themselves or even for their organization.

This humility was part of the ideology. Participatory democracy was non-hierarchical, even antihierarchical. At their meetings, SDS members preferred consensus to majority decisions. They couldn't always get that consensus, but trying to get it was always a goal. Meetings deliberately ran themselves in defiance of Robert's Rules of Order; the chairman was less a leader than a facilitator. One of the SDS slogans was "Let the people decide." Often, they applied it to themselves. Part of the disaffection with established American life was distaste for its drive for success, its egoism, its uncritical approval of personal ambition.

This attitude was not without consequences. Most of the students who worked with SDS went back to college, bringing these new approaches with them. They may have numbered only in the hundreds, but by the time their talk had filtered through the coffee shops, snack bars, and smoking lounges of hundreds of dormitories, their converts numbered in the thousands. When 1964 started, there were barely a thousand SDS members. Before it ended, there were twenty-five hundred, still far from a mass movement, but a significant cadre.

Considering their high regard for self-effacement, it was no surprise that when they gathered for the seventh annual convention in Pine Hill, New York, in June, SDS members elected as their new president a gaunt, introspective twenty-four-year-old named Paul Potter. An Oberlin graduate who'd grown up on a small farm in Illinois, Potter combined a serious moral commitment with extraordinary intellectual integrity. Even when he spoke fervently, as he often did, his language was prudent, as though he were weighing his words that they might not offend the innocent.

His was a radicalism based on an essentially religious outlook. The perfect political organization, he told the convention that elected him,

> would be open, flexible, transparent. It would allow individuals to show themselves to others as they really were. It would be directly democratic, and it would rest on the goodwill and sincerity of each participant. If these images correspond to any former image I have in my mind, it is very definitely that of a church. Not of any church I have directly known or experienced, but of the church I have heard some churchmen talk about, the early revolutionary church, whose followers lived in caves and shared their bread, their persecution and their destiny. I say church, because in spite of what we observe them actually doing, churches stand for the salvation of men's souls, the salvation of humanity (frequently called Godliness) or its members. I say church because church stands for a belief in a radically different, spiritually liberated life which is thought to be so changed as to be unimaginable to people who live in this world. I say church because church stands for communion, and it is the church feeling of communion that I believe must be at the bottom of any organization we build.

No one else in public life talked quite that way. The few others who were thinking similar thoughts, if not expressing them as eloquently, were working for Barry Goldwater.

Nor was it a surprise that the SDS members, convinced though they were of their eventual triumph, understood their own limits. If they were not completely immune from delusions of grandeur, they did not suffer from them as much as most politically active people do. They were students; they could see that an organization of a few thousand people—a few thousand kids, really—would be trivial were it not part of something larger than itself.

That something was the impulse that inspired ERAP. It was the desire on the part of thousands of young people who had grown up in reasonable comfort to assert their authenticity by making common cause with the least comfortable. ERAP was SDS's effort to tap that desire. When it failed, the organization acknowledged that in left-of-center America, the most important initials were not SDS. They were SNCC, they were CORE, and they were COFO.

| | |

That spring, the Council of Federated Organizations seemed to be everywhere: setting up offices in Mississippi, holding meetings in Atlanta and Washington, recruiting students from Harvard to Stanford. Or maybe it was just Al Lowenstein who was everywhere. On Easter Sunday, he was in Atlanta; to be precise, he was held at the Atlanta Municipal Airport, not by the air traffic control system but by Robert Moses, who was meeting downtown with James Forman, who detested Lowenstein.

Forman thought Lowenstein's student acolytes talked too much to their college newspapers, and he blamed Lowenstein for not controlling them. And the two men had argued about the National Lawyers Guild.

They weren't the only ones. Joe Rauh and Jack Greenberg of the NAACP had warned Moses and the others not to accept the guild's offer to send lawyers to Mississippi to represent civil rights workers. The Mississippi Negroes, people like Forman and Lawrence Guyot, simply could not understand what the problem was. Here were prominent attorneys willing to take time from their lucrative law practices and come to Mississippi, knowing the personal dangers involved. Why on earth would anyone refuse?

Because the guild members were communists, or at least they associated with communists, said Lowenstein, Rauh, and the others, who could not understand how anyone could fail to understand the danger. It wasn't just bad politics, though surely any association with communism would be politically risky. The guild, Rauh said, had supported "every Russian mood" for decades. From bitter experience, the Northern liberals harbored a principled distaste for communism and for those who seemed close to it or indifferent to its evils.

It was a distaste they kept trying to explain to the Mississippians, but it was a hard sell. To Guyot and Forman and the young Negroes who had been beaten and threatened and jailed and shot at, the debates that Harrington, Howe, and their friends had endured in scores of wine-soaked Greenwich Village lofts meant nothing. These young men had never had the need or the opportunity to ponder the impacts of oppression. They were oppressed. They'd take help from any competent lawyer who volunteered it.

| | |

Early in April, not long after the Fulbright speech, Johnson invited Bill Moyers and Richard Goodwin to go for a swim in the White House pool. They were in the pool for a long time, but their naked bodies got less exercise than their minds.

"There's a Gallup poll coming out," Johnson told them. "Says that seventy-five percent of the American people approve of what you boys are doing. It's really your work, you and the rest of the staff. I'm just a conduit."

Treading water, nobody had to take this seriously.

"Now, I've got two basic problems—get elected, and pass legislation the country needs," he continued, rattling through the list of John Kennedy's unfinished legislative business. But he wanted to do more than pass the Kennedy program. "We've got to use the Kennedy program as a springboard to take on the Congress, summon the states to new heights, create a Johnson program, different in tone, fighting and aggressive.

"Hell, we've barely begun to solve our problems. And we can do it all. We've got the wherewithal. The country was built by pioneers with an ax in one hand and a rifle in the other. There's nothing we can't do, if the masses are behind us. And they will be, if they think we're behind them. . . . I never thought I'd have the power. Now some men, like Nixon, want power so they can strut around to 'Hail to the Chief'; some, like Connally, want to make money; I wanted power to use it. And I'm going to use it. And use it right if you boys'll help me."

As Goodwin later remembered it, Johnson turned directly toward him, the house intellectual—the Northeasterner, Harvard Law grad, Kennedyite, Jewish intellectual—floating naked beside him, and said, "You would have loved my father. He was a liberal, almost radical, Democrat. He hated the KKK. The day after I was elected to Congress he told me to go up there, support FDR all the way, never shimmy and give 'em hell."

At the time, Goodwin could feel only Johnson's "immense vitality," the extraordinary strength of his will. Not the urgent plea, the almost pathetic plea, from the most powerful man on earth that he be admitted to Goodwin's circle, that he be granted legitimacy.

"Now, boys," Johnson told Goodwin and Moyers, "you let me finish the Kennedy program. You start to put together a Johnson program."

Goodwin took the assignment seriously, especially after he got a deadline. The president was to receive an honorary degree from the University of Michigan in Ann Arbor on May 22, and by then he wanted his Johnson program.

| | |

On Tuesday, April 7, George Wallace got 25 percent of the vote in the Wisconsin primary, and all of a sudden it seemed that every columnist in America was talking about something called the "white backlash."

It was not a new phrase. A year earlier, financial writer Eliot Janeway, operating on the same assumption that inspired that Ad Hoc Committee on the Triple Revolution—the conviction that automation would lead to massive unemployment—had predicted a "backlash" among the unemployed. Now racial resentment, not economic insecurity, seemed the more immediate threat.

The news delighted the Southerners, but it did not surprise them. It was the certainty that these resentments were festering in the North that lay behind Russell's Negro relocation proposal. At least one other Southerner was not surprised and tried to sound unconcerned: "The fact that we got more votes than Wallace is pretty satisfactory to us," Lyndon Johnson told press secretary George Reedy.

Wallace and anti-Negro bigotry were not bothering Johnson that morning as much as columnist James Reston and anti-Southern bigotry. In *The New York Times,* Reston had written that the president's anger about coverage of his Texas automotive antics was misplaced considering that he'd had "a remarkably good press" since taking office.

The president was not comforted. Were he not a Southerner, he was certain, he would not get treated this way. "It shows some of the same attitude toward a Southerner that Mississippi shows toward Harlem," he told Reedy. "I don't know whether I can lead the world . . . if my own people feel this way about me. . . . It may be that they got somebody else that can do it better."

Then he began to plot out how he would tell the country that he would not run again.

"I'd say we're worried from a patriotic standpoint about the future of the country and the world. We've tried to effect the transition and bring labor in and bring business in with a minimum of deep divisions and hate. . . . But we believe that the Eastern press has a feeling. It's kinda like [*Washington Star* columnist Paul] Berryman's cartoons. They always put a string bow tie on me because of where I was born. I never wore one in my life."

| | |

Here was a clash of cultures, no doubt more annoying to the president because his political mind-set held that there was but one American culture, even as he reacted with one culture's resentment of another's perceived dominance. Editorial writers and cartoonists in Washington and New York were part of a Northeastern, urban culture that at least stereotyped, when it did not condescend to, the west Texas rural culture, or the Northeasterner's impression of the west Texas rural culture.

Other cultures outside the mainstream were usually ignored, and preferred it that way. There was, for instance, the Negro culture, which transcended both inequality and the protest movement to overcome inequality. Not that Negroes weren't also part of the general culture; they watched TV, played and went to ball games, read books and newspapers, and, where allowed, voted. But they also had their own tastes, their own pastimes, and, more than anything else, their own music, much of which white radio stations would not play.

They couldn't keep it all to themselves. From Bix Beiderbecke to Elvis Presley, whites had been invading it and borrowing from it for years. By the early 1960s, a few Negro entrepreneurs were producing popular recordings by Negro singers who were so good that the resistance of white radio station managers began to crumble. The biggest and best of these firms was in Detroit, and so it was called Motown. Stevie Wonder recorded for them, and so did Martha and the Vandellas. Five young women who sang in local clubs as the Primettes used to hang around the Motown offices.

The day after the Wisconsin primary, three of the Primettes—Diana Ross, Florence Ballard, and Mary Wilson—cut a record for Motown as the Supremes, a name chosen on the spot by Florence Ballard, because she was the only one in the office when their manager insisted on a new name. The song recorded that day was "Where Did Our Love Go?"

| | |

Allard Lowenstein came to Queens College on Thursday, April 9. There was, then, hardly a college to which Allard Lowenstein did not go. He was thirty-five years old that spring, and he'd graduated from the University of North Carolina fifteen years before, but part of Lowenstein remained a student. He moved easily in the company of his elders—Eleanor Roosevelt and Norman Thomas were among his confidants—but he always felt most at home on campus, where his energy and idealism never failed to attract a small army of followers. Of adulators.

Maybe it wasn't just his energy and idealism. Then and later, there was something about Lowenstein that refused to grow up. He accepted—he embraced—the responsibilities of adulthood while maintaining the demeanor of an adolescent. For many young people, this was irresistible.

And there were many young people who did not want to resist. More serious, more sophisticated, far more political than the teenage Beatles fans, they shared with them their disinclination to follow their elders, their impatience, and their desire to do something new and different.

Lowenstein was a bridge between ideologies as well as generations. He was a liberal, not a radical, but he appealed to the radicals because, like them, he was a romantic, almost a naïf. It wasn't that he really thought American government and politics worked the way the civics book said they did, but he never lost the belief that they might, that they would if only people believed that they should.

That's what he talked about at Queens College. He talked about America and his belief that it could work the way it was supposed to, even in the Deep South. He was not there at random but as part of a well-planned campaign to recruit Northern college students—white Northern college students—to go to Mississippi to work in voter registration drives and to teach in "freedom schools."

The very audacity of the plan made it a romance. The Northerners would live among the poorest of the poor, the most downtrodden folk in America. They would . . . well, they would not raise them up; they would help them raise themselves. They would be bringing light into the darkest corners of the land. Here was the romance: idealistic young people against the armed might of the state of Mississippi.

It was a state of 1.2 million whites and 916,000 Negroes, a higher Negro percentage than any other state. Until the 1930s, Negroes had been a majority, and they still were in twenty-nine of the state's eighty-two counties. More than 60 percent of the people lived on farms or in small rural villages, and in 1960 the median family income of whites was $4,209; of Negroes, $1,444.[2]

Mississippi had the lowest level of education in the country and the most vicious antipathy to racial equality. It wasn't that the average Mississippian was more racist or violent than his counterpart elsewhere in the South. But in Mississippi racial violence was condoned in an organized and institutional manner by state and local authorities. This state, as no other, ever, even had its own secret police force, the Mississippi Sovereignty Commission, dedicated to preserving the state's "way of life," meaning its separate and unequal racial system.

All of which was now being challenged by . . . well, by a bunch of kids. Robert Moses was their leader, nonviolence was their strategy, energy their deadliest weapon. Robert Moses had been a field-worker for the Student Non-violent Coordinating Committee, so he knew how to get poor people together, but he was neither a Mississippian nor a politician. His degrees, from Harvard yet, were in mathematics and philosophy. Philosophy? And he was going to lead his pathetic little army of liberal arts namby-pambies from the North against Mississippi? Most Mississippi men owned guns.

Not that Lowenstein understated the difficulty. Mississippi, he told the students, was "the most totalitarian state in America." Noble this effort might be, but he did not want to delude anyone. There would be, he said, "great danger in going to Mississippi."

That scared some of the students in Lowenstein's audience, but it inspired Andy Goodman, not yet twenty-one but already a veteran of civil rights struggles. As a high school sophomore—at Walden, the private school where Mickey Schwerner had gone a few years earlier—he joined the "Youth March for Integrated Schools" in Washington. Early in his senior year, he and a friend went down to West Virginia to look into the causes of Appalachian poverty. They came back to report that the problem was intractable and that the root of it was capitalism.

A few months later, on February 1, 1960, four young men—David Richmond, Ezell Blair Jr., Franklin McCain, and Joseph McNeil—Negro freshmen at North Carolina Agricultural and Technical College, went to the Woolworth in Greensboro, North Carolina, and sat down at the segregated lunch counter. Nobody told them to do it. They weren't part of any organization. They had just had enough. A month later, Northerners supporting them set up picket lines outside the Woolworth's at New York's Herald Square. Andy was there.

Now, listening to Lowenstein, Andy could see that demonstrating in Manhattan was not enough. The battle was in Mississippi.

|15|

UPRISINGS

The Toronto Maple Leafs had just won their third Stanley Cup in a row beating the Detroit Red Wings four games to three. The Boston Celtics and the San Francisco Warriors were playing their way into the National Basketball Association finals, which the Celtics would win, four games to one.

It was a good time to escape from worldly cares, and there were plenty of appealing escapes. Broadway had a new star, Barbra Streisand, who was playing the role of Fanny Brice in the hit musical *Funny Girl*. In mid-April Arnold Palmer won his fourth, and last, Masters Tournament, and Sidney Poitier won his, or any Negro's, first Academy Award for best actor, for his role in *Lilies of the Field*. The other winners were Margaret Rutherford for *The VIPs,* and two actors who starred in the movie *Hud*, Patricia Neal and Lyndon Johnson's friend Melvyn Douglas.

Actually, Douglas was not as close a friend of Johnson's as was his wife, Helen Gahagan Douglas, who had been a member of the House of Representatives when Johnson came to the Senate in 1949. They were close enough friends that she still called him "Lyndon." The buzz around Hollywood on the morning after was not about who had won but who hadn't, notably the star of Neal and Douglas's movie, Paul Newman.

For devotees of the finer arts, the New York City Ballet led by George Balanchine opened its first season at the new New York State Theater with a performance of *Midsummer Night's Dream* on Sunday, April 24.

Earlier that day, Lady Bird Johnson held a five-minute telephone conversation with Dr. Elizabeth A. Wood, a scientist with the Bell System's laboratories. Mrs. Johnson was in Washington and Dr. Wood in New York, but the two women could see as well as hear each other. It was the public debut of the Picturephone, combining telephone and television technology.

Regular commercial Picturephone service would begin at selected locations immediately, and though the cost would be high at first—sixteen dollars for the first three minutes between New York and Washington—phone company officials predicted that it was only a matter of time before the average home had Picturephone.

Six long months had passed since Joe Pepitone lost Clete Boyer's throw against the background of white shirts in the seventh inning in Los Angeles, allowing Jim Gilliam to get to third base and to score the winning run on Willie Davis's sacrifice fly, ending the 1963 baseball season.

But now, as in every year since the beginning of time, opening day had come again, and Hubert Humphrey had arranged to take some friends to Griffith Stadium. Majority Leader Mike Mansfield was with him, as were Minority Leader Everett Dirksen and that great baseball fan Richard Russell, all sitting together to see the Senators play the California Angels.

But fellowship was not the only thing Humphrey had arranged. He knew how the Senate worked, and he knew that should one of the filibusterers notice a sparsely attended chamber, he would demand a quorum call. In the absence of a quorum, the Senate would recess, giving the Southerners more time and allowing them to conserve energy.

Anticipating such a ploy, Humphrey had told Senate staffer David Gartner to monitor the session and to phone the stadium manager in the event of a quorum call. Humphrey had even composed the message for the announcer. It came in the third inning: "Attention please, there has been a quorum call in the United States Senate. All United States senators are requested to return to the Senate chamber immediately."

Russell stayed.

| | |

On April 15, most of the 65,375,601 Americans who had not already done so filed their tax returns. For most, this was a painless process. Few people owned securities, and although 34 million had savings accounts, most of those accounts were small, a few hundred dollars at most, and the income they got from the 4.85 percent interest rate didn't add up to much. For everyone but a fortunate few, income meant wages or salary.

All they had to do was subtract $600 for each member of their household and either the standard deduction or their itemized deductions, which consisted mostly of their mortgage interest, property taxes, and charity donations. What remained was their taxable income, and most of them paid 15 percent of it. Filling out the form didn't take long, and most taxpayers got a refund that was bigger than last year's, thanks to the recently enacted tax cut. Only the first phase of it had gone into effect this quickly; there would be more savings in the years ahead. Still, that mythical typical household, one with two kids and the median income, saw its tax burden fall from about $750 to about $570.

That was a substantial increase in disposable income, and most people disposed of it, igniting more of that economic growth so important to their president. Despite lower rates, government revenue kept rising. In private life or public, the trend lines were up.

America was getting used to being rich, not just in the aggregate, but in most of its parts. People had money, and it wasn't only the money people who had money. All sorts of average folks had a few bucks left over after they'd paid the bills. This was not unprecedented, but the extent of it was, and so was the sense that the condition had become permanent.

In fact, if there was a single root cause underlying almost everything going on in 1964—suburbia, civil rights, economic concentration, new ballparks and bridges, new theaters, the Goldwater movement, highbrow TV shows, young peace activists—it was money. More people and more institutions had more of it than ever before.

Money in the hands of government, businesses, universities, and foundations financed research and development, leading to new technologies. From these stemmed new processes and products, some of them cheaper, meaning more people could buy them. Some of the new developments were huge, such as the automated earth-moving operation that enabled the contractor on California's 770-foot-high Oroville Dam to move fifty thousand cubic yards of material every day. Some were tiny, such as Enovid, the pill developed by Pfizer in 1960, enabling women to have sex without having children.

Money in the hands of people meant they could buy the products being developed. No, they didn't buy earth-moving systems, but they did buy the electricity produced by dams, and they bought the houses in which they used the electricity. As recently as the end of World War II, most people rented their homes. Now 63 percent of the homes were owner-occupied. That was a pretty good indication that most Americans had a few bucks.

Not that income was evenly distributed. The richest fifth of the population took in 41 percent of the $495 billion in personal income in 1964, and the bottom three fifths got only 35 percent. Just about 31 percent of all families earned less than $5,000; only 6 percent earned more than $15,000.[1] Doctors, who averaged $25,000, were the highest paid professionals, in part because there were so few of them. The American Medical Association's efforts to hold down the number of physicians were working; in 1950, there had been 109 for every 100,000 persons. Now there were 97, and because they were earning more, they were working less. Just a few years earlier, the average doctor made house calls. Now only 7 percent did; the burden of travel had shifted to the patient.[2]

If there was no equality, there was sufficiency for most people. A majority of households earned between $5,000 and $12,000 a year. This wealth, national and individual, was cause for celebration, and it was much celebrated. But affluence, although not a problem, can be a cause of contention. Abundance posed a new challenge. Americans started to debate the purpose of wealth. Everyone agreed that money was worthwhile. What they argued about was why.

There should have been no mystery about why this debate started now. Money may be fungible, but the means by which it is earned are not, and those means affect the earner's attitudes toward it. More than ever before, people in 1964 were affluent because they were educated. It wasn't just doctors and lawyers. The economy now needed engineers, scientists, statisticians, and even writers. Thanks to these demands, to the G.I. Bill, and to bigger state universities, more people had gone to college. They may have gone to learn a trade, but many picked up some real education while they were at it.

Although engineers, scientists, and even writers may work hard, they don't work hard the way farmers, miners, and factory workers do. At the end of the day, the white-collar worker is likely to have enough energy to read a book, to play a musical instrument, or to watch a good play on television.

The result was an unprecedented number of people who valued education for its obvious financial benefits and for more. In the cities and in the middle-income suburban subdivisions, people were joining book clubs, acting in amateur plays, agitating for better schools, taking piano lessons, and learning to draw.

There was quality fiction on the best-seller list—Mary McCarthy's *The Group,* John O'Hara's short story collection *The Hat on the Bed,* John Cheever's *The Wapshot Scandal,* Peter De Vries's *Reuben, Reuben*—and some serious nonfiction, including Alfred Sloan's *Years with General Motors* and Vance Packard's *Naked Society. The Trojan Women* was a success on the New York stage.

No, America had not become a modern Athens. The ballpark and the bowling alley still outdrew the lecture hall and the art class. Weekly Westerns and situation comedies drew larger audiences than Leonard Bernstein's explanations of jazz or symphonies on television. Still, the number of consumers who wanted to buy what used to be called the finer things of life had grown so much that it would now be accurate to consider this group a constituency.

They displayed, among other things, a different attitude toward the natural world. There had always been notable exceptions such as Henry David Thoreau, but the standard American view of nature was that it was there to be used, with little regard for the consequence. A common adjective describing "wilderness" had long been "untamed," implying that taming it was a virtuous act.

To be a young adult in 1964 was to have sat through public school filmstrips celebrating how DDT had conquered malaria and how TVA dams controlled flooding and brought cheap power to impoverished farmers. Altering nature was culturally progressive and politically liberal. No less a leftist than Woody Guthrie had written and sung an anthem to public power and river impoundments: "Your power is turning our darkness to dawn. Roll on, Columbia, roll on."

Now came a reconsideration. One of the books so many Americans read in the first years of the 1960s was Rachel Carson's *Silent Spring,* which pointed out that people altered nature at a price; DDT wiped out fish and birds along with malaria, and the book inspired a movement to get rid of the pesticide. Carson's death at fifty-five in April 1964 revived interest in her book and in the drive to ban DDT.

Although it was considered audacious, the announcement in March that conservationists would oppose the Marble and Bridge Canyon Dams of the Central Arizona Project was not as shocking as it would have been a decade earlier. More than a few Americans had absorbed the notion that perhaps the best thing to do with rivers was to let them flow.

That's because education and affluence also affected recreations less cerebral than art and literature. Among the products a lot of people could afford were tents and sleeping bags. Taking the kids camping became increasingly popular. From 1956 through 1963, although logging in the national forests rose by one-third, recreational visits more than doubled. For the first time in the nation's history, there were more people who wanted to enjoy the public land than to make money off it.

But there was more going on than the specifics of appreciating art, nature, and culture. More generally, although Americans knew they were richer, many were not sure that they were happier. A materialistic people did not begin to question whether material wealth was desirable. They did begin to question whether it was enough. One of the books that was being discussed in the spring of 1964 was by the sociologist David Riesman. It was called *Abundance for What?*

In Riesman's view, too much of America's abundance was devoted to, and dependent on, defense spending. "Military Keynesianism," he called it, and he blamed it for the increasing conformity and specialization of American life. Although more and more Americans could afford the "standard package" of consumer goods, Riesman said, fewer of them could find "meaningful work."

| | |

As the tax returns were being mailed, Andy Goodman, in search of meaningful work, was interviewed by Jim Monsonis, one of SNCC's Northern agents. All the volunteers were required to put up $500 in case they needed to bail themselves out of a Mississippi jail. Andy had been saving money earned at a part-time job loading trucks at United Parcel Service. Without telling his parents where he was going, he would get up early each morning to go to work before heading to class.

| | |

In a column that appeared that day, Joseph Alsop claimed that communist agents were "beginning to infiltrate certain sectors of the Negro civil rights movement" and that Martin Luther King remained in contact with "Communist collaboration and even Communist advice."

King was not just furious, he was almost in a panic. Knowing Alsop to be far more refined and moderate than Paul Scott or Robert S. Allen, King reasonably assumed that this leak came not from the FBI but from the president, who was perhaps testing a retreat on the civil rights bill.

At King's request, his aide Walter Fauntroy sought an immediate meeting with Burke Marshall, who confirmed that Alsop's source had indeed been the FBI but assured him that the administration was standing firm.

King accepted the explanation, not without wondering why Alsop had let himself be used. He never found out. Not until after Martin Luther King was dead was it revealed that J. Edgar Hoover had unusual powers over Alsop, who in 1957 had been seduced into a homosexual encounter in Moscow by KGB agents, who had taken pictures of the encounter. Hoover had the pictures.

| | |

The day of the Wisconsin primary, eight of the nation's largest steel firms—including the Bethlehem, Jones & Laughlin, Armco, and Republic companies—were indicted for conspiring to fix prices. The indictment had academic as well as legal consequences. For years, mainstream academic economists had assumed that the very hugeness of the huge corporations that dominated an industry gave them effective power to "administer" prices, regardless of the market but also without resorting to collusion. The possibility that they had colluded anyway called that assumption into question.

Nine days later, amidst an unprecedented splurge of advertising and public relations, the Ford Motor Company unveiled its new passenger car, the Mustang, designed for the buyer who wanted a sporty but inexpensive vehicle.

Though the Mustang was legal, together the two developments explained some of the economic realities of the day. The most obvious was that not all Americans were questioning the purposes of wealth. Whether or not Calvin Coolidge had been right when he said the business of America was business, the business of *business* was certainly business. Whatever their personal values, corporate executives were supposed to produce goods or services and earn big profits for their companies.

Furthermore, a great many Americans had simple answers to David Riesman's question: abundance for its own sake, for the sake of the ease and comfort it provides, the luxuries it can buy, the satisfaction it grants to those who attain it. Lots of people, including people who liked to go camping and read serious books, also liked zippy cars and labor-saving gadgets. They were snapping them up.

Among the supporters of more consumption and higher profit was the president of the United States. He understood the appeal of having more of everything, and he had an obvious vested interest in the kind of booming economy that generates lots of tax revenue and a slightly less obvious interest in high profits for his new friends who ran the large corporations.

So when his friend and advisor Esther Peterson suggested he take credit for the recent drop in the cost-of-living index, inspired as it was by electric utility refunds ordered by the Federal Power Commission, Johnson replied, "I don't think we ought to do too much crowing or bragging at this time." He didn't want to rub consumer protection liberalism into the faces of the executives he was trying to woo to his party.

The other economic reality illustrated by these two April events was that it was no longer possible for businesses simply to think up a product or process, produce it, and sell it. Things had gotten too intertwined for that. Some of the intertwining took place with government, some with universities, some with the advertising and public relations companies hired by production companies to market their goods.

None of it permitted criminal conspiracies to fix prices, but the executives holding those discussions might have wondered why their actions were wrong if it was right for the secretary of the interior to meet with utility company executives to plot out how to rewire the American West.

In two months, the Interior Department would announce plans for the

Pacific Northwest–Pacific Southwest Intertie, to consist of four extra-high voltage transmission lines to be built by public and private utilities and by the federal government to bring "excess" power from the Columbia River. A department press release said it would be "the most imaginative electric transmission system conceived by any group of engineers throughout the world." It would cost $697 million, $280 million from the government, and those costs would influence the rates.

In this case, then, the government was presiding over a price-fixing process. What was legal in one industry was criminal in another. What was beyond question was that, legally or not, a certain amount of coordination was required to run the economy.

So was a certain amount of size, because firms had to be big in order to coordinate. As of the end of 1962, the twenty largest manufacturing companies held 25 percent of the assets of all manufacturing firms. The 419,000 smallest held 25.2 percent. In some industries, size was indispensable. It was no accident that the smallest of the auto firms, Studebaker, had gone out of business in January.

Testifying before a Senate committee later in the year, economist Gardiner C. Means reported that in 1929, the 200 largest corporations legally controlled 48 percent of the assets of all nonfinancial companies. Twenty-five years later, Means said, "The most I can say with reasonable certainty is that concentration for the economy as a whole is not significantly less than it was in 1929 . . . the atomistic economy around which nineteenth-century economic theory was built has ceased to exist."

There was nothing atomistic about the appearance of the Mustang. Ford did not just decide that it would be a good car and consumers would like it. That's pretty much what Henry Ford had done when he started his company fifty-nine years earlier. He raised some money, designed a product, and arranged to produce as many as the public would buy.

The Mustang had been more than two years in the planning, ever since Lee Iacocca had taken over the company and put a stop to the project begun by his predecessor, Robert McNamara, to create a car known as the Cardinal. Unlike McNamara, Iacocca was a salesman. The Cardinal, he saw almost immediately, was too small. Its fuel economy was great, but it looked too . . . well, too plain. It had no pizzazz.

He sent the designers and engineers back to the drawing boards, and by the time they were done, planning for the Mustang had cost about $50 million.[3] The design and engineering costs alone were $9 million.[4] Nor was this new vehicle's design a matter of anyone's whim, instinct, or creative impulse. Ford did not produce a car and then seek to market it. Instead, through polling and survey techniques, the company tried to figure out what the market wanted; then it produced a car for it.[5]

The Mustang was inspired not by engineering but by demographics. The baby boomers were beginning to go to college and get jobs. Because college graduates were more likely to buy new cars and because the number of families with two cars had shot up to 13 million from only 1 million five years earlier, what this market obviously needed was a vehicle designed to be a second car.

More precisely, what was needed was a second car for people in their twenties or thirties, people who didn't need a big car (the family's first car was probably bigger) and didn't want to spend too much on their second car. The stripped-down, six-cylinder, 101-horsepower version cost only $2,365, FOB Detroit.[6]

Having created the car for the market, Ford commenced to flood the market with publicity and advertising. Automotive reporters for major newspapers were slipped "exclusive" stories on the Mustang weeks before its debut. Ford had some pretty good tub-thumpers; the Mustang made the covers of both *Time* and *Newsweek*. That was the "free" (not counting the cost of the public relations companies) publicity. The company also conducted a saturation bombing of television ads, buying time on such popular programs as *Perry Mason* and reaching 30 million homes on one evening.

Under the chassis, it wasn't even a new car. The Mustang was "virtually a technical reproduction of Ford's Falcon Spring," as *The New York Times* noted. In other words, only the style was new.

But by now, "manufacturing had become a competitively neutral factor" in determining whether automobiles got bought.[7] What was important was not engineering but design, and design only mattered because it was part of image. Auto advertising did not sell its product; it sold customers new impressions of themselves.

One merely had to start a "sleek new 1964 Buick Skylark" to be transformed into "an escape artist." The driver of the Thunderbird was a pilot manqué. The driver's seat was in a "cockpit"; the driver would be "airborne on the luxury of new contoured shell-design front seats." All he had to do was "pick out a runway and prepare to soar," because driving a T-bird "is the nearest thing to flight itself!" They must have needed that exclamation point.

Ford proclaimed that its 55/XL had "super-silent torque," not to mention "deep-foam bucket seats" and a floor-mounted shift. There was something about putting that gearshift lever on the floor that provided the illusion of really handling the vehicle. Not that most people had to shift; most cars were automatics. The targeted customer was the suburban commuter, the kind of guy who "used to take the 6:02," according to one advertisement showing a fellow freed of the tyranny of the commuter train schedule.[8]

The image was more sedate than it had been just a few years earlier. Only the Cadillac still had the tailfin, which began to disappear in 1959, and even the Caddy's fins were diminished. Far more common was the straight-line styling featured on the new Chevelle, striking in its simplicity; the trim Plymouth Barracuda with its elongated rear window; or the Ford Fairlane with its level front and sleek sides.

The two-toned car was pretty much gone, too. In some models, such as the Fairlane, car-buyers could choose a model with a different-colored roof. But the chassis with one color above a chrome strip along the side and another below it was gone, though many models retained a narrow version of the strip, now little more than a symbolic reminder.[9]

When it produced the Mustang, Ford had about two hundred thousand domestic employees, many of whom were among the 580,000 members of the United Automobile Workers Union of America and were paid at least $3.76 an hour.

The jobs were good, but they were neither easy nor enjoyable, and forty thousand UAW workers were sixty years old or older. Most of those older men wanted nothing more than to retire. Walter Reuther had a plan to institute a "share the work" system, which would have allowed those over-sixties to retire early.[10] There would have been lots of available sharers. More than 3.2 million people, constituting more than 5 percent of the civilian labor force, were unemployed.

Reuther couldn't get that plan in the contract that year. Still, the auto workers were relatively well paid and well treated, in part because their union was a strong one. Other workers were having more difficulties.

Ed Ball, the seventy-five-year-old brother-in-law of Alfred I. du Pont, ran the Florida East Coast Railway and, through the du Pont estate, also controlled thirty-one Florida banks. When most of the nation's railroads accepted a wage increase of 10.24 cents an hour for their nonoperating employees, Ball didn't. Instead, he insisted on running his line without his thirteen hundred nonoperating workers, and when some other unions stayed out in sympathy, Ball simply returned to normal operations with seven hundred workers, down from two thousand.

Some reduction in force was possible because the union contract required the company to hire more workers than modern locomotives needed. But Ball cut out more jobs by abolishing passenger service, which wasn't making much money anyway. Senator Wayne Morse of Oregon wanted to investigate, and perhaps to break up, the "interlocked financial–industrial–real estate–railroad empire of the Alfred I. du Pont estate," but nothing ever came of that plan.

Ball was not the only strikebreaker. In Wisconsin, Herbert V. Kohler, a political ally of Barry Goldwater's friend Dean Manion, had successfully been ignoring and defying rulings of the National Labor Relations Board for a decade to keep the United Auto Workers out of his plumbing-ware manufacturing business.

Ball and Kohler may have been onto something. As a percentage of the workforce, union membership had peaked in 1956 and had been dwindling ever since, from 33.4 percent to 28.9 percent of the nonagricultural workforce.[11]

Although business ownership was becoming more concentrated, the workplace was becoming less so; there were slightly more small plants and shops, slightly fewer big ones. It's easier to organize a thousand workers in one plant than a hundred workers in each of ten plants.

The industrial worker of the 1920s through the 1950s was most likely to be an immigrant or a man bred in the city. Most industry was in the North or on the West Coast, regions hospitable to unions. Now more industries were moving south, and Southerners were moving north and west to the workplace, bringing rural attitudes with them.

To some of these displaced farmers, accustomed to fending for themselves, unions were vaguely alien. They were associated with immigrants, and Catholic or Jewish immigrants at that. Even if there was no bias, there was often a cultural disconnect. If he'd moved to pro-union California, the Tennessee farm boy was likely to be wary of the union organizer; if he'd moved to Texas, where the union shop was illegal, he was even harder to reach.

There was little doubt that millions of factory, shop, and office workers were Tennessee farm boys—and girls—moved to Texas and California. As the year began, there were 12,954,000 people living and working on 3.2 million farms, 380,000 fewer than the year before and 2.7 million fewer than in 1960.[12]

Both technology and government were making it easier for the large farm to thrive and harder for the smaller one to survive. By now, almost half of the $3.3 billion in government price supports was going to the biggest and richest farms, which in turn produced almost half the agricultural output. Big farms got bigger by absorbing their less successful neighbors.

On Thursday, April 16, in Washington, Everett Dirksen presented ten amendments to Title VII, the fair employment section of the civil rights bill. Predictably, the most liberal senators and the civil rights lobbyists reacted harshly, but Humphrey understood the real significance. Not long ago, Dirksen had fulminated against the very existence of Title VII. Now he only wanted to change it. He was coming around.

| | |

By now, even the Goldwater campaign was beginning to worry about Henry Cabot Lodge. On Friday, April 17, Richard Kleindienst told Cliff White to get some "research on Lodge." He was asked to "reduce a condensation of it in some kind of printed pamphlet" by not less than a week before the May 15 Oregon primary "so that a last minute 'smear' could not be leveled at us."[13]

That was not the only covert political act of the day. While Kleindienst was writing his memorandum, the joint chiefs of staff were forwarding to the secretary of defense OPLAN 37-64, calling for "graduated overt pressures" against infiltration routes in Laos and Cambodia and targets in North Vietnam.

The plan specified ninety-one targets in North Vietnam and recommended "a sudden sharp blow" as the most effective course.[14]

| | |

On the thirty-fifth day of the filibuster, Sunday, April 19, the advocates of civil rights welcomed a new ally—God, or at least an impressive array of his professional devotees here on earth. That day, Catholic, Protestant, and Jewish seminarians began a continuous prayer vigil at the Lincoln Memorial. Ten days later, six thousand clergy and active lay leaders from churches and synagogues all over the country attended a national interreligious convocation at Georgetown University before ascending Capitol Hill to call on their senators.

Thanks largely to the National Council of Churches, which ended up spending four hundred thousand dollars on grassroots lobbying (and which the FBI had been investigating to see if it was run by communists), ministers had been writing to their representatives for weeks. And during those weeks, the religiously observant of many denominations (though not, usually, Southern Baptists) could expect to hear their clergy sermonize on the evils of discrimination.

Sometimes the effort was more precisely targeted. Shortly before one key vote, Father John Cronin of the U.S. Catholic Conference of Bishops called a colleague in South Dakota, whose Senator Mundt was very much on the fence. More phone calls ensued. After voting the way Dakota's Catholic clergy wished, the senator was heard to say, "I hope that satisfies those two god-damned bishops that called me last night."

On the thirty-seventh day of the filibuster, Tuesday, April 21, the Southerners made their first tactical move. Senator Herman Talmadge of Georgia called up an amendment that would require jury trials in criminal contempt cases arising from any provision of the bill. It was a shrewd move. How could liberals oppose trial by jury?

That day sixty-one crosses were burned in southwest Mississippi. Because he was alarmed, and because he had so little confidence in the FBI, Robert Kennedy sent his friend Walter Sheridan into the state. Sheridan was an experienced and devoted investigator, but there wasn't much he could do by himself, except arouse the wrath of J. Edgar Hoover, who quickly dispatched a note to Burke Marshall about "a man in Mississippi named Walter Sheridan who claims to be doing investigative work for the Department of Justice. This is to inform you that he is not a member of the FBI."[15]

Hoover no doubt knew precisely who Walter Sheridan was and knew that Marshall was at least as up-to-date about what was going on. The director just wanted his superiors to know that they couldn't make an end run around him without his finding out about it.

|16|

MIDDLE-CLASS LIFE

The following day, Wednesday, April 22, the World's Fair opened in New York City. It had been much awaited and not a little feared because some of the city's angrier Negro leaders, led by the Brooklyn chapter of CORE, had threatened to disrupt opening day, including President Johnson's welcoming speech, with a new technique they called a "stall-in." The idea was to tie up the city's intricate network of commuter highways by simply stopping cars right in the traffic lanes. For a city as dependent on mobility as New York, this was a tactic all but guaranteed to cause distress. Mayor Robert Wagner, with his customary eloquence, called the threat "a gun to the heart of the city."

No one was more distressed than the mainstream civil rights leaders, especially Roy Wilkins of the NAACP. Along with their white liberal allies, they were issuing statements of condemnation against the more militant Negroes behind the plan, and they eagerly sought support from Martin Luther King.

In a letter to Wilkins, King agreed that the stall-in was a "tactical error," all but designed to enhance the white backlash. But he refused to join an "outright condemnation" of the angry young Negroes threatening the stall-in.

"Which is worse, a 'Stall-In' at the World's Fair or a 'Stall-In' in the United States Senate?" he wrote. "The former merely ties up the traffic of a single city. But the latter seeks to tie up the traffic of history, and endanger the psychological lives of twenty million people."

The stall-in fizzled, though it may have been responsible for the small opening day attendance of only 92,646, and a few protesters—not on the expressways but at the fair—chanted "Freedom now" and "Jim Crow must go" during the president's speech.

No one could remember the last time Americans had shouted during a speech by their president. Like the proposed stall-in itself, the shouts illustrated how impatient some people were getting with the pace of change, so impatient that they had become angrier at the established leaders who shared their goals than with the forces who opposed them.

Or maybe they were really angry about the fact of established leadership. Earlier, there had been hints of such an attitude from the left-of-center intelligentsia. In February, Nat Hentoff, the well-known critic of jazz and society, had accompanied Labor Secretary Willard Wirtz on a tour of Harlem, where Wirtz asked a teenager whether he was looking for a job.

"Why?" the young man had answered, and Hentoff considered his reply "a healthy reaction."

To Hentoff, the kid was saying, "I've stopped letting myself be conned. I have eyes. I see what jobs are available to the adults in the ghetto. I *know* the lousy schooling I've had. Where am I supposed to look? . . . Nobody out there gives a damn for me."

There was no point urging middle-class values on the poor, Hentoff said, because the "middle-class values which are paramount in this society today are selfishness, hypocrisy and a deep, bitter resentment against being disturbed."

Hentoff's rhetoric may have been overwrought, but he clearly laid out the distinction between consensus liberalism and the rising anger against it from the left. Liberals, led by the president, Bobby Kennedy, Hubert Humphrey, and even Martin Luther King, wanted to open middle-class life to everyone, regardless of race or family income. Now people with some intellectual credentials were stating openly that middle-class life was not worth entering.

The World's Fair itself, hard by Shea Stadium on the same 646-acre site of the 1939 version in the Flushing Meadow section of Queens, was a determined celebration of middle-class life, technology, and the shiny future that awaited all Americans. Its central symbol, the Unisphere, was a tilted globe orbited by a satellite. In the General Motors Pavilion, visitors could see a future of underwater cities with a submarine in every garage, futuristic farming, and cities with wide roads. The General Electric Pavilion simulated a thermonuclear fusion reaction, demonstrating the electric power generation of the future.

Abe Lincoln was in the Disney Pavilion. Using something known as audioanimatronics, the life-size statue of the sixteenth president could make forty-eight separate body movements and seventeen different head movements as he held forth about the dangers of subversion from within the country. It was Disney genius, with a little help from the Defense Department, that had first developed the technology for controlling rocket launchers.[1]

Even the fair's most celebrated premodern attraction—Michelangelo's *Pietà*, shipped over from Italy just for the occasion—"has been improved upon for us," as Wolf Von Eckardt wrote in *The New Republic*, by the addition of flickering blue lights.

Unbeknownst to most, there had been a small effort to subvert the fair's stifling respectability. Philip Johnson, the architect who designed the towering New York State Pavilion, knew and liked Andy Warhol and assigned him to paint a mural of the Ten Most Wanted Men in America on the outside.

Neither the subject matter nor the artist was acceptable to the fair's management, and Warhol didn't like the way his mural was displayed, so by something approaching mutual agreement it was whitewashed. Warhol and a few of his friends went out to Queens to view the desecration, but by the time they got there the job was mostly done. Warhol was just as glad; he wouldn't have wanted to help the cops catch a criminal. And in just a few weeks, a show dearer to his heart would open at the Stable Gallery on East Seventy-fourth Street. There, he was assembling his paintings of consumer cartons, the kind holding Del Monte peach halves, Campbell's tomato soup, and Brillo pads.

| | |

Andy Goodman was one of the protesters at the fair. He was now immersed in writing a sociology term paper titled "The Black Muslims: A Phenomenon of Negro Reaction." Among his conclusions was that "while it is somewhat of a fantasy to believe that all white men are devils, it is true that the white man (and by this I mean Christian civilization in general) has proved himself to be the most depraved devil imaginable in his attitudes toward the Negro race."

White racism, Goodman concluded, "has created a group of rootless degraded people. . . . The road to freedom must be uphill, even if it is arduous and frustrating. A people must have dignity and identity. If they can't do it peacefully, they will do it defensively."

But the civil rights forces were not just playing defense. Two days after the opening of the fair, Robert Moses and a few ten-dollar-a-week SNCC workers opened a Washington, D.C., office of the Mississippi Freedom Democratic Party.[2]

| | |

On the day the fair opened, *The New York Times* ran a page-one story citing earlier congressional testimony by J. Edgar Hoover that communists were infiltrating the civil rights movement. This was secret testimony Hoover had given in 1963 to a congressional subcommittee, testimony that Robert Kennedy had considered so irresponsible that he had not permitted Hoover to make it public and had urged House members not to disseminate it. Now Hoover had simply leaked it.

Martin Luther King was furious. The next day, as President Johnson headed to Chicago to speak to a Democratic fund-raising dinner, King was in San Francisco, where he held a press conference. To the assembled reporters (and FBI agents posing as reporters) he said he only wished that Hoover and his agents "would be as diligent in apprehending those responsible for bombing churches and killing little children as they are in seeking out alleged communist infiltration in the civil rights movement." He found it, he said, "difficult to accept the word of the FBI on communistic infiltration in the civil rights movement when it has been so completely ineffectual in protecting the Negro from brutality in the Deep South."

Back at FBI headquarters, the shock was not so much that King had criticized Hoover but that in doing so he had actually used the director's name.

That night in Chicago, the president tried out a new phrase. "We have been called upon to build a great society of the highest order," he said. Nobody paid attention. The president was at one end of the cavernous McCormack Place arena on the Lake Michigan shore. In front of him were several thousand Chicago Democrats, not known for their attentiveness to original thought even before a few hours of drinking and schmoozing.

"We have been called upon—are you listening?—to build a great society of the highest order," he repeated. He screamed, "A society not just for today or tomorrow, but for three or four generations to come."

He'd get back to it later.[3]

| | |

That night a new play by James Baldwin, *Blues for Mr. Charlie*, opened off-Broadway. Directed by Burgess Meredith and starring Rip Torn, it was well received despite its manifest flaws as a drama and despite, or perhaps because of, its message of racial hatred. "I'm going to make myself well with hatred," the lead character says at one point. The audience, almost all white and affluent, was impressed.

The next day, speaking at Stanford University, Robert Moses told four hundred students and faculty that the nation's problems were "much deeper than civil rights." The dislocations expected from automation, the poverty in the cities, the threat of war, "go to the very root of our society . . . it just happens that the civil rights question is at the spearhead of all of these."

That day Dirksen moved toward a civil rights compromise. He and Mansfield proposed a bipartisan substitute to Talmadge's amendment, under which the judge in any case would decide whether a jury trial was necessary. If it was not, punishment could not exceed a $300 fine or thirty days in jail. Dirksen had thrown in with the civil rights forces. From now on, he had as much at stake in passing the bill as anyone in the Senate.

| | |

On Monday, April 27, the president of the United States lifted his two beagles, Him and Her, by their ears.

"If you ever follow dogs," he said, "you like to hear them yelp. . . . It does them good to let them bark."

Dog lovers all over America were furious, and even the president's old friend Ev Dirksen got in on the act. At a Republican Senate lunch the next day, he said he'd give the Southerners just another week before filing for cloture. But he also called on Johnson to compromise. He would go see his friend that very day, Dirksen told the Republicans, and tell him, "Now it's your play. What do you have to say?"

Then he said Johnson had mistreated his puppies.

"He's acting like a shit-ass," Johnson complained to Mike Mansfield the next day, apparently more upset about the dog criticism than pleased about the civil rights news. "First thing, he said he wouldn't treat his dog like I treated mine. . . . It's none of his damned business how I treat my dog. And I'm a hell of a lot better to dogs and humans, too, than he is."

Dirksen did go visit his old friend the president that day. His old friend the president did not even discuss a civil rights compromise. Dirksen left the White House with nothing.

If only Vietnam were so easy to deal with. "We're not getting it done," the president told McNamara on the last day of the month. "We're losing. So we need something new. If you pitch this old southpaw every day and you wind up as the Washington Senators and you lose, we'd better go and get us a new pitcher."

| | |

On Wednesday, April 29, President Johnson approved an agreement under which the government would lease the Anvil Points experimental oil shale plant to the Colorado School of Mines Research Foundation, which then subleased it to the Mobil and Humble Oil Companies. Shale oil was part of private industry's Grand Plan for exploiting natural resources on Western public lands, though in this case industry did not speak in one voice. The oil business itself was of two minds. Within the shale (actually marlstone, not shale) was a fuel (actually kerogen, not oil) worth billions. But there was no oil shortage, and developing this new fuel source might flood the market. More than a few observers wondered if the oil companies wanted to control the shale project in order to scuttle it.

In the meantime, the companies got complete access to $6 million of publicly owned equipment for which $18 million of taxpayers' money had already been spent. The companies would get to keep ownership of all the technology generated by the project. The government would get just about nothing, but it would grant the oil companies exemption from enforcement of antitrust laws.

This was not the only shale project. A few days earlier, Sohio Petroleum Company, one of the industry's giants, had announced a venture for "the first commercial production of oil from shale in the United States," in cooperation with two other companies. The joint venture, which had neither capital nor employees, would be headed by Huntington Hartford.

| | |

In Hanover, New Hampshire, at 4 o'clock in the morning of Friday, May 1, two student assistants sat down at two General Electric 265 computers in the basement of College Hall at Dartmouth. The computers had been purchased in February with money from a National Science Foundation grant. One of the computers was used as the master to control the flow of information between some teletypewriter terminals and a second—slave—computer that actually performed the calculations.

Under the leadership of Professors John Kemeny and Thomas E. Kurtz, the students had been trying to develop a new programming language. The FORTRAN and ALGOL languages computer designers had been using were too complicated, too cumbersome. Nobody but experts could understand them, so they were useless to the majority of Dartmouth students who did not major in science. The Dartmouth team was working on a simpler plan they called Beginner's All-Purpose Symbolic Instruction Code consisting of only fourteen different statements.

At the two terminals, the students simultaneously typed in "If X=9 THEN GOTO 200" and gave their computers the command to run. Both machines came up with the same answer. BASIC was born. Kemeny and Kurtz started teaching it the following September and then placed it in the public domain.

That May Day teenagers were singing "I Get Around" along with the Beach Boys or dancing as Chuck Berry sang "No Particular Place to Go." John Le Carré's spy novel and James Michener's epic of Afghanistan were still on the best-seller list. The more scholarly were reading Walter Jackson Bate's biography of John Keats or Richard Hofstadter's *Anti-intellectualism in American Life*, both of which would be awarded Pulitzer Prizes three days later. The awards this year were less noteworthy than the decision by the Pulitzer Board that no work of fiction, drama, or music was worthy of a prize.

The Pentagon announced that six American soldiers had been killed in Vietnam in April, for a total of 220 combat deaths since 1961. The U.S. Fish and Wildlife Service announced it had counted thirty-two endangered whooping cranes. President Johnson predicted that a woman would be elected president one day, "although I hope you will forgive me for hoping that day is still a few years off," and Richard Russell told his Southern colleagues that he hoped to keep their filibuster going until George Wallace's presidential campaign alerted Northern politicians to the dangers of supporting civil rights.

Russell had been hearing news from home, and he knew that the next day the once-insignificant Republican Party of his own state would hold its most successful fund-raising dinner of the century and the first without a single Negro guest. "The Negro has been read out of the Republican Party of Georgia here today," one of Barry Goldwater's campaign aides proclaimed, perhaps too candidly, but Russell knew the other side of that coin—whites were finding the Republicans increasingly attractive. As if in support that Saturday, as Willie Hartack was riding Northern Dancer to victory in the Kentucky Derby, Goldwater was sweeping the Republican primary in Texas.

Though Russell and Goldwater probably did not notice it, there was dissension in the civil rights camp. Speaking at Stanford University that day about the summer plans to register Negro voters in Mississippi, Allard Lowenstein said that he had been having "some deeply disturbing disagreements with some of the people I've worked with. We are not far from violence."

Lowenstein had almost dropped out of the Mississippi effort altogether a few weeks earlier. The disagreement was over civil disobedience. He was against it. In his mind, Freedom Summer was for voter registration, meaning that it was politics. "Civil disobedience," he told the Stanford students, "doesn't contribute to what we are trying to do."

But that depends on what you are trying to do. Bob Moses and some of his allies weren't just trying to get people to vote. They were trying to get people to change because they wanted the whole society to change. Lowenstein didn't. He thought society was just fine, or would be if it included everyone.

| | |

To Goldwater's dismay, the newly Republican segregationists were getting no help from their party's leader in the Senate. On Tuesday, May 5, Everett Dirksen invited Attorney General Robert Kennedy and his top deputy, Nicholas Katzenbach, into his office for some bourbon and discussion. They sat around Dirksen's big mahogany dining table under a crystal chandelier, and it wasn't long before discussion became negotiation, as Dirksen and a few other Republicans told the Democrats from Justice how they'd like the civil rights bill altered.

They didn't really want much, perhaps because they knew they couldn't get much. By now, all contestants had played their hands, and Lyndon Johnson, Hubert Humphrey, Bobby Kennedy, and their friends were holding the high cards. There were several reasons for this, one of which was that most people wanted the bill passed. In a democracy, majority support is usually a potent force but rarely a sufficient one. Adding to its strength was how Humphrey was playing on Ev Dirksen's ego. It was no accident that those meetings were in Dirksen's office and that Humphrey never rushed the Minority Leader and rarely passed up an opportunity to praise him. To get the bill passed, Humphrey later said, "I would have kissed Dirksen's ass on the Capitol steps."

He didn't have to, because he could see in Dirksen what he could see in himself but may not have been able to see in Lyndon Johnson: their need for the approval of the political, cultural, and intellectual style-setters of the Northeastern Establishment.

The three of them did not react identically to this Eastern Imperialism. Humphrey embraced its politics and was indifferent to its style. Johnson agreed with most of the politics but despised the style. Dirksen could not accept even the Republican version of Eastern politics, and despite his love of theater, he resented Eastern culture.

But all three were vulnerable to the standards set by the Eastern Elite. Dirksen knew that if he helped pass the civil rights bill, he would become, however briefly, celebrated at Harvard and in *The New York Times*. It wasn't that he had ceased being a conservative; as a member of the Special Committee on Aging, he issued a minority report warning that plans for a federal medical insurance program for the aged would "interfere with the desire of older people to live independently and with maximum freedom of choice. Still, he wanted the approval of the Eastern intellectuals. He didn't want to want it, but he did.

Yet through it all, Dirksen was fooler as much as fooled. Like Russell, he knew that things had changed, that there had to be a bill. He just wasn't sure all his followers knew that. So he, too, was playing a game, pretending to be more hostile to the legislation than he really was so that he could get at least twenty-five Republicans to vote for cloture.

He was acting. It was his greatest gift.

| | |

That day the *Los Angeles Herald-Examiner* quoted Joe Jensen, the chairman of the Los Angeles Metropolitan Water District, saying that 9 million southern Californians faced "grave hazards" to their supply of both water and electricity if the water level of Lake Mead were allowed to fall any further.

Lake Mead, created by Hoover Dam in southern Arizona, was downstream from the new Glen Canyon Dam at the state's northern border, behind which Lake Powell was still filling up. Jensen wanted the Interior Department to open up the gates of Glen Canyon Dam to let more water flow down to Mead and thence to California's reservoirs and turbines. But officials in the Upper Basin states (Colorado, Utah, New Mexico, Idaho) were just as adamant about filling up Powell and were already furious because Interior Secretary Udall had uttered the unutterable, that he might have to pull the plug there.

Knowing it was unutterable, he first had it uttered by his imperious Reclamation Bureau director, Floyd Dominy. Visiting Page, Arizona, on Lake Powell's southern shore, Dominy said on March 2 that it was "conceivable" that the lake's "present level will be reduced to meet downstream requirements for power and irrigation."

The legalities of the situation were intricate, but the politics were simple. Even if pulling that plug endangered Democratic senators in Wyoming and Utah, as Udall feared it would, Boulder Dam and Lake Mead had more clout. Los Angeles and environs depended on them for water and electricity, and there were more congresspersons from California than from the rest of the West combined. On Monday, May 11, calling it "one of the most difficult decisions I have had to make as secretary," Udall ordered Glen Canyon Dam's gates open enough to maintain an elevation of 1,123 feet at Lake Mead. The Upper Basin was aghast. "Are we ready to accept Glen Canyon as a gaping monument to the perfidy of the secretary of the interior?" demanded former Colorado governor Ed Johnson.

Howard Zahniser died of a heart attack on Tuesday, May 5. Crusty as he was as a public man, Wayne Aspinall was a sentimentalist; he had liked Zahniser, even as he had opposed him. Not only did he attend Zahniser's funeral, but he had his committee mark up John Saylor's tougher wilderness bill, not Dingell's.

This didn't guarantee passage, but as it turned out, sentimentality wasn't Aspinall's only weakness. The chairman loved order. And he loved the Congress—his official position in it and his unofficial position as the master of public land law. Knowing history, Aspinall knew that for the first hundred years Congress existed, most of the laws it passed dealt with public land. Inevitably, then, the statutes dealing with public lands were scattered over many sections of the law. It could be confusing. Aspinall did not like confusion. A few years back, he had decided that the best way to make order of this chaos was to create a public land law review commission.

Especially on the Senate side, most Westerners opposed it, not because it was a particularly bad idea but because they thought it unnecessary. "What do we need a commission for?" Nevada's Alan Bible had asked. "We're going to examine the laws anyway."

But the idea had become almost an obsession with Aspinall. The Capital Beltway around Washington was just being completed, so the phrase had not yet been coined, but in this matter Aspinall had fallen victim to what later would be called an "inside-the-Beltway" perspective.

| | |

On Tuesday, May 5, George Wallace got almost 30 percent of the Democratic vote in the Indiana primary. Like many other Americans, Indiana Democrats responded favorably to Wallace's attack on "pointy-headed bureaucrats, tyrannical judges, [and] the ultraliberal press," all euphemisms for civil rights.

Wallace was a problem for civil rights advocates, because if he was unscrupulous, he was not entirely wrong. One of the lines that got the biggest response in Indiana was his claim that "they're building a new bridge over the Potomac for all the white liberals fleeing to Virginia," a statement not disproven by the fact that conservatives, and even a few Negroes, would also use the new Theodore Roosevelt Bridge.

The day after the primary, the civil rights filibuster became the longest in American history.

| | |

Now the Wallace threat was important enough that Martin Luther King had to acknowledge, on *Face the Nation* the following Sunday, May 10, that race was a "national problem" and that the Republican Party might turn into a "white man's party," which would be "tragic for the Republican Party as well as tragic for the nation."

King might have been subdued because just two days earlier Johnson honored the fortieth anniversary of Hoover's command by signing an executive order exempting the director "for an indefinite period of time" from mandatory retirement, which would otherwise have kicked in the following New Year's Day when Hoover turned seventy.

No one seemed to notice that "for an indefinite period of time" meant at the president's pleasure, but how could a president who called a man "a hero to millions of decent citizens and an anathema to evil men" intend anything but endless tenure for him?

Hoover was no doubt pleased. He must have suspected, even if he had not known, that John Kennedy had planned on easing him into retirement. Honored retirement, retirement celebrated by honor guards, jet flyovers, brass bands, and red carpets, but retirement nonetheless.

Johnson was not the only prominent officeholder taking note of Hoover's anniversary. Robert Kennedy also sent his congratulations, regretting that "in the past few months I have not had the pleasure of associating with you as closely as formerly." Hoover sent a courteous reply.

| | |

On Monday, May 11, the Connecticut Supreme Court upheld the state's law prohibiting doctors from prescribing contraceptive devices or birth control pills to their patients. An appeal was planned.

The next day, one of the Grammy Awards was presented to Jack Jones for the song "Wives and Lovers." Other winners were Barbra Streisand for her album *Barbra,* Henry Mancini for "Days of Wine and Roses," and the trio Peter, Paul and Mary for "Blowin' in the Wind."

| | |

The bourbon and the conversation were both flowing in Ev Dirksen's office on Wednesday, May 13, so there was little argument when Dirksen said he wanted to eliminate from the bill the Civil Rights Commission's authority to investigate voting fraud.

Robert Kennedy agreed; the commission was the wrong place for such activity, but Kennedy had promised that provision to William McCulloch, the Ohio Republican congressman who was so helpful in getting the bill passed. Kennedy couldn't go back on his word, and if he did there might be trouble getting the House to agree.

Dirksen went along with that decision, turning his attention to the more serious problem of the section banning job discrimination. He had some amendments, and he wanted Humphrey to look at them. Humphrey nodded. At this point, Senator Joe Clark of Pennsylvania slapped some papers down on the table in front of him and stalked out of the room shouting, "It's a goddamned sellout."

"See what pressure I'm up against?" Humphrey said to Dirksen. "I can't concede any more on this point."

Dirksen, who had similar troubles of his own, nodded and poured everyone a little more bourbon, never knowing he had witnessed a piece of theater written and produced by Humphrey and Clark.

A few hours and a few drinks later, they all emerged with the final version of the civil rights bill of 1964. "We have a good agreement," Dirksen said, and Robert Kennedy pronounced it "perfectly satisfactory."

What they had was the House bill minus authority for the attorney general to initiate court action without a "reasonable cause to believe" that a "pattern or practice" of violations existed, plus the insistence that state antidiscrimination agencies get the first crack at resolving disputes before the feds get called in, minus any mention of busing to eliminate de facto school segregation. Even Joe Rauh called them "minor, face-saving changes."

What they didn't yet have was sixty-seven votes to cut off debate, and the "pattern or practice" solution only enraged the Southerners more, for only their states met that test. This "puts Charles Sumner, Thad Stevens, and Ben Wade to shame," fumed Russell, who also tried a political dig. Dirksen, said Russell, has "killed off a rapidly growing Republican Party in the South, at least so far as his party's prospects in the presidential campaign are concerned."

| | |

The next day, Lady Bird Johnson was walking in the woods near the Middleburg, Virginia, home of family friend George Brown. It was not an idle stroll. She was trying to do some serious thinking. To help her, she invited two friends, Willis Hurst and Jim Cain, for dinner. These friends were physicians. Dr. Hurst, who had treated Lyndon Johnson after his 1955 heart attack, was now one of the White House physicians. Dr. Cain, a family friend and physician since the 1930s, was with the Mayo Clinic. The topic of dinner conversation was their prominent patient's health, physical and mental, and whether he should run for a full term.

The next day the two doctors, along with White House doctors George Burkley and Janet Travell, and Dr. Larry Lamb of San Antonio, would subject

Johnson to a thorough physical examination. But first, his wife wanted to talk to them about his mental state, his psychological strength. More and more, of late, he had been talking like a man who didn't like his job, like a man who hoped his doctors would tell him to quit.

Even before the doctors got to Huntland, as the Browns called their Virginia estate, Mrs. Johnson prepared a nine-page analysis of the pros and cons, including suggested wording of her husband's announcement of withdrawal:

> Having, by the end of this present term, finished some thirty years of public service, ranging from my young years with the NYA [National Youth Administration] to the House of Representatives, the Senate, the Vice Presidency, and this latterly ultimate responsibility, I wish now to announce that I will not be a candidate for reelection. I wish to spend the rest of my life in my home state, in peace with my family, for whom the rigors of my duties have left me too little time for companionship. This decision is made easier by the fact that I can feel my conduct of the presidency, to which I came in such a tragic hour of national rending, has not been without some solid accomplishment, thanks to the grace of God and the sturdy cooperation of the American people.

There would be drawbacks to such a decision, Lady Bird Johnson wrote. Many, especially active Democrats, would feel betrayed, and "there might be periods of depression and frustration."

Not to mention that a bored, retired Lyndon Johnson might take to heavy drinking again. But he would live longer.

| | |

Among the people who agreed with Martin Luther King that it would be tragic for the Republicans to become the party of white people was Nelson Rockefeller. It was this belief, almost as much as his ego, his determination, and his money that kept him in the race for the Republican nomination after New Hampshire, after all the certified experts had proclaimed his campaign dead.

Together the ego, the money, the determination, and the belief resurrected it. With money and old family connections, Rockefeller won the barely contested primary in West Virginia. Then he went to Oregon.

Nobody else did. After their brief effort to find damaging information about Lodge, the Goldwaterites decided they'd be better off ignoring Oregon; it wasn't their kind of state; it only had eighteen delegates; its only impact might be to give the winner a boost for the California vote on June 2. And

Jacqueline Kennedy and Robert
F. Kennedy at John F. Kennedy's
grave, November 25, 1963.
(UPI/Corbis-Bettmann)

LEFT: F. Clifton White, the architect of the Goldwater Revolution, in his campaign office at Citizens for Goldwater-Miller, in October 1964. *(John M. Ashbrook Center for Public Affairs Archival Collections, Ashland University, Ashland, Ohio)*

BELOW: Not the closest of colleagues. FBI Director J. Edgar Hoover and his nominal boss, Attorney General Robert F. Kennedy, not quite looking at each other at the White House. *(UPI/Corbis-Bettmann)*

ABOVE: Five legends-to-be, Cassius Clay and the Beatles, clown for the camera a few days before Clay's fight with Sonny Liston. *(AP/Wide World Photos)*

RIGHT: Liston ducking away from Clay's cocked right fist during the fifth round of their championship fight in Miami Beach. *(AP/Wide World Photos)*

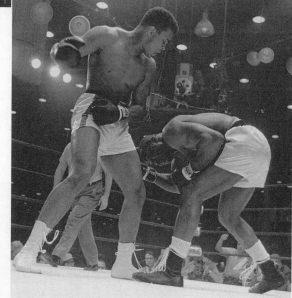

ABOVE, LEFT: And two to go. Senators Hubert Humphrey of Minnesota and Philip Hart of Michigan, with the Reverends Martin Luther King Jr. and Fred Shuttlesworth, celebrate a procedural victory after the Senate agreed to begin debating the House-passed Civil Rights Bill in February 1965. Votes to cut off a Southern filibuster and to pass the bill would not come until the summer. *(UPI/Corbis-Bettmann)*

RIGHT: And here, we would build . . . nothing. Senator Lee Metcalf, a Montana Democrat, and conservationist Howard Zahniser point out some of the proposed wilderness areas that would be created in the legislation they were supporting. *(Courtesy of the Wilderness Society)*

LEFT: UAW President Walter Reuther, flanked by his brother, Victor *(left)*, and his lawyer, Joe Rauh, plot strategy at a political gathering. *(Americans for Democratic Action)*

BELOW: A (literally) star-studded photograph used by the Ford Motor Company to promote its new Mustang, which first appeared in May 1964. *(Ford Photo-media Services)*

ABOVE: Some like him. George Wallace being welcomed by supporters at the airport in Green Bay, Wisconsin, where he campaigned in the Democratic presidential primary. *(AP/Wide World Photos)*

RIGHT: Some don't. Students at St. Norbert College in De Pere, Wisconsin, hissed at Wallace, though he got a polite welcome from Roger Burbach, president of the Young Democrats Club. *(AP/Wide World Photos)*

ABOVE: Happy anniversary. President Johnson congratulates J. Edgar Hoover on spending forty years as FBI director, on the day Johnson issued an executive order waiving the mandatory retirement age for Hoover. *(UPI/Corbis-Bettmann)*

RIGHT: Making his point. Senator Everett Dirksen assumes one of his preferred positions, squatting atop a desk in the Senate Press Gallery to answer reporters' questions about the Civil Rights Bill. *(AP/Wide World Photos)*

BELOW: Conservative hero. Led by members of Young Americans for Freedom, supporters welcome Senator Barry Goldwater to Chicago's O'Hare Airport in February 1964 on his first midwestern swing since announcing his candidacy. *(UPI/Corbis-Bettmann)*

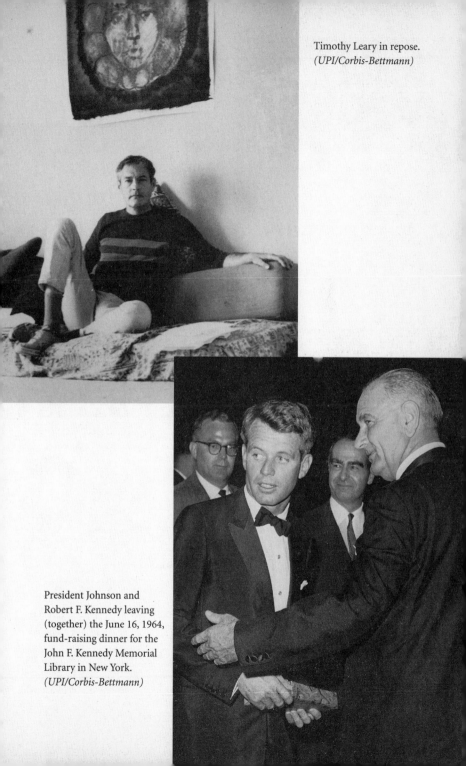

Timothy Leary in repose.
(UPI/Corbis-Bettmann)

President Johnson and
Robert F. Kennedy leaving
(together) the June 16, 1964,
fund-raising dinner for the
John F. Kennedy Memorial
Library in New York.
(UPI/Corbis-Bettmann)

ABOVE: Goatee. Mickey Schwerner, twenty-four years old and dedicated, in a reflective mood. *(UPI/Corbis-Bettman)*

ABOVE, RIGHT: Olan Burrage's dam outside Philadelphia, Mississippi, and the excavating equipment that uncovered the bodies of Schwerner, Goodman, and Chaney. *(UPI/Corbis-Bettmann)*

RIGHT: Missing in action. Thousands of these FBI circulars were distributed in Mississippi, Alabama, Tennessee, Arkansas, and Louisiana after Schwerner, Andrew Goodman, and James Chaney disappeared in Neshoba County, Mississippi. *(UPI/Corbis-Bettmann)*

MISSING CALL FBI

THE FBI IS SEEKING INFORMATION CONCERNING THE DISAPPEARANCE AT PHILADELPHIA, MISSISSIPPI, OF THESE THREE INDIVIDUALS ON JUNE 21, 1964. EXTENSIVE INVESTIGATION IS BEING CONDUCTED TO LOCATE GOODMAN, CHANEY, AND SCHWERNER, WHO ARE DESCRIBED AS FOLLOWS:

	ANDREW GOODMAN	JAMES EARL CHANEY	MICHAEL HENRY SCHWERNER
RACE:	White	Negro	White
SEX:	Male	Male	Male
DOB:	November 23, 1943	May 30, 1943	November 6, 1939
POB:	New York City	Meridian, Mississippi	New York City
AGE:	20 years	21 years	24 years
HEIGHT:	5'10"	5'7"	5'9" to 5'10"
WEIGHT:	150 pounds	135 to 140 pounds	170 to 180 pounds
HAIR:	Dark brown, wavy	Black	Brown
EYES:	Brown	Brown	Light blue
TEETH:		Good, none missing	
SCARS AND MARKS:		1 inch cut scar 2 inches above left ear	Pockmark center of forehead, slight scar on bridge of nose, appendectomy scar, broken leg scar.

SHOULD YOU HAVE OR IN THE FUTURE RECEIVE ANY INFORMATION CONCERNING THE WHEREABOUTS OF THESE INDIVIDUALS, YOU ARE REQUESTED TO NOTIFY ME OR THE NEAREST OFFICE OF THE FBI. TELEPHONE NUMBER IS LISTED BELOW.

Doing business. President Johnson and Senator Hubert Humphrey meet with grain exporter Dwayne Andreas and William Thatcher, president of the National Federation of Grain Cooperatives, to discuss more federal help for grain farmers and exporters. *(UPI/Corbis-Bettmann)*

Attorney General Robert F. Kennedy holding some of the pens President Johnson is using to sign the Civil Rights Act. *(Americans for Democratic Action)*

ABOVE: Responding to an "attack." The National Security Council convenes the day after the U.S. destroyer *Maddox* was or was not attacked by North Vietnamese torpedo boats. President Johnson is flanked by Secretary of State Dean Rusk *(left)* and Defense Secretary Robert McNamara. George Ball is to Rusk's left. Robert Kennedy and Atomic Energy Commission Chairman John McCone are at the end of the table. *(UPI/Corbis-Bettmann)*

RIGHT: Senator Barry M. Goldwater and his wife at the Republican National Convention in San Francisco. *(John M. Ashbrook Center for Public Affairs Archival Collections, Ashland University, Ashland, Ohio)*

ABOVE: An unidentified, but enthusiastic, Illinois delegate expresses her approval of Robert Kennedy at the Democratic National Convention. (AP/Wide World Photos)

ABOVE, RIGHT: "I question America." Fannie Lou Hamer, the sharecropper who was beaten for having the temerity to try to register to vote, tells her story to the Democratic National Convention's Credentials Committee. (UPI/Corbis-Bettmann)

RIGHT: Protest on the Boardwalk. Supporters of Mrs. Hamer and the Freedom Democratic Party outside the convention hall during the second day of the Democratic National Convention in Atlantic City. (AP/Wide World Photos)

ABOVE: President Johnson, with Interior Secretary Stewart Udall behind him to the right, signs the bill creating a 9.2-million-acre National Wilderness System on September 3, 1964. *(Courtesy of the LBJ Memorial Library)*

RIGHT: Cartha DeLoach, J. Edgar Hoover's chief factotum and coordinator of the FBI's political espionage operation at the Democratic National Convention. *(AP/Wide World Photos)*

BELOW: His kind of town. President Johnson, with Illinois Governor Otto Kerner behind him, stands on the back of a car to speak to a crowd at Chicago's O'Hare Airport. *(UPI/Corbis-Bettmann)*

ABOVE: In enemy territory. Campaigning not just in Texas but in Lyndon Johnson's home territory, Barry Goldwater speaks to supporters at the airport in Austin. *(UPI/Corbis-Bettmann)*

BELOW: Allies. Campaigning together in Brooklyn, President Johnson and U.S. Senate candidate Robert F. Kennedy wave to a loyal Democratic crowd. *(UPI/Corbis-Bettmann)*

ABOVE: It's not champagne. But victory barbecue isn't bad either. President Johnson and his vice president elect at the ranch the day after the election. *(UPI/Corbis-Bettmann)*

BELOW: LBJ for USA. The president campaigning in California. In the car behind him are the wife of Governor Edmund Brown and the newly appointed (and soon-to-be-defeated) U.S. senator, Pierre Salinger. *(UPI/Corbis-Bettmann)*

Lodge, who was going to be that winner—he led by more than two to one in the early polls—was no threat in California, where he had no campaign.

But Lodge didn't go to Oregon. As Nelson Rockefeller suspected, Lodge stayed in Saigon, waiting to be crowned the Great Moderate Hope without having to fight for it. Rockefeller went, and he stayed, and he campaigned with the most appropriate slogan—"He cares enough to come"—and the result proved, for neither the first nor the last time, that voters don't like to be taken for granted. On Friday, February 15, Rockefeller got more than a third of the Oregon primary vote, fifteen thousand votes more than Lodge and forty-four thousand more than Goldwater.

| | |

Earlier that day, the Central Intelligence Agency told President Johnson that the South Vietnamese were losing the war. Unless the situation were dealt with quickly, the CIA said, "the anti-Communist position in South Vietnam is likely to become untenable."

Just a few days earlier, General Kanh told Henry Cabot Lodge and Secretary McNamara, who was on yet another trip to Saigon, that his preference was to attack North Vietnam, not because the South Vietnamese Army had the strength to do so, but (he didn't put it quite this bluntly) as a diversion from his own political problems.

McNamara was unconvinced. Lodge was enthusiastic, even though—or perhaps because—he knew how weak Kanh was. He told McNamara that if Kanh were toppled by yet another coup, the United States should forget about who was running Saigon and run the country itself, perhaps from the naval base at Cam Ranh Bay harbor. The United States, Lodge said, could "move into a position of actual control" through a "High Commissioner."

The president was thinking it over.

| | |

The next day was Armed Forces Day. In celebration, twelve young men burned their draft cards, a provocative but not illegal act, at Union Square in New York. What inspired them, they said, was no specific aspect of military or foreign policy but the evil of conscription for whatever cause. "The basic issue is my right of choice," one of them said.

It was an illustrative comment. The young man was saying that he and his friends were less unhappy about their country visiting a war of questionable necessity on a peasant people halfway around the world than about their lack of personal discretion in deciding whether to join it.

| | |

Tuesday, May 19, was Douglas Cater's first day on the job in the White House as special assistant to the president, and he found himself with nothing to do but sit around. Life as a journalist, most recently at the *Reporter* magazine, had been livelier. Late in the afternoon, former secretary of state Dean Acheson invited Cater to his Georgetown home for cocktails. The small-talk portion of the evening did not last long, nor did Cater's illusion that this was merely a social occasion.

"Things are going to hell in a hack in Vietnam," Acheson said, "and if the president does not do something that relates to getting the support of Congress in a Formosa-type resolution, it's going to be too late, and we'll go into this orgasm of a campaign period in which things will just have to stall."

As he assumed he was supposed to, Cater went back to the office and composed a memorandum for the president.[4]

| | |

A few hours earlier, Ev Dirksen met with reporters at the Capitol and explained why he was going to vote for cloture. For support, Dirksen relied on one of the few people in all of human history who might have been wordier than he. On the very night that Victor Hugo died, Dirksen informed the reporters, he had written in his diary that "no army is stronger than an idea whose time has come."

Victor Hugo did not keep a diary. He had written a story called "Histoire d'un Crime," which contained this sentence: "A stand can be made against invasion by an army; no stand can be made against invasion by an idea."

Dirksen had edited Hugo and improved it.

| | |

Oregon affected California, all right. All of a sudden, Rockefeller jumped ahead of Goldwater by a seemingly comfortable 47 to 36 percent margin. And Rockefeller had a superb campaign organization in California. He had the support of the state's top two Republicans, Senator Thomas Kuchel and former governor Goodwin Knight. He was endorsed by the *Los Angeles Times*. He had the expertise of Spencer-Roberts, the oldest and best political consulting firm on earth. They could produce the sharpest television advertising, and Rockefeller could buy all the time that was available.

In sprawling, suburbanized California, as everyone was beginning to learn, political campaigns were won by the side that bought the best and the most TV ads.

Rockefeller had another advantage—Goldwater, who was still prone to outrageous statements. The senator had bowed to some political realities; he was no longer in favor of transforming the Social Security system or selling the Tennessee Valley Authority. But when it came to foreign affairs, he couldn't restrain himself. On Sunday, May 24, he told a questioner on CBS's *Issues and Answers* that "low-yield atomic weapons" could be used in South Vietnam to "defoliate" the jungles, thereby exposing convoys coming down from North Vietnam.

So the reporters, old political hands, and other self-styled experts were all beginning to predict a Rockefeller blowout. They couldn't see where Goldwater's strength lay. That's because his strength was less visible, or, more accurately, because it was not in the usual places.

The day Douglas Cater was drinking Dean Acheson's whiskey and Ev Dirksen was misquoting Victor Hugo was two weeks before the California primary, and Barry Goldwater's volunteers were on the streets. In Los Angeles County alone, more than three hundred thousand voting households were visited by Goldwater canvassers, all reading from the same script, which demanded courtesy.

"DO NOT DEVIATE FROM SUGGESTED QUESTIONING," it insisted. "*NEVER* ASK VOTER *HOW* HE INTENDS TO VOTE. ALWAYS BE FRIENDLY AND DO NOT PRESS."

The message was—be a good neighbor. No message could have been better suited for the situation. The typical southern California suburbanite was a recent immigrant from elsewhere in the country, sociologically out of sorts. The familiarities of home—family, high school, the candy store and parks where people hung out—were back in Michigan or Tennessee. The new communities were subdivisions without downtowns, geographic focus, or much community feeling. A neighbor at the door, friendly but not pushy, was welcome indeed. Thanks to Cliff White, the Goldwater campaign knew that there was more than politics to politics.

| | |

At the end of that day, the ballots from the Maryland primary were counted. George Wallace led in the early returns. Late in the evening, Maryland's secretary of state appeared on television to announce that there had been a "recapitulation" of the results and that Senator Daniel Brewster, President Johnson's stand-in, was now in the lead.

Wallace, who ended with 43 percent of the vote, would tell the story for years, with emphasis on the repeated use of the word *recapitulate,* and conclude by saying, "Now, I don't rightly know what this *recapitulate* means, but lemme tell you folks, anybody ever tell you he goin' *recapitulate* on you, you better watch out."

Even with the recapitulation, 43 percent was a powerful showing. Considering the strong Negro vote in Baltimore, it was obvious that a majority of white Democrats had voted for Wallace. "I wish I had entered California," he said.

| 17 |

A GREAT SOCIETY

In considering his president's orders to come up with "the Johnson Program," Richard Goodwin adopted a rather loose interpretation of *program*. He would develop more than a legislative laundry list; he would give voice to an idea, the idea that affluence was not enough, "that private income, a decent standard of living, was only a foundation," as he later wrote, "that private affluence, no matter how widely distributed, could not remedy many of the public conditions that diminished the possibilities of American life."

This was less an analysis than an attitude, and Goodwin didn't invent it. Betty Friedan's book *The Feminine Mystique* owed its popularity to the growing sense that social realities prevented women, no matter how wealthy, from fulfilling their potential. The forces fighting those dams and saving the wilderness also reflected the growing awareness that "the pursuit of happiness" required more than wealth, more even than the equitable distribution of wealth. Tom Hayden's *Port Huron Statement* had suggested that America's apparent contentment with its prosperity "might . . . better be called a glaze above deeply felt anxieties."

Goodwin played with all these notions, and Thursday night, May 21, he brought the draft of a speech to Moyers. The next morning, they took it to the president, who sat behind his desk reading it slowly while the two of them stood there. Then he read it again. Goodwin was not at ease.

After his second reading, Johnson looked up and said, "It ought to do just fine, boys. Just what I told you."

Then the president called Jack Valenti into the Oval Office and said, "What time's that damn plane leave? And why are we always running out of Fresca?"

III

On Friday, May 22, exactly six months after John F. Kennedy's assassination, his successor bent his head as a sash of blue, maize, and purple—the University of Michigan's colors—was draped around his head in front of a throng of eighty thousand in the fabled stadium where the Wolverines played their Big Ten football games. Then he straightened up, went to the microphone, and preached something more ambitious than the dogmas of social justice and economic growth that he had been advocating.

Being rich isn't good enough, either for individuals or for a country, LBJ said. Instead, "the challenge of the next half-century is whether we have the wisdom to use that wealth to enrich and elevate our national life and to advance the quality of American civilization."

Otherwise, important values might be "buried under unbridled growth." Already, he said, "expansion is eroding the precious . . . value of community with neighbors and communion with nature. The loss of these values breeds loneliness and boredom and indifference."

These were, of course, the difficulties that might convince suburbanites to vote for Barry Goldwater.

Even the world's highest gross national product could not create a civilization "where leisure is a welcome chance to build and reflect, not a feared cause of boredom and restlessness . . . where the city of man serves not only the needs of the body and the demands of commerce, but the desire for beauty and the hunger for community."

Johnson also spoke of creating "a place where man can renew contact with nature . . . which honors creation for its own sake, and for what it adds to the understanding of the race . . . a place where men are more concerned with the quality of their goals than the quantity of their goods . . . where the demands of morality, and the needs of the spirit, can be realized in the life of the nation."

To the attentive graduates and their proud parents, he used the same phrase ignored the previous month by those raucous Chicago Democrats. He called his vision "the Great Society."

It was Richard Goodwin's phrase, of course. Johnson had not told Goodwin what he wanted, but he accepted it as if he had been thinking similar thoughts all his life, without ever uttering them. Maybe he got some of it from J. William Fulbright. For years, Fulbright had been making speeches with a theme often heard from the pulpit, the classroom, or the foundation report but rarely from a politician: the notion that it would be possible to "create a good society" in America.

"Good" was never enough for Johnson.

Neither he nor Goodwin invented the term. Back in 1914, Graham Wallas, an Englishman who taught at Harvard, had written a book called *The Great Society*. Among his students was Walter Lippmann, who later wrote a book with the more modest title *The Good Society*, which helped inspire Fulbright's speeches. Then, in the mid-1950s, historian Arthur Schlesinger Jr. wrote an essay called "The Future of Liberalism—The Challenge of Abundance," which drew a distinction between "quantitative liberalism" and "qualitative liberalism," the latter possible in this new age of material abundance.[1]

There is no evidence that Lyndon Johnson read any of those works. He was a politician, not a scholar, and a politician whose own wife once described him as a man with "no natural cultural bent."[2] But he was a thoughtful and observant politician who was reacting to, and reflecting, the society that was changing around him.

Or maybe he had more of a natural cultural bent than even his own wife recognized. Certainly, he had been brought up to have one. Rebekah Johnson read poetry to her little boy, repeating passages by Longfellow and Tennyson so often that three-year-old Lyndon could recite them. When he finished reciting, she would hug him. Nothing delighted her more. Nothing provided this cultured, genteel woman more solace from her unsatisfying marriage to hard-drinking, tough-talking Sam Ealy Johnson, who had neither the wealth nor the social distinction with which she was raised.

She taught Lyndon the alphabet when he was two and made sure he could read before he went to school. She kept his hair in long curls, which she would comb as lovingly as she brushed her own dark hair. When he got a little older, she bought him a violin.

Sam Johnson did not like his son's curls. One Sunday morning when Rebekah was at church, Sam, not a churchgoing man, took a big pair of scissors and cut them off. No one was going to turn his boy into a namby-pamby. Like many a hard-drinking Texas farmer, Sam Johnson did not simply ignore culture; he disdained it as unmanly. Rebekah tried to instill a love of literature, music, and gentility into her son, and Sam wanted him to be a tough Texan. In another time and place, a boy as smart as Lyndon might have figured out that these were not mutually exclusive directions. In west Texas in the second decade of the twentieth century, Lyndon could not. He had to choose.

At some point, he chose Sam's way. In his middle elementary school years, Lyndon grew closer to his father. He stopped being a good pupil and began to be a troublemaker at school. He started drinking as a young teenager.

He went squirrel and rabbit hunting with the other guys, and though he was at first reluctant to kill an animal, he shot a rabbit after his father taunted him about being the only boy in the neighborhood who hadn't brought home some game. He became Sam Johnson's tough kid.

But how can a boy who slept in his mother's bed and hungered for her hugs reject her without regret? Rebekah Johnson was still alive in 1964, still idolized by her son. The Great Society may have been repentance as well as policy.

| | |

The day after the Ann Arbor speech, a new kind of newspaper that openly billed itself as offbeat and "underground" began publishing in Los Angeles. It was called the *Los Angeles Free Press*. Two days later, New York's Museum of Modern Art opened two new wings, one of which contained the first permanent photography gallery in an American museum.

That night, a new play called *The Subject Was Roses* opened on Broadway. The critics loved it; Walter Kerr called it "quite the most interesting new American play to be offered on Broadway this season." Unfortunately, the public did not feel the same way.

There was a similar disconnect between popularity and critical acclaim reflected in the Emmy Awards presented that same evening, some of them to programs that had attracted modest audiences. Jack Klugman won for his role in *Blacklist*, and other awards went to *The Defenders*, to Shelley Winters, and to both Dick Van Dyke and Mary Tyler Moore for *The Dick Van Dyke Show* (this one did have a big audience), which was also named the best comedy series.

| | |

The senior staff of the Warren Commission flew to Dallas on Sunday, May 24, to observe an elaborate re-creation of President Kennedy's assassination. FBI agents posing as Kennedy and Governor John Connally sat in a limousine identical to the one the men rode in on November 22. The re-creation was not an academic exercise. Test firings with a rifle identical to Oswald's had raised grave doubts that even an expert marksman could have squeezed off three shots accurately enough to hit Kennedy and Connally in the time Oswald had to aim and fire from his sixth-story window.

But Arlen Specter of the Warren Commission had come up with a possible explanation: Perhaps one of the two bullets that hit Kennedy was also the one that wounded Governor Connally. The re-creation of the motorcade was to test out this "single bullet" theory.

| | |

On Tuesday, May 26, Mike Mansfield, Hubert Humphrey, Everett Dirksen, and Thomas Kuchel introduced a seventy-four-page substitute for the civil rights bill. Humphrey announced that he would call for cloture vote on June 9. He also referred to the measure as "the Dirksen substitute."

For the civil rights forces, this was such good news that President Johnson generously praised Robert Kennedy on the phone. But Johnson still doubted that the Senate would vote to cut off debate. So deep was the mutual distrust of the two sides that liberal senators and their allies continued to watch for Southern dirty tricks. But there were to be no tricks, dirty or otherwise. Russell and his Southerners were out of spirit as they were out of favor. Only arithmetic was on their side. With eighteen segregationist Southern Democrats plus John Tower of Texas manning the barricades, they needed but twelve more votes to stave off defeat. Considering that there were twenty-one conservative Republicans, that didn't seem out of reach.

But Russell had no strategy. Like Humphrey, he had tactics: His troops were organized so that six of the Southerners were on the floor at all times in the same three-platoon system that had worked before. But Russell's only plan was to keep talking until the civil rights liberals started fighting among themselves. They always had. Maybe Russell thought nothing had changed.

Or perhaps he knew that everything already had changed. He was leading this fight in part so that white Southerners would know that he and his colleagues had done everything that could have been done to block the bill. If they lost a fair and hard fight, he thought, white Southerners would be more likely to accept the changes in their day-to-day lives the bill would dictate.[3] His sense of national responsibility challenged, if it did not conquer, his passion for his parochial past.

| | |

The day after the Dirksen substitute was announced, a troubled Lyndon Johnson called his old friend Dick Russell.

"What do you think of this Vietnam thing?" the president said. "I'd like to hear you talk a little bit."

There was a context to this question. The president knew that he could not long avoid making the pivotal decision over what to do about Vietnam. A few days earlier, he had asked McGeorge Bundy to prepare a new set of recommendations, and Bundy had immediately set up four "working groups" of foreign policy and military experts. Johnson wanted to consult one expert whom Bundy would not.

"It's the damn worst mess I ever saw," Russell said, "and I don't see how we're ever going to get out of it without fighting a major war with the Chinese and all of them down there in those rice paddies and jungles."

The Chinese, of course, were not there. Russell was extrapolating. But he was also thinking, and he told the president that he had an idea that might get them out of this fix. How about arranging another coup?

"I'd get the same crowd that got rid of old Diem and get rid of those people and get some fellow in there that said he wished to hell we would get out," he said. After all, Vietnam "isn't important a damn bit, with all these new missile systems."

This was such wise advice that it is a wonder Johnson did not accept it, or even consider it. A few years earlier, he might have. Until Russell became known primarily as the leader of the anti–civil rights forces, his open support would insulate any president from the charge that he wasn't tough enough or anticommunist enough. But the race issue and his stand on the civil rights bill had marginalized Russell. Johnson must have known that his old friend was no longer capable of providing political cover to anyone.

|||

John F. Kennedy would have been forty-seven years old on Friday, May 29. His widow took her children to Arlington National Cemetery, where they placed flowers on his grave before attending a memorial Mass at St. Matthew's. From there, they flew to Hyannis Port.

The picture on the cover of the May 29 issue of *Life* magazine was of Mrs. Kennedy, her dark hair dipped over one eye, her gaze both firm and mysterious, as though she were a cross between the Mona Lisa and Veronica Lake. Inside, under her byline, was a short essay about John Kennedy's favorite possessions, his books, his love of poetry. His literary appreciation inspired him, Mrs. Kennedy said, to scorn the children's poetry that bored him and teach their daughter, Caroline, Shakespeare's "Where the bee sucks, there suck I." There was no mention of whether either adult Kennedy was aware of the erotic undertone of the verse.

Nor was there any public announcement of the fact that Mrs. Kennedy had decided to leave Washington, in part because she was tired of being a tourist attraction. Every day, crowds gathered near her N Street house in hopes of catching a glimpse of her. Photographers, amateur and professional, hung around, too, and if she did not precisely consider them predators, she certainly felt as though she were someone's prey. At the suggestion of her sister, Lee Radziwell, Mrs. Kennedy put her Georgetown house on the market.

That Monday, in preparation for the strategy session on Vietnam to be held in Honolulu during the first two days of June, McGeorge Bundy and his working groups completed the report the president had requested ten days earlier suggesting just what Lyndon Johnson didn't want—an American war in Vietnam.

This report, *Basic Recommendations and Projected Course of Action on Southeast Asia,* proposed getting from the Congress a resolution giving the president the right to use force in defense of any nation in Southeast Asia menaced by communist "aggression or subversion." The politically astute drafters even prepared a scenario of replies to "disagreeable questions" that might emanate from the representatives of the people.

Were one of them to ask, for instance, whether this resolution implied a blank check, the answer proposed was that "hostilities on a larger scale are not envisaged."

| | |

Two personal events took place that same day. In a telephone call from Los Angeles, a tired Martin Luther King had a bitter quarrel with his wife, who was upset over his frequent absences from home. Their distress was welcomed by the FBI agents who overheard the discussion.

And in New York's Lying-In Hospital, Margaretta Rockefeller gave birth to a healthy seven-pound, ten-ounce baby boy. They named him Nelson Rockefeller Jr. When asked about the event, Barry Goldwater said he thought it was "great."

In Shea Stadium the next day, the San Francisco Giants and the New York Mets played the longest game in history. After seven hours and twenty-three minutes, the Giants won the twenty-three-inning game 8 to 6. It was the second game of a doubleheader.

| | |

On Memorial Day, Sunday, May 31, Mickey Schwerner made a speech at the Mount Zion Church in Neshoba County to convince the congregation to allow a freedom school to be set up. There was no time to spare. By the third week of June, the student volunteers would be coming down from the North, ready to teach, but they needed classrooms to work in. For now, they were in Oxford, Ohio, at Western College for Women, learning what to expect when they got to Mississippi and how to deal with it.

Mickey and James Chaney would be going up to Oxford to help out with the training. About the same time they started out, in that blue Ford wagon, Andy Goodman was packing his bag in his parents' New York apartment. He was heading to Oxford, too.

The lead story in that morning's *New York Times* was a preview and prediction of the pivotal California primary two days hence. "The long and strange Republican Presidential primary election campaign is now virtually finished," wrote James Reston, "and so, apparently, are the two principal candidates."

Though the polls said that Rockefeller would win the final primary, Reston wrote, the "professional politicians swear" that they will not nominate him at the convention. "The hunt for a compromise is now centering on Gov. William W. Scranton of Pennsylvania and former Vice President Richard M. Nixon," Reston informed an anxious world.

At least one man was taking him seriously. The previous day Richard Nixon had once again invited some of his closest advisors to a suite at the Waldorf-Astoria to consider what to do should Rockefeller win California.

| | |

On Monday, June 1, the Philadelphia Phillies and Chicago White Sox were in first place. The Boston Red Sox were far from the lead, but fans were flocking to Fenway Park every night, some of them hoping their team would get into just enough trouble to call on colorful relief pitcher Dick "The Monster" Radatz, who would kick the dirt, yell and scream at himself or no one, and then usually pitch his way out of a jam. On the radio the Beach Boys were singing about how they get around and the Four Seasons were serenading their "Rag Doll." Readers were gobbling up Ernest Hemingway's posthumous memoir, *A Moveable Feast,* and moviegoers transported themselves into medieval tragedy in *Becket* with Peter O'Toole as Henry II and Richard Burton as his doomed prelate or into the fantastic present in *From Russia with Love.*

In the mundane present, the secretaries of state and defense met in Honolulu with the American civilian and military chiefs based in Vietnam. Ambassador Lodge and General William Westmoreland, the new military commander, told them things were looking better, and Westmoreland was particularly enthusiastic about his "crash pacification program" in eight critical provinces. Before the month was out, he would ask for 900 more advisors.

The Honolulu meetings ended on Tuesday, June 2, Nelson Rockefeller Jr.'s third day on earth and, for all practical purposes, his father's last as a presidential candidate. Nelson senior got 1,030,180 votes in that day's California primary, only 48,953 fewer than Barry Goldwater got, but the margin didn't matter. At this stage of the campaign, coming in second in a two-man race was defeat.

Clad in a big white nightshirt with red polka dots, Goldwater watched the good news unfold in the Royal Suite of the Ambassador Hotel in Los Angeles. The loser was back in New York with the wife and baby who might have cost him victory.

The results confounded the pollsters, whose last surveys had indicated that Rockefeller would win. Had people been lying to the pollsters? Or did some thousands of Rockefeller voters stay home, perhaps even switch to Goldwater, when Nelson junior's arrival reminded them about Nelson senior's past?

No one can ever know, nor does it matter. By that night, there was no real doubt about who the Republican presidential nominee would be.

| | |

On Wednesday, June 3, President Johnson told the graduating class at the U.S. Coast Guard Academy that the military strength of the United States surpassed "the combined might of all the nations in the history of the world."

Even the mightiest find that their strength flags now and then. For the superpower known as Sandy Koufax, this had been a disappointing spring. By early June, he had only five wins against an astounding four losses, just one less than he'd had the entire previous season.

His next start came on Thursday, June 4, in Philadelphia, and now the left arm was crackling. Richie Allen walked, but was thrown out trying to steal second. Nobody else got on base. With two out in the bottom of the ninth and the Dodgers leading 3 to 0, Bobby Wine took ball one, fouled a pitch off umpire Ed Bargo's leg, and then swung and missed for strike two. He did not swing at the next pitch, but Bargo called him out. Koufax had his third no-hitter, and he would lose but one more game all year long.

That was mighty.

| | |

The next day Senator Bourke Hickenlooper, Republican of Iowa, claiming the support of at least seventeen other Republicans, arose to say he wanted the cloture vote put off one day, until June 10, so that the Senate could debate and vote on three amendments he and his colleagues wished to propose. He asked for unanimous consent.

He got it. Humphrey and Hickenlooper had talked. Two of the amendments were unobjectionable, and the other couldn't pass, so Humphrey was willing to let them come to a vote. In fact, he went a step further: If the Senate's majority accepted any of these amendments, why, by golly, so would he.

Wait a minute, said Russell; he had been accorded no such courtesy.

"Well, Dick," Humphrey said, "you haven't any votes to give us for cloture, and these fellows do."[4]

In fact, they'd already given them. In return for allowing a vote on the amendments, Humphrey had gotten the votes of Hickenlooper, Norris Cotton, Roman Hruska, and Karl Mundt. Hickenlooper came cheap, as Humphrey, who understood both Senate politics and human psychology, knew he would. He knew that what was really bothering Hickenlooper had nothing to do with the legislation; it had to do with all the attention Dirksen was getting. Hickenlooper wanted to be courted; he wanted his name in some paper other than the *Des Moines Register*.

Hubert could deal with that. Especially because by picking off those four conservatives, he had all but isolated Goldwater. Now only four other senators would join the nominee-presumptive as anti–civil rights Republicans. Goldwater took pains in those days to assure the world that he was no bigot. He was not. His store had been one of the first in Phoenix to employ Negroes, and he had helped integrate the Arizona Air National Guard. He was even a member of the Tucson chapter of the NAACP. "I don't like segregation in any form, any place, amongst any people," he said.

But neither was he all that bothered by it. "There was never a lot of it [in Phoenix]," he once said, in sincerity and ignorance. He grew up in a segregated setting without noticing its segregation. For years, his store gave a wristwatch to the top graduate of all the high schools in Phoenix, all except George Washington Carver, where the Negro kids went. As soon as someone brought this to Goldwater's attention, he added Carver to the list.

This insensitivity was consistent with Goldwater's individualism. In his worldview, there were no groups; everyone was in an equal position of personal autonomy. To recognize that Negroes might have collective grievances requiring collective remedy would come dangerously close to recognizing something similar about factory workers, miners, or store clerks.

Not that any of this really mattered. Politically, Goldwater had no choice but to oppose cloture and the civil rights bill. The Cliff White strategy was a Southern white strategy, abetted by Northern conservatives who were not racist but who somehow never found an expression of Negro aspirations they could admire. The *National Review,* typically, had described the 1963 March on Washington as "mob deployment."

Like Goldwater, Cliff White was no racist. But as a conservative political strategist, he knew what George Wallace knew, that race was conservatism's entree to support from the broader public. For decades, a few conservative intellectuals and a few entrepreneurs disliked government. Rank-and-file voters never did. They liked highways, clean water in their faucets, public schools, parks, a strong military, Social Security, and protection for workers. Hating the government never got political legs until the government made it against the law to discriminate against people because of the color of their skin.

From the beginning, White's nomination strategy was based on the South. He needed 661 delegate votes, and he started with a base of 451 he thought he could win easily. All 451 came from nine Southern states, the whole Confederacy except Tennessee and Georgia, and they were in his second tier of target states.[5] There were reasons other than resistance to racial equality that helped explain the rise of Southern conservatism. But all those other reasons paled in comparison. Only the West depended on the federal government more than the South did. Only the civil rights movement made Goldwaterism strong in the South, where 75 percent of Negro adults were not registered.

Opposition to civil rights, or at least to this bill, was central to the Goldwater campaign. It was nothing he had to be talked into. As early as 1961, Goldwater had told a Republican audience in Atlanta that their party wasn't going to get many Negro votes anyway, "so we ought to go hunting where the ducks are."[6] He would vote no.

| | |

On Friday, June 5, President Johnson received two items of information on the matter of racial politics, one merely annoying, one deeply disturbing. The annoyance was George Wallace's announcement that he would run for president as an independent candidate. Johnson had expected that news, and anyway, Wallace was likely to take more votes from Goldwater than from the president.

He was not expecting a memorandum from Attorney General Robert Kennedy warning him that the situation in Mississippi was becoming increasingly dangerous. Terrorism, often abetted by the local sheriffs, was common. "It seems to me," he wrote, "that this situation presents new and quite unprecedented problems of law enforcement."

The president was convinced that Kennedy was right, and a few days later Al Rosen, the assistant director in charge of the FBI's criminal division, sent inspector Joseph Sullivan into the state, where the FBI had no office. Sullivan was a six-foot two-inch experienced, capable, and honest cop, and for all his loyalty to the Bureau, he was not impressed with its agents in Memphis, who were responsible for Mississippi but rarely went there. He decided to wait in Memphis through the weekend of June 19–21, when the first Northern students would arrive in Mississippi.

|||

That afternoon, Chief Justice Warren went to Jacqueline Kennedy's Georgetown home to take her testimony for his commission's investigation. The visit was as much courtesy as substance; there was little she could tell him that he and his staff did not already know. Two days later, Warren and Gerald Ford went to Dallas to interrogate Jack Ruby, who repeated his earlier insistence that he killed Oswald only out of sympathy for President Kennedy's family and anger at his murderer.

"A fellow whom I sort of idolized is of the Catholic faith and a gambler," Ruby told Warren and Ford, "and I knew that Kennedy, being Catholic, I knew how heartbroken he was, and even his picture—of this Mr. McWillie— flashed across me, because I have a great fondness for him. All that blended into the thing that, like a screwball, the way it turned out, that I thought I would sacrifice myself for the few moments of saving Mrs. Kennedy the discomfiture of coming back to trial." The commissioners seemed unimpressed. Ruby, Ford later wrote, was "unstable." He "spoke in a rambling fashion and didn't contribute much."[7]

|||

Attorney General Kennedy brought suit on Friday, June 19, to prevent the General Telephone and Electronics Corporation from acquiring three large independent telephone companies out West. In the view of the Justice Department, the merger would violate Section 7 of the Clayton Act banning mergers that would "substantially lessen competition."

In this case, said the government, competition would diminish because General Telephone manufactured much of the telephone equipment it used, and after the merger it could be expected to insist that its new subsidiaries buy from it instead of on the open market.

But more was at stake here than the specifics of this case. Emboldened by an April Supreme Court ruling against corporate mergers, the Justice Department was asserting itself and the authority of government at the same time that the nation's largest corporations were asserting themselves.

Corporate America was in the throes of its third major consolidation era, as companies combined to achieve greater control over their markets and their suppliers. Manufacturers were buying up the stores that sold their products. Cement producers were acquiring ready-mixed concrete firms. The Minnesota Mining and Manufacturing Company, which made the tapes used by radio stations, bought the Mutual Broadcasting System. The Gannett newspaper chain gobbled up eight suburban newspapers on Wednesday, April 1, when it bought the Macy newspapers of New York's Westchester County suburbs.

Big businesses, like presidents, had to have nationwide scope. That's why Standard Oil paid $329 million for John Getty's Tidewater Oil Company, taking over a refinery and thirty-nine hundred service stations in seven Western states. Soon, Esso signs would be seen not just east of the Mississippi but coast to coast.

While moving together, the largest companies were also moving away. Two electronics firms, General Instrument Corporation and First Capacitator, were building electronic assembly plants in Taiwan. Fairchild, which already had a plant in Hong Kong, was expanding its operations there.[8]

For these companies, this was good business. Electronic components are tiny and therefore cheap to ship. They were also easy to manufacture and inexpensive as long as the cost of labor was low. In Asia, it was very low.

Big business had big plans—to move jobs overseas, to consolidate, to develop new products. It didn't want the government interfering.

Neither, as it turns out, did Attorney General Kennedy's boss. Lyndon Johnson was opposed to these antitrust cases. His plan was not to bother corporate America but to seduce it. Robert Kennedy's aggressiveness in this matter was one more thing Johnson would discuss with him, when he got around to talking to him.

| | |

In politics, the process creates its own dynamic. Even though the contest is over, until the process ends, the contest continues. That's why, although the race for the Republican presidential nomination was over, it went on. There was still a convention.

Conventions didn't matter anymore, but hardly anyone had figured that out yet. Some people still believed that there were powerful men in the world who could operate behind the scenes and who could "make things happen." James Reston obviously thought this, and so did Lyndon Johnson. Reston was certain that, in the end, the powerful men—Henry Luce, perhaps, or the bankers—would throw the Republican convention to Scranton or Lodge or even Nixon. Henry Luce and the bankers agreed that they had such power. Only twelve years earlier, they had outwitted this same yahoo faction to nominate Eisenhower. The folks who had run the Republican Party for years were really miffed that they had been beaten by this conservative juggernaut, and beaten by a fellow and a force that were a touch déclassé. But they were also a legitimate constituency, and if there was snobbery and bitterness in their hostility to Goldwater, there was also policy, even principle. Theirs had been the party of caution, of conciliation. Most important, theirs had been the party of civil rights.

Certainly, that was most important to Nelson Rockefeller. His great-grandfather, Harvey Buel Spelman, was the abolitionist who had helped escaped slaves in Ohio. Not just the Rockefellers, but also the Spelmans and the Aldriches had always supported Negro causes. The family had endowed the first Negro women's college, Spelman College, back in 1876. For Nelson Rockefeller, abandoning civil rights would have been a rejection of his heritage.

And this was one part of his heritage he had embraced enthusiastically. Openly, the Rockefellers gave money to Negro colleges, to the NAACP, even to Martin Luther King's Southern Christian Leadership Conference. Secretly, Nelson Rockefeller gave money to CORE, to King, and, yes, even to SNCC.

So Nelson Rockefeller was not going to let the Republican Party become an anti–civil rights party without a fight. Barely had the California votes been counted than he deputized his chief political aide, a young lawyer named Robert Douglass, to see if anything could be done to head off Goldwater's nomination.

Douglass immediately got together with Thomas E. Dewey's political circle. Dewey himself was busy, so Douglass met with New York Brahmins Lucius Clay and John McCloy and later reported to Dewey by phone. They only had one choice, so that's the choice they made. They were going to try to stop Goldwater with Bill Scranton. Money would not be a problem. Douglass then went to Harrisburg, Pennsylvania, to put himself into Scranton's service.

Thus began one of the most bizarre, if ultimately meaningless, little episodes in American political history—the "Stop Goldwater" campaign, featuring William Scranton, Dwight Eisenhower, George Romney, Richard Nixon, and Nelson Rockefeller, all of whom, save Rockefeller, succeeded only in making fools of themselves.

Even before the California primary, Scranton had asked Pennsylvania Republican senator Hugh Scott to ask Eisenhower's brother Milton to ask Dwight Eisenhower to ask Scranton to visit him at his farm in Gettysburg. This was not a subtle hint, and Ike took it. Scranton toodled out to Gettysburg on Saturday, June 6, hoping for the patriarch's blessing. All he got was the suggestion that he make himself "more available."[9]

Toward that end, he betook himself the next day to Cleveland, to the National Governors Conference. Most of the sixteen Republican governors were moderates—governors have to govern—and most were against Goldwater. Scranton had it all figured out. On Sunday, he would appear on *Face the Nation,* and armed with Eisenhower's endorsement, he would announce right there on CBS that he was a presidential candidate.

But then something went awry. Ike went to the conference, too, but if he ever planned to back Scranton, he changed his mind, perhaps influenced by his host and former treasury secretary, the very conservative George Humphrey. On Sunday morning, Ike called Scranton and told him he'd be part of no "cabal."

Shaken, and telling no one about the phone call, Scranton went to the Sunday breakfast meeting of the Republican governors, most of whom were worried about what would happen in their states if Goldwater led the ticket. The most vociferous was Romney, who had words with Paul Fannin of Arizona, one of the few pro-Goldwater governors. After a few minutes, Rockefeller backer Mark Hatfield of Oregon entered the fray, but not on Romney's side.

"Where have you been for the last six months?" he asked Romney, and he looked over at Scranton, too. "Rockefeller has been working his head off day and night for the past six months while both of you have remained gloriously silent. Any stop-Goldwater movement now by you eleventh-hour warriors is an exercise in futility."

Scranton, adept at futility if nothing else, went from the breakfast to the studios of KYW-TV for his *Face the Nation* appearance. In his pocket, on a sheet of white paper, was the statement announcing his candidacy. As he sat down, he pulled it out of his pocket and laid it, folded in thirds, on the table in front of him.

Where it sat, untouched, unopened, and unmentioned, for half an hour, while he hemmed, hawed, hedged, and said nothing stronger than "If the majority of the delegates at the convention want me, I would serve."

Who wouldn't?

The extent of his failure was illustrated by the response of his most important ally, Nelson Rockefeller, when asked whether Scranton was displaying the "responsibilities of leadership."

"Did you see him on television?" Rockefeller asked.

By evening, Scranton had regained his bearings, and he began to hold meetings with his fellow-governors. Late at night, in the suite of Governor John Rhodes of Ohio, Scranton, Rhodes, and Rockefeller had a new stop-Goldwater candidate—George Romney.

| | |

Back in May, Walter Jenkins had commissioned the Oliver Quayle firm to do a poll of Maryland. Quayle did it quickly, and Johnson read his fifty-five-page report immediately. He liked what he saw, and soon enough Quayle's interviewers were making calls to Indiana and Wisconsin, too, to all the states where George Wallace had done well.

The results were conclusive. The white backlash was not a threat, at least not yet. Yes, some urban Democrats were mad enough about civil rights that they might vote Republican. But they were outnumbered by the Republicans who were going to vote for Johnson.

This didn't mean only that the president was as close to unbeatable as any mortal ever is; it meant that he could pick Humphrey, McCarthy, or the Man in the Moon to be his running mate, and it wouldn't matter. If there was ever any doubt in his mind, it was gone by mid-June: He was totally liberated from any need to consider Robert Kennedy.

| | |

At 4:30 A.M. on Saturday, a few hours before Bill Scranton went to see Ike, McGeorge Bundy woke up Lyndon Johnson with the news that an American reconnaissance plane had been shot down over Laos. The next day, the Laotian communists knocked another U.S. plane out of the sky, a fighter jet this time. The jet pilot was recovered, but the pilot of the first plane was not.

The obvious response was to take out the antiaircraft batteries firing at the planes, but Laotian prince Souvanna Phouma had agreed only to American reconnaissance flights, not to American attacks on his territory.

Johnson decided to attack anyway, on Monday night, June 8. It failed.

This seemed to be in keeping with everything else that was failing in Vietnam. "It's a very weak situation," Robert McNamara told the president on Tuesday, June 9, in a conversation in which the president made it clear he was rejecting Dick Russell's advice to find an excuse to abandon Vietnam.

Majority Leader Mike Mansfield had made a similar suggestion to the president, and in his conversation with McNamara, Johnson was referring to Mansfield, not Russell, but their suggestions were interchangeable. "What he comes out and says is he thinks we ought to get out of there," Johnson said. "Which we can't and are not going to do."

He never said why.

18

OUR FREEDOM YEAR

As U.S. planes were bombing Laos, J. Edgar Hoover sent Robert Kennedy a note informing him that one Frank Capell, the publisher of a right-wing newsletter called the *Herald of Freedom,* had advised the New York FBI office that he was publishing a seventy-page paperback called *The Strange Death of Marilyn Monroe.* The book, Hoover wrote, "will make reference to your alleged friendship [with Monroe]. He will indicate in his book that you and Miss Monroe were intimate and that you were in Miss Monroe's apartment at the time of her death."

For Kennedy, this information was more annoyance than problem. Capell's books were self-published, narrowly marketed, and barely noticed outside his tiny circle of conspiracy-theory right-wingers. But for Hoover, the move was a twofer; he was earning Kennedy's gratitude and hinting as subtly as he ever hinted that he might have some damaging, if spurious, information about the attorney general.

| | |

That Tuesday, Humphrey told Johnson that the votes for cloture were in hand, and Richard Nixon got to Cleveland. He checked into the Sheraton-Cleveland at 12:30 and started to hold court, mostly with aides to Ohio governor John Rhodes, whose latest news, that Romney was now the man, surprised even Nixon, who did not surprise easily.

As it happened, Romney was Nixon's breakfast guest at 7 A.M. You're the man, Nixon told him, sipping black coffee, to stop Goldwater and become the nominee. Romney, a Mormon who eschewed coffee, sipped his breakfast milk and protested that he had pledged to serve a full term as governor.

But Nixon had a plan, and the more he discussed it, the more interested Romney became. Ohio chairman Ray Bliss might throw his state's delegates to Romney. The only trouble was that Nixon had never discussed this with Bliss, who said he would not endorse anyone except his governor, James Rhodes, as a favorite son. Romney's enthusiasm quickly faded.

Nonetheless, at a press conference the next morning, Nixon said that "it would be a tragedy if Senator Goldwater's views, as previously stated, were not challenged—and repudiated."

Nixon was still playing for a convention deadlock.

| | |

At 7:58 P.M. on Tuesday, June 9, Senator Robert Byrd of West Virginia took the floor of the Senate. He began by reading the entire text of the Magna Carta, which would be 749 years old the following week. He was still talking when the dawn broke, explaining now how he had "attempted to reach some understanding as to the Scriptural basis upon which we are implored to enact the proposed legislation." To no one's surprise, he proclaimed, "I find none."

Indeed, he reported, the Bible barely mentioned race, and neither had most of the American evangelists. "Shall responsible men and women be persuaded that throughout the religious history of this country, they failed to preach the truth?" he asked. If so, "I might say to Christians that Christ died in vain."

If anything, he went on, Scripture endorsed segregation. Did not Leviticus prohibit letting "thy cattle gender with a diverse kind"? Yes, it says we must love our neighbor, but it "does not say that we may not *choose* our neighbor."

At 10:11 A.M., he sat down.

It was now Wednesday, June 10, the seventy-fifth day of the filibuster. Old Carl Hayden, the president pro tem, had never voted for cloture and said he never would, not out of opposition to civil rights but out of conviction that the filibuster rule protected small states such as his. So Lee Metcalf of Montana presided in his place. The chamber had never been both so full and so quiet. With a red rose in his lapel, Humphrey stood to begin the brief procedural debate on taking up the cloture vote.

"I say to my colleagues of the Senate that perhaps in your lives you will be able to tell your children's children that you were here for America to make the year 1964 our freedom year. I urge my colleagues to make that dream of full freedom, full justice, and full citizenship for every American a reality by their votes on this day, and it will be remembered until the ending of the world."

Because he didn't care who'd get credit, because he knew he'd get his share, because he'd promised, Humphrey left the closing oration to Dirksen, who rose to the occasion. Considering the occasion, it was no small ascent.

Dirksen went back to his misquote of Victor Hugo: "Stronger than an army is an idea whose time has come," he intoned, pompously but perfectly. "The time has come for equality of opportunity in government, in education, and in employment. It will not be stayed or denied. It is here."

Just before he finished, Metcalf banged the gavel. It was time to vote.

"The chair submits to the Senate, without debate, the question: Is it the sense of the Senate that the debate shall be brought to a close? The Secretary will call the roll."

"Mr. Aiken," began Secretary Felton Johnson.

"Aye," said the Vermont Republican.

"Mr. Allot."

"Aye."

"Mr. Anderson," and at that moment a rear door opened and a wheelchair bearing Senator Clair Engle of California entered the chamber. Unable to walk or talk, near death from cancer, Engle had had two brain operations and had not come to the Capitol since April. When his name was called, he tried to speak for a moment, then lifted his partially paralyzed left arm, pointing to his eye.

"Aye," declared the secretary. The staff aide standing behind the chair wheeled it about and took Clair Engle out of the Senate chamber. He never returned.

To no one's surprise, Barry Goldwater responded to his name with a brusque "No."

Republican John Williams of Delaware cast the sixty-seventh vote for cloture, bringing Carl Hayden out of the cloakroom where he'd been hiding. "It's all right, Carl," Mansfield said. "We've got it."

Metcalf announced the result—71 to 29—four votes more than needed. Almost a hundred years after it abolished slavery, the United States Government was about to outlaw racial discrimination. America would never be quite the same again.

| | |

That night, Lyndon Johnson was huddled with McGeorge Bundy discussing what to do about Vietnam, when Robert Kennedy showed up. The president was so pleased about the cloture vote, and no doubt so eager to stop talking about Vietnam even for a moment, that he was downright effusive with his attorney general.

"Hello, Hero," he said.

"Wasn't that good?" Kennedy said, before taking his leave.

The next day, Martin Luther King was arrested for trying to eat in a restaurant in St. Augustine, Florida.

| | |

Disgraced and furious, Bill Scranton flew back to Pennsylvania, where he proved himself at the very least a glutton for punishment. He decided to run anyway. He announced on Friday, June 12, and flew to Baltimore for the first stop of what would be five weeks of campaigning. "I've come here to offer the party a real choice," he said. He did pick up a few delegates, but Goldwater, who already had more than enough to win, kept adding to his total. Rockefeller officially ended his candidacy on Monday, June 15, "because I believe it is my duty to do everything I can to help Governor Scranton to win his contest for the Republican nomination."

But all the help in the world couldn't help Scranton, who was in over his head. In Washington, he sought out Dirksen. "You know," he told the Minority Leader, "you'd make a great favorite son."

But Dirksen had had his moment of glory for the year, and anyway, this was just too silly. To Scranton he said, "This thing has gone too far."[1] To someone else, he said, "What does he think I am? A rookie or a patsy?"[2]

| | |

On Sunday, June 14, Henry Cabot Lodge told President Johnson he didn't want to stay in his job, and President Johnson told his wife that he didn't want to stay in his, either. Johnson didn't hear about Lodge's decision until the evening, when Secretary of State Dean Rusk handed him a wire from the ambassador. Just what he needed, another dangerous decision to make about Vietnam. He didn't want to deal with Vietnam, or with Laos or Cyprus or civil rights. That's what he told Lady Bird that afternoon. He would rather be back at the ranch.[3]

A few days later, he ordered officials at the Democratic National Committee to postpone showing a filmed memorial to John F. Kennedy until the final night of the national convention, after the president and his running mate had been nominated, when it would be too late for the delegates to be so swept away by emotion that they would ignore their president and nominate Robert Kennedy.

| | |

On June 15, the first three hundred Freedom Summer volunteers gathered at Western College for Women in Oxford, Ohio, along with psychiatrists, psychologists, and lawyers. The lawyers were from the National Lawyers Guild. Allard Lowenstein was in Europe.

The volunteers were young and almost all white, and most of them had never known hardship, much less danger. They were from Harvard, Swarthmore, Wisconsin, Berkeley, and other citadels of learning, contemplation, and privilege. One volunteer, W. Donald Edwards, was the son of Representative Don Edwards of California. Another, Harold Ickes, was the son of Franklin Roosevelt's interior secretary.

On the morning of their first full day, they gathered in the college auditorium, with pencils sharpened and clipboards in their laps, as if ready for the first day of the new semester. They got their instructions about the ten or more community centers they were to run, the arts and crafts they would teach, the libraries they would set up, and the voter registration drives they would lead.

They sang. Fannie Lou Hamer led them, the large black woman from Ruleville, in the Delta, who had been beaten two years earlier for having the temerity to try to register to vote. First she told them that they might be beaten, might even be killed; then she started singing "Go Tell It on the Mountain," and they all joined the hymn, though few of them understood how deeply the civil rights movement was grounded in Christianity. She led them in one of the anthems of the civil rights movement, "I'll Be Sitting Right There."

Then Bob Moses came to the front of the room, not onto the stage but on the same level as the volunteers. He didn't introduce himself. He didn't have to. Despite his advanced academic degrees and his scholarly-looking horn-rimmed glasses, he dressed like a sharecropper, in T-shirt and denim overalls. He put his hands in the bib of the overalls, and he gave it to them straight.

"When Mrs. Hamer sang 'If you miss me from the freedom fight, you can't find me nowhere, come on over to the graveyard, I'll be buried over there,' . . . that's true."

Only then did he go up to the stage, where he drew a map of Mississippi on the blackboard and gave a short course in the history, economy, and sociology of the place they'd be going to. He stopped. He put down the chalk, and he turned to them. "When you come South," he said, "you bring with you the concern of the country—because the people of the country don't identify with Negroes. The guerrilla war in Mississippi is not much different from that in Vietnam. But when we tried to see President Johnson, his secretary said that Vietnam was popping up all over his calendar and he hadn't time to talk to us."

Now, only because of the summer project, the FBI was sending a team of its best agents into Mississippi. "We have been asking for them for three years," he said. "Now the federal government is concerned."

It was a chilling statement. With just a touch of subtlety, Moses was confirming the vilest charges being used against him and the entire project by the segregationists—that its aim was to use young white people as sacrificial lambs, that only if white people—respectable, upper-middle-class white people—were exposed to the same dangers that Mississippi's Negroes faced every day would the electorate, and therefore the government, care enough to act. "No administration is going to commit political suicide over the rights of Negroes," he said. "This is part of what we are doing . . . getting the country involved through yourselves. Our goals are limited. If we can go and come back alive, then that is something."

Not that their education was only political and social. They were taught how to stop a charging dog (a sharp chop across the snout), why to carry a jacket even on the hottest days (to wrap around the head in case of attack), how to curl up like a baby while being beaten, not to stand too long before a lighted window lest one become an easy target for snipers. But it wasn't all work and horror stories. In the afternoons, they played soccer and volleyball beneath the sycamore trees of the campus. At night they sang folk songs, confided in one another, paired off for long walks.

One official of the Johnson administration came to speak to them. John Doar, the deputy chief of the Justice Department's civil rights division, proffered his respect and admiration. "The real heroes in this country today are the students, and particularly those students who have given their time and energy and dedication to correct the very bad and evil problems in the South with respect to the way in which American Negro citizens are treated before the law."

But he did not proffer assistance, not even to help these young idealists survive the summer. When someone asked what he would do "to enable us to see the fall," he was blunt. "Nothing. There is no federal police force. The responsibility for protection is that of the local police. We can only investigate."

|||

Joseph Alsop, Clark Clifford, and their wives came to dinner at the White House on Monday, June 15, and during a postprandial walk on the southwest grounds, Alsop told the president that if he did not commit U.S. combat troops to battle in Vietnam, he would go down in history as the first American president to lose a war.

There is no record that Johnson asked Alsop whether he had read James Madison out of the list of former presidents.

III

On Tuesday, June 16, social critic Jane Jacobs spoke at a White House lunch, and the president and Mrs. Johnson joined the Kennedy family for a fund-raising dinner in New York for the John F. Kennedy Presidential Library. Sitting with the Johnsons on the plane up from Washington, Senator Edward Kennedy took the opportunity to lobby on behalf of Boston's naval bases. At the reception on the roof of the St. Regis Hotel, Jacqueline Kennedy, clad in a simple black dress, greeted the three hundred guests who had each contributed $10,000, then sat next to the president at dinner. Mrs. Johnson sat next to the attorney general.

After dinner, Fredric March read some of John Kennedy's favorite poems, selected by his widow. Then the Johnsons, Mrs. Kennedy, and Robert Kennedy got into a car for the ride to the hotel where the president and his wife would spend the night. Cordially, the president and his attorney general discussed what to do after the civil rights bill passed.

While the elites of Manhattan and the federal government were dining formally, listening to poetry, and discussing policy, the elites of Neshoba and Lauderdale counties, gathered as the combined klaverns of the White Knights of the Ku Klux Klan, met in the gymnasium of an abandoned school just east of Philadelphia, Mississippi.

It wasn't the first time officials of the two chapters had gotten together. Neshoba County "kleagle" Edgar Ray Killen, known as the Preacher because he was an ordained Baptist minister, had been going to Lauderdale meetings at Akin's Mobil Homes, owned by Klan member Bernard Akin, or at the Longhorn Drive-in, managed by Frank Herndon, the forty-six-year-old Exalted Cyclops of the Lauderdale klavern.

But this was a special meeting. More than seventy men attended, and most of them had one thing on their mind—Goatee. They were furious at how he and that wife of his paraded around with the Negroes. Their leaders had promised they would do something about this Jewish invader, and the members were getting impatient.

No sooner had the meeting started than Ethel Glen "Hop" Barnett, a former Neshoba County sheriff, announced that on his way to the school he'd noticed some kind of meeting under way at the Mount Zion Church. Maybe, someone suggested, some civil rights workers were there, perhaps even Goatee. Preacher Killen asked for volunteers to find out.

Within minutes, a group of armed men, all of them from the Lauderdale klavern, all of them armed, were in their vehicles headed for the church.

| | |

June 16 was Precinct Meeting day in Mississippi, the day when Democrats (and in theory, even Republicans) were to meet in the 1,884 precincts to select delegates to the county conventions, which in turn would elect delegates to the congressional district conventions, who would select the state convention delegates, who would elect the delegates to the national convention.

In Ruleville, eight Negro voters went to the regular polling place, the community house, at the appointed hour of 10 A.M. It was locked and empty, so they convened the precinct meeting on the lawn. Similar accounts were received from throughout the state. For the most part, there were no precinct meetings.

| | |

The meeting of the officers of Mount Zion Church ended at 9:30 P.M. Cornelius Steele, his wife, and their two children got into the cab of their truck, while a friend named Jim Cole hopped into the flatback behind them. The truck never got out of the driveway. A pickup truck blocked the exit to the clay road. Five or six white men appeared out of the darkness and ordered them out of the truck.

"Where are those white boys?" one of the men said.

"What white boys?" Jim Cole said.

"The white boys who've been coming around here."

There was a gunshot, a warning apparently, because the white men got into the pickup truck and roared off.

They were lucky. Cole's brother, fifty-eight-year-old Junior Roosevelt Cole, known as Bud, had gotten out of the driveway and turned down the road before he was halted some fifty yards from the church. He was dragged from his car, knocked to the ground, and repeatedly beaten with some kind of heavy stick—he never knew what it was—while his wife, Beatrice, watched and prayed.

Finally, the beating stopped, and somehow Bud managed to drive home. He wouldn't let Beatrice go for the doctor until morning. She couldn't sleep. At about 1:00 A.M., Beatrice heard a truck roar up the road toward the church, then back again. A few minutes later, she saw a glow in the sky. The Mount Zion Church was burning to the ground.

|||

Someone called Hubert Humphrey off the Senate floor on Wednesday, June 17, to take a phone call from his wife. She told him that their son, Bob, had a malignant growth on his neck and would have to undergo major surgery to clean out his lymphatic system.

He had taken the call in his whip office, just off the Senate floor, and was sitting there, crying and unable to move, when Joe Rauh and Clarence Mitchell came in, ebullient with their impending success. Tormented, Humphrey went back to the Senate floor, where he belonged. He didn't see his son until after the final vote.

On Thursday, June 18, Barry Goldwater announced that he would vote against the civil rights bill. "I am unalterably opposed to discrimination of any sort," he said on the Senate floor, "and I believe that though the problem is fundamentally one of the heart, some law can help—but not law that embodies features like these, provisions which fly in the face of the Constitution and which require for their effective execution the creation of a police state."

Then he flew to Dwight Eisenhower's ranch to explain his vote to the party patriarch. Ike was not entirely satisfied, but when Goldwater returned to Washington, he found a warmer welcome from the chairmen of the Mississippi and Alabama Republican parties, and suggestions to stand firm from his new legal advisors, William Rehnquist and Robert Bork.

Rehnquist and Bork were longtime foes of integration. As a clerk to Justice Robert Jackson ten years earlier, Rehnquist had railed against the plaintiff's case in *Brown* v. *the Board of Education of Topeka*. The Jim Crow doctrine of separate but equal, he wrote, was "right and should be affirmed." Instead of joining "a pathological search for discrimination," engaged in by liberal politicians, Rehnquist proclaimed, "it is about time the Court faced the fact that white people in the South don't like the colored people." The tone of his memorandum left little doubt that he agreed with them.

Bork, a Yale Law School professor, described the civil rights bill as "an unwanted intrusion on the right of individuals to choose with whom to associate." After consulting with these two attorneys, Goldwater called the civil rights bill a "threat to the very essence of our basic system."

|||

At 10:50 P.M. on the night of Friday, June 19, a chartered Aero Commander airplane on approach to Barnes Municipal Airport in Springfield, Massachusetts, crashed into Walter Bashista's apple orchard. The plane carried two United States senators, Birch Bayh of Indiana and Edward Kennedy of Massachusetts, who were on their way to the Massachusetts Democratic Convention that would nominate Kennedy for his first full term.

They were late because they had been forced to stay in Washington for the final Senate vote on the civil rights bill. "Everyone knows that I am a candidate this year," Kennedy had wired the delegates, "even though I am hundreds of miles away. We are now fifteen minutes away from the vote on Civil Rights," and he urged them "not to nominate Joan [his wife] until I get there."

After the vote, they had stopped briefly at John Kennedy's grave before heading for the plane, piloted by Edwin Zinny, the regular pilot for the plane's owner, a Massachusetts businessman. Kennedy's aide, Ed Moss, sat next to the pilot. Kennedy was behind him, in a seat facing the rear. Bayh and wife Marvella were facing him.

North of New York the fog and wind got worse, and by the time they got to the Springfield area there was just enough visibility for an instrument landing. Kennedy loosened his seat belt so he could turn around and watch the plane land. He could see the altimeter dropping from 1,100 feet to 600 feet, but this felt less like a landing than "like a toboggan ride, right along the tops of the trees for a few seconds. Then there was a terrific impact into a tree."

The plane spun into the orchard. Birch Bayh got himself and his wife out of the plane, and then he went back in to save whoever was savable. The first thing he saw was Ted Kennedy's pale hand, which he grabbed. Kennedy told Bayh he couldn't move from the waist down. Bayh told Kennedy to grab him around the neck. Somehow, he got Kennedy out of the plane and laid him down on the ground; the Bashistas' daughter gave him a drink of water. An ambulance took him to Cooley-Dickenson hospital in Northampton. His pulse was weak, his left lung was punctured and partially collapsed, and three vertebrae were smashed; at first the doctors were not sure he'd live.

Pilot Zinny and Ed Moss did not.

| | |

The attorney general was in Hyannis Port, which is about as far away from Springfield as one can get and still be in Massachusetts. He got to the hospital just as Ted Kennedy regained consciousness, recognized his brother, and said, "Is it true that you are ruthless?"

The injuries were bad but not life threatening, and a relieved Robert Kennedy walked out of the hospital with his friend Walter Sheridan. They lay down in the grass, and Kennedy, looking up into the summer sky, said, "Somebody up there doesn't like me." Then he asked Sheridan whether he should try to become vice president or run for the Senate in New York. Sheridan suggested the vice presidency.

But by then he was already on the verge of the other choice. Had Lyndon Johnson offered him the second spot on the ticket, he would have taken it. But he knew how unlikely that was, and he had made contact with some of the leading Democrats in New York, especially John F. English, the Democratic chairman in Nassau County on Long Island, and Peter Crotty, the chairman of the big county in the state's opposite corner, the Buffalo area.

Together, they'd even commissioned a poll to find out how badly Kennedy might be hurt by being labeled a "carpetbagger."

Not too badly, was the early judgment.

| | |

Lyndon Johnson woke up at 5:30 on the morning of Friday, June 19. The morning papers would not get there for an hour, so he read from his "night reading" envelope and did his exercises.

He'd been better about his exercises lately. It was kind of like the praying.

The helicopter that would take him to Andrews Air Force Base for the plane ride to California would leave at seven, and at ten minutes before the hour, he walked to his bedroom door. There he stopped, turned, and came back to the bed where his wife lay. He leaned close to her and whispered, "Get me out of this, won't you?"

He didn't mean the California trip.

|19|

A SIMPLE CASE OF MURDER

Mickey Schwerner and James Chaney left Oxford on Saturday, June 20, at 3 A.M. so they'd be sure to get to Meridian before dark. With them were two new colleagues who were going to join them in Meridian, Andrew Goodman and a twenty-one-year-old Drew University student named Louise Hermey, and four other volunteers, three men and a woman. They were in that powder-blue Ford station wagon CORE had given them; J.E. drove as far as Bowling Green, Kentucky, where they stopped for breakfast and gas.

When they got back in the car, Mickey was driving. As they passed through Birmingham, Alabama, a carload of white teenagers in a passing car shouted "Nigger-lovers," so they changed the seating arrangements so that Chaney, the only Negro among them, would not be sitting next to a white woman. Without further incident, they got to Meridian on schedule, at about 5:10 A.M., and drove right to the office.

Inside, up the thirty-one stairs to the office, Mickey gave the newcomers a quick tour of the five rooms and explained how to use the phones, how they needed to log calls, and where they kept the lists of jails and police stations for all the counties around as well as the numbers for law enforcement offices, the state highway patrol, and the FBI.

They had to be very careful, he explained. They were to use 482-6103 for outgoing calls, leaving 485-9286 for incoming. Every hour on the hour, someone was to check in with the Jackson office to say "all is well." He'd learned a lot in less than six months.

While Mickey was acting as the tour guide, James Chaney had been getting some news; he invited Mickey into the small inner office where the sink and the mimeo machine were and told him that Mount Zion had been burned down. There was no doubt about what they had to do. They would have to go, first thing next morning, and Andy Goodman should go with them because he was set to run the freedom school in Neshoba.

They all had supper at Beal's café, across the street from the community center. Then the new volunteers got their housing assignments, all except Andy, who hadn't been scheduled to come to Meridian. He was going to stay with the Schwerners for a few days, until he could find a place in Longdale. James, Mickey, and Andy dropped the other volunteers at their assigned places and then went to Chaney's house to visit his mother, Fannie Lee, and to have a piece of her lemon pie.

Early in the morning, using the outgoing-call phone, Chaney got a weather report from the Meridian weather bureau. Then he grabbed two hours of sleep, got up, drove to the Phillips 66 station on Fifth Avenue, filled the tank, and had the tires checked.

At 9:30 A.M., Schwerner told Louise Hermey where they were going. "There's an immutable rule here," he said. "No one is to remain in Neshoba after 4 P.M. If for any reason we aren't back by 4 P.M., you should alert Jackson and begin checking every city jail, county jail, sheriff's office, police station, and hospital between Meridian and Neshoba. OK?" He put on his Mets cap and headed downstairs.

They only spent about fifteen minutes at the church, or at the cold ashes that had been the church. It wasn't as though there was anything they could do about it. They visited Bud and Beatrice Cole, and then they went over to Ernest Kirkland's folks' house for about half an hour. Mrs. Kirkland offered chocolate cake, and James Chaney had a piece. Andy Goodman spent the visit talking with Gwendolyn Kirkland, Ernest's younger sister, gathering information for his impending assignment at a Longdale freedom school, even though they'd have to find a new site for it now.

Pretty soon Mickey said it was time to go; they had to be back in Meridian by four. The four young men got back into the blue Ford wagon, Chaney at the wheel as usual. They dropped Ernest Kirkland at a friend's house, then headed back to the highway, south toward Meridian.

They were subdued. First of all, the Coles had made it clear that the terrorists had been looking for them, probably for Mickey most of all. And now they couldn't be sure that the Longdale Negroes would still welcome a freedom school or a voter registration drive. Beatrice had been the one who wanted them to come; Bud had always been wary, fearing . . . well, fearing just what had occurred.

Chaney pulled up to the stop sign at the corner of Longdale Road and State Highway 16, the east-west route that went through Philadelphia, just a few miles to the west. The quickest way home was to go east a few miles, then some twenty-five miles south on Highway 491 to Meridian. But 491 was a narrow, clay road, lined by abandoned farmhouses and empty pastures—a perfect place for ambushers to lie in wait.

The other way, back through Philadelphia and then down State Highway 19, was longer, but it was all paved highway, with more traffic. Besides, they'd come up 491; one of the rules was not to go back the way you came. Chaney turned right, toward Philadelphia.

It was about 3 P.M. on the longest day of the year. The temperature was about 100 degrees, and it was humid. Chaney made sure to keep his speed at the legal limit of 65 mph, especially when he noticed a big white Chevy sedan with a red light on its dashboard go past him as it headed east. Then he passed a state police cruiser parked by the side of the road. Nobody bothered them.

But the big Chevy, driven by Deputy Price, soon turned around and pulled up behind the Ford wagon. At the Philadelphia city line, where the speed limit drops to 35, Price flipped on the dashboard bubble light. Chaney didn't stop right away, and Price's siren wasn't working, so he honked his horn. After going less than half a mile, Chaney pulled over. He was just inside the city limits, near the First Methodist Church.

Price asked the three men for identification and then told them they were under arrest, not just for speeding but for suspicion in the fire-bombing of the Mount Zion Church. That may have been absurd, but Price was no fool. One look into the car told him what a bonanza he had come upon. He'd never met the man in the front passenger seat, but he knew who it was—the round face, the long nose, the bright blue Mets cap, the little beard. It was Goatee.

By now the state troopers in that parked car had been summoned, and they helped take the three young men to jail. As they herded their prisoners into the patrol car, Patrolman E. R. Poe realized that he'd taken his gunbelt off, as he often did on hot days, and left it in the backseat. When he turned around to get it, he saw that Schwerner had it and was in the process of handing it to him. It was, he remembered later, "the first time a prisoner ever handed me my own gun."

They took them to the jail in town, on Myrtle Street, not far from the courthouse. Philadelphia was one of those typical, sleepy Southern county seats with the big redbrick courthouse in the center of a grassy common, surrounded by a small business district. The stores and shops faced the square, with a common wooden overhang protecting pedestrians from sun and rain as they trod along sidewalks raised well above street level.

But the appearance was deceiving; Philadelphia was more remote, more insular, more backward than even the typical rural county seat. It sits where the Choctaws lived, before they were forcibly removed in the 1830s to open the Mississippi frontier for white settlers. The surrounding soil is fertile, and for a while the area prospered from rich cotton fields. After the railroad came through in 1905, Philadelphia was a thriving cotton market. But when cotton farming declined a few years later, there was nothing to take its place. Philadelphia isn't even on the way from one large city to another, so there was never any pressure to improve the highway system. Most of the roads were unpaved until the late 1940s.

In 1964, almost all Philadelphians were descended from people who had lived there, or on nearby farms, since before the Civil War. The place didn't attract newcomers. There simply wasn't much reason for anyone from anywhere else to move there. As local historian Florence Mars wrote, in Neshoba County, "the basement of the past is not very deep."

The jail was run by an elderly couple named Herring. Mrs. Herring had been a Posey, and her nephew, Billie Wayne Posey, was one of the Klan members who had gone to Mount Zion the previous Tuesday. Mrs. Herring was out front when Deputy Price brought his prisoners to the jail at 4 P.M., just when they were expected back in Meridian.

Mickey asked Price if he could make a phone call.

He could not.

But Price did. He called the Preacher.

This was what Edgar Ray Killen had been waiting for. He got two of his trusted fellow-Klansmen, Jerry McGrew Sharpe and Jimmy Lee Townsend, both young men. The three got into Sharpe's car and drove down to Meridian, to the Longhorn, where they told Herndon that Goatee was in jail. Herndon went right to the phone.

He wasn't the only one working the phones. On the other side of town, Louise Hermey called the COFO office in Jackson to report that she hadn't heard from the three young men. At five, she started calling all the jails and hospitals in the area. So did Mary King, an idealistic young white woman in the Jackson office, claiming to be an Atlanta newspaper reporter.

For Mickey, being in jail was no big deal. He asked again for permission to make a phone call and was again denied. He introduced himself to the other white prisoner in the cell where he and Goodman were placed; Chaney was in another cell with a Negro prisoner.

At one point, Mickey asked Herring if he'd buy him a pack of cigarettes with money from his wallet, which had been taken from him. Herring agreed but then came back and reported that Price had taken all three wallets with him. Mickey the smoker would have to wait without a smoke, and Mickey the Mets fan would not know that Philadelphia Phillies pitcher Jim Bunning was pitching the first regular-season perfect game since 1922 against the New York Mets at Shea Stadium that evening.

Back at the Longhorn, Killen and his friends were having trouble recruiting enough men. After a while, James Jordan, a thirty-eight-year-old salesman at Akin's Mobile Homes, came to the restaurant to meet his wife, who was a waitress there, and he agreed to join them. Jordan and Sharpe rode over to the home of Wayne Roberts, a big, dishonorably discharged ex-Marine who had done much of the beating of Bud Cole the previous Tuesday. Finally, four others were rounded up, and Killen explained the plan. Goatee and the other two would be released. A highway patrol car would chase them down on an isolated stretch of road and turn them over to the Klansmen. They bought some rubber gloves. Then they got into two cars and headed for Philadelphia.

Shortly before 5:30 P.M., Mrs. Herring cooked up a supper of chicken and dumplings, green salad, green beans, potatoes, corn bread, cake, and iced tea for her prisoners. While she was cooking, the phone rang. The COFO log reported that the Neshoba County Jail was called at 5:30. The Herrings later said they never got such a call. They do remember that all the prisoners devoured their meals.

At 10 P.M., Cecil Price came back and told Chaney they'd be free to leave if he paid a twenty-dollar fine. He agreed, the fine was paid, and the men were given back their billfolds and released. "Now," the deputy said, "let's see how quick y'all can get out of Neshoba County." He escorted them to their car.

Back in the powder-blue Ford, Chaney at the wheel, they went east on Myrtle Street to Pecan Avenue, then east on Main. Price, accompanied by Officer Richard Willis, tailed them.

Chaney turned south onto Highway 19. Price and Willis followed for about another half mile, then turned back to the courthouse at just about the moment that seventy-one-year-old Otha Neal Burkes, a World War I veteran and former Philadelphia police officer, pulled his car alongside Doyle Barnette's, parked behind a warehouse on the south side of town.

"They're going on Nineteen toward Meridian," Burkes said. "Follow them."

Barnette went to Route 19, where he was soon overtaken by Billy Wayne Posey's red and white 1958 Chevy. Posey had three passengers—Jerry McGrew Sharpe, Jimmy Townsend, and Wayne Roberts. They'd been drinking.

A few minutes later, Chaney saw headlights in his rearview mirror and stepped on the gas. But the car behind him was faster, so he tried an evasive maneuver, swerving off Highway 19 onto Highway 492, a gravel road heading southwest toward the little hamlet of Union. Price, who knew the territory, was not fooled. On the narrow road, Price turned on his flashing red lights, and Chaney—no one knows why—stopped.

Price got out of his car just as Barnette's Fairlane reached them, carrying five passengers including Posey, whose own car had broken down a few miles back. He had left Sharpe and Townsend with his crippled auto.

"I thought you were going back to Meridian if we let you out of jail," Price said to the civil rights workers.

"We were going there," Chaney said.

"Well, you were taking the long way around. Get out of the car."

He ordered them into the backseat of his car. Chaney hesitated, and Price hit him on the back of his head with his blackjack. All three vehicles then turned around and drove back the way they came, back to Highway 19, back toward Philadelphia.

They picked up Jerry Sharpe at Posey's car, leaving young Jimmy Townsend to stay with the vehicle, then continued north a few miles until Price turned left down a dark dirt road, full of curves angling up and down red-dirt hills. The locals called it Rock Cut Road.

When the cars stopped, Klansman Wayne Roberts walked immediately to Price's car and pulled the left rear door open. He grabbed Mickey by the shirt, pulled him to his feet, and spun him around so that they faced each other. Roberts put his left hand on Schwerner's shoulder. His right hand held his gun.

"Are you that nigger-lover?" he shouted.

"Sir, I know just how you feel," Mickey said, just before Roberts shot him in the heart. He fell to his left.

Roberts went back to the car, pulled Andy Goodman out of it, and killed him. James Jordan shot Chaney in the lower back, and Roberts put another bullet into his brain.

"You didn't leave me nothing but a nigger," Jordan said, "but at least I killed me a nigger."[1]

"Better pick up those shells," Deputy Price said.

"I've already got mine," said Wayne Roberts.

"All right," said Posey. "Let's load these guys in the wagon and take them to the spot."[2]

They had already worked out a place to bury them, thanks to one of their neighbors and the United States government. With the help of a grant from the U.S. Agriculture Department's Soil Conservation Service, Olen Burrage, a local trucker, was planning to dam up a small stream to create a cattle pond. He'd hired Herman Tucker, one of his part-time drivers, who also ran a bulldozer, to do the work for him. The Klan had arranged for Posey to get there at midnight with the bodies, which would be placed in the center of the dam, at least fifteen feet down. Then Tucker would seal it with a bulldozer. After the pond filled, all traces of the bodies would be obliterated.

Barnette, Sharpe, and Roberts drove to the site, found Tucker, and threw the bodies on the damsite. Tucker started up his CAT D-4-d bulldozer and scooped away an indentation at what would be the center of the dam. Then he backed the CAT away and watched as the Klansmen carried the bodies and dumped them into the hole. It took Tucker only about fifteen minutes to cover them over.

| | |

Later that Monday morning, June 22, Robert Moses spoke to the next group of volunteers at Oxford. "Our goals are limited," he said. "If we can go and come back alive, then that is something. If you can go into Negro homes and just sit and talk, that will be a huge job. We're not thinking of integrating the lunch counters. The Negroes in Mississippi haven't the money to eat in those places anyway. They still don't dare go into the white half of the integrated bus terminals. They must weigh that against having their houses bombed or losing their jobs."

He paused, and he stood very still for a while before continuing.

"We've had discussions all winter about race hatred," he said. "There is an analogy to *The Plague* by Camus. The country isn't willing to admit it has the plague, but it pervades the whole society. Everyone must come to grips with this, because it affects us all. We must discuss it openly and honestly, even with the danger that we get too analytic and tangled up. If we ignore it, it's going to blow up in our faces."

There was an interruption at the side entrance. A few staff members had come in and were whispering. One went over to the stage and sprang up to whisper to Moses, who bent on his knees to hear. Then he was alone again, crouched, gazing at his feet.

Then he stood. "Yesterday morning, three of our people left Meridian, Mississippi, to investigate a church-burning in Neshoba County. They haven't come back, and we haven't had any word from them."

| | |

At 6:20 on Monday morning, June 22, FBI agent Joseph Sullivan was informed that Mickey Schwerner, Andrew Goodman, and James Chaney had disappeared. He was ordered to Meridian later in the day. He wouldn't leave for nine months.

For the next several days, the United States government mobilized its law enforcement and military establishments to try to find the three young men, or their bodies, and their killers; white Mississippi organized its political and public relations establishments to portray the disappearances as a hoax.

"Why, I don't think there's a damn thing to it," Senator James Eastland told the president on Tuesday. "I think it's a publicity stunt."

By then some Choctaw Indians had found a smoldering Ford station wagon in a thicket near Bogue Chito Creek some thirteen miles south of Philadelphia. There were no bodies in it. J. Edgar Hoover relayed the news to the president just before he met, quite reluctantly, with Schwerner's and Goodman's parents. "Every goddamn time somebody's going to be missing I got to meet with all those parents," he complained.

Sometime that day, the president decided to send CIA director Allen Dulles as his personal emissary to Mississippi. To puzzled aides he explained that Hoover, who really wanted to be CIA director himself, hated Dulles, hated the fact that he was on the Warren Commission, and would be provoked into doing a better job by the Dulles mission.

The imperious, impeccably dressed, and seemingly upright CIA director—he was actually a notorious womanizer—got to Jackson Wednesday night. So did Rita Schwerner, furious in her sorrow.

The next day, the two of them met. It was not a happy occasion. She refused to shake his hand, saying she wanted her husband back, not sympathy, and when he said the government was doing all it could, she replied that it was not doing much of anything.

Dulles also met with Robert Moses, Aaron Henry, David Dennis, and Lawrence Guyot.

"We want this mess cleaned up," Dulles told them; when they asked what mess he referred to, he said, "These civil rights demonstrations are causing this kind of friction, and we're just not gonna have it, even if we have to bring troops in here."

"Wait a minute. You're talking to the wrong people," Henry told him.

That day Norman Thomas, the eighty-year-old idol of the American Left, sent a telegram to his onetime protégé, Allard Lowenstein: "Your return imperative since you recruited students."

| | |

Robert and Ethel Kennedy left for Europe on Thursday, June 25. Robert was to dedicate a memorial to President Kennedy in Berlin. Through McGeorge

Bundy, President Johnson had made it clear that he preferred that Kennedy not go. The administration's stated reason was that the attorney general should stick around in case he was needed for talks on the civil rights bill. The unstated reason was that the president didn't want to see Bobby Kennedy looking good on the television news.

Shortly before Kennedy's departure, he telephoned Johnson, explaining that he'd also been invited to Poland, not by the Communist government, but by students. Of course, Kennedy said, he would not "want to go or even contemplate going unless you thought it was advisable or helpful."

It is neither on record nor difficult to imagine what Lyndon Johnson said in his own mind at that moment. To Kennedy, he said, "If you think you ought to, go ahead." The president of the United States would neither be sending his attorney general to Poland nor interfering with his desire to go there.

While in Berlin, the Kennedys dedicated the memorial. Then they headed to Poland, where the government had pointedly refused to provide its citizens any information about his "nonofficial" visit. If folks wanted to know where Kennedy would be, they'd have to find out for themselves. And it seems they did. The day after the Kennedys arrived, they went to church with Ambassador John Moors Cabot, whose limousine was enveloped by a crowd of young people. Kennedy and his wife climbed up on the car roof to wave to the crowd. The ambassador did not object until the roof started caving in.

In Krakow a throng sang "Sto Lat," a Polish song wishing long life, and the Kennedys replied by singing "When Polish Eyes Are Smiling." When another crowd gathered in front of Ambassador Cabot's residence, where the Kennedys were to dine, Kennedy got up on yet another car top to address them. After a few minutes, he said, "I have to go to dinner now. Would you like to come in with me?"

Sure they would. So he held a mock consultation with Cabot over the wall of the embassy grounds, and then said, "The ambassador says you can't come." The crowd jeered and laughed.

Something had happened here. Over the past four or five years, Robert Kennedy had gotten himself a reputation as a tough, smart, political inside man. But he'd never been much of a campaigner. Maybe it was just that he'd never campaigned for himself, but he was stiff on a podium. He read speeches in a monotone. It was as though he had no persona in public.

Every good politician plays a role; campaigning is a performance. The difference between an honest and a dishonest politician is that the honest one plays himself. But it takes a while for anyone to know who that self really is, how it should perform. Never having run for office—never having performed—Robert Kennedy had to figure that out. Now, it seemed, he had. He was the fervent but gentle, polite yet irreverent young man. Like his brother, he could combine serious discourse with ironic wit. Like his brother's, the wit was usually aimed at himself, so he could tease others without seeming too much the wise guy (though at that moment, Ambassador Cabot might not have agreed).

Kennedy was smaller and slighter than his brother had been. The tone of his voice was perhaps half an octave higher, a bit reedier. Less imposing, less threatening, he could seem more endearing. He had figured that out. Whereas John Kennedy's face and eyes could be impassive, Robert's were expressive. His eyes sparkled when he was pleased, glowered when he was not. Rarely did no emotion at all show through. He'd figured that out, too. Now he knew who he was in public. He could connect with a crowd, especially a young one.

He was young. He was thirty-eight that spring, only eight years younger than John Kennedy would have been had he lived, but they were eight big years. When Jack Kennedy went off to war, Robert was in high school, and though he enlisted in the Navy at seventeen, World War II ended before he could get into it. Unlike all those men just a few years his senior, he had no war stories to tell. He was, in effect, of a different generation.

So he was open to newer ideas. The change coming over Robert Kennedy in the spring of 1964 transcended his campaigning skills. The tough, centrist politician was now ready to listen to—if not yet to agree with—those outside the political mainstream, especially if they were young. He retained a large dose of skepticism toward intense and sentimental liberals, but he seemed to have a new respect for vigorous radicals. He seemed, in some respects, a different man.

Later, some would suggest that he had emerged an entirely different man, that before John Kennedy's murder Robert had been a narrow-minded moralist who would work for Joe McCarthy and hound Jimmy Hoffa to jail and that afterward he became the sensitive scholar who could quote Aeschylus on the night of Martin Luther King's murder and care deeply about the poor and put-upon.

This is gross oversimplification. He never stopped being a moralist. He had expressed concern about poverty and racial injustice long before November 22, 1963. If he was better able to recognize gray areas at the age of forty than he was at thirty, who is not? Nor did he discover the classics only in mourning for his brother. A Harvard education is not, usually, a complete waste of time. Robert Kennedy had been reading poetry, and underlining some of it, all his adult life.

Still, the experiences of the last year had not left him unchanged. Robert Kennedy was now the family patriarch and its political heir apparent. He was free to carve out his own political identity. And that he did.

| | |

On Friday, June 26, the Mississippi Freedom Democratic Party held its state convention. Unlike the regular (white) Democrats, the MFDP had followed the regular Democratic Party rules. It had held open precinct meetings and conventions at the county and congressional district levels. Now, in Jackson, it elected Lawrence Guyot as party chairman and Aaron Henry as chairman of the delegation that would go to Atlantic City to seek its credentials as the real Mississippi Democratic Party.

Toward that end, it endorsed Lyndon Johnson for president. The "regular" Democrats, meeting a few days later, came out for Goldwater and against the United Nations.

| | |

John Doar of the Justice Department's Civil Rights Division made his second appearance at Oxford on Friday, June 26. Once again he offered much praise but little protection, but this time he was challenged not by a student but by a teacher.

Yale historian Staughton Lynd arose from the audience to contend that when violence accompanied an 1890 Illinois Railroad strike, the federal government sent troops in, and the Supreme Court upheld the action.

"If you have this power to act, and if you have the moral responsibility yet choose not to act, how in the world do all of you live with this?" Lynd asked.

Doar was not intimidated. "I believe we are a government of law," he said. "I have taken a vow to uphold the law. I just try to do the best I can under law. I have no trouble living with myself. The people I know in the federal government and administration are fine people, and they have no trouble living with themselves either."

On the last evening, there was one more general meeting. Jim Forman spoke, and they all sang, and finally it was Moses's turn. As usual, he swayed as he talked; he held the microphone, and he started talking about . . . Tolkien. He wondered how many of them had read *The Fellowship of the Ring*.

"There is a weariness," he said, "from constant attention to the things you are doing, the struggle of good against evil."

He stopped for a moment and looked at the ground before speaking again.

"The kids are dead."

He stopped again, not for effect, but to let them absorb, and then he went on: "When we heard the news at the beginning, I knew they were dead. When we heard they had been arrested, I knew there had to be a frame-up. We didn't say this earlier because of Rita, because she was really holding out for every hope."

He looked out at them again and told them that more might be killed, that they were all taking risks.

"The way some people characterize this project is that it is an attempt to get some people killed so the federal government will move into Mississippi. And the way some of us feel about it is that in our country we have some real evil."

He did not, then, deny the way some people were characterizing the project.

That night there was a bonfire in a clearing. The young volunteers drank beer and sang songs, but harmony did not reign. The racial tensions that had always been there, but buried, began to surface. Even though two of the murdered men were white, some of the young Negroes were starting to complain that none of these white people could truly understand what they'd been through.

|||

Rita Schwerner had her day in Washington on Monday, June 29. First she met with Deputy Attorney General Nicholas Katzenbach, to whom she complained that the search for her husband and his friends, or their bodies, was "only a PR job, and not a very good one."

"What makes you qualified to say whether or not an investigation is under way?" Katzenbach said.

"I haven't been bought off like you have by Southern politicians," she said.

Later, with the help of her congressman, Republican Ogden Reid, she spent five minutes with Lyndon Johnson, whose willingness to grant her an audience was probably not unrelated to Walter Cronkite's calling the search for the civil rights workers "the focus of the whole country's concern" on *The CBS Evening News* the previous Thursday.

Mrs. Schwerner told the president that the two hundred sailors were not enough, that five thousand men were needed. He told her there "would be nowhere near thousands of men" but assured her that the federal government "was doing everything it possibly can." A few hours later, at a press conference at SNCC headquarters, Mrs. Schwerner derided the president's statements as "contradictory."

She was, of course, distraught, and immune for the moment from the criticism that would have been so easy to level at her: What made her an expert on the logistics of searching? Where was her evidence that Nick Katzenbach had been bought off by anyone?

But beyond her sorrow and her innate toughness, there was a political message in her rudeness. The movement of which she was a part had grown so impatient with mainstream politics that it was beginning to reject mainstream culture, including its manners. Without planning it, without basing it on any theory, movement folks were evolving a political attitude, one that disdained middle-class values.

It was as though they would taunt their enemies by living up to their negative stereotype. "The hard core of this group is your beatnik-type people," Governor Paul Johnson said of the civil rights workers. "Nonconformists, hair down to their shoulder blades, some that you'd call weirdos."

Then they would play the part. At Berkeley, in Mississippi, at the Oxford training sessions, one could display the depth of one's devotion to the movement by using improper speech, by being assertive. The movement's leaders—Robert Moses, Martin Luther King—were known for their gentle demeanor. Some of their followers were adopting a toughness, even surliness, to set themselves apart.

There was also a more specific political tactic at work. From the beginning, some in the movement tried to present the case that the federal government abandoned Schwerner, Goodman, and Chaney, that if officials in the Justice Department and the FBI really cared, they might have prevented the murders. If there were more FBI agents in Mississippi, this argument went—and goes to this day—or perhaps if U.S. marshals had been deployed, their lives might have been saved.

It is a flimsy case. There aren't that many U.S. marshals, and half of them are in no physical shape to protect anyone. Nor were there enough FBI agents to patrol the rural South.

But there is this possibility: If there had been an FBI office in Jackson, and if somebody had reached it early on the evening of June 21, perhaps an FBI agent, not Louise Hermey or Mary King, would have called the Neshoba County Jail, and perhaps Rainey or Price or the Herrings would have been sufficiently impressed, or intimidated, that they would have let the young men go.

That's a lot of "perhapses," and because there was no FBI office in the state, the others don't really matter. As to why there was no FBI office in Mississippi, well, J. Edgar Hoover didn't see the need for one, and nobody in the Justice Department, including Robert Kennedy, tried to change his mind.

Clearly, had Hoover been committed to the cause of civil rights, there would have been a Jackson office. But he was not. Hoover described himself as a "states-righter," and he displayed more concern about real and (mostly) imagined communist influence on the civil rights movement than about segregation. At one point, he briefed Burke Marshall about the "subversive activities" of Nathan Schwerner, Mickey's father. At another, he noted that Allard Lowenstein was an opponent of . . . apartheid and that, furthermore, he had once appeared at a dinner party given by Senator Fulbright. Hoover needed no firmer evidence to prove Lowenstein's disloyalty.

20

THE COMEDY CONTINUES

On the first of July, the population of the United States was 191,334,000, and for the first time more people lived in California than in New York, or anyplace else. A new Beatles song called "A Hard Day's Night" was all over the radio, along with a lilting tune called "Yesterday's Gone" by Chad & Jeremy and Chuck Berry's rollicking bit of nonsense, "No Particular Place to Go."

Chekhov's *Three Sisters* was being revived on Broadway, and so was Rodgers and Hammerstein's *The King and I,* with Rise Stevens and Darren McGavin. The movie versions of Tennessee Williams's *The Night of the Iguana* and Harold Robbins's *The Carpetbaggers* opened to mixed reviews, and Gore Vidal's novel *Julian* hit the best-seller lists.

Sailors and FBI agents were crawling all over Neshoba County, Mississippi. Civil rights advocates, instead of celebrating the imminent passage of their bill, were clamoring for the intervention of some kind of federal force in Mississippi.

They didn't get that, but they did get the law, a bit quicker than expected. On the morning of Thursday, July 2, the last bit of resistance in the House of Representatives evaporated, despite Howard Smith's description of the measure as a "monstrous instrument of oppression upon all of the American people."

That day was also Robert Kennedy's first back in the office after his European trip, and after an article in *Newsweek* said that Kennedy wanted the vice presidency but assumed he was "the last man in the world" Johnson would choose "because my name is Kennedy, because he wants a Johnson Administration with no Kennedys in it . . . because I suppose some businessmen would object, and because I'd cost them a few votes in the South."

It was a remarkably perceptive, and excessively candid, piece of political analysis. In an effort to maintain cordiality, Kennedy called Johnson that morning. "I just spoke about all of these matters quite frankly and openly, as I always have," he said.

The president was gracious. It was "unfortunate," he said, but "let's forget it. There're too few left in the family and let's hold together as much as we can."

The conversation then turned to the timing of the president's signature on the civil rights bill. For the symbolism, some liberals wanted him to wait two days so he could sign it on the Fourth of July. Kennedy offered another, more practical reason. If it were signed immediately, he said, "we're going to have a rather difficult weekend, a holiday weekend . . . with Negroes running all over the South figuring that they get the day off and that they're going to go into every hotel and motel and every restaurant."

Johnson would have none of it. "You tell your publicity man over there," he said, an unmistakable touch of irritation in his voice, "don't say a damned word about what I'm gonna do."

The president didn't exactly say that he blamed Bobby Kennedy for coming up with the Fourth of July idea. But considering that he blamed him for every other problem, it's a reasonable conclusion.

By late afternoon of July 2, the House passed the Senate bill, and the president signed it a few hours later. "We have come now to a time of testing," he said at the televised signing ceremony. Behind him, Kennedy sat next to Dirksen in the front row, Martin Luther King sat in the second row, J. Edgar Hoover in the third.

It was a test, Johnson said, that "we must not fail. Let us close the springs of racial poison."

Privately, Johnson had already asked the Negro leaders for restraint, and they had agreed to discourage demonstrations. Richard Russell was equally conciliatory, or at least resigned. "As long as it is there, it must be obeyed," he said of the new law.

But the owner of the Heart of Atlanta Hotel filed suit immediately, claiming that the law violated his constitutional rights in requiring him to rent rooms to Negroes. Nearby, Lester Maddox, the feisty owner of the Pickrick, a fried chicken restaurant, chased three Negroes away from his establishment, resting on the slogan "A man's house is his castle," seemingly unaware that it was his restaurant, not his house, being integrated.

Robert Kennedy's fear of rowdy celebration turned out to be ill-founded. Instead, in cities throughout the South, Negroes claimed their new civil rights civilly, walking into restaurants that had barred them only days before. And Maddox turned out to be far more the exception than the rule. Though there was bitter, and sometimes violent, resistance in some rural areas, throughout the South the vast majority of businesses quietly complied. Before the law was two weeks old, Martin Luther King's Southern Christian Leadership Conference met in Birmingham, where King had been arrested fifteen months earlier. There were almost forty members, and they were welcomed as they checked into the Parliament House.

Most of the reaction was favorable, though there was intellectual opposition of a sort. William Buckley's *National Review* said the law gave the White House "the powers of a despot."

In only a few places did resistance find official sanction. One, needless to say, was Mississippi, where Governor Paul Johnson urged businesses to disobey the law. Despite this defiance, or perhaps because of it, the president called the governor on Friday, July 3, at 3:17 P.M. The governor was unhappy about the way newspapers and television were portraying his state.

"They have really made this state look like the worst thing on earth . . . [a] bunch of barefoot hooligans who want to kill everyone we see."

"I think you've done extremely well under the circumstances," the President said.

But the governor could see only trouble ahead as Negroes started to assert their new rights.

"Big niggers like to move," he said. "Could make it mighty, mighty rough."

"Well," said Johnson, "you keep a stiff upper lip and if you need me, call me. . . . I know you got a great problem."

| | |

The president celebrated the Fourth of July at his ranch with family and friends, almost relaxed. He lunched with John Connally and his brother and two other old Texas buddies and their wives. It was both a social gathering and a business lunch. The business at hand was the vice presidency.

Judge Homer Thornberry and his wife were for Gene McCarthy. The Connally brothers and their wives were for McNamara, as were Congressman Frank Ikard and his wife. Humphrey was deemed acceptable, but barely, to the South.

After lunch, the president went for a boat ride on the lake on the ranch. That evening, he had a friendly telephone conversation with Jacqueline Kennedy, who had spent the holiday in Hyannis Port. She told him that Ambassador Maxwell Taylor had been to visit her and the children.

"How are the children?" Johnson asked her.

"Oh, fine, thank you, and yours?"

"Good. Lynda's with us. Lucy's in Washington having dates."

"I noticed she didn't come," Mrs. Kennedy said. "I thought it was something sinister like that."

"You know," Johnson said, "she came in and said that she wanted a very special birthday present on July the second, and we asked her what it was, and she said she just wanted to go one whole day without an agent."

They both laughed at that and about what might have happened on that unchaperoned date.

"It's sure good to hear your voice," Johnson said, "and I hope that you're feeling all right."

"Oh, yes," Mrs. Kennedy said. "It was nice to talk to you. Give my love to Lady Bird."

"All right. I long to see you."

"Okay, we'll see you soon."

"Thank you, dear," said the president of the United States.

| | |

Ever hopeful, Bill Scranton flew to Chicago on the day of the All-Star Game, Tuesday, July 7, for the caucus of the Republican delegates from Illinois. "You are the fifty-eight most important people in the United States today," he told them, perhaps unaware that more than forty of them were for Barry Goldwater, who had gotten to the O'Hare Inn first and had pledged that if he were president he'd enforce the Civil Rights Act he had just opposed.

Emerging from the closed meeting, Ev Dirksen ended the fight for the nomination as clearly as he had ended the fight over civil rights, and with similarly Baroque language. "Too long," he intoned into the microphones, "have we ridden the gray ghost of me-tooism. When the roll is called, I shall cast my vote for Barry Goldwater."

The American League didn't do much better than Scranton, losing to the National League, 7 to 4, in that new ballpark New York City had built for the Mets.

| | |

A. J. Muste, a Dutch-born pacifist with vaguely left-wing leanings, was both the editor of *Liberation* magazine and the leader of a small but devoted faction that opposed American foreign policy, especially on the subjects of nuclear weapons and Cuba. Earlier in the year, Muste and his followers had begun a "peace march" from Quebec to Guantánamo, the U.S. base in Cuba.

For reasons that defy understanding, Muste and his little band of marchers enraged officials of the Johnson administration, and the White House wanted to go to court for an injunction to prevent Muste and his group from boarding a Cuba-bound boat in Florida. The attorney general had to sign the letter of authorization, and in due course one of his deputies, Norbert Schlei, brought it to him.

"Now wait a minute," he said. "What am I supposed to sign here?"

"It's a letter," Schlei said. "The White House wants it signed. It's important."

"Now wait a minute. Let me get this straight. You want me to sign that letter so that an 80 year old man can't walk 800 miles. Fuck it. I don't think he's a threat to the security of the United States. I won't sign that piece of paper."[1]

If he really craved the vice presidency, he would have signed it. By then, he knew that he wouldn't be chosen, even though he had not given up all hope. For Johnson, running with Kennedy would have been a psychological impossibility, and he said so. "I don't want history to say I was elected to this office because I had Bobby on the ticket with me," he said, only three weeks after the assassination.

More than anything, Johnson wanted, needed, an election victory that was his alone, not one that would be attributed in part to the Kennedy family. He craved the kind of unqualified approval he had never gotten at home, or even from the voters. He never had forgotten losing his first bid for the Senate in 1941 and then winning by eighty-seven votes in 1948. The only decision Johnson had to make was how and when to tell Kennedy and the rest of the political world. It shouldn't have been difficult. It turned out to be almost impossible.

| | |

On Friday, July 10, J. Edgar Hoover flew to Jackson for the ceremonial opening of the new FBI office. He was greeted as a hero and delighted local officials when he said that the Bureau "most certainly does not and will not give protection to civil rights workers." Despite his devotion to law, he refused to criticize Governor Johnson's call to defy the latest one passed. However, he did spend the night in an integrated hotel, and to Robert Kennedy's relief, he did not say anything about the civil rights movement being run by communists.

It was not surprising that Martin Luther King did not come to the opening. He was in Florida. But his absence did not mean that there was no communication between him and Hoover, whose agents had installed a bug in King's hotel room.

Without knowing this, his anxieties were enough to keep him awake much of the night. Soon, he would go to Mississippi to offer his support to the voter registration effort and the Freedom Party, and he had reasonable fears about his safety. "I want to live a normal life," he told a friend, "but the staff was trying to say 'You have no normal life. You are not an ordinary man.'"

|||

It was an eclectic crowd of some forty thousand folks that gathered at San Francisco's civic center on Sunday, July 12, the day before the Republican National Convention opened. There were moderate Republicans who had come to hear speeches by Nelson Rockefeller, Henry Cabot Lodge, and Senators Jacob Javits and Kenneth Keating of New York. There were members of San Francisco Negro organizations. There were liberal Democrats who just wanted to maximize the size of any anti-Goldwater crowd. There were student and nonstudent left-wingers from Berkeley, gathered by the same protest organizations that had handled the demonstration at the Sheraton Center.

The stated purpose of the demonstration was support for civil rights, not opposition to Goldwater. But no one was fooled, not even the moderate Republican speakers who pointedly declined to criticize their candidate-to-be or to mention his name.

A. Philip Randolph, the president of the Brotherhood of Sleeping Car Porters, was less restrained. "I cannot see how any Negro with any self-respect can even give the slightest presumption to Barry Goldwater as president of the United States," he said.

Finally, the young people near the edges of the crowd could cheer: the college guys in Beatle haircuts and the girls in unkempt blue jeans, the ones bearing signs reading "Defoliate Goldwater" or "Vote for Goldwater: Courage, Integrity, Bigotry."

Many of them had come across the bay from Berkeley, where they went to school or once had gone to school. To many on the University of California campus, Goldwater was evil incarnate, so much so that they were trying to help Scranton even though they hardly shared his politics.

At the university's main entrance, at the T-intersection of Telegraph Avenue and Bancroft Way, some students had set up tables on the twenty-nine-foot by ninety-foot plaza outside the Sather Gate to pass out Scranton leaflets and to urge students to do volunteer work for him. According to a university rule, partisan political activity was forbidden on campus. There were a few Goldwater supporters at the University, and they complained to the campus authorities.

||||

A few days earlier, Republican State Chairman Jim Martin of Alabama had been outside mowing his lawn in Gadsden, Alabama, when his wife came to the door to tell him Governor George Wallace was on the phone. It was no social call. A state plane was already on the way to the Gadsden airport, Wallace said, to bring Martin to Montgomery for a secret meeting at the Jefferson Davis Hotel. He wouldn't even have time to change out of his lawn-mowing clothes.

The meeting lasted three hours, but the governor was blunt. He wanted Martin to tell Barry Goldwater to choose him—Wallace—as his running mate. "With all my big victories of the past two years," he said, "it must be apparent to a one-eyed nigguh who can't see good out of his other eye that me and Goldwater would be a winning ticket. We'd have the South locked up, then him and me could concentrate on the industrial states of the North and win."

Wallace wanted Martin to pretend that this was his idea, not Wallace's. "It didn't come from me," the governor told him.

Martin was somewhat dumbfounded, but he agreed to "tell Mr. Goldwater" as soon as he got to San Francisco.

"No," Wallace said. "I want you to go tonight."

Martin looked down at his grass-spattered old clothes and dirty shoes.

"I'm not prepared to go you know," he said. "I don't have any money with me."

"That's no problem," said Wallace, and one of his aides counted out a thousand dollars in cash.

Martin did go home to change his clothes, but he got to San Francisco earlier than scheduled, and that Sunday before the convention opened, he kept his promise, meeting with Goldwater on the roof of the Mark Hopkins Hotel.

"Mr. Wallace has suggested that he would like to be a candidate with you as your vice presidential nominee on the Republican ticket," he said as a photographer on an adjacent roof began snapping pictures of the nominee-to-be, one of his aides, and this other fellow.

One of his pictures showed Goldwater appearing stunned—but not witless. The suggestion, he said, was impossible. Yes, he had been trying none too subtly to hint that Wallace should drop his third-party candidacy. But, well, he was going to carry most of the South with or without Wallace, and Wallace was still a Democrat, and "this *was* a Republican convention."

|||

Tim Leary was upstairs on a trip when the Pranksters arrived.

The trip was Ken Kesey's idea. Kesey was one of those artists for whom mind-expanding drugs were a supplement to enormous talent, not an excuse for lack of it. A high school football player and college wrestling champ in Oregon, Kesey discovered intellectuals (Larry McMurtry and Wendell Berry were classmates) and mind-altering substances as a graduate student at Stanford. In his mind, the two would be forever connected.

In nearby San Francisco's North Beach, Kesey found the jazz musicians, junkies, writers, and artists who had been influenced by Ginsberg's poetry and Kerouac's *On the Road*. Kesey considered Kerouac more reporter than novelist but was drawn to him anyway. Kesey knew that there was something of himself in Kerouac's *Road* companion, Dean Moriarty, the car-obsessed, speed-loving outlaw who lived on drugs and instinct.

Kesey first tried LSD under the auspices of the United States government, which was doing experiments on volunteers at Menlo Park Veterans Hospital. "Suddenly, I was shifted over to where I had been looking full front at the world," he said, "and by shifting over, I was seeing it from another position."

What a great situation for a young novelist. Soon enough, Kesey began working the late shift at the hospital as a psychiatric aide. Another great situation for a young novelist, and from it came a fine novel, *One Flew Over the Cuckoo's Nest,* written out of experience, prodigious talent, and the haze of peyote. It was published in February 1962 to rave reviews.

Now, in the summer of 1964, Kesey wanted to see the country, to go to the World's Fair, to be in New York for a publication party for his new novel, *Sometimes a Great Notion.* And he wanted to make a movie. With some of the royalties from *Cuckoo's Nest,* he'd been buying cameras, film, and lighting equipment, and somehow it came to him that it would be a neat idea to take his friends across the country with him and make a movie about their trip, a new version of *On the Road.*

Especially because Neal Cassady would be the main driver. Cassady was the real-life model of Kerouac's Dean Moriarty. Cassady, on parole after serving half of a five-year sentence in San Quentin on a trumped-up marijuana conviction, had showed up at Kesey's house two years earlier, talking nonstop. He was a great talker and a great driver and, best of all, a mythical character, a living icon.

So Kesey bought a prewar International Harvester bus, reconfigured it as a traveling home, wired in a sound system, and embarked on a voyage of discovery, a fantasy of sorts. As such, his group had to have fantasy names. Kesey was the Chief. Cassady was Speed Limit. The whole group was the Merry Pranksters. Even the bus had to have a name. Somebody painted the bus exterior with bright Day-Glo paint, wrote the word FUURTHER on the front, the warning CAUTION: WEIRD LOAD on the back, and A VOTE FOR BARRY IS A VOTE FOR FUN on one side. On Sunday, June 14, they left Oregon.

They went to Arizona, then to Houston to visit Larry McMurtry, on to Louisiana and Florida, and up the coast to New York, where a friend who was going to be out of town made available an apartment at Madison Avenue and Ninetieth Street.

Cassady wanted to see his old road buddies. He wanted to get them together with his new road buddies. Ginsberg was easy to find, but Jack Kerouac was staying out in Northport, on Long Island, with his mother, and he was reluctant to come into town. Neal drove out to Northport to bring him to a party.

It wasn't much fun. By the time Cassady and Kerouac got back from Long Island, it was almost 11 P.M. Ginsberg was there with Alan Orlovsky and Orlovsky's brother, Julius, who had just been released from a state mental hospital. The Pranksters set up their movie and recording equipment, and Ginsberg started in on a Krishna chant. Kerouac sat on a sofa, drinking whiskey from a bottle in a paper bag. Cassady put a set of earphones on Kerouac's head while the Pranksters sang, and one of them draped an American flag around his shoulders.

Kerouac was not comfortable. They hadn't realized how he had changed. He was drinking a lot and had become quite conservative. He was going to church. He was offended at the casual use of the flag. After a few minutes, he took the earphones off his head, removed the flag from the Prankster's shoulders, folded it, laid it down on the sofa, and left. At that point, someone realized that Julius Orlovsky was missing.

But there were other worlds to conquer. A few days later, the Pranksters got back in the bus and headed north. They'd heard about what was going on at Millbrook and thought they'd be welcomed there.

They were wrong. Most of the regulars were coming off what Richard Alpert called "a very intense and profound" all-night LSD trip when the bus pulled up in the morning. American flags flying, rock 'n' roll blaring from the speakers, the bus rolled onto the grounds, the Pranksters announcing themselves by throwing green smoke bombs from the bus.

Alpert, a polite fellow, went outside to welcome them, but he was not glad to see them, feeling, he later said, "like we're a pastoral Indian village invaded by a whooping cowboy band of Wild West saloon carousers." But he made them feel at home, gave them the run of the place, went upstairs to tell Tim who had arrived. The Pranksters bathed. They ate. They slept. They realized they were intruders, and they left.

Tim Leary stayed upstairs, down with a touch of flu and on a three-day trip. "In many ways," Alpert later said, "it was a moment in history that didn't happen." All that quietude and Eastern mysticism was strange to the Pranksters, who began referring to their brief stay at Millbrook as "The Crypt Trip." To Kesey, all this Oriental stuff was objectionable, an aping of someone else's cultural ideas, not America's.

Like Andy Warhol, Ken Kesey was attracted to American sights and sounds, not exotic re-creations of somewhere else. They were not alone. California artists such as Wallace Berman, Bruce Conner, Ed Kienholz, and Connor Everts, along with the beats and some of the more conventional writers and artists, found their frame of reference not in Greek myths, Renaissance painting, European philosophy, or classical music but in the objects of everyday life. Warhol was not the only artist painting what he saw, what everyone saw: highways, office buildings, transistor radios, movie stars, Brillo boxes.

In rebelling against abstract expressionism and its self-conscious intellectualism, Warhol, Red Grooms, Roy Lichtenstein, Robert Rauschenberg, Claes Oldenburg, and Jasper Johns were, aesthetically at least, making common cause with common folks. They disdained the disdain for everyday life and commercial culture expressed by so many artists and intellectuals. "The real American architecture," Lichtenstein said, "is McDonald's and not Mies van der Rohe."

You go paint the abstract vision inside your cultured, oh-so-sensitive head, these artists were saying to their elders; we're going to paint Marilyn Monroe, hamburgers, or a comic strip. Or we're going to place objects on our paintings, stick junk from the street right onto the canvas. Maybe art shouldn't imitate life so much as blend into it.

Wallace Berman used an old copier machine to make collages from magazine clips, building them layer by layer, sometimes painting over them with bright acrylics. His constant image was the transistor radio. Just as radio, with many stations to listen to, provided an unprecedented variety of listening opportunities, Berman's collages provided an almost infinite variety of images. The viewer could take in the entire work or focus on a piece of it.

Artist Allan Kaprow, who helped invent "happenings" in the late 1950s, wrote that the paintings of the last great abstract expressionist, Jackson Pollock, were really "environments" and that artists should "learn to go beyond paint and canvas in order to immerse themselves in the environment of everyday life."[2]

A similar democratizing point of view had entered the dance world. Choreographers Merce Cunningham and Paul Taylor were creating dance movements based on such quotidian actions as walking, sitting down in a chair, and yawning, not the grand gestures of *grands hommes* and *grandes dames* but the stuff most folks do every day.

This attempt to erase the distinction between "high art" and the day-to-day world was part of the aesthetic theory of the day. "Everyone is an artist," proclaimed Joseph Beuys. Arthur Danto, the philosopher and art critic, said that at that time artists "recognized that there was no special way a work of art had to be," and so "artists were liberated to do whatever they wanted to do."[3]

Sort of like Muhammad Ali.

Lawrence Alloway, the art critic for *The Nation*, came up with a name for it: he called it "pop art." It was descriptive, but pop was not an organized movement of cooperating artists, as, say, impressionism had been in Paris in the 1870s. Instead, it was what critic Bob Adelman called "the spontaneous convergence of low culture and high spirits." Warhol thought he was the only one using comic strip characters in his works until he came across Lichtenstein's paintings at the Leo Castelli Gallery.

None of this sprang full-blown in 1964. It had been going on since the late 1950s, and most of the pop artists were somewhat older than the draft resisters and college dropouts who began making their presence known in 1964 with a similar appeal to the ordinary and distrust of the established. But like youthful political rebellion, pop emerged into the general culture in 1964. That was the year Lichtenstein started making enough money from his art that he could quit teaching, even though *Life* magazine wondered whether he was "the worst artist in America." It was the year, Warhol said, when "everything went young."

Arthur Danto was also part of the school of analytical philosophy, which by the early 1960s had begun to displace the more traditional metaphysical philosophers. Though it might seem absurd to call any school of philosophy "populist," analytical philosophy is more down to earth than its predecessors. It is, Danto wrote, "tied to human experience . . . and ordinary discourse."

There was a similar populism of personal behavior, at least among young people. Or perhaps it was a reverse populism; instead of the elite adopting the practices of the middle class, much of the middle class was imitating the avant-garde. The political and cultural rebels of 1964 were likely to be middle-income children of suburban parents, liberated from the constraints of their elders by affluence and by one particular product of technology—the oral contraceptive. It was not a beat poet in Greenwich Village but a senior at Ohio State, of all places, who said that today's undergraduates had "discarded the idea that loss of virginity is related to degeneracy. Premarital sex doesn't mean the downfall of society, at least not the kind of society we're going to build."[4]

Considering that the "monokini," a Rudi Gernreich–designed bathing suit composed of wool-knit shorts held up by narrow halter straps, was already at the stores (though it was illegal to wear it on almost every public beach), such comments should have come as no surprise. Other designers were experimenting with transparent blouses, bare-backed evening dresses, plunging necklines open to the navel in front and going to the top of the spine in back. By October, Warner's would introduce the brief nylon body stocking, the cling of which left little to the imagination.[5]

Neither the established culture nor established authority was willing to surrender on this front. When Connor Everts, a California avant-gardist, arranged an exhibit at the Zora Gallery in Los Angeles for a series of lithographs called *Studies in Desperation,* works about the assassination of President Kennedy and the 1960 execution of California rapist Caryl Chessman, five vice cops came to the gallery and said that three "offensive" works in the window and thirteen others in the gallery should be removed. When Everts refused, he was arrested.

The "offensive" works were not sexual. They were abstract (but not so abstract that the average person wouldn't know the subject) depictions of a child emerging from the womb, then returning to it. The point being made was that America was a dangerous place for children, and Everts, who didn't think these lithographs were his best work, was convinced that what the cops were trying to censor was his statement, not obscenity.

| | |

The Republican National Convention opened at the Cow Palace on Monday, July 13, and now, finally, Cliff White was in charge, in his element, and in the closest proximity to heaven he would know on this earth.

Literally and otherwise, he had the place wired. From his air-conditioned fifty-five-foot unmarked green and white trailer, appropriately protected from unauthorized entry by uniformed Pinkerton guards, White and six regional directors were connected to the world by twenty-nine telephone lines and three television sets. Seventeen phone lines went to the convention floor, two to Barry Goldwater's suite, five to the main Goldwater switchboard, and two to the general world. Then there was the "all-call" line, by which White could talk to all the state delegations at once.

In addition to the telephones, eighteen walkie-talkies were distributed to the Goldwater floor operation, so that if trouble broke out anywhere, anytime, a responsible campaign worker could be quickly dispatched to deal with it.

Some days before the convention started, Nicholas Volcheff of the phone company and Jim Day of White's staff had climbed the rafters and catwalks above the Cow Palace and installed a master antenna connected to White's trailer. Invisible to the eye—as if any eye would think to search that far up—but audibly powerful, the antenna could pick up the voices on walkie-talkies.

Scranton's walkie-talkies. Volcheff and Day had equipped the Goldwater walkie-talkies with a parallel set of ultra-high-frequency equipment more difficult to spy on.

Nor was that the only bit of electronic hanky-panky. High in the Cow Palace's loft area, White's minions marked every cable of every television and radio station, and they were prepared to cause "cable trouble" should the coverage become what Goldwater later called "a little too obnoxious to us."[6]

Each delegation had two Goldwater chairmen. The "inside man" took instructions from White and his regional directors, and the "outside man" kept tabs on all the Goldwater delegates, contacting each one every day, often two or three times a day, to make sure no one wavered.

This was made easier by the accumulation of what would later be called a database. In a master card file there was a card for each delegate containing political and biographical information, though not, White insisted, personal information.

Then there was security. This was run by White's friend Charley Barr and a small army of volunteers, each with a small recorder and/or a Polaroid camera. Strangers hanging around the Goldwater trailer were likely to be photographed, perhaps interviewed.

At the Mark Hopkins, entry to the fifteenth floor was barred; with the Scranton headquarters just two floors below, one couldn't be too careful. Visitors had to get off on the fourteenth floor and walk up, past a guard at the top of the stairs. Authorized staff wore lapel pins with the presidential seal on them. Senior staff pins had the numerals "3505" across the seal. Closed-circuit television cameras acted as auxiliary guards.

It was elaborate, it was unprecedented, it was efficient, and it was unnecessary. White did all this because he had the money for it; because Goldwater, who loved gadgetry and didn't want to have to talk to White any more than necessary, gave it his quick approval; and because it was fun. For White, it was like the days when he was younger and ran roughshod over the opposition at Young Republican meetings. Considering what he'd been through, White deserved to play with toys.

But this convention would have nominated Barry Goldwater if White had no more sophisticated a communications system than a megaphone, no more of a political organization than a delegate list, and no security at all. He had seen to that months ago. These were the delegates he had arranged for. This was not a Republican convention but a Goldwater convention; an astounding 74.3 percent of the delegates had not been at either the 1960 or the 1956 convention. Most of them had never been to any convention at all. There was no need to worry about waverers. These delegates would not have wavered had Barry Goldwater been found wandering naked in front of the Mark Hopkins at noon.

Goldwater came pretty close to the political equivalent of that in an interview in the German magazine *Der Spiegel,* which hit the newsstands a few days before the convention opened. "The Eastern money interests, the large banks, the financial houses have most always been able to control the selection of the Republican candidates," he told the interviewers. Considering his background, Goldwater would have made an unlikely anti-Semite, but especially in a German magazine, his sentiments brought to mind paranoia about claques of international bankers trying to rule the world. For good measure, he complained that the American press takes "slanted views that just can't be associated with honest reporting."

The delegates, even those who didn't agree, didn't care. Besides, you can't beat somebody with nobody, and Scranton, the only opponent remaining, was effectively nobody. He had a headquarters. He had walkie-talkies. That was about it.

The day before the convention began, Scranton released an open letter to Goldwater, accusing him of "casually prescribing nuclear war as a solution to a troubled world, [allowing] radical extremists to use you, [displaying] irresponsibility in the serious question of a racial holocaust."

Save for that last word, the contents of the letter were arguably accurate. Considering the timing, the tone approached hysteria, and Goldwater had little trouble ignoring him.

What nobody realized at the time was that this was the first of the meaningless conventions. Even Cliff White did not fully understand the extent to which television, affluence, and a more educated electorate had taken the nominating process out of the hands of political leaders who could control delegates and put it into the hands of ordinary citizens who went to caucuses and voted in primaries.

But if this convention, like those that followed it, was insignificant as a nominating mechanism, it was momentous as theater, and in their determination to enjoy their own performance, the delegates and speakers put on a dreadful show in the eyes of the larger audience watching them on television.

First, there was Dwight Eisenhower's speech on Tuesday, unmemorable save for his expression of disdain for "sensation-seeking columnists and commentators." To any other crowd, this was a remark that might have passed unnoticed as the grouchiness of a geezer. To this crowd, it was red meat. They filled the Cow Palace with raucous cheers of approval. Like their candidate, they despised the "liberal" press.

Their sentiment was not without foundation. Most reporters were at least mildly liberal, if not on all issues at least on the two that most engaged conservative Republicans—foreign policy and civil rights. The typical successful journalists (and it was the successful ones who got to cover presidential campaigns) approved of the United Nations and disapproved of racial segregation.

It was hardly unanimous, and Goldwater had supporters among influential journalists. Just weeks earlier in Newport, Rhode Island, *New York Times* columnist Arthur Krock and William Buckley had discussed ways of "getting the senator off of the defensive in re: the armament-disarmament situation and the missile reliability versus the bombers." Krock had suggested that "either the senator or his chief aides . . . read the John Paton Davies book, *Foreign and Other Affairs.*"

Still, most reporters tended to view Barry Goldwater as a political oddity. Reporters who covered his campaign grew to like him personally, but few of them liked his politics.

The trouble was that the average American, although perhaps not enamored of reporters, harbored no particular dislike for them, either. In fact, the average American found some of them downright likable. Chief among these was John Chancellor of *NBC News*, so that it was particularly inconvenient that he was the correspondent escorted off the floor by White's security forces just hours after Ike's speech for the crime of interviewing someone on the convention floor, which he was authorized to do.

To the average viewer, Chancellor seemed a gentleman. The appearance fit the reality; Chancellor was in fact a gentle man, and though he disagreed with Goldwater on almost everything, especially civil rights, he was a scrupulously fair reporter. He also had a quick wit. As he was being led off the floor, live to the world, he signed off: "This is John Chancellor, somewhere in custody."

White's security forces were hardly the Gestapo, but the comparison was impossible to ignore, especially after other credentialed journalists reported that they had been kept off the convention floor by guards who told them only delegates could enter. In fact, a few delegates with valid floor passes but Rockefeller buttons were kept out, too. That these were petty abuses of power made them no less distasteful.

That night was the platform debate, and the moderates had decided to make their stand over a proposal to insert a plank condemning extremism. How could anybody be against condemning extremism?

Easily, in this case. The Goldwater delegates saw the resolution as an attack on them, a conviction confirmed for them by the news that the main speaker for the proposal was to be their archenemy, Nelson Rockefeller.

Senator Thruston Morton, presiding, had barely introduced Rockefeller when the booing started. It came down from the galleries and echoed off the huge ceiling down to the delegates, who joined in. As it echoed, it crescendoed.

It was animal, an outpouring of frustration and resentment by people whose politics were driven by resentment. They had won. They had beaten Rockefeller, and now, instead of displaying graciousness in victory, they were venting their spleen at him and everything he stood for in their eyes: civil rights, internationalism, restraint, activist government, personal immorality. They tried to shout him down.

They failed. Rockefeller stood there and took it. They didn't bother him. He had lost the nomination and he knew he would lose this vote, but he was, after all, Nelson Rockefeller, and he was not to be driven off the podium by anyone, certainly not these people.

"This is still a free country, ladies and gentlemen," his gravelly voice shouted into the microphone, and the boos grew louder again. White hit his "all-call" button and ordered the delegation chairmen: "If there is any booing in your delegation or surrounding delegations, stop it"; but some of the delegates were beyond control.

Finally, after sixteen minutes, Rockefeller was able to speak. He had five minutes, and he had prepared a five-minute speech, but when he was not quite done, Mel Laird, now the presiding officer, came up behind him, having judged his time to be over, and grabbed him by the left sleeve.

Rockefeller turned briskly to his left and pushed Laird away. It was not a gentle push. He had a five-minute speech prepared, and he would deliver it. In millions of living rooms, he looked like a hero.

| | |

On Thursday, July 16, as the Republican National Convention was preparing to nominate Barry Goldwater, an apartment building superintendent was hosing down the sidewalk and watering the trees and flowers of his building on East Seventy-sixth Street in New York.

Some of the water splashed on a small group of teenagers who were in the neighborhood as part of a summer jobs program. One of them, fifteen-year-old James Powell, grabbed a garbage can cover to use as a shield and a bottle to throw at the superintendent. An off-duty police officer passing by saw what was happening, shouted, and fired a warning shot.

Powell turned and lunged at the cop, cutting his right forearm. The officer, Thomas Gilligan, fired again, twice, at the teenager. He killed him.[7]

| | |

That afternoon, shortly before the balloting began in San Francisco, Goldwater called the president "the biggest faker in the United States. He opposed civil rights until this year." Johnson, said Goldwater, is "the phoniest individual who ever came down the pike."

Hours later, Goldwater was nominated overwhelmingly. Shortly after the balloting, he told reporters he would not level personal attacks at the president. He then announced the choice of William Miller, an undistinguished congressman from upstate New York, as his running mate. There would be no gesture to the center in his selection, nor would such a gesture come in his speech the next evening, much of which was an eloquent exposition of the kind of conservatism almost any American could accept. The Republican Party, Goldwater said, "with its every action, every word, every breath, and every heartbeat, has but a single resolve and that is:

"*Freedom!*

"*Freedom*—made orderly for this nation by our constitutional government.

"*Freedom*—under a government limited by the laws of nature and nature's God.

"*Freedom*—*balanced* so that order, lacking liberty, will not become the slavery of the prison cell; *balanced* so that liberty, lacking order, will not become the license of the mob and jungle."

Alas, all that reasonable eloquence was overshadowed by two sentences in the speech. "I would remind you," he said, "that extremism in the defense of liberty is no vice." The cheers now were as enthusiastic as had been the boos for Rockefeller, and Goldwater had to pause a moment before completing the thought.

"And let me remind you that moderation in the pursuit of justice is no virtue."

The applause was deafening in the hall, but in the trailer, Cliff White was grim. He knew it was coming, of course, and had expressed his disapproval. But who was listening to him?

Goldwater had been listening to a small coterie of conservative scholars, including historian Harry Jaffa, who helped write the speech and who was impressed by a line of Thomas Paine's: "Moderation in temper is always a virtue, but moderation in principle is always a vice."

In the abstract, Paine's contention and Jaffa's paraphrase of it were interesting and arguable propositions. In the context of this convention, they were politically destructive. Goldwater seemed to be defending the Birchers and their ilk, rejecting pragmatism and endorsing zealotry. Tom Paine, to be sure, had no distaste for zealotry. But the American electorate did.

When the convention was over, Cliff White, his wife, and his friends held their long-planned celebration in the Crystal Room of the Fairmont Hotel. They partied until 3 A.M., reveling in their hard-earned accomplishment. Then White and his wife drove to the home of family friends where Mrs. White and their children had been staying. In the morning, White called his convention office and asked if Senator Goldwater had been looking for him.

He had not.

White then went back to his room at the Mark Hopkins to start packing. A few minutes later, there was a knock on his door. Two reporters wanted his comment on the news: Goldwater had named Dean Burch as Republican national chairman. It was the only job White had ever craved.

As soon as the reporters left, he sat down and wrote Burch a note of congratulations. He had not finished before an old New York friend dropped by. White told him what had happened and said, "I guess my job is done."

|21|

SECURITY AND ITS DISCONTENTS

In New York, CORE organized a rally to protest the killing of James Powell on Saturday evening, July 18. The Reverend Nelson Dukes of the Fountain Street Baptist Church urged the crowd to march on the Twenty-eighth Precinct Station House, where the group became unruly. As garbage can covers and bottles began to fly, Dukes said, "If I knew this was going to happen I wouldn't have said anything." Then he walked away.[1]

The rioting spread, and it got political support. The tiny but loud Progressive Labor Party proclaimed the Revolution. Rent strike leader Jesse Gray called for a "hundred revolutionaries willing to die." Horrified that Negro rioting could only help Goldwater, NAACP leader Roy Wilkins cut short a Wyoming vacation. "I don't care how angry Negroes are," he said. "We can't leave [our cause] to bottle throwers and rock throwers."

But many young Negroes were now more receptive to the Progressive Labor Party than to Roy Wilkins. To them, he was just another proper, middle-aged leader. The same youthful impatience that inspired college students to risk their lives in Mississippi inspired high school dropouts to violence in New York.

| | |

Earlier that day, Jack Ruby, at his insistence, was hooked up to a polygraph and questioned in Dallas by Arlen Specter of the Warren Commission staff. Ruby swore, again, that he had never met Lee Harvey Oswald and had shot him only to save Mrs. Kennedy the ordeal of a trial. The polygraph indicated that Ruby was telling the truth.

The next day, caving in to both reality and pressure from conservative segregationists such as Roger Milliken, George Wallace said he would not run as an independent candidate after all.[2]

||||

Robert Kennedy went to Chicago on Monday, July 20, to have lunch with Mayor Richard J. Daley, who called President Johnson the next day with an account of the discussion. Daley was a busy fellow over the next few days. He also met with Hubert Humphrey and Eugene McCarthy. To each of them, he said, "You'd make a fine candidate." McCarthy alone interpreted these words as an endorsement, telling reporters that Daley indicated he was "partial to me."

Daley was partial to Robert Kennedy, but he was loyal to the president, to whom he reported on each of his meetings. Early in August, Daley visited the White House, where Johnson invited him to stay overnight. In his room, Daley decided he wanted a beer. The steward said there was no beer, but there was good scotch—Chivas Regal. Daley accepted the Chivas, but sipping it while sitting on his bed he complained, "When Jack Kennedy was here, they had beer."

Even so, he was delighted the next day to be summoned into the presidential bedroom. In he strode, proper as always in suit and tie, to be welcomed by a pajama-clad Lyndon Johnson still abed, newspapers spread out on the covers and all three television sets on, one tuned to each network. Along with Daley's favorite young protégé, Congressman Dan Rostenkowski, the mayor spent fifteen minutes listening to Johnson talk about the three television sets.[3]

||||

Shortly after noon on Tuesday, July 21, Robert Kennedy called the president. "Martin Luther King is going down to Greenwood, Mississippi, tonight and he's going to address a mass rally there," Kennedy said, and local law enforcement officers had declined to provide an escort. "It's a ticklish problem because if he gets killed, uh, uh . . . it creates all kinds of problems, not just being dead but also a lot of other kinds of problems."

"Can we have FBI people there?" Johnson said.

"Well, it's difficult. . . . I have no dealings with the FBI anymore, but I think maybe if you ask them, perhaps."

No dealings with the FBI? The attorney general? The president appeared confused. Had Kennedy not recently received an FBI document?

Instead of answering that question, Kennedy told Johnson that he understood Hoover "sends all kinds of reports over to you . . . about me and about the Department of Justice."

"Not any that I've seen. What are you talking about?"

"Well, well, I just understand that—about me planning and plotting things."

"No, no," Johnson said. "He hasn't sent me any report on you or on the department at any time."

"I had understood that he had sent reports over about me plotting the overthrow of the government by force and violence, leading a coup."

Kennedy laughed when he said that. It was offhand hyperbole. What he meant was that he had heard that Hoover was sending Johnson reports that Kennedy was engaged in political mischief, efforts to make the president look bad.

"No, no, that's an error," Johnson said. "He never has said that or given any indication of it."

Kennedy didn't believe that. He didn't believe much of what Johnson said to him.

| | |

The New York City riots must have been organized.

Such, at least, was the assumption of Lyndon Johnson, J. Edgar Hoover, Governor Rockefeller, and Mayor Wagner. Johnson ordered the FBI to investigate whether political subversives had incited the violence, and then asked Thomas E. Dewey to help evaluate the Bureau's information and to serve as a public "sponsor" of the final report. Still worried about the backlash despite comforting poll results, the president was seeking bipartisan cover for whatever emerged.

The most obvious culprits were radical Negroes and what Hoover called "left-wing labor groups," but Nelson Rockefeller had another thought. At the convention, he said, Goldwaterites had taunted him with predictions about embarrassing race riots in his state. So the scope of the investigation was broadened to seek out operatives from both the left and right wings.

On Thursday, July 23, 242 of the nation's most powerful businessmen descended on Washington—so many that more than ninety company planes had to be diverted from National Airport to Dulles—to have lunch at the White House. The stated purpose of the event was to get the business community to help "persuade others that the law of the land must be obeyed." The subtext was that the heads of some of the nation's biggest corporations had recognized that government was their ally, not their adversary. Lyndon Johnson's seduction of big business was working.

It had been working for a while. Already Henry Ford II had endorsed the president for reelection; soon he would become one of the forty-five sponsors of the National Independent Committee for President Johnson and Senator Humphrey. Even earlier, Ford had supported the tax cut and had convinced a few other corporate executives to join him, including the presidents of Westinghouse and the Norfolk and Western Railway. By Election Day, forty-five heretofore Republican executives of major companies would endorse the president.

And by endorsing him they would be endorsing his policies, including the managed economy and the planned deficit. Here was the key element for completing the New Deal, which had fought deflation (that's what the Great Depression was) by deficit spending. It was the only thing that worked. It had even been the only thing that worked for Eisenhower, his economic advisors, and their corporate friends, who had decided to accept deficits in 1958 and 1959 rather than risk a recession. Now, with Goldwater scaring businessmen with his statements on foreign affairs and civil rights, Johnson had the chance to bring them over to his side of the debate and to forge with them a lasting prosperity built around modest deficit spending. It was an opportunity he would not let pass.

After lunch, Johnson turned to crasser political matters. He told John Connally that his running mate would not be Kennedy, who "thinks he can probably make me throw the election and he would like to see me a defeated man like Stevenson."

Connally agreed, calling Kennedy an "egotistical selfish person who feels like he's almost anointed and he is so power-mad that it's unbelievable." Connally, who always liked a good fight, encouraged Johnson in his. "If you have to take Bobby on in a goddamned fight, let's take him on."

| | |

Barry Goldwater, now the Republican nominee for president, went to the White House the next day and surrendered. "I do not believe it is in the best interest of the United States to make the Vietnam War or its conduct a political issue in this campaign," he said. "I have come to promise I will not do so."

Neither would he attack Johnson on civil rights, because "it could polarize the country." The president, obviously pleased, was grateful but otherwise noncommittal.

Late that evening, the president met with his closest aides to discuss the vice presidential choice. Among the names thrown about: Dean Rusk, Bob McNamara, Gene McCarthy, Hubert Humphrey, Senator Edmund Muskie of Maine, and Robert Kennedy.

And Robert Kennedy?

Perhaps Johnson, fearing that even his most senior staff included disloyal leakers, was simply putting on an act, making it seem as though Kennedy were still in the running until he, himself, could make it clear to his attorney general and the world that he was not.

Or perhaps, when it came to Robert Kennedy, the president was so befuddled, so defensive, and so enraged that he was unable to act. If so, the paralysis was not political but psychological. Johnson feared Kennedy. He feared him more than he disliked him. He no doubt disliked him less than he was disliked by him. As that little tête-à-tête in the White House kitchen showed, Johnson would have welcomed Kennedy's friendship. Kennedy was not interested.

Perhaps that was one reason Johnson feared him. Another reason was the insecurity that the president could not escape when confronting members of the Eastern meritocracy. Kennedy was a rich man's son who had gone to Harvard. He held those "seminars" at his home in Virginia at which prominent intellectuals held forth for invited guests. He mixed easily with John Kenneth Galbraith and Arthur Schlesinger and their friends who knew their way around Harvard Square, quoted poets, and read *The New York Review of Books*. For all Johnson knew, Kennedy read it himself. Johnson wasn't much of a reader. In the presence of such men, the president of the United States felt inadequate.

But there was a more specific reason that Kennedy made Johnson uncomfortable, more specific and more personal. Kennedy was living evidence that the great, wrenching decision Lyndon Johnson had made as a young man—a decision that required nothing less than a rejection of his mother—had been unnecessary. Bobby Kennedy was a tough little son of a bitch who liked to read poetry. He was a vicious political infighter, a hard-nosed attorney general, and he was even physically tough enough to have made the Harvard football team as a scrawny 155-pounder, none of which stopped him from at least dabbling at the edges of the world of culture and intellect.

Johnson could see this—he could see so many things—and it must have tortured him. In early adulthood he had decided to become the tough Texan his father wanted him to be and not the literate gentleman of his mother's dreams. Now here was this . . . this spoiled, obnoxious whippersnapper who barely tolerated him and who stood as a constant reminder of the turning point in his own life he had never quite gotten over.

| | |

On Monday, July 27, at the urgent pleading of Mayor Robert Wagner, Martin Luther King went to New York to meet with the mayor and Roy Wilkins. King suggested that Wagner establish a civilian police review board and arrange for more economic development in the Negro community. The three of them then toured Harlem, where they were booed, including King. Even the local leadership was not in thrall to the great man. "No leader outside Harlem should come into this town and tell us what to do," proclaimed Congressman Adam Clayton Powell from his pulpit at Abyssinian Baptist Church.

No wonder. Powell had a political machine that depended on low voter turnout. Only 25 percent of the eligible voters in his district cast ballots in 1964. A guy like King might inspire more people to register. Powell had no more interest in having more Negroes register to vote than did Paul Johnson.[4]

Later that day, the president of the United States finally called his attorney general and asked him to come by for a little talk.

Sure, Kennedy said; he'd even cancel his scheduled trip to New York the next day for a meeting about the Kennedy Memorial Library.

Oh, no hurry, said the president. Wednesday would be fine.

"He's going to tell me I'm not going to be vice president," Kennedy said as he hung up. "I wondered when he'd get around to it."[5]

Johnson was just as glad for the delay. He had to prepare for this.

The previous evening, David McDonald of the United Steelworkers Union had come to dinner at the White House, bearing bad news. His members liked Barry Goldwater. One private poll, McDonald told the president, actually showed Goldwater leading among union members.

| | |

On Tuesday, July 28, Jacqueline Kennedy bought a fifteen-room apartment at 1040 Fifth Avenue, overlooking Central Park at Eighty-fifth Street. It cost her $200,000, and she spent another $125,000 refurbishing it to her taste.

| | |

On Wednesday morning, July 29, President Johnson called Clark Clifford.

"I'm going to have that meeting today," the president said. "I've talked to one or two folks. He knows what it's about. He also wants to know who it is."

"I have believed all along that all you do is tell him," Clifford said. "Now

I think it is appropriate and courteous to give some reasons for your decision, but you are not asking him at any time for his reaction. . . . Say I have not made the final decision as yet."

But Johnson wanted more than advice. He wanted Clifford to write the statement that Johnson would make, in private, to Kennedy. Clifford complied.

There were two summit meetings on the afternoon of Wednesday, July 29. In New York, Whitney Young of the Urban League, John Lewis of SNCC, James Farmer of CORE, and Martin Luther King went to the NAACP offices of Roy Wilkins, who had summoned them with a telegram warning of "violent and futile disorder." A. Philip Randolph of the Sleeping Car Porters and Bayard Rustin also attended.

At the meeting, Wilkins and Young suggested that they all declare a nationwide "moratorium" on marches and demonstrations until after the election; demonstrations, Wilkins warned, too easily degenerated into riots, and for the moment, Negro riots were "Goldwater rallies."

But Lewis and Farmer objected, pointing out that the NAACP and the Urban League rarely engaged in protest demonstrations anyway, so they would be giving up nothing. Besides, they said, to announce a moratorium on all demonstrations would play into the hands of their enemies, who refused to recognize the distinction between peaceful protest and riot.

Rustin and Randolph agreed with Wilkins. Here, again, was the essential cleavage—as much generational as ideological, as much a difference of attitude as of analysis—between conventional liberals and the uneasy allies to their left. To the liberals, political action was . . . political! Its purpose was to win political power, the better to accomplish specific policy goals.

To the younger Negro leaders such as Lewis, specific policy goals were not enough. As they saw it, there was substance in the process; the method by which one achieved one's goal was part of the goal. To them, political action was not just political; it was also personal, moral, perhaps existential.

And where was Martin Luther King in this debate?

Either right in the middle, or nowhere, or once again seeking synthesis by saying he found merit in both arguments. Under his guidance, the Negro leaders altered Wilkins's draft statement; instead of an outright "moratorium" on all demonstrations, it called for "broad curtailment if not total moratorium."

| | |

At almost the same hour the Negro leaders met in New York, Robert Kennedy entered the Oval Office. The president did not escort him to the sofa near the fireplace but sat formally behind his official desk, with

Kennedy in a high-backed chair next to the desk. From where Kennedy sat, he could see the lights indicating that a tape recorder was on. Johnson looked at the wall, looked at the floor, and then read Clark Clifford's words aloud:

> I have asked you to come over to discuss with me a subject that is an important one to you and me. As you might suppose, I have been giving a great deal of thought and consideration to the selection of the Democratic candidate for Vice President. . . .
>
> I have reached a decision in this regard and I wanted you to learn of my decision directly from me. . . . I have concluded, for a number of reasons, that it would be inadvisable for you to be the Democratic candidate for Vice President in this year's election. . . .
>
> I believe strongly that the Democratic ticket must be constituted so as to have as much appeal in the Middle West and Border States; also it should be so constituted as to create as little an adverse reaction as possible upon the Southern States. . . .
>
> I am sure that you will understand the basis of my decision and the factors that have entered into it, because President Kennedy had to make a similar decision in 1960.[6]

Fine, said Kennedy, on his best behavior perhaps because of those red lights.

As Kennedy later remembered it, Johnson offered him an ambassador-ship or another cabinet position but urged him to stay at Justice, with its "outstanding staff." His own staff, Johnson said, wasn't much. He couldn't really count on Valenti, Jenkins, or Reedy. Moyers was good, but "his most useful function was rewriting what other people did."

Kennedy was appalled. Johnson was bad-mouthing people who were de-voting their lives to him. "It convinced me that I could not have worked closely with him," he later recalled. Johnson went on to discuss the Bobby Baker case, to insist that he'd had only one inconsequential business dealing with Baker, to describe how there were more Republican senators involved in illegal activities with Baker than Democrats.

From the way Johnson spoke, Kennedy remembered, "it was obvious . . . that he was receiving detailed reports from the FBI on the activities of several of the congressmen and senators."

Still, it was not an unpleasant conversation. After forty minutes or so, Kennedy got up to leave, paused at the door, and said, "I think I could have been of help to you."

"Well, you are going to be a lot of help to me," Johnson said, "and a hell of a lot of help to yourself."

Kennedy immediately walked over to McGeorge Bundy's office. He was not gloomy. In fact, Bundy told the president that Kennedy seemed to have been "cheered up" by the conversation. The attorney general then went back to the Justice Department, where he reported the details of his meeting to a few close advisors and said, "Aw, what the hell. Let's go form our own country."

| | |

And that should have been that.

But it wasn't. Johnson wanted it both ways. He had rejected Kennedy in private, but he insisted that Kennedy take himself out of consideration in public. So the president first told McNamara, who refused, and then Bundy to get Kennedy to announce that he had decided, all by himself, to take his name out of consideration.

No dice. "First, it wasn't true," Kennedy told Bundy. Besides, what kind of a message would it send to all those who'd urged him to seek the spot? This left Johnson in a pickle. He'd finally told Kennedy, but now he had to tell the world without making Kennedy appear a sympathetic character and making himself look like a grouch. Thus was born the "no-cabinet-member" dodge, with the president appearing before television cameras at the White House on Thursday, July 30, and intoning: "I have reached the conclusion that it would be inadvisable for me to recommend to the convention any member of my cabinet or any of those who meet regularly with the cabinet."

As a figleaf, it was transparent, but it did serve the purpose of providing Kennedy with something to make fun of. He was sorry, he said, "that I had to take so many nice fellows over the side with me." He wondered whether it was "premature to stop the vice presidential boomlet for Dean Rusk."

Later that day, Walter Jenkins drove over to the Sheraton Hotel to find Cartha DeLoach, who'd made a speech there, and to give him the news.

"How did Bobby take it?" DeLoach asked.

"Like a spoiled child," said Jenkins.

But he had not come simply to inform; he wanted a favor. "The president wants you to come to the White House and look at the seventy-two telegrams that have arrived since the public announcement this morning. He wants to know if you think they're the real thing or just something Bobby's people cooked up."

Seventy-two telegrams? In a nation of 190 million people, seventy-two telegrams represented something less than revolution in embryo. But De-Loach sat at a desk outside the Oval Office and dutifully went through them. Having determined that twenty of them came from the Boston area, that forty were signed with names that were either Irish or otherwise ethnic Catholic, he made the judgment dearest to the president's heart—that "this is a campaign orchestrated by some of Bobby's old supporters. I don't see a groundswell."

Did they all relax then?

The next day, Friday, Johnson invited three White House correspondents to a lunch of sherry, broiled half-lobster, tomato salad, watermelon, iced tea, and revenge. For four hours, the president provided an account of his session with Kennedy designed to humiliate him. He claimed that Kennedy had visibly gulped when given the news that he would not be chosen, "his Adam's apple going up and down like a yo-yo."

As it had to, as Johnson knew it would, all of official Washington spent the weekend discussing Johnson's version of the July 29 meeting. Kennedy spent the weekend in Hyannis Port, effectively a Washington neighborhood in this context, and when he heard the gossip, he was not amused. He'd thought their meeting was confidential.

Back in Washington a few days later, he waited until the end of a cabinet meeting to protest what he considered a breach of confidence, whereupon the president of the United States told his attorney general that he had not discussed their meeting with another living soul. Whereupon the attorney general stopped just short of calling his president a liar; he simply said that the president could not be telling the truth.

Whereupon Lyndon Johnson blinked.

He said he'd check his records to see whether he might have had some conversation that had subsequently slipped his mind.

He didn't, of course, but Kennedy never expected it. "He tells so many lies," Kennedy noted a week later, "that he convinces himself after a while he's telling the truth. He just doesn't recognize truth or falsehood."

| | |

One of the little band of staff people who shuttled between the two sides of the Capitol working on legislation in those days was Robert Wolf, a former forester and a Republican who had been hired by Mike Mansfield to work on resource issues. One day he was in the office of Senate Interior Committee chairman Anderson, who asked him just how badly Wayne Aspinall wanted that Public Law Land Review Commission.

Very badly indeed, Wolf told him.

Whereupon Anderson leaned back in his desk chair, put his hands behind his head, and said, "And I want a wilderness bill. I guess Wayne's got his Mongolian idiot."[7]

It was an infelicitous phrase, and not even accurately put—"Mongoloid idiot" was the crude term for someone suffering from Down syndrome—but it captured the political situation. In return for his commission, Aspinall allowed the wilderness bill to go through.

It wasn't a straight logroll, the commission for the Wilderness System. Aspinall knew that the idea had too much public support to stop it. But he did hold out for his commission, and he weakened the final bill in two important ways: He cut the acreage, and he made sure that only Congress, not the president, could add to the system.

On July 30 the bill passed by a lopsided vote of 373 to 1. The one was Joe Poole of Texas. After a few more changes in conference, the measure was sent to Johnson, who signed it on Friday, September 4.

It wasn't a complete victory for the preservationists. The law allowed mining in the protected areas until December 31, 1983, and claims valid in 1964 were granted eternal life. Motorboats were to be allowed in much of the canoe area in northern Minnesota, and where grazing had been permitted it would remain permitted.

But neither was it an inconsequential victory. The law designated 9.14 million acres of wilderness, all of it in existing national forests, and if the protection of this land was not total, it was strong. And it had all happened rather quickly—from an all-but-ignored idea in 1949, to an equally ignored piece of legislation seven years later, to law eight years after that. Neither the resource-extracting industries nor the technocratic bureaucrats quite knew what had hit them.

What hit them was a country that was now rich enough, educated enough, and sufficiently at leisure to have created a sizable number of people receptive to the argument that their government should enhance their appreciation of what Aldo Leopold years earlier had called "multiform emotional, intellectual, and scientific values."

Emotional and intellectual values? These had not heretofore been meet subject for congressional action. Even more than creation of the national parks, inspired in part by railroad and resort moguls trying to gain customers, this was legislation not to bolster the economy or to protect the public but to gratify the soul.

So W. Howard Gray had not been entirely wrong. The purpose of this law was to provide some individuals "with wilderness pleasures." Gray just underestimated how many people were interested in such pleasures.

| | |

That day, *Ranger 7* radioed to Earth four thousand close-up pictures of the moon, just seventeen minutes before it crashed northwest of the Sea of Clouds. The pictures indicated that the moon's surface was suitable for spacecraft landings.

The next day, President Johnson held a public conversation with Dr. Homer Newell, an assistant administrator of the National Aeronautics and Space Administration. Were there any doubts, the president said, that going to the moon would be a good idea?

"Not in my mind, not at all," Newell said. "I would feel that we were backing down from a real challenge, the kind we've never backed down from before." Should we do so now, Newel said, we would "lose leadership."

"In the world?"

"In the world."

"Do you think we can be first in the world and second in space?" Johnson asked.

"No, sir."

There were to be no doubts that Lyndon Johnson was not the kind to back down from challenges.

| | |

At a few minutes before 6 P.M., the president called his friend Jim Rowe, directing him "to have a good set-to with this good man from Minnesota." Johnson wanted to make sure, again, that if Hubert Humphrey were his vice president he would be "as loyal to me like I was to Kennedy."

Johnson had just been given another reason to doubt the totality of Humphrey's subservience, which is what he really meant by loyalty. Three days earlier, columnist Drew Pearson had reported that at the last Democratic leadership breakfast, Hubert Humphrey himself had complained to the president that the Federal Power Commission had "too many oil and gas men" on it and that he should make sure that "a consumer's man," such as Charles Ross, should fill the new vacancy.

Johnson assumed, reasonably, that Hubert Humphrey himself had leaked this tidbit to Pearson, and he told Rowe he didn't like information "about what happened at my breakfast table" being bandied about like that and that Humphrey "oughtn't to have done it."

By no means, the president said, was Rowe to allow Humphrey to think that the choice had been made. On the contrary, he was to be informed that "we're gonna be doing some exploring with other people."

And one more thing: "The first he'd better do is try to put a stop to this hell-raising so we don't throw out fifteen states. That'll defeat us."

The "hell-raising" was the Mississippi Freedom Democratic Party challenge. Humphrey was to "get his Reuthers and the rest of 'em in here—and Joe Rauhs—and make 'em behave. That's the first thing."

So there was no doubt about what Hubert Humphrey's Atlantic City assignment was. It was his test. Pass it, and he'd be on the ticket. Fail it. . . . Well, there was always Gene McCarthy.

Less than an hour later, Rowe had completed his mission; he was in Humphrey's office when the senator called the president to report that Rowe was with him, having "brought me over a little message that you sent along . . . and I want to come right to the point with you. If your judgment leads you to select me, I can assure you—unqualifiedly, personally, and with all the sincerity in my heart—complete loyalty."

"Yeah," Lyndon Johnson said, so quietly that it he almost mumbled, "I know that."

| | |

As Washington was beginning the business day on Thursday, the day Lyndon Johnson had his chat with Homer Newell and Joe Poole cast his dissenting vote, a contingent of South Vietnamese commandos left their base at Danang, heading north in four boats.

It was twelve hours later in Vietnam than in Washington, so the boats soon had the cover of darkness, and shortly after midnight commandos in two of them tried to storm the island of Hen Me, knocking out its radar installation.

But the island, seven miles off the North Vietnamese shore, was too heavily guarded, and the commandos withdrew. Meanwhile, the soldiers in the other two boats bombarded another island, Hon Ngu, three miles from the port city of Vinh, one of North Vietnam's busiest ports.

A U.S. destroyer, the *Maddox*, cruised nearby. Captain John Herrick, the skipper, was not expecting any trouble. But he had his orders.

22

ANOTHER STING

The *Maddox* didn't just happen to be in the neighborhood. It was monitoring the South Vietnamese commando raids of O-PLAN 34A, trying to appear as inconspicuous as a destroyer can possibly look. There were lots of fishing boats around.

On Sunday, August 2, Captain Herrick saw three PT boats speed into the main body of Tonkin Bay from the leeward side of Hon Me Island. They could go almost twice as fast as the *Maddox,* and Herrick, a prudent man, was in no mood to start a war. He retreated farther out to sea, the better to preserve O-PLAN 34A's secrecy, and he was more than a little surprised when the boats followed him for almost twenty-five miles and attacked the *Maddox* with torpedoes and machine gun fire.

It wasn't much of a fight. Herrick sent a distress signal, which caused pilots on the nearby carrier *Ticonderoga* to scramble to attack. At a few minutes after 3 P.M. (3 A.M. the previous morning in Washington), Herrick ordered the *Maddox*'s guns to open fire.

After only twenty minutes, one of the North Vietnamese boats had sunk, and the other two, badly damaged, were limping homeward. One bullet hit the *Maddox,* causing no damage.

| | |

The president got the news first thing in the morning and was as prudent as Captain Herrick. He drafted a note of protest to Hanoi. For the first time in his presidency, he got on the "hot line" to Nikita Khrushchev to assure him that the United States had no desire to make this war any more serious than it already was. He wondered, hoping, whether some local, hotheaded Vietnamese commander had acted on his own.*

But he did order another destroyer and more planes into the area, and late Monday morning he called the White House press corps into the Oval Office to tell them what had happened and to explain that the Navy had been ordered to meet any new threat "not only with the objective of driving off the attack force but of destroying them."

Secretary of State Dean Rusk also played it cool. "The other side got a sting out of this," he said. "If they do it again, they'll get another sting."

But he also told his staff to find that resolution Mac Bundy had drafted in May to see if it needed to be updated. And from Honolulu, Admiral Ulysses S. Grant Sharp, the commander of the Pacific Fleet, ordered another destroyer, the *C. Turner Joy,* to join the *Maddox* in more vigorous maneuvers to "assert the right of freedom of the seas."

None of this was enough for Ambassador Maxwell Taylor. From Saigon he wrote that unless there was a stronger response, the world would say that the United States "flinches from direct confrontation with the North Vietnamese."

There was no countervailing pressure. Some of the president's aides told him his prudent course was the right one; others argued it was too prudent. Almost nobody—in Congress, the administration, or the press—suggested pulling back for a few days to let things cool off.

Of course only a few people in the administration, and none at all in Congress or the press, knew about O-PLAN 34A. Even when Johnson acknowledged that "we've been playing around up there" to his old friend Robert Anderson, who was one of his links to moderate, corporate Republicanism, the response was to get tougher. Calling Goldwater "a wild man on this subject," Anderson warned against "any lack of firmness."

There would be no such lack. The orders from Washington were to continue all operations and, in the event of a second attack, to strike back. Hard.

Later that day, rioting broke out in a Negro section of Jersey City. Before it ended two days later, fifty-six people had been injured, including twenty-two police officers.

If that wasn't enough to concern the president, the other news he got that day was that Jacqueline Kennedy was going to come to the Democratic National Convention. On top of all his other worries, he now had to consider

---

*Quite possibly this was the case. In 1997, General Nguyen Dinh Voc, the director of the Institute of Military History in Hanoi, said that the decision to attack was made on the ground, not in Hanoi (*New York Times Magazine,* August 10, 1997).

the possibility of an emotionally driven runaway convention that would dump its incumbent president to nominate his predecessor's brother.

| | |

As August began, the New York Yankees were in first place over the Orioles in the American League, and the Philadelphia Phillies were minimally ahead of the San Francisco Giants. But the Cincinnati Reds and Pittsburgh Pirates were still in the running. Only the most devoted fans could sustain any hope for the Milwaukee Braves, however, six and a half games out of first place, or the St. Louis Cardinals, half a game behind them.

The biggest-selling books were still *The Spy Who Came In from the Cold* and *A Moveable Feast.* But two new books had joined the best-seller list: *Mississippi: The Closed Society* by Charles Silver and *Crisis in Black and White* by Charles Silberman. The reading public, at least, was taking civil rights seriously.

Because no one had suggested suspending them, the O-PLAN 34A raids resumed the next day. Commando boats left Danang on the afternoon of Monday, August 3, headed for two objectives on the North Vietnamese mainland some seventy-five miles north of the Seventeenth Parallel division of the two Vietnams.

Captain Herrick proposed monitoring them from a bit farther away, but Admiral Sharp ordered him to hold his course near the coast. The North Vietnamese, Sharp said, had "thrown down the gauntlet," and their vessels should be regarded "as belligerents from first detection."

The next night, Herrick put both ships into evasive maneuvers near the Chinese island of Hainan. Late on a cloudy, windy night, the sonar screens on the *Maddox* detected . . . something. Vessels? Aircraft? Perhaps enemy PT boats? It was hard to tell on a starless, stormy night, full of thunderclaps. Electricity in the air does weird things to sonar.

From the *Ticonderoga*, two F-8 fighters, two A-4D jet attack planes, and four propeller-driven A-11s took off to see what they could see. They saw two unidentified vessels and three unidentified aircraft near the destroyers.

At about 9 P.M. in the Gulf of Tonkin, guns on the *Maddox* and the *C. Turner Joy* began firing at what they thought were torpedoes. Sonar on the ships counted twenty-two of them, none of which hit, and officers reported sinking two or three craft in more than four hours of firing.

Minutes later Robert McNamara told President Johnson that the *Maddox* was under torpedo attack. They agreed that only one option was open to the United States—retaliation. To lay the groundwork, they planned to brief congressional leaders that evening.

There was just one problem. They weren't absolutely sure that an attack had taken place. In fact, while the two of them and Dean Rusk were having lunch at the White House, Captain Herrick was telling his superiors that "any reported contacts and torpedoes fired appear doubtful. Freak weather effects on radar and overeager sonar men may have accounted for many reports. No actual visual sightings by *Maddox*. Suggest complete evaluation before any further action."

Admiral Sharp wasn't buying it. From the advantage of remoteness, he assured his staff that the attacks were real. And sure enough, just before dawn Captain Herrick sent a new note: "Certain that original ambush was bona fide."

By then, someone, probably a member of Congress, had leaked news of the second attack to the press. "The story has broken on the AP and the UP," McNamara told Johnson at 5:09 P.M. At that moment, any chance of greater restraint evaporated. With Barry Goldwater calling for "victory" in Vietnam, the politics of the moment required an attack.

But it was not just politics. Johnson did not want to be vulnerable to the "soft on communism" charge, but neither did he want war. Nor did Rusk, McNamara, or Bundy. But they had prepared the infrastructure for war, and all the momentum was toward action. Once Bundy's staff put together that draft resolution in May, putting it into effect one day became . . . well, not quite inevitable but very, very likely. The raids now ordered had been prepared months in advance in the expectation, perhaps the subconscious hope, that they would one day be needed.

| | |

It was hot in central Mississippi that afternoon when the FBI agents told the heavy equipment operators to stop excavating. Puffing cigars to keep away the bugs and the stench of death, the agents took up garden tools and began digging near the center of Olen Burrage's dam.

It had not been easy, getting information out of people in Neshoba County, but neither had it been impossible. Slowly, federal lawmen had picked up bits of information, some of it about their local counterparts such as Sheriff Lawrence Rainey, whose distaste for Negroes did not keep him from having used a few of them as casual sex partners. They learned that arresting Negroes and then releasing them to the mercies of Klansmen was standard operating procedure. In exchange for $30,000 in cash, probably to Burrage himself, they had been told it might be productive to dig at the dam.

Soon they came upon the body of a shirtless man, facedown, his arms outstretched. In the left back pocket of his jeans was a wallet with Michael Schwerner's draft card inside it.

"We've uncapped one oil well" was Inspector Joseph Sullivan's coded telephone message to Washington.

| | |

The congressional leaders had no quarrel with the president's decision to retaliate. Neither did Barry Goldwater when Johnson finally reached him at 10 P.M. Carefully, the president first briefed his opponent by reading a prepared statement.

"As president and commander-in-chief," said the president and commander-in-chief, "it is my duty to the American people to report that renewed hostile actions against U.S. ships on the high seas in the Gulf of Tonkin have today required me to order the military forces of the United States to take action and reply."

Then he used his own words. "Now, when I say the reply is being given, Barry, I may elaborate on that a little bit, depending on how safe I can be at the time I deliver the statement. Do you follow me?"

Goldwater followed and agreed. The unofficial treaty the two men had made on July 24 held.

Shortly before midnight, the president spoke to the nation, or as much of it that was awake: "Repeated acts of violence against the armed forces of the United States must be met not only with alert defense but with positive reply," he said. "That reply is being given as I speak to you tonight. Air action is now in execution against gunboats and certain supporting facilities in North Vietnam."

As he spoke, his senior cabinet invented a new Washington institution. Dean Rusk met privately with reporters at the State Department and Mc-Namara did the same at the Pentagon, both cabinet members speaking on the condition that they be cited only as "U.S. officials." With the midwifery of the journalists, they thus gave birth to the "background briefing," by which senior officials have been manipulating reporters and public opinion ever since.[1]

The targets, which McNamara had pointed out to Johnson in the White House dining room earlier in the evening, were four patrol boat bases and an oil depot.

"We seek no wider war," the president made clear. But just in case, he was submitting to Congress a resolution authorizing him to do it again. It was the resolution that Bundy's working groups had put together in May. It gave the president the authority "to take all necessary measures to repel any armed attack against the forces of the United States." And it declared the United States "prepared, as the president determines, to take all necessary steps, including the use of armed force, to assist any member or protocol state of the Southeast Asia Collective Defense Treaty requesting assistance in defense of its freedom."

The resolution contained no expiration date.

| | |

The retaliatory raids met some resistance. Though described as "limited in scale," there were sixty-four sorties, and two planes were lost. Lieutenant (jg) Everett Alvarez Jr. of San Diego became the first of almost six hundred Americans captured and held in the prison camp that came to be known as the Hanoi Hilton. He was released eight years later.

The Southeast Asia Resolution submitted to Congress fared better, though it contained no language limiting the American role in the war, which disturbed Senator Gaylord Nelson of Wisconsin. He offered an amendment making it clear that U.S. forces were still going to act as advisors, nothing more.

Otherwise, he said, "the Congress [would be] appearing to tell the executive branch or the public that we would endorse a complete change in our mission."

Senator William Fulbright, the resolution's chief sponsor, immediately rose to explain that such an amendment was not needed, that the resolution as written "is quite consistent with our existing mission and our understanding of what we have been doing in South Vietnam for the past ten years."

Asked whether the resolution might lead to a general war in the region, Fulbright was adamant and eloquent.

"The last thing we want to do is become involved in a land war in Asia," he said.

Nelson was not convinced. So Humphrey went up to him to warn him that it was this resolution that offered the best hope of averting a messy war. "There are people in the Pentagon who think we ought to send three hundred thousand troops over there," Humphrey told him. The implication was clear: The administration was the peace party, standing up to the Pentagon hotheads and their Republican allies. To weaken the president would be to strengthen the war hawks. Nelson withdrew his amendment.[2]

The only real debate came in a secret joint session of the Senate Armed Services and Foreign Relations Committees when Senator Wayne Morse of

Oregon, no longer ignorant of the commando raids, asked McNamara whether the Vietnamese attacks could have been retaliation.

Our Navy, McNamara said, was in no way involved with those raids "if there were any." Morse was unconvinced and spoke heatedly against the resolution, but he was a man without a following. A onetime Republican who had switched parties, he was a garrulous, self-absorbed teetotaler. His colleagues found him boring, irritating, rather funny, but not credible.

It's hard to know what would have happened had Nelson, Fulbright, Frank Church of Idaho, or a respected Republican such as Clifford Case been the dissenter. Probably the resolution would have passed, anyway, but perhaps not before a serious debate had occurred.

As it was, Morse carried the debate, without influence, though not without prescience: "We're going to be bogged down in Southeast Asia for years to come if we follow this course of action and we're going to kill thousands of American boys until, finally, let me say, the American people are going to say what the French people finally said: they've had enough."

| | |

On Wednesday, August 5, President Johnson spoke at the opening of the Newhouse School of Communications at Syracuse University, where he told students and faculty "that attack was repeated. The attacks were unprovoked." Then what had he been talking about with Bob Anderson?

| | |

The founding convention of the Mississippi Freedom Democratic Party (MFDP) took place at the Masonic Temple in Jackson on the morning of Thursday, August 6. It looked like a real convention, with signs marking the seating areas of the county delegations.

But the singing was better. "Go Tell It on the Mountain," sang the share-croppers and woodchoppers who had been singing it since childhood, swaying, clapping, "Go tell it on the mountain that Jesus Christ is born," and in another verse, "Go tell it on the mountain to let my people go."

This was politics with a twist. For these delegates neither Christianity nor liberation was an abstraction; their devotion to the first was as great as their commitment to the second, and the two were intertwined.

This may have explained why Charles Evers of the Mississippi NAACP stayed in his office upstairs in the same building. SNCC and the NAACP had become the uneasiest of allies, and anyway, Evers would have felt out of place downstairs.

The keynote speech by Ella Baker was not at all typical. She spoke neither of defeating the opposition nor of building coalitions but of the purpose of existence. "Young men and women want some meaning in their lives," she told the sweltering delegates. "Big cars do not give meaning. Place in the power structure does not give meaning." Being part of a community, being part of something greater than the self—that's what gives meaning, she said.

But politics did intrude. Joe Rauh was there to talk about the convention, and he was not talking inspiration; he was talking numbers. The numbers were eleven and eight. It would take eleven votes on the 108-member Credentials Committee to take a minority report to the convention floor, and eight delegations to demand a roll call vote. Then they'd win; how many Democratic delegates could vote against these struggling heroes, especially when their opposition was a bunch of segregationists who'd endorsed Barry Goldwater?

Rauh, the establishment lawyer with his bow tie and horn-rims, got caught up in the spirit. Somehow he found himself on that podium shouting, "Do we have the eleven?" and reveling in the response. "Do we have the eight states?" he called out to the crowd, and they shouted back their hopeful answer.

That evening, watching the film on all three networks on his three television sets, Lyndon Johnson watched this performance, shuddered, and issued an order.

"That's gonna ruin us," he told Humphrey. "Nothing good can come from it. We already got the Negro vote. We already got the liberal vote. But we got a fighting chance in Texas to win, and if you can't do this you haven't met your first test as vice president. It's up to you."

If only Johnson had known that Rauh had found the perfect solution, and a Texas solution at that.

A little research had informed Rauh about the 1944 dispute in which two rival Texas delegations showed up at the Democratic Convention. Both were seated, with each delegate getting half a vote. It was simple.

"And why?" Rauh later recalled. "Because nobody was going to vote in the 1944 convention. Roosevelt was going to be renominated, so what was the use of fighting?" That was precisely the case again. The 1964 Democratic Convention would make no decisions. It would renominate the incumbent president and ratify both his platform and his choice of a running mate. Who could complain about simply seating both delegations?

Everyone. A lot had changed in twenty years, especially now that television had made the theatrics of politics even more important than they had been, the substance accordingly smaller. Television had also democratized those theatrics. Now it was not only congressional leaders and presidential candidates who got to strut on the political stage; it was anyone who chose to walk in from the wings.

There was, then, a constant incentive to intensify the drama. Unable, or at least unwilling, to be seen back home in any compromise with civil rights forces, the Southern segregationists had to threaten to walk out if the MFDP delegates were seated. It wasn't just the segregationist hard-liners, either. Supposed Southern moderates such as Governors John Connally of Texas and Carl Sanders of Georgia threatened to take their delegates home. "It looks like we're turning the Democratic Party over to the nigras," Sanders told the president.

But the participants were motivated by more than mere love of the spotlight. Politics, regrettably, had also become more sincere. Like Martin Luther King, Robert Moses based his politics on a stern intellectual foundation, and it didn't matter that Christianity was not as central to his foundation as to King's; a religious sensibility was a sense of the moral responsibility of the individual as practiced and understood by Christians, whatever their notion of God and Jesus.

There was no doubt at all about how central Christianity was to most of the MFDP rank and file. If its dominance in their lives had any rival it was their recently acquired sense of being part of a democratic polity, a role theoretically guaranteed but actually denied them. Having achieved it at the risk of their lives, they did not want to hear talk of compromise. For them, the MFDP was not a mere political organization. It was the purpose of existence.

Finally, Lyndon Johnson was not Franklin D. Roosevelt. FDR was a supremely confident politician who gladly delegated authority and rarely let himself be bogged down in detail. Lyndon Johnson, despite what the polls told him, was becoming increasingly insecure about his reelection. He had somehow convinced himself not just that all the Southerners would walk out, but that their electoral votes, and those of the border states, would vanish with them.

Here, plenty of his allies were anxious to intensify his fears. "It doesn't matter what you do about unseating the whites," John Connally told the president, "but you let those bugaboos march in and the whole South will march out."

Without adopting Connally's terminology, Johnson accepted his analysis. "There's not a damn vote that we get by seating these folks," he told Walter Reuther. "I don't want to run off fourteen border states like Oklahoma and Kentucky."

| | |

With 85 percent of the people supporting the president and his raids in Southeast Asia, Congress overwhelmingly approved the Tonkin Gulf Resolution on Friday, August 7. For this first (and last) congressional sanction of military action in Southeast Asia, there were no dissenting votes in the House and just two—Morse and Alaska's Ernest Gruening—in the Senate. Nor was there visible opposition outside of government. And no wonder. America had long ago learned this basic lesson: When it is attacked, it must strike back. And had it not been attacked?

Probably not.

Yes, Captain Herrick had intercepted North Vietnamese messages about preparing for "military operations," but these were as likely to have been defensive. Then or later, nobody ever claimed to have seen a North Vietnamese ship or plane fire any kind of weapon at the *Maddox*. Navy pilot James B. Stockdale, later briefly famous as the honorable if inept running mate for independent presidential candidate Ross Perot in 1992, was one of the pilots from the *Ticonderoga*. He later wrote that he saw no sign of hostile activity.

Even Lyndon Johnson, years later, acknowledged that "those dumb stupid sailors were just shooting at flying fish."

| | |

That same day the rainmaking dream effectively died. G. V. McCarthy, the chief of the Reclamation Bureau's Division of Project Development, wrote to his boss, Floyd Dominy, that the "snow augmentation" and other climate control experiments launched with such hope last winter had come a cropper.

The simple problem, said McCarthy, was that none of the tests indicated that it was possible to alter the climate, at least not without creating problems worse than aridity. "Climate control is a dream that, misapplied, could lead to disaster," he wrote.

That was about it for climate control. The previous month, Leland Haworth, the director of the National Science Foundation, had told Senator Warren Magnuson that there was no evidence that "seeding (clouds) affects the amount or character of the precipitation over flat country," though there were "slight increases" in cold, mountainous conditions. In some cases, Haworth wrote, seeding "may decrease precipitation."

So there were limits, after all.

| | |

James Chaney was buried that afternoon in Meridian.

At least one man who was disturbed about Chaney's death did not attend the funeral. James Jordan drove around Meridian that evening, occasionally stopping for a drink or food or to get cigarettes. Near the corner of Eighth Street and Thirty-fifth Avenue he encountered two women he knew, Beverly Rawlings and Gladys McCormick.

"I'm way past due now," he told the women. "I'm looking for the FBI to pick me up most anytime."

Confused, one of the women asked him what he meant.

"You'll find out," he said. "I'd just as soon kill another nigger right now."

| | |

One late-August day a doctor and a law enforcement officer from the Food and Drug Administration came to Millbrook. The doctor pronounced himself "shocked" by what was going on, and the cop said he and his colleagues "can't wait for these drugs to be made illegal so they can bust your ass."

"Maybe Kennedy went along with this kind of thinking," the doctor said, "but Johnson is different." In fact, he said, "President Johnson has made it clear he wants a drug-free America."

Poor Lyndon, Tim Leary thought, as he watched the two men drive away.

| | |

Now, as the Tonkin Gulf Resolution was sailing through, the poverty bill was in trouble. Southern Democrats, upset because antipoverty programs such as the proposed Job Corps would be integrated, saw a way to get some revenge for losing on civil rights. This time, the Republicans were on their side, not because of race but because the Republicans were certain the government couldn't do much about poverty, and they weren't sure it should try.

With Sargent Shriver on Capitol Hill and Lyndon Johnson on the phone, the administration lobbied as hard as it could. They bought about twenty Republicans who fancied themselves conservationists by promising that 40 percent of the Job Corps projects would deal with parks and outdoor recreation. But they were still about twenty votes shy of a majority on Friday, August 7, when the Southerners, through Speaker McCormack, named their price: Adam Yarmolinsky's head.

Yarmolinsky was one of the public policy intellectuals who had helped put the antipoverty program together. Though technically still on the Pentagon payroll, he was working full-time with Shriver, and he would obviously become a top deputy in the new Office of Economic Opportunity once the bill passed.

But he had also been the Defense Department official in charge of placing segregated rental apartments off-limits to military personnel, rendering him off-limits to segregationists, who had dug up some dirt about his family. Yarmolinsky's mother had once joined the leftist John Reed Club, and his father was head of the Slavic Language Division of the New York Public Library.

Mrs. Yarmolinsky's association with the John Reed Club was brief and predated the war—World War I—and Mr. Yarmolinsky was known around the library, and the Soviet Union, for his fierce anticommunism. No matter. Adam Yarmolinsky would have to go.

Desperately trying to avoid the shame of having to dismiss a loyal and capable associate for no reason, Shriver told McCormack that only the president could hire and fire in the executive branch.

"That isn't going to satisfy those people," McCormack said.

Shriver went to a pay phone in a Capitol corridor to call the president and Bill Moyers. They told him to do whatever was necessary.

At this point Lyndon Johnson may have been starting to wonder whether he even wanted this War on Poverty, at least the way the Adam Yarmolinskys had designed it. Johnson was a Texas New Dealer who thought government services should be provided by governments. Now these Eastern intellectuals had come up with something else entirely.

"I thought we were gonna have CCC camps," he said to Bill Moyers, "community action where ... some government agency sponsors a project and we'd pay the labor. ... I'm against subsidizing any private organization ... I'd a whole lot rather Dick Daley do it than the Urban League."

Daley's sentiments exactly.

So Shriver went back to McCormack's office and pledged that he would not recommend Yarmolinsky for any position in his agency. Then he went back to his temporary office on Connecticut Avenue to inform the sacrifice of his immolation.

"Well, we've just thrown you to the wolves, and this is the worst day of my life," Shriver said. At the moment, Yarmolinsky felt worse for Shriver than for himself.[3] That betrayal did get the bill passed, and with that and the war resolution out of the way, the president flew to his ranch, where at a press conference the next day, he was asked about the betrayal of Adam

Yarmolinsky. He denied it, denied that Yarmolinsky had been working with Shriver at all.

"Your thoughts are wrong," he told the reporter. "He never left [the Pentagon]."

Among those surprised at this answer was Joseph Califano, who had replaced Yarmolinsky at the Pentagon.

| | |

That was the week the Columbia Broadcasting System bought the New York Yankees, seventeen first-graders in Biloxi became the first Negro children to go to school with whites in Mississippi, Lady Bird Johnson and Stew Udall set off on a trip to national parks in the West, the Beatles returned to America, and the president of the United States moved toward the edge of a breakdown.

| | |

When Walter Reuther gently mentioned Joe Rauh's preferred "seat everyone" solution in Mississippi, LBJ's response was immediate and close to irrational. "We'd have more damn wars than you ever saw," he said. "Who's gonna haul the banner in demonstrations?"

Almost as soon as he hung up with Reuther, he placed a call to James Rowe and gave him a mission: Identify every MFDP supporter on the Credentials Committee and find out each one's vulnerability. Then he called Roy Wilkins. Not that he wanted to be "panicky or desperate," Johnson said, but "the cause you fought for all your life is likely to be reversed and go right down the drain."

Wilkins's distaste for Martin Luther King was such that he was receptive even to this absurdity. By now, Wilkins was almost as convinced as J. Edgar Hoover that King was controlled by subversives, if he was not one himself. "You know some of the forces behind him," the NAACP leader told the president.

By now, Humphrey had come up with what he considered a fair compromise: The regular (white) delegates would not be seated unless they signed a loyalty oath to the national ticket; the MFDP delegates would be seated on the convention floor as "honored guests"; and no future Democratic Convention would seat a delegation selected in a racially segregated process.

On Wednesday, August 19, just five days before the convention was to begin, Wilkins and most of the other civil rights leaders met with the president in the White House. Martin Luther King did not come. He had pleaded a schedule conflict, but Johnson knew that the real reason was that King did not want to get himself into a position where he'd have to endorse LBJ's stance on the Mississippi delegation. Johnson knew that because the FBI had told him so, courtesy of the tapes they had made of phone conversations between King and Bayard Rustin. As it was, the convention never came up during the meeting, perhaps because Johnson had seen no need to raise it.

The next day, Sheriff Rainey and Deputy Price served summonses on the COFO civil rights workers in Philadelphia and evicted them from their offices.

The following day, the Freedom Party delegates left Tougaloo by bus headed for Atlantic City. There were sixty-eight of them. Most had never been out of Mississippi; many had never spent a night in a hotel.[4] They were nervous. They sang.

But they were not naive. A week earlier, Robert Moses had asked the Reverend Ed King to try to figure out what kind of compromises they would be offered, the better to figure out what kind of compromise to accept. King came up with about thirty possibilities.

As they headed north, the $947 million Economic Opportunity Act was being signed at a White House ceremony. "For so long as man has lived on this earth, poverty has been his curse," President Johnson said, implying without actually saying that by this law the curse would be lifted.

As is common, the president used many pens to complete his signature, the better to hand them out as souvenirs to those who made the occasion possible. Adam Clayton Powell got the first one. Adam Yarmolinsky got one of the last.

| | |

The Credentials Committee of the Democratic National Convention met on Saturday, August 22, in a ballroom of the Pageant Hotel, the challengers seated across the aisle from the regular delegation, each side with an hour to present its case. The dissidents went first. Rauh called on Aaron Henry and the Reverend Edwin King to make brief remarks, and then he brought his star witness to the chair. Fannie Lou Hamer, a large woman lame from childhood polio, limped to the witness chair, put her purse on the table, and calmly transfixed the nation.

"It was the thirty-first of August in 1962 that eighteen of us traveled twenty-six miles to the county courthouse in Indianola to try to register to try to become first-class citizens," she began. She spoke slowly, and though there were errors of grammar aplenty, there was also a haunting and persuasive rhythm to her cadence. It was the rhythm of the only book she really knew: the Bible.

"We was met in Indianola by Mississippi men, highway patrolmens. My husband came and said the plantation owner was raising Cain because I had tried to register," she said.

The owner of the plantation where she and her husband worked told her, she said, " 'If you don't go down and withdraw your registration you will have to leave.' And I addressed him and told him and said, 'I didn't try to register for you. I tried to register for myself.' I had to leave that same night. . . .

"And in June, the ninth, 1963, I had attended a voter registration workshop, was returning back to Mississippi. Ten of us was traveling by the Continental Trailway bus."

The bus was stopped in Winona, and Hamer testified that when she got off, she was arrested and taken to the local jail and into a cell where there were two Negro prisoners.

Click!

At that moment, eight minutes into her testimony, all three networks switched to the White House, where the president was hosting thirty Democratic governors. Informed only that the president had some kind of announcement, the networks assumed it had to do with the vice presidency. In fact, he just wanted to get Fannie Lou Hamer off the screen.

But it didn't work. The networks knew they'd been fooled, and they had film. As soon as it was obvious that Johnson had nothing to say, they showed it, so the country could hear Mrs. Hamer:

> I was carried out of the cell into another cell where they had two Negro prisoners. The state highway patrolman ordered the first Negro to take the blackjack.
>
> The first Negro prisoner ordered me, by orders from the state highway patrolman, for me to lay down on a bunk bed on my face, and I laid on my face. The first Negro began to beat, and I was beat until he was exhausted. . . . After the first Negro . . . was exhausted, the state highway patrolmen ordered the second Negro to take the blackjack. The second Negro began to beat and I began to work my feet, and the state highway patrolman ordered the first Negro who had beat to set on my feet to keep me from working my feet. I began to scream, and one white man got up and began to beat me on my head and tell me to "hush."
>
> One white man—my dress had worked up high—he walked over and pulled my dress down and he pulled my dress back, back up. I was in jail when Medgar Evers was murdered. All of this is on account we want to register, to become first-class citizens, and if the Freedom Democratic Party is not seated now, I question America.

She wasn't the only one.

23

BREAKDOWNS

The polls seemed too good to be true. Johnson was leading Goldwater by better than two-to-one margins, not just in New York and Wisconsin but in usually Republican Maine.

What a glorious time this should have been for Lyndon Johnson. In a week, on Thursday, August 27, he would turn fifty-six years old, and by coincidence or quirk of fate, he would on that very day accept the Democratic nomination for president of the United States, to begin an election campaign he would dominate. He should have been euphoric, but instead he was afraid he was going to lose.

He told Walter Reuther that his candidacy was doomed if the Freedom Democratic Party prevailed. At least that's what Reuther told Joe Rauh, trying to convince him to call off the challenge.

"Are you serious?" Rauh said. "Goldwater has been nominated. How can you lose it?"

"We both think the backlash is so tremendous that either we're going to lose the Negro vote if you go through with this and don't win, or if you do win, the picture of your all-black delegation going on the floor to replace the white one is going to add to the backlash. We really think that Goldwater's going to be president."*

It was hard to believe either one of them really was this frightened. Yes, the Goldwater forces were gearing up for a major-league campaign, and their far-right-wing allies were working with them. From Dallas the president received word that Goldwaterites and John Birchers had rented offices in Dallas, from which they were mailing out millions of free copies of *A Texan Looks*

---

*These were Rauh's words recorded years later, when "black" had become preferred usage. Reuther probably said "Negro."

at Lyndon: A Study in Illegitimate Power, by J. Evetts Haley, a Texas segregationist who had run for governor in 1956.

The report was true, with one twist. The books weren't free. The Goldwater campaign was getting them for twelve and a half cents a copy and planning to resell them for twenty-five cents or more, pocketing what Cliff White called "a substantial campaign profit."

No one ever doubted that Goldwater had his supporters or that the Republican Party could put together an effective campaign structure. What mattered was the majority, and it was squarely behind Lyndon Johnson.

No matter. By now, the president was close to panic; he was not in control. And it wasn't just panic that he might lose the election. He was still worried about losing the nomination. Without a hint of evidence and contrary to all knowledge, he had convinced himself that the Mississippi Freedom Democratic Party had been born in the Justice Department, as part of Robert Kennedy's plot to steal the nomination.

Maybe he'd just let him have it.

| | |

If Johnson could not have total control, he could seek total information, a task made easier by the special political intelligence organization at his disposal. At the president's behest, J. Edgar Hoover sent Cartha DeLoach, twenty-seven agents, one radio technician, and two stenographers to Atlantic City.

They got there on the afternoon of Sunday, August 23, set up a command post in the Post Office building, and took rooms at the Claridge House, where Martin Luther King was staying. This presumably made it easier to tap King's room telephone, though for reasons never explained the technicians didn't get a working bug installed in his room. They did better with the microphones at the Gem Hotel, where the MFDP delegates were staying, and at the SNCC-CORE headquarters in the Union Baptist Church in the Negro section of the city. The real targets, DeLoach said, were the "sixty members of the SNCC from Jackson, Mississippi, [who] plan to . . . assist in seating the Mississippi Freedom Democratic Party delegation."

Four times a day the FBI agents telephoned their information to Robert Wick in the Crime Records Office in Washington. Wick dictated a summary to stenographers, who typed it up on plain bond paper and sent it by messenger to the White House. But some of the White House was already in Atlantic City. Walter Jenkins and Bill Moyers were staying at the Pageant House, and DeLoach reported regularly to them, too.

On Sunday, Representative Edith Green of Oregon proposed a compromise similar to Rauh's original plan—to seat everyone from both delegations who would sign an oath of loyalty to the national ticket. Considering that the regulars, having endorsed Goldwater, could not sign such an oath, it was a pro-MFDP compromise, and the MFDP accepted it. The president did not.

| | |

That day both Hubert Humphrey and Gene McCarthy appeared on *Meet the Press.* McCarthy said that were he offered the vice presidency he would accept it as "a matter of obligation." Humphrey, in his half hour (minus commercial breaks), praised Lyndon Johnson thirty-two times. The president called them both afterward, telling each man he'd done well.

| | |

At noon on the convention's opening day—Monday, August 24—Hubert Humphrey invited Credentials Committee members on both sides of the Mississippi dispute to his suite. He had already convinced the committee, and its chairman David Lawrence, to appoint a special subcommittee to propose a solution, and it was Humphrey, not Lawrence, who chose the subcommittee chairman: thirty-six-year-old Walter Mondale, a Humphrey protégé who was attorney general of Minnesota.

So far the subcommittee had not found a solution, and neither did those who attended the meeting in Humphrey's suite, so that afternoon Rauh convinced Lawrence to postpone a decision for twenty-four hours. That meant that the convention would open with empty chairs where the Mississippi delegation should be sitting, but empty chairs wouldn't look as bad as walk-outs.

One new idea did emerge from Humphrey's meeting. Al Ullman, a young congressman from Oregon, suggested seating some of the MFDP members as "at-large" voting delegates. Humphrey immediately rejected the idea; he knew of those Southern threats to walk out if any of "those people" were seated.

| | |

That afternoon, the president of the United States invited the reporters covering him for a walk around the White House. They walked, and as they walked, he talked. He told them he had not decided on a running mate but that he would be happy to tell them what he wanted in a vice president: a partner, someone who knew Congress, an advocate of civil rights, a man qualified to become president, a man who would be loyal and energetic. "I expect to work hell out of him," Johnson said.

He made this comment while he himself was working the hell out of the press corps. They walked around the White House, and then they walked around again, and again, and after they had walked around it *nine times,* he invited them into his office for more talking.

The reporters were hot, but happy. It was a good story. They'd all be on page one the next day. But some of them found the whole experience bizarre.

| | |

For days now, the president had been spending much of the afternoons in his bedroom. Lady Bird wasn't sure he was getting enough sleep, and she was concerned that he'd let his exercise regimen lapse. He was on the phone almost constantly to Atlantic City—to Moyers, to Reuther, to Humphrey. He seemed distracted.

The day the convention opened, a wire from Martin Luther King arrived for the president. "Only you are in a position to make clear the Democratic Party's position" on the Mississippi dispute. Dispirited, the president called Dick Russell, who as usual was spending the convention period at home.

"They are getting ready to take charge of the convention," said Lyndon Johnson, whose control of the convention was all but complete. "I don't think there's any question but what Martin Luther King and that group wants me to be in a position of giving them an excuse to say that I have turned on the Negro," he told Russell.

"I don't believe they can sell that to the Negro, even," Russell said.

"Yeah, I think that's Bobby's strategy though, Dick."

"Suppose Bobby would like to see Goldwater elected president?" Russell asked.

"No," Johnson said, "but I think he'd like to see me caused all the damned trouble he can."

After he hung up, Johnson gave the FBI an additional mission in Atlantic City; he told it to put a tail on the attorney general.

| | |

It was not a fancy dinner in the bedroom at the White House. With trays propped on laps, the president and First Lady watched the opening session of the convention Monday evening with the president's new, temporary speechwriter—John Steinbeck. Along with his wife, Elaine, the novelist had been fetched by government plane from their Long Island home to spend some time with the Johnsons while Steinbeck worked on Johnson's acceptance speech.

| | |·

The attorney general, who did not know that FBI agents, whose boss he was, had been dispatched to Atlantic City, was planning to run for the Senate from New York. Toward that end, he resigned as a delegate from Massachusetts, designating his sister-in-law, Joan Kennedy, as his replacement. Briefly, Johnson wondered whether this signaled some nefarious plot to subvert the convention, then thought better of it.

The FBI happily fueled the president's distress. When Kennedy told reporters in New York he would have a statement the next day, the analysis to Johnson from the FBI made much of the fact that Kennedy "refused to elaborate." Perhaps this meant he was concocting some kind of effort to get the convention to turn to him. As ever, the FBI's talent for political analysis was less than impressive. Robert Kennedy was concocting a Senate candidacy.

Kennedy wasn't the only target, though. In fact, not all those targeted were in Atlantic City. The Bureau was also investigating the student activists who stayed in Mississippi. Division 5 had directed field agents to identify the students, whereupon their names were run through the Bureau files.[1] Before long, the Bureau had a file on every resident of every COFO Freedom House, including one whose residents included a Catholic nun, a former FBI agent, the son-in-law of a newspaper publisher, the daughter of a Communist Party member, a newspaper reporter, and "an oversexed Vassar girl."

Whether they were oversexed or adequately sexed, the young women of Freedom Summer were doing a lot of thinking about sex. One reason they were thinking about it a lot is that they were engaging in it frequently, more frequently than they could have imagined just a year or so earlier, and with a greater variety of partners.

In particular, quite a few of the Northern college women were involved with Southern Negro men—leaders of the movement or rank-and-file Mississippians who had been sharecroppers before they became civil rights workers.

To a young woman raised in suburbia and schooled at Smith or Oberlin, there was an earthy exoticness to the Negro Mississippian. Perhaps subconsciously, the liaison was something of a political statement, a way of validating to others and to oneself the depth of one's commitment to the cause. For the Southern Negro men, liaisons with white women were, among other things, a rebellion against the grand and petty attacks on their manhood they had known since birth.

Some of this psychologizing may not be necessary; throw together men and women aged eighteen to twenty-five who are involved in a crusade and are living at a high emotional pitch, and passion will ensue.

It did, as their opponents throughout the South loved to relate as evidence of the immorality of the civil rights movement. Even Yale historian Staughton Lynd, a sympathetic (older) observer who went to Oxford to help in the training, noted that "every black SNCC worker with perhaps a few exceptions counted it a notch on his gun to have slept with a white woman—as many as possible. And I think that it was just very traumatic for the women who encountered that."[2]

Meanwhile, some of the Negro women were feeling left out, and soon enough a few of them broke their silence. Rather than coming out and blaming the white women for stealing their men—that would have been embarrassing—they asked a simple question: How come, considering that the women get beaten up and arrested as much as the men, it was the women who had to do all the cooking and cleaning?

| | |

At midnight more than a hundred MFDP supporters gathered on the boardwalk in front of Convention Hall, forming a picket line, pledging to keep a twenty-four-hour vigil until their delegation was seated. Some held posters bearing the likenesses of Schwerner, Goodman, and Chaney.

As always, they sang to keep up their spirits. "This little light of mine," they sang to Fannie Lou Hamer's lead,

> I'm gonna let it shine
> Down in Mississippi
> I'm gonna let it shine,
> Here in Atlantic City
> I'm gonna let it shine,
> Let it shine, let it shine, let it shine.

It was both jolly and moving, and by dawn there were more than three hundred people gathered about. They were spirited but hardly threatening. Something about their demeanor exuded gentleness. A determined gentleness to be sure, but gentleness nonetheless. Between chanted slogans, they laughed easily. They had the supreme confidence of people who had no doubt about the rightness of their cause, and this confidence somehow included a hint of snobbery, surprising from some of the poorest, least educated people in America. But they wanted nothing except what they deserved.

Then and later, the argument against them was that though they held the moral high ground, their segregationist adversaries had the better legal argument. But it was the Mississippi regulars who had been chosen in a most irregular (if then common) manner, simply by appointment from the governor and his acolytes. The MFDP had attempted to follow a rational political procedure to choose its delegation. Yes, that process had been extralegal, but only because the law, illegally, excluded them.

Despite their firmness, their irregular tactics, their sometimes cloying sense of self-righteousness, the MFDP should have appeared threatening only to the racist or the irrational. The president of the United States was no racist; at one point he had erupted at Governor Carl Sanders of Georgia that "these goddamn fellas down there have to stop eatin' [Negroes] for breakfast every morning. They have got to quit that. And they got to let 'em vote and let 'em shave and let 'em eat and things like that."

For the moment, however, he was irrational. On Tuesday morning the president had his breakfast in bed. He did not do his morning exercises. Before 8 A.M. he called his old Texas buddy A. W. Moursund and told him he was thinking of announcing that he would not run for president. Three hours later, in the Oval Office, he called his press secretary, George Reedy.

"I'm just writing out a little statement," he said to Reedy, who informed him that Robert Kennedy had just announced his Senate candidacy.

"Here's what I think I'm gonna say to 'em," he said, reading from a statement he had written out by hand:

Forty-four months ago I was selected to be the Democratic vice president. . . . On that fateful November day last year, I accepted the responsibility for the president, asking God's guidance and the help of all of our people. For nine months I've carried on as effectively as I could. Our country faces grave dangers. These dangers must be faced and met by a united people under a leader they do not doubt. After thirty-three years in political life most men acquire political enemies as ships accumulate barnacles. The times require leadership about which there is no doubt and a voice that men of all parties and sections and color can follow. I've learned, after trying very hard, that I am not that voice or that leader. Therefore . . . I suggest that the representatives of all states of this union . . . proceed to do their duty and that no consideration be given to me because I am absolutely unavailable.

Then they can just pick the two they want for the two places. We'll . . . do the best we can to help till January. Then . . . they can have a new and fresh fellow without any of these old scars. And I don't want this power of the Bomb. I just don't want these decisions I'm being required to make. I don't want the conniving that's required. I don't want the disloyalty that's around.

After the tiniest of pauses, and in a deadpan voice that would do honor to a stand-up comic, Reedy said, "This would throw the nation in quite an uproar, sir." There was no more emotion in Reedy's voice than there would have been had Johnson told him he was knocking off early for the day, but there was method in the press secretary's apparent excess of caution; he knew his man, he did not dismiss the possibility that his man meant exactly what he said, and he knew the best course was to let his man talk on.

Talk on he did:

"I cannot lead the North and the South," Johnson said. "I'm very convinced that the Negroes will not listen to me."

Now, gently, Reedy began to argue. "I think it's too late, sir. I know it's your decision because you're the man that has to bear the burden. But right now I think this just gives the country to Goldwater."

"Well, that's all right. I don't care," Johnson said. "He can do better than I can."

"He can't, sir," Reedy said. "He's just a child, and look at our side. We don't have anybody."

But that was not the point. Johnson, at that moment, was indifferent to the Democratic Party or the country. He was thinking of his own life.

"I don't feel I ought to live . . . my wife and my daughters and things they're going through like *Time* magazine this week . . . the lies they publish [*Time* had just run a major story about Johnson's personal finances]. . . . I don't have the hide of a rhinoceros, and I'm not seeking happiness. I'm just seeking comfort. . . . I think I've earned it."

"I think you've earned it too, sir. But I don't think it's a question of having a hide of a rhinoceros. It's kind of a question of rising above these things."

"Well, I can't do that," Johnson said. "I have a desire to unite people. And the South is against me, and the North is against me, and the Negroes are against me, and the press doesn't really have any affection for me, or an understanding. And I'm unable to give it to 'em. I try, but just look in the *Philadelphia Inquirer* this morning. Our friend Henry Brandon, whom I do not know, but—'a textbook caricature of fast-dealing politician . . . he has not aroused any excitement as a person or any emotion or enthusiasm as a human being, he lacks dignity and charm because he is not sufficiently detached about himself.' "

Suppressing any impulse to suggest that the substance of this phone call could provide support for Brandon's analysis, Reedy recalled Edmund Burke's "dictum about the presumptuous judgment of the ignorant" and reminded his boss that "much worse things than that have been said about presidents, sir. Abraham Lincoln was called a baboon."

But this president, he said, was "not debating." He knew that "another Johnson sat in this same place and suffered more anguish than I'm suffering. But I don't see any reason why I *need* to."

If he could not be in control, he'd just go back to Johnson City.

| | |

In New York, Robert Kennedy, having resigned as attorney general, announced that he was running for the Senate as the strongest possible supporter of Lyndon Johnson. He was running, Kennedy said, because "all that President Johnson is trying to accomplish, all the progress that has been made, is threatened by a new and dangerous Republican assault."

Senator Kenneth Keating, the incumbent Republican who had carefully avoided endorsing his own party's presidential candidate but would not support its opposition, ignored that argument in favor of one calling attention to his new opponent's recent status as a New Yorker. He offered to send Kennedy a map of New York State and a guidebook.

| | |

No sooner had the president hung up with Reedy than he called Walter Jenkins to deliver a similar message, elaborating that he would withdraw in part to remove the Vietnam situation from partisan politics. "I don't believe there'll be many attacks on the orders I issue on Tonkin Gulf if I'm not a candidate," he said. Best to give his replacement, probably Robert Kennedy, "a mandate."

"I don't believe a white Southerner is the man to unite the nation at this hour," he told Jenkins. Humphrey or Kennedy could "get along with the nigras better than I can." Besides, even the people around him were disloyal.

"Here at the crowning point of my life when I need people's help I ain't even got the loyal here . . . so I just don't see any reason why I ought to seek the right to endure anguish."

He doubted "whether a man born where I was born . . . raised like I was raised could ever satisfy the Northern Jews, and Catholics, union people. And I don't feel good about throwing Alabama out, and Mississippi, and making them take an oath. . . . I don't want to have to fight to carry Texas. I just don't want Texas to have to say yes to me any more."

Just for a moment, and just in private, the tribal Southerner in Lyndon Johnson overcame the rational nationalist he had become, giving some indication of how difficult a journey he had taken from the first to the second.

"There's so much hatred of Mississippi," said the president, who had risked everything to eviscerate the foundation of Mississippi society. As much as anyone, he had hated that foundation; but he would not hate the people who had lived on it. They were his people, and not only because he was their president. Or maybe he was just feeling a little more tolerant of white Mississippi because he was convinced that Negro Mississippi was being used by his political enemy.

"I think this Freedom Party was born in the Justice Department," he told Jenkins.

"Now there are younger men and better prepared men and Harvard-educated men," he continued, who would perform better in the presidency, and he would make his final decision "during the lunch hour."

Then he said he'd have to decide on his running mate that very day. And that evening he called Illinois congressman Dan Rostenkowski in Atlantic City to ask him to make one of the seconding speeches for the vice presidential nominee. Rostenkowski agreed, hung up, and was halfway back to his seat in the convention hall before he realized Johnson had not told him whom he would be seconding. Somewhat reluctantly, Walter Jenkins told him it would be Humphrey, which was more than Humphrey knew at the time.

| | |

In Atlantic City, Jim Rowe and his friends had whittled four Credentials Committee votes away from supporting the MFDP; three more, and there would not be enough votes to send a minority report to the floor. It was old-fashioned hardball politics; Verna Canson of California, for instance, was told that if she wanted her husband to get the federal judgeship he'd been craving she'd best not defy the president who could appoint him.

Power politics, however, has its limits, especially at conventions. Unlike congressmen, who know they might need help next week or next month, a delegate spends only four days in office, and some of them don't need a job, an honor, or any other quid exchangeable for a quo. They can be true to their principles at no cost.

By Tuesday morning, Rowe and Humphrey realized that they weren't going to whittle away those last few votes unless they somehow sweetened their offer. They knew what their own vote count was, and thanks to the FBI's eavesdropping, they knew that the MFDP's vote count confirmed their own. Then they remembered Al Ullman's plan of the previous day: How about giving the MFDP two actual convention votes—at-large, not Mississippi—and to make it even more attractive, give one of them to a Negro, Aaron Henry, and one to a white, the Reverend Ed King.

Somewhat reluctantly, the president approved. Why worry about two votes when nothing would be voted on, anyway? Although Mississippi might walk out, and perhaps Alabama, the other Southern states would hardly bolt a convention over two civil rights delegates, one of them a white minister.

| | |

In the morning, Joe Rauh was outside the Credentials Committee room when he was told Walter Reuther was holding for him on a pay phone down the hall. "The convention has decided" how to resolve the dispute, Reuther said. How Reuther could speak for a convention to which he was not a delegate remained unexplained, but he called the solution "a tremendous victory," and he ordered Rauh "to go in there and accept it," at the risk of his UAW retainers.

"I want to make my position clear," Rauh said. "It's quite a good offer, but it's unacceptable to me."

"Why?"

"Because any offer is unacceptable until I've talked to Aaron Henry. Aaron and I shook hands on the proposition that neither of us would accept anything until the other had agreed to it."

"This is an order," Reuther said.

"You can't give me an order," Rauh told him, and he hung up, to find himself surrounded by reporters. He told them he'd been talking to a pretty girl and then asked the committee for a recess so he could consult with his clients.

| | |

At 1 P.M., the president had lunch with Rusk, McNamara, and Bundy. After lunch, he went to his room, drew the shades, and lay down. But sleep would not come. He made a few more phone calls, and then he told Lady Bird what he had told Reedy and Jenkins, that he would not accept the nomination. He didn't even want to go to Atlantic City.

She had been down this road before and knew better than to dismiss what he said as nothing but a transient bad mood. Instead, she sought the solace of her daughter Lynda, and the two of them walked along the south grounds of the White House. At one point, they stopped to lie down under one of the evergreen trees.

Late in the afternoon, Mrs. Johnson sat at her desk and wrote her husband a note:

Beloved:

You are as brave a man as Harry Truman—or FDR—or Lincoln. You can go on to find some peace, some achievement amidst all the pain. You have been strong, patient, determined beyond any words of mine to express.

I honor you for it. So does most of the country.

To step out now would be wrong for your country, and I can see nothing but a lonely wasteland for your future. Your friends would be frozen in embarrassed silence and your enemies jeering.

I am not afraid of *Time* or lies or losing money or defeat.

In the final analysis I can't carry any of the burdens you talked of—so I know it's only *your* choice. But I know you are as brave as any of the thirty-five.

I love you always
Bird.

If Lyndon Johnson could not control George Wallace or Fannie Lou Hamer, could not control Joe Rauh or the Credentials Committee, he could always control Hubert Humphrey.

So he did.

In his gloom, Johnson stayed atop the Mississippi credentials fight and, in doing so, stayed in Humphrey's face. One of those phone conversations he held while unable to sleep on Tuesday was with Humphrey and Walter Reuther, reporting in from Atlantic City about their latest proposal.

"We think we've made some progress . . . in reference to our little problem on credentials," Humphrey told him.

Actually, Humphrey made a speech to him, outlining not only what they had done but the reasons for it—"Since the Freedom Party itself is not a party but a protest movement it surely cannot be considered a legal entity," and more in that vein—reasons Johnson didn't need to hear.

Johnson called it a "good solution," and perhaps under Humphrey's influence, he orated back: "Our party's always been a group that you can come to with any bellyache and injustice, whether it was a pecan-shelling plant that paid four cents an hour or sweatshop wages or usurious interest rates or discrimination. . . . That's what the Democratic Party's for. That's why it was born. And that's why it survives. . . . Long as the poor and the downtrodden and the bended know that they can come to us and be heard. And that's what we're doing. We're hearing them."

But no one must know that the president himself played any role in settling this dispute.

"Don't have people saying that I'm making you do this," said the man who was making them do that. "I never heard of it. It's your proposal. And my name's Joe Glutz. . . . We understand each other, right?. . . . Don't tell anybody. Just you talked to Joe Glutz. That's my name."

Oh, and one other item: "Hubert, I'm not a sadistic person as you well know . . . I'm not just trying to play coy. . . . Since our conversation on the phone, I don't think we need to have any more. . . . You don't have to spell out everything."

Hanging up in Atlantic City, Humphrey might have begged to differ. Had Johnson just promised him the vice presidency? Or not?

| | |

Rauh was right; it was a pretty good offer, and he knew that it was good enough to dislodge at least three of the thirteen committee delegates who had been supporting his cause. The battle was essentially over, and considering that it had always been a symbolic battle anyway, it was now entirely within the power of the MFDP to declare it a symbolic victory, a declaration that would automatically render itself true.

But as he also knew, the MFDP might not see things that way. Picking one delegate of each race may have seemed like a great idea to Humphrey and Reuther, but to the MFDP delegates, this was just another case of other people trying to tell them what to do. Nothing could have been more offensive to their devotion to bottom-up democracy, to what Ed King called "the Gandhian get-our-neighbors-together grassroots approach."

So when Humphrey invited Henry and King to his suite for a Tuesday afternoon meeting, the delegation sent Moses and Fannie Lou Hamer along with them. When the four Mississippians got there, they found Rustin, Reuther, Martin Luther King, and one of his aides, Andrew Young.

They came tantalizingly close to agreement. The basic plan was acceptable, Ed King said, but the Freedom Party rank and file, not a couple of party bigwigs, should choose which of them should get the two at-large seats. To show how serious he was, King said that he would decline the honor and withdraw in favor of a sharecropper.

But Humphrey was worried that the MFDP would name Hamer to one of the slots, and he knew Johnson would never accept that. Earlier, he had told Rauh that "the president will not allow that illiterate woman to speak from the floor of the convention," though it was surely her eloquence, not her illiteracy, that scared Johnson.

Now, in Hamer's presence, Humphrey only pleaded with the Mississippians not to complicate matters any more. He began to talk about his agenda, his and Lyndon Johnson's and the Democratic Party's, about the great unfinished work of the New Deal and the New Frontier, about everything the Democratic Party had meant to America these last thirty years.

As he talked the tears began to flow, because what he was describing was something close to paradise. Once they were elected—Lyndon Johnson and him, with a strong Democratic Congress and a real mandate from the electorate—they would abolish poverty, they would bring the best health care to the poorest of the elderly, they would abolish the slums and improve the schools, and they would make sure that this war in Vietnam did not get out of hand. They would, in short, do everything that Fannie Lou Hamer wanted done.

He was pleading with her. He was one of the most powerful men in the United States—in the world—and he was pleading, tearfully, with a barely literate woman whose last job had been as a field hand on a plantation in Ruleville.

She turned him down.

"Senator Humphrey," she said, "do you mean to tell me that your position is more important to you than four hundred thousand black people's lives?

"I know lots of people in Mississippi who have lost their jobs for trying to register to vote. I had to leave the plantation where I worked in Sunflower County. But God took care of me. Now, if you lose this job of vice president because you do what is right, because you help the MFDP, everything will be all right. God will take care of you. But if you do not do right with the Mississippi Freedom Democratic Party, why, you will never be able to do any good for civil rights, for poor people, for peace, or any of those things you talk about.

"Senator Humphrey, I'm going to pray to Jesus for you."

Humphrey couldn't understand. Not the part about Jesus—Humphrey was a churchgoer—but that people should care as much about the way things got done as about whether they got done at all.

He probably couldn't understand why Mississippi's four hundred thousand Negroes would be any better off if the entire MFDP delegation was seated, either, and Mrs. Hamer offered no explanation, there being none. However moving she may have been, Mrs. Hamer did not convince all her fellow-delegates. Aaron Henry, for one, was willing to entertain the compromise, and he told Mrs. Hamer that the time had come for them "to listen to some of them that know much more about politics than we know."

Once again, there was a chance for an agreement. Humphrey and Reuther turned expectantly to Martin Luther King—a political realist, their friend, and not incidentally a man whose organization depended on Walter Reuther's union for much of its funding.

But King disappointed them. He had been moved by Mrs. Hamer's statement, he said, and, anyway, this was a decision to be made by the MFDP delegates, without pressure from outsiders such as himself.

Then Moses told Humphrey and Reuther that if King or Rustin or another moderate Negro leader tried to convince the delegates to accept the deal, he himself would make the case for rejection. We're still for the Edith Green proposal, Moses told them, and we'll take our chances with the Credentials Committee.

Too late.

By the time he spoke, the committee had voted, having rejected Rauh's appeal for a recess. Chairman David Lawrence moved the Humphrey compromise, and the committee approved it, with only seven other delegates joining Rauh in opposition.

Except as a symbol, this fight was over. But since it had never been anything *but* a symbol, it survived, with the moment and the method of victory only adding fuel to the unstable mix. The MFDP delegates who had met with Humphrey now assumed that it was all a setup, that they had been called not to negotiate but to surrender.

They were right, of course. He who has the votes does not have to negotiate.

|||

Joe Glutz. Now he was kidding around. Now he was a happy man. There would be no roll call. There would be no convention stampede to Robert Kennedy. Never again would he speak to anyone about quitting.

All the talk about quitting was just that—talk—and every *action* that Johnson took was that of a man intent on running and winning. Still, those closest to him did not think he was bluffing.

But Reedy remembers the night Johnson kept him up late, walking up and down the South Lawn so late that Reedy didn't get home until midnight, with the president still saying he would not run, saying it so often and so profanely that Reedy believed him, believed Barry Goldwater would become president.

So it is not frivolous to consider what would have happened had the Mississippi compromise blown up, deepening the president's depression so much that he released that statement of withdrawal. Probably, the convention would have nominated him anyway. When a president is eligible for reelection, his party's convention is his servant. A Johnson withdrawal would probably have been followed by a Johnson draft.

If not, there seems little doubt that the convention would have nominated Robert Kennedy. And Kennedy would probably have beaten Barry Goldwater. It would have been a much closer election, to be sure, for Kennedy was a polarizing figure. When he ran in the primaries in 1968, he won all but one of them, but he never got a majority.

Still, on the reasonable assumption that he would have taken all the states Johnson carried by 59 percent or more (minus Texas), he would have ended up with a strong majority of 335 electoral votes.

|||

Late Tuesday afternoon, the president called Walter Jenkins in Atlantic City and said, "Get Humphrey and tell him—no, let Jim do it, and this is what I want to tell him. Tell Jim to find a copy of the interview in today's *Star*. That says it."

The interview, the one held during that marathon walk around the White House, was with the president of the United States outlining what he would require from his vice president: absolute loyalty. Johnson wanted Jim Rowe to show the article to Humphrey so that he could, again, pledge his fealty.

There was one little problem. The *Star* wasn't easy to find in Atlantic City. Rowe found a copy of the *Post*, whose account had the same basic content, though apparently in a version less comforting to the president.

There was another problem. Humphrey was meeting with the MFDP delegates. Rowe "had to knock on seven or eight doors before I got all the way in to find him. It took me forty-five minutes."

Humphrey broke away from the meeting and, with his wife and two of his political aides, went to Rowe's suite at the Colony Hotel, where Rowe insisted that Humphrey join him in the bedroom, alone.

There, finally, he told him: "You're it, and you're to fly immediately to the White House for an official announcement."

But of course it wasn't that simple.

Hubert was "it" pending his agreement to the stipulations outlined in the interview, one of which was "you can be against me in our conferences until as president I make up my mind; then I want you to follow my policies."

Fine, Humphrey said.

Now he was "it." He would immediately tell Muriel, his wife.

No, Rowe said, you can't tell anybody, not even Muriel.

This was too much even for Humphrey.

"This is ridiculous," he said. "A man can't even tell his own wife?"

No, they could only say that Humphrey was heading to Washington for a meeting with Johnson.

Humphrey was furious. What sort of petty game was Johnson playing?

"Hubert," Rowe said, "tonight you're just a senator from Minnesota, but this time tomorrow night you'll be a candidate for vice president, and then we both can tell Johnson he's a shit."

A few minutes later, Walter Jenkins called to inform Rowe and Humphrey that the trip to Washington had been put off for a day; it was foggy.

It was, but that may not have been the reason. The president was still playing games; he would have both of Minnesota's senators fly to Washington to meet with him in the White House—Humphrey and Gene McCarthy.

| | |

In his hotel room, Gene McCarthy figured out that he was being played the fool, that he would not be the anointed one. With the help of his wife, Abigail, he composed a telegram to the president:

> I HAVE, AS YOU KNOW, DURING THIS CONVENTION AND FOR SEVERAL WEEKS NOT BEEN INDIFFERENT TO THE CHOICE YOU MUST MAKE. THE ACTION THAT I HAVE TAKEN HAS BEEN TO THIS END AND TO THIS PURPOSE: THAT YOUR CHOICE WOULD BE A FREE ONE AND THAT THOSE WHOM YOU MIGHT CONSULT, OR WHO MIGHT MAKE RECOMMENDATIONS TO YOU, MIGHT BE WELL-INFORMED.... IT IS MY OPINION THE QUALIFICATIONS THAT YOU HAVE LISTED, OR WHICH YOU ARE SAID TO HAVE LISTED AS MOST DESIRABLE IN THE MAN WHO WOULD BE VICE PRESIDENT WITH YOU WOULD BE MET MOST ADMIRABLY BY SENATOR HUMPHREY.

It was good politics and good self-therapy, and not just because McCarthy had trumped Lyndon Johnson at his own game. McCarthy had made himself seem less the toady than Humphrey, though perhaps he had merely figured out that he was the less successful toady.

Still, there was this distinction: Though both men were used, and misused, by Johnson, Humphrey accepted the terms, and McCarthy, in the end, did not.

Nor would he forget how misused he'd been.

| | |

On Wednesday morning, the MFDP gathered in the Union Temple Baptist Church to consider the compromise. This time, the consideration was only for themselves. The Credentials Committee report had been accepted; the deed had been done. The decision to be made now was not official but political.

Joe Rauh told them to take it, told them that it was a victory. Aaron Henry told them to take it. Bayard Rustin agreed. The movement was now a political force, he told them, not just a voice of protest, and it had to broaden its outlook accordingly.

"You're a traitor, Bayard, a traitor. Sit down," shouted Mendy Samstein, a white veteran of SNCC.

Al Lowenstein would have agreed with Rustin but uncharacteristically decided that perhaps he had spoken enough to this group.

And Martin Luther King? Once again, he declined to recommend.

"I am not going to counsel you to accept or reject," he said. "That is your decision."

Yes, he said, from a national, pragmatic, political perspective, they should accept. But from a moral, parochial, Mississippi perspective, they should not.

"So, being a Negro leader, I want you to take this," he said, "but if I were a Mississippi Negro, I would vote against it."

Where synthesis was impossible, abstention was his refuge. It was King's version of going back to Johnson City if he could not be in control.

Were there any flickering chance that the delegates would go along, Bob Moses ended it. "We're not here to bring politics to our morality, but to bring morality to our politics."

And so they did, rejecting the compromise because . . . well, because they had gone through too much, suffered too much to pay attention to pragmatism, to politics, to coalition. They held the moral high ground. Their light would shine. Let it shine.

| | |

Back in Mississippi, the light was being questioned by some of their own. The women of Freedom Summer had made some progress in getting the men to help with the dishes. Still, many of them had the feeling that they were being used—as servants, as concubines.

Sometime that summer, a thought occurred first to one or two, then to a few others, and as they discussed it—hesitantly—with each other, the thought evolved, until somebody—nobody knows exactly who—put it this way: Being a woman in this country wasn't much different from being a Negro; either way, you weren't treated equally.

A month earlier, two of the white women veterans of the movement, Mary King and Casey Hayden, Tom Hayden's former wife, had tried to put some of their frustrations down on paper. But they were uncertain, aware of their position as whites in a Negro-dominated organization. So they didn't show their writings to anyone else.

| | |

At two o'clock that morning, while Humphrey was in his suite getting a rubdown, Rowe called, saying that if word of his selection leaked out, Johnson would change his mind.

24

RECOVERY

On the morning of Wednesday, August 26, President Johnson signed the bill allowing the Atomic Energy Commission to sell nuclear fuels to private utility companies. He was in a good mood. The Mississippi Freedom Democratic Party crisis was over. He could get back to the usual business of the presidency.

Shortly after noon, the president invited the White House press corps on another walk. It was 89 degrees and humid in Washington, and this time they did fifteen laps around the South Lawn drive, a total of roughly four miles. They didn't all make it. Now and then one of the older reporters would drop out of the procession, seeking the relative cool of a shade tree. Johnson, older by far than most of them, never broke his step. He told them how much effort he was giving to this matter of the vice presidency. That very day, he said, he had spoken to Mayors Daley and Wagner, Governor Connally, Senators George Smathers and John Pastore, Speaker John McCormack, even Robert Kennedy.

Still, he had not yet decided, he told the surviving reporters. When one of them asked about Humphrey, Johnson said he'd invited him over that very afternoon, just to talk things over. "If he can come down, I'll let you know," the president said. It was almost three o'clock when he stopped doing laps and invited them all into the Oval Office for some cold orange drink.

| | |

That morning, Rowe had told Humphrey to stay close to the phone. But when the call came, telling Humphrey to get on a plane to Washington, it came with the news that he'd have a companion—Senator Tom Dodd of Connecticut.

"What?" Humphrey asked Rowe. "Is Tom Dodd being considered, too?"

"No," Rowe said, "this is just a cover." Something, he said, to "keep the press off balance."

But it didn't do Humphrey's balance much good, either.

Nor was that all. When the twin-engine Beech got to Washington, it was met by a White House limousine, with Jack Valenti in attendance. Valenti informed the two senators that the president was not quite ready to receive them, that they would have to ride around for a while.

It wasn't that the president was busy. He just didn't want anything to interfere with live television coverage of Lady Bird's arrival in Atlantic City. And he was playing games, trying to keep the White House reporters wondering why Tom Dodd had come along.

Dodd had come along for the ride. An ethically challenged, undistinguished senator with a drinking problem, Dodd was no more likely to be Johnson's choice than was J. Edgar Hoover. Still, the limo driver went aimlessly around Washington for fifteen minutes before going to the White House and parking near the south entrance. Dodd was invited into the presidential presence first; Humphrey fell asleep in the backseat. After a while he was awakened by a knock on the window from a White House flunky, who showed Humphrey into the Fish Room outside the Oval Office. In a moment, Johnson appeared and escorted Humphrey into the cabinet room.

"Hubert," he said, "do you want to be vice president?"

Yes, as a matter of fact, he did.

But Johnson was not through torturing Humphrey. "This is like a marriage with no chance of divorce," he told him. "I need complete and unswerving loyalty."

When he was finished, he got the reply he wanted.

"You can trust me, Mr. President," Humphrey said.

It was the president, not the husband, who called Muriel Humphrey to tell her the news. And he pledged Humphrey to secrecy so that he, himself, could set a precedent, could go himself to the convention that evening, the day before he was to give his acceptance speech, to stand before the delegates and announce his choice.

|||

On the plane to Atlantic City, the president was buoyant but also philosophical. Relaxing with his closest aides, he held up a whiskey glass. "You know," he said, "every family has a certain thread that runs through it. In the Kennedys it was women. All those town houses and all those women . . . like an animal need, the need for women. . . . For other families it's money, or skiing, or meat. In ours it was alcohol."

He finished his drink and asked for a refill.

It was after eleven before he got to the convention hall. Waiting for no invitation or introduction, he strode to the podium, impatiently pounding the gavel, quieting the crowd to tell it what it knew, that he wanted Hubert Humphrey to be his vice president.

| | |

FBI Agent Bill Barry drove Robert Kennedy to the airport in New York, where Kennedy asked him to come along to Atlantic City. "Ethel's pregnant and I have nobody in Atlantic City and I really want you to go," Kennedy said. Atlantic City was outside his division, but Barry went, just to be friendly.

Barry's colleagues were not pleased. To his surprise, one of the first people he ran into was Cartha DeLoach, who told him to leave town.

"There's some thought that Attorney General Kennedy might try to stampede the convention," DeLoach said. "If he does that and he's got an FBI agent by his side, the president will not be too happy with the FBI organization, so you're immediately to leave Atlantic City."

He did.

In the afternoon there were the two events that had convinced the president that this "stampede" was possible. One was Jacqueline Kennedy's reception for the delegates. Again, Fredric March read from some of the late president's favorite poetry, and more than five thousand delegates streamed through. Mrs. Kennedy shook the hand of every one of them.

The other was the touring exhibit of the John F. Kennedy Library held on the boardwalk. Part of it was a short film about John Kennedy. Robert Kennedy was there when it was shown; his face was impassive as he stared at the screen, his hands grasped together in front of him, held so tightly that his knuckles turned white.

Later, Kennedy and his friend John Seigenthaler went to the convention hall to prepare for Kennedy's introduction of the longer memorial film to his brother, the one Lyndon Johnson had made sure would not be shown until after he and his running mate were nominated.

The two of them were led through the darkness into a small, windowless dressing room under the platform. "We can't hear anything back here," Kennedy said. "I think Lyndon may just have put us back here with orders to forget us. They'll probably let us out the day after tomorrow."

He had already prepared his short speech of introduction, with a little help from Jacqueline Kennedy, who had told him about an appropriate quote from *Romeo and Juliet*.

Shortly after the convention was called to order, Kennedy was taken to a runway behind the speaker's platform where the other dignitaries were already assembled. Only Jim Farley, who no longer had anything to lose, attempted to speak with him; it was as though the others feared any apparent kindness would be reported back to the president. Kennedy took out a pencil and the copy of his speech to scribble small changes in the manuscript.

Scoop Jackson—Senator Henry Jackson of Washington—presiding over the convention, introduced Kennedy, and before he could reach the podium the roaring began. It was not simply applause. It was not even an ovation. It was a torrent of pent-up emotion, an indication less of approval than of longing. Something had been taken from these people, and they were letting the world—they were letting themselves—know how much they missed it.

The roar went on. So slender that he seemed almost a waif, a stick being tossed about on this sea of noise, Kennedy made a few feeble efforts to quiet the throng. He held up his hand. He said, "Thank you very much." Nothing worked.

"Let it go on," Jackson told him. "Just let them do it, Bob, let them get it out of their system."

It took them twenty-two minutes, and then he began to speak. It was a very short speech, just to introduce the film, and all that was memorable about it was the quotation Jackie Kennedy had found:

> When he shall die
> Take him and cut him out in little stars
> And he will make the face of heaven so fine
> That all the world will be in love with night,
> And pay no worship to the garish sun.

Judging from the ensuing roar, maybe Lyndon Johnson—was he the "garish sun"?—hadn't been totally wrong in believing that he would have trouble keeping control of this convention.

| | |

The next day, after a false rumor that police had killed a Negro woman made its way around west Philadelphia, rioting erupted in the city. Governor William Scranton issued an executive order closing the bars in the city, and Negro leaders praised the policy for "a remarkable degree of restraint." No one was killed, but 250 people were hurt badly enough to be hospitalized.

| | |

A novelist's skills are not necessarily those of a speechwriter. Johnson accepted his nomination with the dullest speech of the campaign. But neither the stodgy construction of his talk nor the lingering MFDP protests on the boardwalk dampened the spirits of the delegates, who were more amused than enraged to see the new boardwalk billboard with Barry Goldwater's face and the huge letters: "In your heart, you know he's right." After all, they knew in their minds that Goldwater would lose.

And the winner-to-be could not suppress his glee. If he had been near depression just three days earlier, Lyndon Johnson now approached mania. At the airport on Friday morning, he saw *Washington Post* publisher Katherine Graham and invited her onto Air Force One with him for the trip to his ranch, ignoring her complaints that she didn't have a change of clothing.

Once there, with the same irresistible, or at least overwhelming, power, he cajoled Humphrey, no horseman, onto the back of one of the tallest horses in Texas, where the vice presidential candidate posed awkwardly, cowboy hat on head, city shoes on feet.

| | |

Optimism was all around, but wasn't it always in early September? New York City police lieutenant Thomas Gilligan was no doubt relieved after he was cleared by a grand jury in the shooting death of James Powell, and there was optimism, though combined with nervousness, in Philadelphia and Chicago, where baseball teams were in first place.

On the radio, Ray Charles was rejoicing about being "Smack Dab in the Middle," and Fats Domino was explaining just how "Sally Was a Good Old Girl." The Beatles were everywhere, on the radio and in the movie theaters with a jaunty, irreverent romp called *A Hard Day's Night,* which many a reluctant adult found irresistible.

Despite the polls, Barry Goldwater seemed jolly, too. He formally opened the campaign on Thursday, September 3, in Prescott, Arizona, promising a government under which "every American can stand on his own, make up his own mind, chart his own future, keep and control his own family asking for help only when truly overwhelming problems beyond his control beset him." No one asked him just how that differed from the present situation.

"There is a stir in the air," Goldwater intoned, more hopefully than convincingly. The stir he was hoping for was the one that would inspire the "hidden conservatives," the millions who had been staying home from the polls all these decades for lack of a true conservative option. It had long been either the hopeful insight or the delusion of a few conservative political analysts that these folks were somehow being missed by the pollsters, but that the Goldwater candidacy would reveal them as a mighty host.

There were no such millions. Long before then, the sampling techniques used by pollsters were sophisticated enough to find the nonvoter as well as the voter and to make at least a rough estimate of how many people were refusing to vote because the Republicans had put up moderate candidates. Not many. The real Republican hope, which could not be stated publicly, was for hidden racists. This hope was not without foundation. In the South, at least, the reaction against the Democratic Party for supporting the Civil Rights Law was overt, as Lady Bird Johnson found out when she was planning her "Dixieland Special" whistle-stop campaign tour through the South.

On Friday, September 4, she began to call Southern Democratic politicians, men she'd known for years, men who'd supped at her table. The reaction often fell short of the usual standards of Southern hospitality.

Senator Harry Byrd of Virginia declined to help, citing the recent death of his wife. His Virginia colleague Willis Robertson declined without benefit of such a convenient excuse. From South Carolina, Strom Thurmond's message was more ominous. He could not help, he said, because he had to make a "really basic decision within the next two weeks."

| | |

Late in August, on a fifty-two-acre site on Waukegan Avenue in Deerfield, Illinois, the Sara Lee Company began operating a new 500,000-square-foot computer-operated bakery. In a freezer room that could hold almost eight million cakes, a computer-controlled giant crane deposited pallet loads of cakes in each of 650,000 pigeonholes in storage racks.

Because the H610 Honeywell computer memorized where it had placed each pallet load, it could quickly extract the right pallet for each order. With the computer updating its memory every fifteen seconds, the system could almost instantly pick out exactly the right mix of cakes each customer demanded, thereby integrating the shipping and packing functions. For the first time, all the diverse elements of a process were under the control of one computer system.

Robert Theobald and his allies at the Triple Revolution Committee may have had a point.

| | |

Labor Day was September 7, and as Democratic candidates had done for years, Lyndon Johnson formally opened his campaign with a speech at

Detroit's Cadillac Square. What he said that day was not memorable. What he said that night, and the context in which he said it, was.

The 50 million or so people who were watching Gregory Peck and Susan Hayward in the boring but spectacular movie *David and Bathsheba* on NBC that night were startled during the first commercial break to see a film of a sweet young girl picking the petals off a daisy, one at a time, counting from one to ten.

Then her voice was replaced by another, male and menacing, counting backward, from ten. At zero, the girl faded away, her image dissolving into that of the mushroom cloud of a nuclear explosion, and as it rose, the unidentified but unmistakable voice of the president of the United States issued a pronouncement: "These are the stakes—to make a world in which all of God's children can live, or to go into the dark. We must either love each other, or we must die."

Then the screen was blank and dark, except for these words printed in white: "Vote for President Johnson on November 3."

In millions of living rooms, people wondered just what they had seen. Was this a political advertisement? Obviously it was, considering its concluding tag line. But it was unlike any political ad they had ever seen before. Until then, political commercials had been about candidates. Usually the candidates themselves appeared to display their strengths. On rarer occasions, ordinary citizens (or actors portraying them) would praise the candidate.

But this advertisement wasn't about a candidate at all. It was about . . . well, what was it about? Nuclear war? And was it implying that if Goldwater were elected the H-bombs would fall?

The immediate reaction to the commercial was one of outrage, not only from Goldwater but from most of the (pro-Johnson) press and from academic and journalistic advocates of fairness. Even Hubert Humphrey called the ad "unfortunate."

The Johnson campaign didn't care. The men who ran it—Moyers, Jim Rowe, Richard Goodwin, Jack Valenti—and the advertising genius Tony Schwartz knew that respectable opinion would condemn them. Too bad. The "daisy ad" ran just that once, but more than any other political commercial in history, it was *news*. So all three networks kept showing it on their newscasts. The message got across, but the Johnson campaign could not be blamed.

And this was a campaign that would seek every advantage. Soon after the Democratic Convention, Walter Jenkins asked Cartha DeLoach to come to the White House for a conversation inappropriate to hold over the phone. When DeLoach got there, Jenkins asked him for everything in the FBI files on Barry Goldwater, his Senate staff, and his campaign staff.

This was too much even for Hoover, who called it "pure politics." After a few days of delay, DeLoach called Jenkins and told him the Bureau had no information about Goldwater or his associates.[1]

| | |

That Tuesday, as politicians were debating the propriety of the commercial, new and returning students were swarming around the Sather Gate at Berkeley, some of them stopping at one of the tables set up by student advocates or opponents of one political cause or another.

Mario Savio stopped by the table manned by opponents of the proposition to repeal the housing discrimination law to put up a poster with news of the latest outrages from his summer stomping grounds in McComb. At another table, students were planning to picket the nearby *Oakland Tribune,* which supported both the anti–fair housing proposition and Barry Goldwater, and whose fifteen hundred employees, according to the local CORE chapter, included only seventeen Negroes. Jack Weinberg was going to join that demonstration.

| | |

All of a sudden, student political troublemaking wasn't confined to Berkeley. All over the country, students going back to college were getting political. In the fall of 1963 there had been five fully functioning chapters of SDS; this fall there were *twenty-nine,* with new chapters at Reed, Oklahoma, Kansas, the University of Chicago, and even Berkeley, where it had to compete with up-and-running left-of-center student groups.

With paid membership rising above one thousand, with radical energies spurred by Freedom Summer, by the civil rights bill, by the discovery that political activity—the association of yourself with your generation—could provide an emotional home more stable than a suburban subdivision had ever been, the usually sober Dick Flacks wrote, "We are in a new state. . . . It is tremendously exciting—one sign of it is that no one person can actually keep up with everything which is going on . . . another sign is the extent to which people are willing to commit themselves. . . . 'The times they are a-changing,' and we are part of it."

That may have been so, but the September National Council meeting in Philadelphia was not such a rousing success. A new fault line had developed, in SDS and the rest of the left. A few on the National Council were convinced the fighting in Vietnam would soon become a real war and that Lyndon Johnson would wage it. They got some money from an outfit called the

Institute for World Peace and started a new subunit called the Peace Research and Education Project, based in Ann Arbor.

But this was hardly a unanimous outlook on the part of the left. "We must tread delicately on the Vietnam question because lots of SDS people are far from being for withdrawal," Paul Potter wrote. Some SDS members agreed that communism should be stopped in Vietnam. Even more of them were worried only about beating Goldwater, despite lack of enthusiasm for Johnson. "Part of the Way with LBJ" was their semimocking motto. The big issue was still civil rights. Students, especially, were not worried about going to war. They had draft deferments.

| | |

On Thursday, September 10, Cartha DeLoach sent a friendly note to Bill Moyers, using the nickname Moyers was known by at the FBI:

> Dear Bishop. Thank you for your very thoughtful and generous note concerning our operation in Atlantic City. Please be assured that it was a pleasure to be able to be of assistance to the president, and all the boys that were with me felt honored in being selected for the assignment. I think everything worked out well, and I'm certainly glad that we were able to come through with vital tidbits from time to time which were of assistance to you and Walter.

It was rookie FBI agent Roy Mitchell who first made contact with Wallace Miller, an easygoing Meridian police officer who liked to cook and who had joined the Lauderdale kleagle of the White Knights because he thought civil rights workers were communists and because he got five bucks each time he brought in a new recruit.

He hadn't known they were going to kill folks, and by mid-September, Mitchell noticed Miller's discomfort every time the subject of the murders came up. The young federal agent kept the young Meridian policeman talking, and soon enough he was talking about some of his fellow Klansmen, including the klavern's chaplain, Delmar Dennis.

"I've been expecting you," Dennis told the two FBI agents who came to see him, and for a hundred dollars a week he agreed to talk and to spy on his Klan friends. When leaders of the White Knights held a meeting in a factory outside Meridian on Sunday, September 27, both Wallace Miller and Delmar Dennis took their memories immediately to the agents, reporting on who had said what within.

| | |

Robert Kennedy had been scheduled to get to Glens Falls at 8 P.M. on Sunday, September 13. As campaigns usually are, his was late, and then some. It was one o'clock the next morning when his plane touched down in the industrial town north of Albany. But there were a thousand people at the airport, and on the drive into town hundreds more, in pajamas and bathrobes, lined the road to see him.

It was an extraordinary outpouring of affection, but as he well knew, he was not its object. "They're for him," he muttered.

Nobody had to ask to whom he referred.

It had been the same a few days earlier when he'd won the support of the New York City Teamsters. Quite a coup, Teamsters for Robert Kennedy, especially considering that John O'Rourke, the union's top honcho in New York, owed his job to Jimmy Hoffa.

But Johnny O'Rourke was also a West Side Irishman, and when Hoffa had ordered the flag put back at full mast the previous November 22, O'Rourke marked whatever he owed his boss as paid in full. As West Side Irishmen will be, O'Rourke was something of a sentimentalist, and he had not lost all touch with his working-class roots. As he saw it, there was now little Hoffa could ask of him and little that Robert Kennedy could not.

But Kennedy knew that for both O'Rourke and the pajama-clad Democrats of Glens Falls, he was less himself than surrogate, that they saw his candidacy as a way somehow to revive his brother.

And didn't he?

It was the unlikeliest of his associates who snapped him out of it. "Get out of this mysticism. Get out of your daze," Paul Corbin barked at him one day. The Democratic National Committee had fired Corbin after his New Hampshire "draft Kennedy" efforts had so enraged Lyndon Johnson. Now, openly on the Kennedy payroll, he spoke more bluntly than anyone to the boss. "God damn, Bob, be yourself . . . you're real. Your brother's dead."

Or maybe not so unlikely. Corbin was beyond embarrassment.

| | |

A few days earlier, lawyers for the *Oakland Tribune,* having done research in preparation for the promised CORE picketing of their establishment, forwarded to officials of the University of California the information that the little strip of land between the Sather Gate and Bancroft Way belonged to the university, not the city of Berkeley.

This information, the accuracy of which remains in doubt, meant that the university administration could apply its long-standing "no politics" rule to the tables set up on the strip, and it announced its intention to do so, claiming, at first, that the tables interfered with pedestrian traffic.

They did not.

| | |

The new television season was allegedly funny.

That is to say, two-thirds of the programs were situation comedies, sixteen returnees from last season and new offerings such as *Gilligan's Island, Flipper, Gomer Pyle U.S.M.C., The Munsters, The Famous Adventures of Mr. Magoo,* and *Bewitched,* a series so daring that for the first time in television history a married couple shared a double bed. Even Rob and Laura Petrie had slept in twin beds.

There was one serious new drama series dealing with public affairs, *Slattery's People,* which dared to try to make state legislatures interesting. And there was one salacious new drama series, *Peyton Place,* which Jack Paar called "television's first situation orgy," starring two interesting young actors, Ryan O'Neal and Mia Farrow.

Not that the networks were devoid of new ideas. NBC had one; it contracted with Universal Studios to produce movies just for television. They didn't give Universal much money, so what they got wasn't much. In fact, the network rejected the first offer, a gangster potboiler loosely based on a Hemingway short story. *The Killers* starred Lee Marvin, Angie Dickinson, John Cassavetes, and Ronald Reagan as a crime kingpin. The network found it too violent.

According to Hollywood scuttlebutt, the big loser in the rejection was Reagan, whose film career could optimistically be described as on hold and who hoped to revive it by playing "heavies," a departure from his earlier roles but one he thought he could manage. In *The Killers,* he slaps Angie Dickinson. Universal's second try, *See How They Run,* starring John Forsythe and Jane Wyatt, was accepted by the network.

But comedy was clearly the rule, and it took no great insight to grasp the two most obvious characteristics of the sitcoms: They were bland and their humor was pitched toward adolescents. Nor was it difficult to see why. Blandness avoided controversy; the great comedians—Berle and Caesar, Benny and Burns—had been off the air for years, and the good writers they had insisted on hiring had gone off to try the movies, the theater, or retirement. And why shouldn't television aim at sixteen-year-olds? There were so many of them.

In past years, parents might have pulled rank to decide what the family would watch. But these days the kids seemed to have the power as well as the numbers.

| | |

After retreating on the "pedestrian traffic" argument, the campus administration reaffirmed that "university facilities may not, of course, be used to support or advocate off-campus political or social action."

Chancellor Edward Strong then issued the first of many "clarifications," saying students could use the steps of nearby Sproul Hall as a "free speech area" and could maintain tables on the strip outside the gate, but not for partisan political causes. The students ignored this restriction, and the administration, wisely, ignored the violations.

| | |

In New Orleans, business leaders took out advertisements urging compliance with the Civil Rights Law. The Holiday Inns of America told its 488 motels to observe the law, and even Morrison's, the South's largest cafeteria chain, announced that its restaurants would be integrated, as the law demanded.

Exceptions there were aplenty, especially in rural areas of Mississippi and Alabama. Even in Jackson, the owners of the fabled Robert E. Lee Hotel on North Lamar Street posted a sign on its front door reading, CLOSED IN DESPAIR—CIVIL RIGHTS BILL UNCONSTITUTIONAL. But the Community Relations Service of the Justice Department found widespread compliance, and even Martin Luther King noted, "The South has complied quite surprisingly."[2]

But nobody in the civil rights organizations even thought to ask whether this success constituted victory, whether, having outlawed discrimination, their movement should evolve from one demanding basic rights for Negroes to . . . well, to something else, perhaps one demanding more economic equality for everyone.

The question would have been premature; the next year, more marches would be required to force the Voting Rights Act, guaranteeing a democracy's most essential right. But if nobody actually asked the question, one man indicated he was thinking along those lines. Martin Luther King in mid-September was turning at least some of his attention from civil rights to the fight against poverty, and not just Negro poverty; he was seeking a biracial coalition to exert pressure on Congress. "The solution to our full citizenship, political and economic, cannot be achieved by the Negro or civil rights forces alone," he said.

By then, though, part of his own movement was slipping away from him and going in precisely the opposite direction. At a meeting in Atlanta, members of the SNCC Executive Committee were in no mood for coalition. The meaning of their failure in Atlantic City, as they saw it, was that neither the federal government nor mainstream liberals could be trusted.

Even some of the not-so-mainstream liberals, such as Aaron Henry and Al Lowenstein, had trouble understanding the depth of anger and alienation Atlantic City had spawned. That's because Henry and Lowenstein, if slightly left of liberal, were political traditionalists; politics, to them, was the path to power. Not power for its own sake—these were men with a social vision and social values—but power as a means to improve the world.

At SNCC, inspired by the religious devotion to "bearing witness," by the Gandhian devotion to self-denial, and (from its educated elite) by Camus's *The Rebel* and its distrust of all organization, politics was a path to personal fulfillment, an art form as much as a social device. If SNCC members had a devotion to anything, it was to what they were now calling "the Movement," which was not just SNCC; it was a general uprising.

Then there was the more primitive divide. Increasingly, the young Negroes of the movement were calling themselves blacks and distrusting all whites, even the ones who came to Mississippi and wore bib overalls. The civil rights movement never came close to evolving into a biracial movement because it was already degenerating into a Negro nationalist movement.

| | |

On the second Monday of September, thousands of white children in the New York City borough of Queens stayed home to protest a "cross-busing" plan designed to integrate two schools by putting all the kindergarten through second graders in P.S. 148 and all the third- through sixth-graders in P.S. 127.

This was a new idea—using bus transportation to bring racial integration to schools that were not legally segregated. Though the schools were less than a mile apart, one was 87 percent white, the other 94 percent Negro. Only 197 children were to be bused, and for some of them, it meant a shorter trip to school. On the other hand, one child was to be bused fourteen blocks, mo' than a mile, to P.S. 127, though P.S. 148 was right across the street from apartment building.

So there were reasons other than bigotry to oppose the plan. On the hand, one of the signs held by a protesting white parent read "You' into a nigger."

| | |

Senator Strom Thurmond announced his "really basic decision" on Wednesday, September 16; he was now declaring himself a Republican.

"The Democratic Party has abandoned the people," he said. "The Democratic Party has invaded the private lives of people. The Democratic Party has succored and assisted our communist enemies . . . worships at the throne of power and materialism . . . has protected the Supreme Court in a reign of judicial tyranny." The Civil Rights Act, Thurmond said, amounted to "another Reconstruction, [and] freedom as we have known it in this country is doomed."

The next day, wearing a Republican elephant gold tie clip, Thurmond welcomed Goldwater on his first campaign trip to South Carolina, a state no Republican had won in this century. Leander Perez of Louisiana, the ruler of Plaquemines Parish, who had been excommunicated from the Roman Catholic Church for his efforts on behalf of segregation, came along.

Outside the South, things were not looking good for Goldwater. On the Republican Great Plains, Thomas W. Taylor reported from Sioux Falls that "most of the candidates for [South Dakota] state constitutional offices are not mentioning Goldwater's name in their speeches."

But they weren't giving up, and now came Cliff White and his friends to the rescue. White, Tom Van Sickle of Kansas, and Rus Walton of California scraped together forty-five thousand dollars and created a film.

But first they created an organization, or at least the shell of an organization. They called it Mothers for a Moral Majority, though there were no mothers involved. This was an organization without members, officers, or dues. Its sole purpose was to distribute the film.

First, they called the film *Violence,* but before it was completed, the name had been changed to *Choice.* It was a cobbling together of newsreels designed to make the point that "now there are two Americas," as the narrator intoned near the beginning.

But the real theme was in the opening shots: a car zooming down a dark country road, scantily clad young people writhing to some kind of music (not heard; what was heard was a twangy, menacing guitar, a sort of fifth-rate version of the theme from *The Man with the Golden Arm*), punks being arrested by cops, a beer can being thrown out the window of that car, still on that same country road. Then came the other, more admirable America, the one our forefathers built out of "virgin land [and] marked it with a cross." Here were the trains, dams, steel girders, rockets, and power plants of a vigorous America now threatened by "love of soft living and the get-rich-quick theory of life."

For all its Republicanism, the film was full of praise for that "dedicated young leader," John Kennedy. But look what followed him. In "eight short months more riots across the United States than in the last eight years," and there were the rioters, Negroes throwing rocks and taunting cops. Now, said the narrator, "it isn't the lawbreaker who is handcuffed; it is the police," and as he spoke the viewer saw the marquees of porno movie theaters, gambling tables, and people rioting and looting. Not all of them Negroes. But a lot of them.

Then came John Wayne telling the voter, "You've got the strongest hand in the world," and urging him or her to use it to vote for Barry Goldwater.

Fade-out.

The film was amateurish, almost laughable, and probably would have had no impact at all, but no one will ever know. Barry Goldwater took one look at it and said, "It's nothing but a racist film." It was never shown.

Once again, Goldwater proved that he was shrewder than some of his associates, though by now the fact that White had anything to do with the project might have prejudiced Goldwater against it. But he could see, as they could not, first, that *Choice* would do him no good, and second, that if he was going to lose—and he knew he would—he ought to do it gracefully. This film was not graceful.

| | |

The Beatles ended their second tumultuous American tour on Saturday night, September 19, with a one-hundred-dollar-a-ticket charity concert at New York's Paramount Theater. Half the audience consisted of the usual charity concert crowd: men in tuxedos, women in gowns. The other half consisted of screaming teenagers in blue jeans. During the performance, a skinny young man kept coming onto the stage and being escorted off by security guards until one of the Beatles entourage recognized him as Bob Dylan.

After the show, Dylan went back to the hotel with John, Paul, George, and Ringo. Mostly, they talked music, but sometime before the sun rose, Dylan introduced his four new British friends to marijuana.

| | |

In the New York State Senate campaign, the carpetbagger argum/ against Robert Kennedy was hitting home, and as the end of Septer/

loomed, Senator Kenneth Keating was sitting on a comfortable lead over Kennedy, who had at least two other problems. One was that he was a boring campaigner, mumbling his speeches in a monotone and unable to attack his opponent for fear of raising the "ruthless" label.

The other problem was that the label was raised anyway. Kennedy ruthlessness, in fact, was generally accepted among much of New York's intelligentsia, whose visceral distaste for the Democratic candidate outweighed their political agreement with him. Author Gore Vidal was the chairman of "Democrats for Keating," and leftist writer Nat Hentoff endorsed the Republican.

Had he sat on his lead, Keating might well have won. But he did not. Perhaps inspired by Herbert Brownell, Ike's attorney general and a political gut-fighter, Keating decided to go for the knockout blow: On Sunday, September 20, he charged that as attorney general, Kennedy had made a deal with a "huge Nazi cartel . . . the chemical arsenal for Nazi Germany."

Keating was referring to the settlement of the case involving the General Aniline and Film Corporation, which had been seized as enemy property during the war and later sold to a Swiss concern, with the approval of Kennedy's Justice Department and also of Keating.

The politics of this ploy were obvious. Of all the subdivisions of the Democratic constituency in New York, the one wariest of Robert Kennedy was the Jews. If Keating could now imply that Kennedy was insufficiently anti-Nazi, he could destroy Kennedy with Jewish voters.

Kennedy struck back quickly. "If this kind of charge were true, I wouldn't deserve to be elected to any public office. The charge isn't true."

Kennedy was right, and he could easily demonstrate it. It was a terrible blunder on Keating's part, not only because he couldn't back up the charge, but because now Kennedy could attack him without being seen as the bad guy.

| | |

On Tuesday, September 22, the ten corporations leading the WEST consortium announced plans to spend $105 billion over the next twenty years to build coal, hydropowered, and nuclear plants that would produce 36 million kilowatts of electricity. One of the projects, expanding the coal-fired power plant near Glen Canyon Dam in Page, Arizona, had been suggested by Interior Secretary Udall as part of a bargain between the Interior Department and the private companies.

Under the agreement, in exchange for promoting instead of opposing the private plans, the Bureau of Reclamation would get 24 percent of the power from the enlarged plant. The companies would get more coal from Indian lands in the Southwest. Nothing better illustrated the assumption by both private and public officials that the only way to provide enough power to the West was by building large, centralized power plants and transmitting the electricity over long distances.

| | |

To the disappointment of many, including, almost surely, its boss, the FBI reported on Saturday, September 26, that the riots of July had not been instigated by subversives. Neither, reported the Bureau, were they "race riots" as the term is usually understood.

"They were not riots of Negroes against whites or whites against Negroes . . . [but were] a senseless attack on all constituted authority without purpose or objective." That there were those in the body politic who no longer considered such attacks senseless seems not to have occurred to the report's authors, themselves devoted to constituted authority.

The next day, amidst great fanfare, came the big report, the Warren Commission's conclusion that Lee Harvey Oswald had shot and killed President Kennedy with no help from anyone.

The conclusions were widely praised by the press, leaders of the government, and academic experts, and they were just as widely disbelieved by the public in general. James Reston, a flawed political predictor, did better here, calling the assassination "so involved in the complicated and elemental conflicts of the age that many vital questions remain, and the philosophers, novelists and dramatists will have to take it from there."

|25|

THE YOUNG AND THE RESTLESS

The president left Washington early Monday morning, September 28, to campaign in Providence, Rhode Island. This was not his kind of town. It was Jack Kennedy's kind of town: Catholic, crowded, full of factory workers who lived in four-family frame houses and whose families had not been in America for more than two generations, if that.

But there were three thousand people at the airport and so many more choking the streets as his open limousine inched past that some of the reporters there figured the crowd outnumbered the city's total population of just over two hundred thousand.

Providence was a good Democratic town with a good Democratic organization that knew how to bring out a crowd. But not this kind of crowd. This was a genuine outpouring of support, all of it for him, for Lyndon Johnson. Some of it was just fear of Goldwater, but not all of it; fear alone could not inspire this kind of reception. They must really like him.

He loved this reception, and in response to the enthusiasm, he tried to tell the crowd what he planned to do. At the corner of Ninth and Broadway, he said, "We're in favor of a lot of things, and we're against mighty few," and then he played the role of cheerleader for himself. "I want to ask you just one question—are you going to vote Democratic in November?" He would cup his ear, and though the answer was loud, he'd say, "I didn't hear you. Did you say yes?"

They did. By nightfall, his hand had been shaken so often, so hard, that it was bloody.

That was the day Chancellor Edward Strong decided he'd have to put a stop to the constant violations of university rules, but gently. Declaring the whole matter "closed," he also announced an amnesty for those who had been setting up the tables in defiance of his earlier orders.

Yet he could not simply ignore all the violations. He was, after all, an administrator. Like so many others in charge of institutions, starting with the president of the United States, he had to believe that dissent from within must be fomented by identifiable fomenters; to believe otherwise would be to acknowledge flaws in the institution itself.

He had his deans select eight students from among the hundreds who had violated the regulations, and he did not simply suspend them, he suspended them "indefinitely," which he lacked the power to do. Mario Savio was one of them.

The next day it seemed that half of undergraduate Berkeley had a table outside the Sather Gate. SNCC was there, and CORE, and a student leftist group known as Slate, and the Young Socialist Alliance, and the Barry Goldwater supporters—each with its table. Campus officials did not attempt to dismantle the tables, but they did take the names of some of those sitting behind them.

The day after that, the last day of the month, some four hundred students signed petitions to the deans proclaiming that they were as guilty as those who had given their names the day before. By now the politically active students had organized themselves, albeit loosely, into something known as the United Federation.

The petition signing was not a spontaneous or improvised act. It was a well-organized response on the part of young people who had been learning how to organize responses in the face of beatings and death threats.

And learning to love it. Mario Savio, effectively the chief organizer even before the rebellious students had formed an organization, was one of perhaps thirty Berkeley students who had gone to Freedom Summer, and Mississippi that summer had been like war—dangerous but thrilling in its existential intensity. Like many a returning veteran of a decade earlier, they were relieved to be back, but also disappointed. After the months of helping to change the world, getting to know and admire the poorest of the poor, risking the fists and guns of the Klan, singing and arguing and talking together, and making love in cotton fields and church basements, they now faced the prospect of . . . going to class? It's no wonder that fighting the chancellor was much more fun—especially because he was so dense, because they were right and he was wrong.

This was only one reason all the student organizations, even the conservatives, were willing to go along with Savio's plan. The other reason was Savio. Like Robert Moses, he was a powerful personality precisely because of his apparent reluctance to assert his personal power. Savio allowed others to see him in the act of trying to control his towering ego, which gave him the appearance of being without ego—gentle, almost mystical, yet strong and never forgetting to apply his stern moral sense as strongly to himself as to any adversary. It was pretty appealing, especially to young people who claimed they wanted no direction from anybody but who may in fact have been looking for a strong leader.

A substitute for Jack Kennedy? Or maybe for a father who would command instead of indulge.

It also helped that Savio was incredibly clever. Instead of debating (though it was debatable) the administration's contention—based on that information from the *Oakland Tribune* lawyers—that the strip outside the Sather Gate was part of the campus, the response of the rebellious students was . . . Okay, we'll apply the same free speech standards to the whole campus. This response had the advantages of being simple, reasonable, and as American as apple pie. If a university was not a fit place for free expression, what was?

Although the administration, in its denseness, could not see this, it was also a bargaining opener. Savio and his friends would have been quite willing then to accept a return to the status quo ante, with campus political activity restricted to the strip between Sather Gate and Bancroft Way.

They set up their tables that Wednesday morning, September 30, and when university officials told them to leave, they replied, "I'm not authorized to leave this table." To encourage the troops and keep up spirits, Savio and Jack Weinberg made speeches, a few songs were sung, and there was a sign-up sheet for students to proclaim that they were breaking the rules as much as were those who sat at the tables.

The eight students who were going to take the fall for all the days of semiauthorized rule breaking were due for their disciplinary hearing at 3 P.M. At that hour, two hundred students (and nonstudents) marched into the administration building, effectively occupying it and paralyzing the administration. They did not stay all night. New as it was, the United Federation had a steering committee, which met in the night and decided it was not strong enough to try to occupy the administration building until morning.

Already, the embryonic student movement had a little network. Weeks earlier, a handful of students at the University of Chicago had conducted a similar sit-in, and after they were kicked out of the university building they occupied, their fellow students did nothing. The lesson—build up support within your constituency before you try civil disobedience—was obvious, and it was transmitted by phone around the country.

A few minutes before midnight, the Berkeley student rebels walked out into the night. But they'd be back at their tables the next day, and they scheduled a rally for noon.

| | |

On Thursday, October 1, the Beach Boys song "Wendy" was number one, but "It Ain't Me Babe," a Bob Dylan creation sung by Johnny Cash, was more popular on college campuses. Within two weeks, *The Physicists*, a new play by Friedrich Dürrenmatt, would open on Broadway to favorable reviews but close within seven weeks even though it starred Broadway veterans Hume Cronin and Jessica Tandy.

By the end of the month, the Supreme Court would strike yet another blow for free expression, regardless of status or even taste, by ruling that *Mad* magazine did not infringe on Irving Berlin's copyright when it parodied his songs. At Johnson campaign headquarters in Washington, John Bartlow Martin was worried. "Goldwater has probably reached his low point. And we are stalled," he wrote in a memorandum to Bill Moyers, the first of many indications that some Democrats still thought they could lose the election.

That day, five hundred delegates to the Southern Christian Leadership Conference met in Savannah to hear their leader, Martin Luther King, explain that "the Negro is not asking charity, he does not want to languish on welfare rolls any more than the next man."

And in Berkeley, California, Jack Weinberg, wearing a plaid pullover and sporting a mustache, sat behind the CORE table outside Sather Gate. It was a long table, and he wasn't alone; there was a sizable CORE contingent, and the members were making a ruckus, trying to call attention to themselves.

Soon enough, someone from the dean's office came up and asked Weinberg for his student identification card.

"I'm sorry," said Weinberg, who of course had no card. "I'm not authorized to give you my ID."

They told him to leave. Instead, he made a speech, which got him arrested. But university officials thought it would be unwise to parade him, handcuffed, through the crowded strip area to the police car, so they ordered a campus police car to drive up to the table, right in the midst of hundreds of students.

Politely—these were campus police—officers placed Weinberg under arrest. Weinberg, who had not been to Mississippi, nonetheless knew the drill and was delighted to play his part. He went limp. Two cops put him in the backseat of the car, then they got into the front seat, ready to drive him off to the pokey, when a shout rang out from somewhere in the middle of the student crowd.

"Sit down!"

They did.

That car wasn't going anywhere.

| | |

In Michigan, Governor George Romney refused to appear with Goldwater, as did Senator Milton Young of North Dakota. Ray Bliss of Ohio, the shrewdest of the Republican state chairman, recalled his party's electoral disaster at the time of Franklin Roosevelt's landslide reelection when he confided to a friend, "We face another 1936 and any goddam fool that doesn't believe it had better."

Barry Goldwater was right. There *was* a stir in the air. But the breeze was not blowing his way.

| | |

The Berkeley campus cops were no fools. Right away, they told Weinberg that he could go to the bathroom in the nearest building, as long as he came right back to the police car. They knew he wouldn't return, and they probably couldn't understand why he declined their offer.

They weren't fools, but they didn't get the point.

Jack Weinberg was having the time of his life. He was in that car, surrounded by hundreds of students, and right now he was the center of their world. It wasn't that Weinberg was some kind of egomaniac; it was the cause that mattered, not him personally. But he was serving his cause. He didn't want to go anywhere. To keep bodily functions to a minimum, he didn't eat solid food. Every once in a while, he'd open the back window and ask one of the students to get him a paper cup. He'd urinate into the cup, hand it back out again to a supporter, and say, "Here, take care of this."

A few minutes before noon, Mario Savio arrived for the rally, saw what had transpired, and rejoiced. Taking off his shoes, he politely asked the campus cops if he could stand on top of the car. The cops by now were ready to surrender anything, including their prisoner if they could find a graceful way to do it, so they agreed.

Barefoot, Savio climbed onto the roof, which immediately sagged (the student organization later paid $455.01 in damages), and accused the administration of repression, both artistic and sexual. The university, he said, "is well structured, well tooled, to turn out people with all the sharp edges worn off." Taking away the tables was not simply an effort to suppress the "creative impulses" of the students but was an act of "attempted emasculation," and for support, he cited scripture.

"The Bible says what knowledge is when it writes that a man knows a woman," he said. "Knowledge and action are inseparable." Like Nelson Rockefeller in New Hampshire the previous January, Savio knew his audience. He was talking to unmarried men and women between the ages of eighteen and twenty-five, hormones a-raging.

As he finished, the president of the student government asked him to join negotiations with the administration and the more moderate students. Sure, Savio said, "but I want it understood that until this person in this car is placed, you know, *out* of arrest, nobody will move from here."

As it turned out, many moved from there, but many replaced them. All day and all night, students came and students went, but there were always several hundred of them around the car while a pleased Jack Weinberg, who had a jacket to shield him from the evening cold, sat in the backseat.

All day and all night, other students wandered by. Many, perhaps most, were not sympathetic to the protesters. One law school student, the son of governor Edmund Brown, found the spectacle somewhat distasteful and walked by quickly. A few aggressive fraternity boys tossed lit cigarettes at them, and at least once a band of counterprotesters stood nearby and, from the heart of the popular culture, sang their own impression of the demonstration: "M-I-C-K-E-Y M-O-U-S-E."

The protesters answered with civil rights songs: "We Shall Overcome," "We Shall Not Be Moved." Theirs was not a mass uprising; no more than a few thousand of the twenty-five thousand undergraduates joined them. But for now, at least, they had the energy, and much better music.

| | |

On the morning of Thursday, October 2, Sheriff Lawrence Rainey, Deputy Cecil Price, and two other Neshoba County law enforcement officers were indicted on charges of depriving seven Negroes of their civil rights. The charges were unrelated to the three murders, but they did indicate that the FBI was on the move.

One prominent Mississippian was out of state that day. Charles Evers of the NAACP spoke at the convention of the association's New York State branch in Rochester, a convention to which Kenneth Keating was invited and Robert Kennedy was not.

In fact, before Evers spoke, the president of the New York chapter scribbled a note to him: "I know Bobby's your man, but not here, Evers." He might have saved his energy. From the podium, Evers told the New Yorkers they were "fortunate to have a man of Kennedy's caliber even visit New York, much less running for senator." Turning to Keating, Evers said, "Bobby Kennedy means more to us in Mississippi than any white man I know, including yourself, Senator."

The Mississippian won few friends, but he did convince the state chapter not to endorse Keating; it opted for neutrality.

| | |

In Berkeley that morning, Chancellor Strong said his disciplinary decisions were not negotiable, whereupon some members of the faculty went around him to Clark Kerr, president of the university system, to negotiate. Kerr agreed, and a deal was worked out quickly. The students would abandon their demonstration. The university would submit the cases of the eight chosen ones to a committee of the Academic Senate, drop charges against Weinberg, and establish a "tripartite" committee made up of faculty, students, and demonstrators to study the whole question of the rules.

At 7:20 P.M. the agreement was signed, and ten minutes later Savio was back on top of the police car to announce the settlement, the victory. "Let us agree by acclamation to accept this document. I ask you to rise quickly and with dignity, and go home."

They did, watched by some of the 643 police officers Kerr had called in just in case the negotiations did not work.

Two days later several of the student activists met to discuss their plans. They didn't know each other very well; Savio thought that Bettina Aptheker, another radical, whose father was one of the country's leading Communist Party members, was named "Patina."

As one might expect from the daughter of a communist, Aptheker knew how to organize. At her suggestion, the group agreed to form an executive committee of fifty members, which would in turn elect a smaller steering committee.

The next day, Monday, October 5, this smaller group met until 1 A.M. and came up with a new name for their cause, the Free Speech Movement.

| | |

That day another Johnson campaign official, Shannon Ratliff, saw disaster ahead. In a memorandum to Walter Jenkins, he said that "only a miracle" would lead to victory in Florida and that "California is worrisome" because an intraparty split had not healed. In another confidential memo, campaign consultant David Garth reported that "Ohio is in terrible shape."

Johnson was ahead in Ohio by more than twenty points.

But one Democratic campaign was really in trouble. On Tuesday, October 6, Robert Kennedy's pollster reported that "it ain't good" and that even though Kenneth Keating's lead was small, it was holding.

| | |

One day earlier, James Jordan left Meridian for Gulfport with an old buddy of his. The friend, Alfred Keene, had come to Meridian to flee the Gulf Coast when Hurricane Hilda came through, and when Jordan complained about a shortage of jobs in Meridian, Keene urged him to relocate to the Gulf Coast, where NASA had opened a new test site.

Jordan was glad to have the job opportunity and was glad to have someone to talk to. He seemed to need to talk. At one point, he told Keene that he had "gone on a job" for the Klan. Another time, he mentioned something about being responsible for the deaths of the civil rights workers. A few days after he got to Gulfport, Jordan was hired by NASA—he was not averse to working for the federal government—as a grade surveyor.

| | |

It was not recorded whether religious observance increased in and around St. Louis in early October, but even some doubters may have been reassessing their dismissal of the possibility of miracles. With but twelve games to play in late September, the St. Louis Cardinals were in third place, and the league-leading Philadelphia Phillies were a comfortable six and a half games ahead of Cincinnati.

The Phillies then lost ten straight games, losing first place to the Cincinnati Reds, who, on the last weekend of the season, were swept by . . . the Phillies. And who should slip into the World Series but the Cardinals?

So it was with some sense of wonder, if not awe, that the home crowd gathered on the afternoon of Wednesday, October 7, for the opening game of the World Series against the New York Yankees, who had also come from behind late in the season.

In this year of civil rights, there was a racial element even to the World Series. The Yankees were one of the last teams to integrate, and though catcher Elston Howard was one of their top players, he was the only Negro in the daily lineup. The Cardinals, on the other hand, despite their semi-Southern location (and their intense resistance, under other ownership, to Jackie Robinson in 1947) had been signing Negro players for years. Their top pitcher, Bob Gibson, was a Negro, as were three of their top everyday players: first baseman Bill White and outfielders Curt Flood and Lou Brock.

It was Flood's triple that drove in the winning runs in the bottom of the sixth.

| | |

That night, Walter Jenkins worked late at the White House and then went to the party celebrating the opening of *Newsweek*'s new Washington office. He had a few drinks there, maybe more than a few, and in his fatigue and his giddiness he was swept away by an old compulsion he thought he had conquered.

From the party, Jenkins walked two short blocks to the men's room in the basement of the Washington YMCA, where he found what he knew he'd find, what he needed—a man who wanted sex with another man.

But he was not the only one who knew about the reputation of the men's room. So did the District of Columbia police, who had drilled peepholes in the walls. A cop saw Jenkins involved in a sex act with an Army veteran now residing in the Old Soldiers Home, and the two of them were arrested.

| | |

Readers of *The New York Times Magazine* might have been surprised on Sunday morning, October 11, to find that Barry Goldwater's economic policies weren't so radical, after all. As described by Professor Milton Friedman, the Republican candidate was less a right-wing extremist than a second Eisenhower, committed "only to a slowing down in the growing rate of spending, not an absolute decline."

Goldwater, said his economic guru, was not even "in favor of balancing the budget every single year," only over a period of years. As for government assistance to the poor, there ought to be a social welfare floor that "is truly there and truly universal."

Quite a few readers wondered how this moderation squared with Goldwater's campaign speeches, which continued to assail government spending, government debt, and government welfare, or with Friedman's previous writings.

More characteristic, if less public, was the advice Goldwater got from Texas billionaire Bunker Hunt, who suggested that in the closing weeks the candidate stress "1-Immorality in government; 2-the so-called 'civil rights' question; 3-softness on Communism." And remember, Hunt said, "THE ESTABLISHMENT demands subservience."

That night Lady Bird Johnson's whistle-stop campaign through the South reached its final destination, New Orleans, where her husband joined her for a final event—speeches and dinner in the ballroom of the Jung Hotel.

Senator Russell Long and Congressman Hale Boggs were there, but Governor McKeithen, all but officially for Goldwater, was not, and neither were most of the state's leading Democrats. Inspired or enraged, the president was more Southern than usual. He expressed his respect for Senator Long's late father, the Kingfish, who had a "heart for the people." He played on Southern resentment of Northerners who "all these years . . . have kept their foot on our necks by appealing to our animosities and dividing us."

Then he left no doubt, as if there was any, about where he stood on civil rights.

"Whatever your views are, we have a Constitution and a Bill of Rights and we have the law of the land," he said. "And two-thirds of the Democrats in the Senate voted for it, and three-fourths of the Republicans. I signed it, and I am going to enforce it, and I am going to observe it."

And then he started to tell a story, one he may have been making up at the moment, about the Southern senator—"whose name I won't call"—who on his deathbed asked Sam Rayburn for the encouragement he'd need to make one last speech for his state.*

" 'I feel like I have one in me,' said the old senator. 'The poor old state, they haven't heard a Democratic speech in thirty years. All they ever hear at election time is—Nigger! Nigger! Nigger!' "

Total silence.

Then a few brave souls started to clap and then a few more, and it picked up into thunderous applause that lasted seven full minutes. It was an extraordinary moment but only to those in the room. The rest of the world would not know what Lyndon Johnson said. Neither the television news nor newspapers quoted him, at least not accurately. The local *Times-Picayune* rendered the words as "Negro, Negro, Negro," and *The New York Times* ignored that part of the speech altogether.

But the president had more than race on his mind. He was still intent on wooing the corporate community, and toward that end he made sure Hubert Humphrey, with his populist background, got the message. It was a message delivered, not surprisingly, as part of a diatribe against Robert Kennedy. "How did we get this antibusiness reputation?" Johnson said. "I'll tell you why we got it, Hubert. That young fellow in the Justice Department. And,

*In his memoirs, *The Vantage Point*, Johnson identified the senator as Joe Bailey, Mississippi-bred but a senator from Texas.

boy, did I have a talk with him about three months ago. I told him: 'Young man, you know as well as I do what your crowd is doing over there. You're harassing businessmen all over the country. I told him, Young man, today is the last damn day for that kind of business. Hubert, if you and I are going to be in the saddle, we'll get good law enforcement men, and we'll see to it that they behave themselves. That kid has done more damage to this party with those shenanigans than you and I can ever imagine—and it's all over with."

Johnson must have been referring to his July meeting with Kennedy, though neither man had mentioned that this subject came up then. Kennedy, however, agreed that Johnson's view of the corporate world was different from his own. "Lyndon Johnson's explained quite clearly that it's not the Democratic Party anymore," Kennedy told his friends. "It's an all-American party, and the businessmen like it. All the people who were opposed to the president [meaning JFK] like it. I don't like it much."

The next day Johnson was in the West, where ten thousand supporters greeted him at the airport in Denver and so many lined the route from there to the coliseum downtown that it took more than an hour to cover seven miles. Seven times on that trip he ordered the limousine to stop so he could thank the crowd. "You take care of me in November, and I'll take care of you for the next four years," he said.

In his confidence, he would now wear his thick-rimmed glasses while campaigning; against Goldwater, he had to look more responsible, not more dynamic. In the autumn air, he would keep his white overcoat on and play the part of the earnest schoolteacher he once was as he urged all of America to help him "help the weak and the meek and lift them up."

At Thirty-second Street, the motorcade turned onto Monaco Street, in a Negro section of the city, and Johnson turned to Congressmen Wayne Aspinall and Byron Rogers and said, "Where did these people come from?"

"Mr. President, this is their residential area," Aspinall said.

"What?" Johnson said. "Their residential area? Stop this car!"

It was a pleasant neighborhood of single- and two-family homes with small yards on tree-lined streets. Johnson got out, looked around, shook some hands, and returned to his limo.

"I've never seen a Negro district that's taken care of like this," he said.

To fourteen thousand at the stockyards, he quoted Goldwater's recent statement—"your children don't have the right to an education"—and announced a five-point program for more federal aid to schools, including more teachers in poor areas, more adult education, and more community colleges.

Agent John Proctor found James Jordan in Gulfport on Tuesday, October 13, and surprised him. Proctor knew Jordan's secret Klan number—twelve. Jordan's collapse was immediate and almost grateful.

"I know I might have to do some time," he told Proctor, "but I'm worried because I'd like to see my daddy once more before he passes on. He's over in Georgia."

That could be arranged. So could a $35,000 payment for his wife to get through his years of imprisonment; so could a theatrically produced arrest the next day so that no one would know he had squealed. He would tell all, he promised.

He did not. He continued to insist that he had not gone down the Rock Cut Road with Roberts, Price, and the others, had not been present at the actual killings. But he told the agents most of what had happened in Neshoba County on June 21. The case was broken.

| | |

Later that day a summary of polls for all the states at Goldwater's headquarters showed the campaign running behind almost everywhere. The faculty of the University of California at Berkeley affirmed its support for "maximum freedom for student political activity."

The next day, word came from Oslo that Martin Luther King Jr. had won the Nobel Peace Prize. Enraged, J. Edgar Hoover sent damaging reports about King's character to the White House, the State Department, the Justice Department, and American embassies in Europe.[1]

| | |

Lyndon Johnson was one of the last to know that his chief of staff had been arrested. FBI agents are more likely to have Republican friends than Democratic, and within forty-eight hours someone at the Republican National Committee knew about Walter Jenkins. By Monday, October 12, the day Lyndon Johnson was discovering middle-income Negroes in Denver, a Republican had informed a reporter friend on the *Chicago Tribune,* and someone told Barry Goldwater.

The *Tribune* held the story, as did the *Cincinnati Post.* And so, to the consternation of some of his associates, did Goldwater.

Here was their big break. For weeks, Goldwater had been campaigning against the moral decay of society almost as much as against government. This was the respectable backlash, not of whites against Negroes but of law-abiding, churchgoing people of conventional behavior against the ever-more visible flouters of convention. Now, the most objectionable of all unconventional behavior had been revealed right next to the incumbent. If anything could turn the campaign around, this was it.

Goldwater wouldn't do it. However narrow his intellectual horizon may have been, his personal tolerance was broad and his personal kindness deep. He knew Jenkins, liked him well enough, and scrupled to hurt a man already hurting. Besides, Goldwater, always a bit of an outsider, knew and liked some men who were, he knew, secretly homosexual. He may not have entirely approved or understood, but neither did he demonize. Besides, his political instincts may have told him that it wouldn't have done any good. It wasn't Lyndon Johnson who'd gotten caught in that men's room.

The next day, the news got to the *Washington Star,* and as any good reporter would, assistant managing editor Charles Seib called Jenkins. Jenkins had to know it was coming, or maybe he had somehow convinced himself that the events of the previous Tuesday had never happened. At any rate, as soon as he hung up he left his office and sought the help first of Abe Fortas, then of Clark Clifford.

Their first reaction was to try to get the news organizations not to run the story, a doomed effort. Then they got Jenkins admitted to George Washington University Hospital. At 8:25 P.M., United Press International moved the story over the wires, and Americans knew that the president's number one assistant, who could see government secrets, who attended National Security Council meetings, was what was then widely known as a sexual deviant.

The president didn't find out about it much sooner than the public did. He was campaigning in New York, campaigning with Robert Kennedy, and his first reaction was to hope that it was some kind of Republican plot.

"It's a frame," he told Cartha DeLoach. "Somehow the Republicans have engineered this because we're whipping their butts."

"I only wish that were true," DeLoach said, explaining that it was not.

Johnson told DeLoach to start an FBI investigation to make sure Jenkins had not been blackmailed into some kind of national security leak. DeLoach did so, first informing his boss of what had transpired.

Hoover sent a bouquet of flowers to Jenkins in the hospital.

Despite being plagued by a cold, the president finished his campaign schedule and retreated to his suite at the Waldorf-Astoria. At midnight, Jack Valenti called pollster Oliver Quayle and summoned him to the Waldorf. When Quayle arrived, Lyndon Johnson was in bed in his pajamas, lying next to a steaming vaporizer. His orders were so simple they could as easily have been issued by phone: Take an instant poll to see how many voters might turn away from Lyndon Johnson because his top aide is a homosexual.

Quayle's telephone banks were up and running first thing in the morning. By midafternoon, he had enough responses that he could tell the president to stop worrying.

Maybe he did, but he didn't stop thinking about it. It kept bothering him. It seemed like such a great campaign day. There he was with Kennedy, who needed him, who was calling him "already one of the great presidents." Now there was no doubt which of them was dominant. Kennedy's position wasn't much different from Hubert Humphrey's. He needed the laying on of Lyndon Johnson's hands.

He got it. "This is ma' boy," the president would say.

At some point in their travels that day, Johnson reminded Kennedy that Barry Goldwater had been Walter Jenkins's commanding officer in the Air National Guard, that he and Jenkins had been "closely identified," and that perhaps they should try "to develop information regarding Barry Goldwater" in this context.

Kennedy said he didn't think that was a good idea.

Such, at least, is how Robert Kennedy remembered, or interpreted their conversation. But talking to Acting Attorney General Nicholas Katzenbach the next day, Johnson used the Goldwater-Jenkins connection not to suggest that Goldwater had homosexual leanings but to convey the message that Goldwater had also been Jenkins's boss and had been just as much in the dark about Jenkins as Johnson had been.

"I'd go to the efficiency ratings and see how Goldwater rated [Jenkins]," the president said. "If he worked for him and he rated him highly and that got leaked out . . . that would at least show I was not the one fellow who got misled."

But the president's problems in the Jenkins matter were not over for the day. An hour later, he had to deal with one person to whom he could not give orders.

"I would like to do two things about Walter," Lady Bird Johnson told her husband on the telephone. "I would like to offer him the number two job at KTBC. Do you hear me?"

He heard. He did not agree.

"I wouldn't do anything along that line now," he said. Yes, he was all for helping the Jenkins family with the financial problems it now faced without an employed breadwinner. But not such visible help at one of the Johnson family's television stations.

"I don't think that's right," Mrs. Johnson said. "Second, when questioned, and I will be questioned, I'm going to say that this is incredible for a man that I've known all these years, a devout Catholic, the father of six children, a happily married husband. It can only be a . . . period of nervous breakdown, balanced against . . ."

"I wouldn't say anything," her husband interrupted. "I just wouldn't be available for anything because it's not something for you to get involved in now. . . . I don't want you to hurt him any more than he's hurt and when we move into it we do that. We blow it up more."

Lady Bird was not convinced. "I think if we don't express some support to him I think we will lose the entire love and devotion of all the people who have been with us," she said.

Somewhat impatiently, the president told his wife to do nothing without talking to Clark Clifford and Abe Fortas, two of his shrewdest advisors. "Talk to them about it. Anything you can get them to approve, let me know."

"All right," Mrs. Johnson said. "Abe approves of the job offer. Abe approves of the statement."

"What?"

Very slowly, enunciating each word as though it were a separate sentence, Lady Bird Johnson repeated herself: "Abe approves of the job offer. Abe approves of the statement, when questioned," though Clark Clifford, she acknowledged, did not approve of the statement.

The president was flummoxed. Going public with her support, he said, would immerse them too deeply in the Jenkins mess. "You just can't do that to the presidency, honey," he said. For several seconds, neither of them spoke, until Lyndon Johnson once again urged his wife to get Fortas and Clifford to talk to Mrs. Jenkins.

"All right. She called me this morning, honey," Mrs. Johnson said.

"All right. What did she say?"

"She is so hysterical and bitter. . . . It's dreadful. She feels that her life is ruined, that their life is ruined, and it's all been laid at the altar of working for us."

"Is she angry at us?"

"Yes. You see, she doesn't believe any of this. She thinks it's a frame, a put-up job."

"Well," said Lyndon Johnson, who had thought the same when he first heard the news, "I think somebody better go talk to her and tell her the facts."

But privately, he insisted. "I don't think I would put myself in the position of defending what we say in public in a situation like this because we just can't win it." Voters, he said, would not distinguish between sympathy for Jenkins and condoning his conduct, "any more than they can [condone] Acheson not turning his back."

The reference to former secretary of state Dean Acheson's refusal to "turn my back" on his old friend Alger Hiss despite Hiss's apparent treason was oblique, and by then more than a decade old, but no doubt clear to Mrs. Johnson.

Not that she replied to it. Instead she asked whether her husband was "unalterably opposed to the job offer."

"I am publicly," the president said. "I'm not unalterably opposed to giving him anything and everything we have, all of it. . . . But I see no reason why I ought to be tried again and blow it up and make the headlines that I gave him advancement because he did this. I don't think you have a license five minutes with a station being operated with something like that."

"I would almost rather make the offer to do it and then let the license go down the drain," Mrs. Johnson said, but not before she had said something else indicating that while her generosity was undoubtedly sincere, it was not without an element of self-interest.

Mrs. Jenkins, Lady Bird Johnson told her husband, "sees her life being ruined around her and she's got to reach out and lash at somebody," and in her anger at Johnson, that lashing could include an alliance with Republicans. "I think a gesture of support on some of our part is necessary to hold our own forces together," she told her husband.

The president was concerned, too, and wanted to make sure Mrs. Jenkins did not start "talking to the papers" or making contact with the Goldwater campaign. He told his wife to get Fortas, Clifford, and Tom Corcoran to tell Mrs. Jenkins the truth, to assure her that Lyndon Johnson was her friend, to remind her that the Republicans knew as much about the event as the Democrats, and to ask her to "ride this thing out for two weeks."

"Abe or Eddie Weisl or somebody better go see her this morning," he said. But he did not want Lady Bird Johnson to go with them. She was not just Mrs. Johnson, he reminded her, but the First Lady.

"My love, my love," she said. "I pray for you along with Walter."

"Have Abe go see her."

"You're a brave, good guy."

Offer Jenkins another kind of job, Johnson said, such as running the ranch.

"All right," she said. "Okay. Okay. All right."

"Better get 'em out there right away, though," the president said.

| | |

As if the Fates were conspiring against Goldwater, the world tumbled forth so much news that Thursday, October 15, that Walter Jenkins and his troubles were pushed below the fold, if not completely off the front page.

In St. Louis, despite Mickey Mantle's eighteenth (and last) World Series home run, the Cardinals won the seventh and deciding game of the World Series, Bob Gibson pitching a complete game on only two days' rest. In Washington, the Defense Department announced that 204 American servicemen had been killed in action in Vietnam since 1961.

In Moscow, Nikita Khrushchev was ousted in a coup led by Leonid Brezhnev. In Peking, the Chinese government announced the results of its first successful nuclear bomb test, and in London, Labor's Harold Wilson ousted the Conservative Party in Britain's elections.

The next day, Chalmers Roberts's column in the *Washington Post* claimed that because of the Jenkins affair the White House was "deeply worried" about the election.

| | |

In Mississippi, Mary King and Casey Hayden still weren't willing to sign their document about the mistreatment of women, but they were prepared to show it. They were getting ready for a big SNCC conference scheduled for the week after the election, and they were polishing the position paper, one of many that would be presented and discussed at the meeting in Waveland, Alabama.

"The woman in SNCC," they wrote, "is often in the same position as that token Negro hired in a corporation. The management thinks that it has done its bit. Yet, every day the Negro bears an atmosphere, attitudes and actions which are tinged with condescensions and paternalism."

Hence, they explained, their anonymity. "Think about the kinds of things the authors, if made known, would have to suffer because of raising this kind of discussion . . . insinuations, ridicule, over-exaggerated compensations."

Then, like the Port Huron and Sharon statements, they listed their specific grievances: the lack of women in leading positions, the assumption that men would make the decisions while women did the clerical work, being referred to as "girls."

Their purpose, the authors said, was less to convert men to their cause than to expand the discussion among women. Then, "maybe sometime in the future the whole of the women in this movement will become so alert as to force the rest of the movement to stop the discrimination and start the slow process of changing values and ideas so that all of us gradually come to understand that this is no more a man's world than it is a white world."[2]

| | |

Postprotest, postvictory, Jack Weinberg was quite the rage. For the first time in his life, he was a star, sought out by fellow-protesters, would-be protesters, and reporters. Weinberg, who was not averse to the publicity, was a hot interview.

Most of the questions were straightforward, but in almost every interview he would be asked about the forces behind the movement, as though students could not be dissatisfied unless they were incited by nefarious influences, probably communists.

By the time he was interviewed by the education reporter for the *San Francisco Examiner,* Weinberg was inured to, as well as amused and annoyed by, such questions, so when one came up again, the pixie in him emerged:

"We have a saying in the movement," he said, making up the saying on the spot. "Never trust anyone over thirty."

It was metaphor. Weinberg was asserting the authenticity, the originality, the youthfulness of his cause; he was resenting the implied insults in all the red-baiting questions, the assumption that these young people couldn't make decisions and take action on their own.

The *Examiner* reporter appeared to understand this, but a few days later, Ralph Gleason, then the jazz critic for the paper, led his column with Weinberg's offhand remark, and within days it was the most quoted sentence in America. Taking it literally, many adults and most conservatives concluded that there was something adolescent, if not infantile, about this "movement." Taking it literally, many teenagers and young adults had themselves a new slogan, one that helped render them and their future political activity adolescent, if not infantile.

26

VICTORY AND OTHER DEFEATS

It wasn't that Andy Warhol didn't like the Beatles. They were fine. But they were a little too bland for his taste and maybe a little too popular. He preferred the harsher, earthier sound of another English group, the Rolling Stones.

So when the Stones arrived on their second American visit—the first, in June, had not been a rousing success—he threw a party for them. On Friday, October 23, two days before the Stones were to appear on *The Ed Sullivan Show,* Andy helped arrange a huge bash at a photography studio on Park Avenue South.

Technically, the host was Warhol's friend Nicky Haslam, who was the art director of Huntington Hartford's new magazine, *Show.* Haslam arranged for an all-female band with gold lamé outfits and stiletto heels. Then he went to a "leather bar" on East Thirty-third Street, a hangout for young men whose taste in sexual pleasure ran to sadomasochism.

He had been there just a few days earlier with his friend Jane Ormsby Gore, the daughter of the British ambassador, who dressed as a boy for the occasion. On his second, solo, visit, Haslam arranged for some of the leather-clad S and M crowd to crash the party for the Stones. It played into the theme he had chosen: "Mods versus Rockers," after the battling British youth sub-cultures.

It was a great party, even if the Rolling Stones didn't enjoy it. They stayed in an upstairs apartment most of the time. But they were only the guests of honor. The important people were the reporters and the gossips who called the reporters the next day. The point of the party was publicity, and it got a good deal of it, for the Stones and for a young model named Jane Holzer, who was co–guest of honor because it was her twenty-fourth birthday. The party became the opening scene in an article about her by pop journalist Tom Wolfe called "Girl of the Year," whatever that means.

Andy Warhol had a good time. These days, though, the parties weren't keeping him away from his new passion, making movies. They were unusual films, often showing nothing but one person sitting in a chair. One of them, *Drink,* showed a friend of his drinking a quart of scotch whiskey and then crawling around drunk on all fours. Another, *Empire,* was eight hours of the camera focused on the Empire State Building.

There was a reason for all this frenetic activity by Warhol. He was obsessed by the desire for fame. He wanted to be celebrated as an artist even more than he wanted respect from the cognoscenti. At another party in October, someone pointed out Susan Sontag to him, along with the information that she didn't like his work. He didn't care that much, even though Sontag was the talk of the town, or at least its intelligentsia, thanks to her essay in the new issue of *Partisan Review.*

The essay was called "Notes on Camp," camp being defined as a way of relating to the world that valued "style at the expense of content." Camp, Sontag said, "turns its back on the good-bad axis of ordinary esthetic judgment." Its whole point "is to dethrone the serious." It was "the modern dandyism," which reveled in "detachment [which] is the prerogative of an elite."

Perhaps not entirely. However limited its direct impact, Sontag's insight seemed to speak to and for a broader audience. A detached self-indulgence in which style was at least as important as substance was part of what was motivating both Barry Goldwater's movement and SNCC.

| | |

If it is not the first rule of campaigning, it is the second: You don't debate your opponent if you're ahead. In September, when Robert Kennedy was ahead, he evaded Kenneth Keating's challenge to debate. In early October, when he was behind, he accepted, but then, of course, Keating delayed.

On Monday, October 19, the *Daily News* poll showed Kennedy ahead. Keating wanted to debate again, and now Kennedy stalled. So Keating bought half an hour of time on WCBS-TV for Tuesday evening, October 27, and invited his opponent to join him. Kennedy declined.

Just as Keating hoped. Kennedy had fallen into the trap. Now Keating announced that he and his Republican colleague, Senator Jacob Javits, would debate an empty chair marked ROBERT F. KENNEDY as a symbol of his opponent's cowardice and of his "ruthless [one never missed an opportunity to use that word] contempt" for the electorate. At this point, not surprisingly, Kennedy decided he'd appear after all.

He didn't tell Keating, or WCBS-TV, or anyone but a few of his closest aides. He just showed up.

The guards at the studio turned him away, leaving him staring at a sign reading PLEASE KEEP OUT. Keating and Javits debated the empty chair and lost, especially after Keating, leaving the studio, was photographed running away from reporters and photographers. In contrast to the polite but determined Kennedy, barred from the studio, the jogging Keating appeared cowardly.

With a week to go before the voting, Robert Kennedy had won himself a Senate seat.

| | |

That same evening, the Goldwater campaign got a boost, the only one it would get all fall. In a half-hour, paid political commercial, movie actor Ronald Reagan delivered an impassioned appeal for the Republican candidate and an assertion that civil rights laws and antipoverty programs were worse than Hitler or Stalin.

"A perversion has taken place," Reagan told the television audience. "Our natural, unalienable rights are now presumed to be a dispensation of government. . . . We are faced with the most evil enemy mankind has known in his long climb from the swamp to the stars."

So favorable was the response that the Goldwater campaign bought another half hour and showed the speech again on Saturday night, October 31.

On Sunday, November 1, the American base in Bien Hoa, in Vietnam, was attacked by guerrillas. Four U.S. soldiers were killed and five jet bombers destroyed. Bien Hua was only a few miles from Saigon.

| | |

The day before Election Day, Martin Luther King learned that he was a presidential candidate against his will. Under the name of a front group called the Committee for Negroes in Government, someone was sending telegrams and handing out leaflets to Negro voters in several cities urging them to write in King's name. The committee, which King assumed was a Goldwater front group, was even trying to buy time on radio stations that catered to Negro audiences.

In Atlanta, King held a press conference on Monday, November 2, urging all supporters to ignore the write-in effort.

| | |

By 9 P.M. that night, someone in the West Wing of the White House decided that the campaign insiders gathered therein could switch drinks. At the bar, the beer bottles were put aside, and the champagne bottles were uncorked. This was going to be a blowout.

Only some of the white South and his home state of Arizona voted for Barry Goldwater, and his margin in Arizona was so close that only Lyndon Johnson's charitable decision not to campaign there kept him from embarrassing his opponent.

Johnson kept the Southern rim states—North Carolina, Kentucky, Tennessee, Florida, Arkansas, and Texas—where Negroes were allowed to vote and where there were constituencies other than traditional Southerners. In South Carolina, Georgia, Mississippi, Alabama, and Louisiana, where few Negroes were enfranchised, Goldwater won easily.*

That was all. The rest of the country was solid Johnson. Even traditionally Republican northern New England and the Great Plains overwhelmingly rejected their party's nominee. Outside the South, only one state, Nebraska, was close, and even there Johnson got 52.6 percent of the vote.

When the counting was done, Lyndon Johnson had 43,126, 218 votes, or more than 61 percent of the total.

Many Republicans voted for him: He carried 140 congressional districts represented by Republicans, and in 27 of those, he carried a Democratic challenger into Congress. By contrast, Goldwater carried only 33 districts with Democratic members of Congress, and all but one of those were in the South.

Outside the South, in fact, Goldwater carried only sixteen districts: six in southern California, five in the Chicago suburbs, and one each in Arizona, Idaho, Nebraska, Oklahoma, and Kentucky.

This was not just Johnson's victory; it was a party sweep. The Democrats picked up two seats in the Senate, one of them in New York, where Robert Kennedy beat Kenneth Keating, and forty-eight seats in the House of Representatives. They also won control of many state legislatures, including New York's, where they had been in the minority for decades.

Not one member of Congress from either party in either house who voted for the Civil Rights Act was defeated; half the Northerners who opposed the law were beaten. But in Alabama, the Republicans won all five congressional

---

*Alabama listed no Democratic electors pledged to Johnson; its unpledged Democratic electors got 210,000 votes, far fewer than the 479,000 for Goldwater.

districts, as well as one in Georgia and one in Mississippi, and in thirty-five Southern districts, the Democratic vote was lower than it was in 1960. As recently as 1962, the Republicans had managed 40 percent of the vote in only twenty-six Southern districts; they did that well in thirty-five of them in 1964.

Proposition 14 won easily, succeeding in fifty-seven of California's fifty-eight counties, even outpolling the president, who got 59 percent of California's vote. The networks won, too. Californians overwhelmingly outlawed pay television.

In the Democratic euphoria, hardly anybody paused to ponder the significance of this fact: A candidate who opposed the centrist consensus that had governed the country since the end of World War II, who wanted to dismantle the New Deal, who ran as an opponent of almost all domestic government activity, had won 40 percent of the vote. And he was a bad candidate, one who scared millions of ordinary citizens because they thought he might start a war. How many votes would a gentler, less abrasive, more appealing fellow with the same ideas have gotten? Forty-five percent? Maybe more. What did this say about the centrist consensus?

That it was shaky, a conclusion soon confirmed by the survey teams working for the American National Election Study coordinated by the University of Michigan's Political Behavior Program. The pollsters had actually been in the field earlier, interviewing 1,571 respondents before the election. All but 121 of them were reinterviewed between the election and the following February.

What the study revealed was a conflicted, if not confused, electorate. It overwhelmingly elected Lyndon Johnson even though it agreed with Barry Goldwater on several important issues. Majorities favored government assistance in getting doctors and hospital care at low cost but opposed federal aid to public schools, and an overwhelming majority thought schools "should be allowed to start each day with a prayer."

The public was overwhelmingly in favor of trying "to settle our differences" with communist countries, and was convinced Democrats would do a better job of that than Republicans. And in general, most people favored foreign aid. But not foreign aid to communist countries. On this issue, Karl Mundt and Otto Passman had been the voices of the people late in 1963.

When it came to racial relations, there was even more ambiguity. Most voters pronounced themselves opposed to discrimination, but wary of federal intervention, divided on whether schools should be integrated at all, and opposed to integrating schools by busing children out of their neighborhoods. Most Americans thought the civil rights movement was pushing for change too fast, had used violence, and had hurt its own cause.[1]

Still, it was surely a happier evening for the Democrats, hence that White House champagne. And it must have been the happiest evening of all for the president. There would be nothing accidental about his next years in office, and only triumph loomed before him.

His political plan was working. He and his party had lost much of the white South, but they had captured part of the most important Republican constituency, big business. Now he could prove to them what he always knew, that they were better off under Democrats, who kept the consumer economy humming, than under the penny-pinching Republicans. Cooperation and consolidation, not conflict, would lead to business prosperity.

In his moment of triumph, reelected with the largest popular majority in American history, Lyndon Johnson still worried whether he was sufficiently appreciated. What about Robert Kennedy? Had Kennedy thanked Johnson for his help in the campaign?

No, the president was told, his name had not been mentioned in Kennedy's brief victory statement.

The president scowled. "I wonder why he doesn't mention me," he said.

And in New York, when one of his friends congratulated Robert Kennedy on his victory, the new senator-elect got a blank look in his eyes and said, "If my brother was alive, I wouldn't be here. I'd rather have it that way."

EPILOGUE

A few postscripts from the remaining weeks of 1964: J. Edgar Hoover spoke to a group of women reporters on Wednesday, November 18. In his usual blunt manner, Hoover called Martin Luther King "the most notorious liar in the country." This was too blunt even for the loyal Cartha DeLoach, who not once, not twice, but thrice sent notes from his chair in the audience to his boss on the podium urging him to retract the statement. Hoover threw the notes away.

On Saturday, November 21, William Sullivan of the FBI gave one of his agents an unmarked package and instructions to fly to Miami. From Miami, the agent called headquarters and was told to mail the package to Martin Luther King at his Atlanta office. Inside the package was a tape with excerpts of the recordings made in King's hotel room a year earlier and an unsigned note urging King to commit suicide: "You are done.... There is only one thing left for you to do. You know what it is. You have just 34 days in which to do (this exact number has been selected for a specific reason, it has definite practical significant [sic]). You are done. There is but one way out for you. You better take it before your filthy, abnormal fraudulent self is bared to the nation." The letter was dated thirty-four days before Christmas.

| | |

Late in November, the battered but game staff members of SNCC held a retreat at a church facility on the Gulf of Mexico. There were the usual speeches, debates, and position papers, but now not everyone wanted to be black and white together. Some of the young blacks wanted nothing to do with whites, even the whites who had been risking their lives for equality. For the first time, Mary King felt herself unwelcome among black people, an injury greater than the one caused by the general disdain that greeted the position paper she and Casey Hayden had circulated but not signed.

The racial antagonism was hardly universal, and on the last night of the retreat, some old friends of both races ended up on the edge of the water, under a full moon, with a gallon of wine and a great many memories. After a few glasses of wine, Stokely Carmichael surrendered to his natural tendency to perform. Standing on the pier sticking out into the bay, he began a comedy monologue. As was his wont, he made fun of folks, starting with himself and his fellow Trinidadians. Then he mocked the poor, black Mississippians they had been working so hard to help. Ultimately, he turned to the business at hand, including the position papers so common at these meetings, especially the much-discussed paper about how women were treated.

"What is the position of women in SNCC?" he asked. And he answered, "The position of women in SNCC is prone."

This was, by any reasonable interpretation, a joke, perhaps not too funny except to those who were there, who thought it quite funny indeed. Later, some feminist writers were to take it quite seriously, to claim that others did also, and to argue that it represented Carmichael's view that women existed to provide sexual pleasure. But Carmichael was one of those who liked the Mary King–Casey Hayden paper, and King was one of those cracking up at Carmichael's monologue.

| | |

On Friday, December 4, Sheriff Rainey, Deputy Price, and nineteen others were arrested and charged with violating the civil rights of Michael Schwerner, James Chaney, and Andrew Goodman. Less than a week later, all charges were dropped. However, they were refiled, and in 1965 the two law enforcement officers and seventeen others were convicted. They served between two and five and a half years in prison. The state of Mississippi never charged anyone with murder in the Schwerner, Goodman, and Chaney killings.

| | |

On Friday, November 20, the University of California Regents met at University Hall. As Joan Baez sang "We Shall Overcome," several thousand students marched from the Sather Gate across campus to rally in front of the hall. At the urging of Mario Savio, most of the male students wore coats and ties. So orderly was the march that the student monitors wore yellow signs marked "Monitor," except for one whose sign said "Merrimac."

President Kerr persuaded the regents to overturn the prohibition against all on-campus political activity. Because they could not simply ignore past infractions, however, the regents refused to expunge charges against the eight students who had been dismissed. After days of rallies and indecision, Chancellor Strong sent letters to four of the students, including Savio, informing them that the university intended to bring charges for actions committed eight weeks earlier.

On Wednesday, December 2, a thousand students rallied outside the university's administration building, Sproul Hall. Then they filed into the building for a sit-in aimed at nothing less than disabling the university. They had come, Savio said, to

> a time when the operation of the machine becomes so odious, makes you so sick at heart, that you can't take part; you can't even passively take part, and you've got to put your bodies upon the gears and upon the wheels, upon the levers, upon all the apparatus and you've got to make it stop. And you've got to indicate to the people who run it, to the people that own it, that unless you're free, the machines will be prevented from working at all.

The next day another grown-up made a mistake. Governor Edmund Brown called in six hundred cops to clear the hall and arrest the protesters. Immediately, much of the faculty rallied to the student cause. Professors provided cars to fetch bailed-out students from jail, and the bail fund set up by the faculty was quickly oversubscribed. Graduate students organized a strike, which stopped most classes for two days. The machine had been prevented from working at all. Within days, the administration and the regents capitulated.

A week later the United States Supreme Court unanimously upheld the public accommodations section of the Civil Rights Act.

| | |

Richard Russell was wrong. Everett Dirksen's support of civil rights did not "kill off the rapidly growing Republican party in the South," less because the South came to accept Dirksen's outlook than because his party came to reject it. But Barry Goldwater and Strom Thurmond were wrong, too. The Civil Rights Act worked, and without the "judicial tyranny" Thurmond predicted. Forced to change their behavior, many people also changed their attitudes. What was really imprisoning the South, as it turned out, was not the federal government but legal racism. Freed of this slave driver, the South prospered as it never had before, as it would not have without the 1964 law and the Voting Rights Act passed the following year.

Robert Theobald was wrong. The "cybernetic revolution" changed the country, all right, but it did not lead to massive unemployment; whether it would have done so absent massive government spending on the military, space flight, and highways, and absent massive corporate advertising to transform thousands of frivolous products into necessities, might be an interesting topic of discussion. As the twenty-first century approaches, so does a glut of consumer goods. Maybe Theobald wasn't all wrong.

Stewart Udall and the experts consulted by that Senate committee were wrong. America and the West grew, but in the year 2000 the nation's population will still be short of 300 million. Indeed, it would hardly be growing at all were it not for immigration, much of it to the integrated South, almost all of it inspired by a level of prosperity of which Robert Theobald despaired and even Lyndon Johnson hardly dared to dream.

On the other hand, Udall and his reluctant allies in the private utility industry were right that any growth in southern California and environs depended on getting enough water and power into the region and that some kind of centralized public-private planning mechanism was the only practical means for getting that done.

And Udall was right—indeed, prescient—when he noticed that Westerners had become as hostile to the federal government as Southerners, perhaps because the West became more dependent on the federal government than the South.

No one will ever know whether Lyndon Johnson and his advisors were wrong in their conviction that the several programs that made up the War on Poverty could have worked. The billion dollars a year the president proposed was a paltry sum considering the extent of the problem. The amount was never increased, and when Richard Nixon became president five years later, he began to dismantle the entire effort.

In fact, the number of Americans living in poverty declined throughout the rest of the 1960s and the 1970s, thanks largely to the cost-of-living increases in Social Security benefits. The rate did not begin to inch up again until the early 1980s, during Ronald Reagan's presidency. At last count, in March of 1997, 36.5 million people, or 13.7 percent of the population, lived in poverty.

Johnson's other two grand designs to alter the course of history—enticing corporate America into the Democratic Party and creating a Great Society in which culture and wisdom would be as important as wealth and power—both came a cropper thanks to the petty design he inherited, the Vietnam War. The war and the protest against it tore the Democratic Party into pieces, and they have not been reassembled three decades later. Rich and powerful people do not join fractious institutions, even if it may be in their interest to do so.

As for the Great Society, Johnson seemed to have forgotten about it. After his speech at the Michigan graduation ceremony, he rarely used the slogan except in a few campaign speeches. Maybe it was just politics to begin with or some combination of politics and personal expiation. More likely, it was another casualty of the war. Presidents can only concentrate on so many things at a time, and by 1965 Vietnam absorbed so much of Johnson's time that he had little time for anything else.

Also, the antiwar protests may have soured him on the values he had boldly advanced in that Michigan speech. After the academic and cultural elites turned so bitterly against the war, and him, Johnson was less likely to pay them any heed, much less to propose policies that might please them.

| | |

Though it is but a blink in world history, thirty-four years is a long time in dynamic modern America, and much has changed since Lyndon Johnson's landslide reelection. A majority of Americans now live in the suburbs, students are more likely to rebel against regulations concerning beer drinking than against social injustice, and the music of the Beatles, in retrospect, seems rather sweet and gentle.

From the perspective of the last years of the twentieth century, it seems unreal that a publisher could go to prison for material as bland as the pictures in Ralph Ginzburg's *Eros* or that a film with explicit sexual content could be banned.

In fact, this change of social attitude did not have to wait thirty-four years. In 1965, the obscenity charge against California artist Connor Everts was decisively thrown out of court by Judge Andrew J. Weisz, who declared that "we no longer live in a tender, unexposed age. Not only are our major commodities sold by the artful use of the outthrust bosom and bared leg, but we are deluged from every side with what once were known as 'girly' magazines but are now merely expensive (and thus sophisticated) ones."

In the 1970s, the FBI's misuse of its powers to spy on political enemies was exposed, and laws were passed to protect individuals against such abuses in the future. It is more difficult, if not impossible, to get permission to tap someone's telephone these days simply because a cop does not approve of that person's politics or personal life.

The John Kennedy–Lyndon Johnson tax cut turned out not to be the last one. Tax rates were reduced in 1981 and again in 1986. Even though taxes were raised slightly for upper-income taxpayers in 1990 and 1993, the average wealthy American pays a lower percentage of income in total taxes now than his or her counterpart did in 1964. The average middle-income and lower-middle-income American does not.

One thing has not changed: American business continues to consolidate, and the largest consolidations continue to dominate. Corporate mergers resumed in the 1980s, and they continued through the 1990s; as the century neared its end, more than a quarter of all the world's business was done by its two hundred largest firms.

In defiance of all evidence, most Americans still do not believe that Lee Harvey Oswald alone killed John F. Kennedy. The many government lies told during the Vietnam War and in connection with the Watergate scandal only solidified popular cynicism about the official version of just about anything.

Those two dams on either end of the Grand Canyon never did get built. Public and private officials had to make alternative plans for a somewhat scaled-down Central Arizona Project, and thirty-five years later there are more proposals to demolish old dams than to construct new ones. The Federal Bureau of Reclamation no longer considers itself "a construction agency" but is instead a "resource management agency."

But the Central Arizona Project lives on, as does the Colorado River Storage Project, still using more than a hundred million dollars a year of tax money between them, and still pregnant with the same political irony in that the beneficiaries of these programs purport to disdain government.

Perhaps the biggest change of all is that Lyndon Johnson's political party no longer dominates the nation's politics. The active, expansive government he advocated is viewed with suspicion. His conviction that prosperity depended on a federal budget deficit has been reversed; however, there is so much more state and local government debt, and so much federal spending is "off-budget," that the United States effectively practices deficit spending despite a budget surplus. Whether the prosperity at century's end depends on that deficit spending is a debate for the economists.

Not that Lyndon Johnson's legacy has disappeared. In fact, it is so pervasive that it blends into the landscape, rendering it hard to see. Every day thousands of Americans get their medical bills paid, millions of low-income children get free breakfasts, millions of poor people get more food than they can afford, and thousands hike in unspoiled woodland and desert thanks to legislation proposed and signed by the thirty-sixth president.

Indeed, many of Johnson's initiatives have grown. The number of acres protected as wilderness has increased more than tenfold, and under Johnson's successor, Richard Nixon, the nation adopted stronger laws against air and water pollution than Johnson would have dared to propose. Ironically, America's love of the outdoors has grown so much that it has become one of the threats to the healthy environment that engendered it.

But there has been a qualitative shift in attitude, perhaps best illustrated by the derision that now greets any mention of the Great Society. It is not just that Republicans—and even some Democrats—use the term as shorthand for excessive government spending; it is that the very idea that people should care about the quality of their society has become questionable. In the late 1990s, the personal has replaced the political. People who work to improve the lives of those around them, rather than to make themselves rich, are regarded as quaint throwbacks, and they have become progressively harder to find.

Now and then there is a story in the newspaper about the increase in income inequality, and someone, usually a professor, laments a situation in which an affluent minority of the people become ever richer while the income of most folks stagnates or even declines. The general reaction, even from the nonaffluent majority, is passive acceptance.

Johnson would have been neither passive nor accepting, not because he had anything against rich people getting richer—he was all for it—but because he thought nonrich people should also be getting richer. In fact, he was convinced that over the long term, a modern capitalist economy could remain prosperous only if it extended opportunity to everyone. In 1964, that was close to a consensus outlook. It isn't anymore, but then not much is.

With the passage of time, of course, people have expired even more inevitably than ideas, and most of the people who made the world of the early and middle 1960s are gone, some of them before their time. Martin Luther King was murdered in Memphis on Thursday, April 4, 1968. Robert Kennedy, challenging Lyndon Johnson for the Democratic presidential nomination, got the news just before he was scheduled to speak to a gathering in the Negro section—by then called the black section—of Indianapolis. He quoted, from memory, those lines of Aeschylus he had discovered in *The Greek Way*, the lines about how suffering can lead to wisdom. Indianapolis was one of the few large cities in which black citizens did not riot that night.

Two months later, after winning the California primary, Robert Kennedy was shot and killed in Los Angeles.

Three months after that, while Hubert Humphrey, Richard Nixon, and George Wallace were campaigning for president, Jacqueline Kennedy married Aristotle Onassis, the multimillionaire Greek shipping tycoon. Americans were shocked, and many were displeased, but the former Mrs. Kennedy, now known as "Jackie O" in gossip columns and women's magazines, remained a figure of fascination until her death in 1994.

In 1980, while working in the campaign of the next Kennedy, Senator Edward Kennedy, Allard K. Lowenstein was murdered by Dennis Sweeney, one of the students Lowenstein had inspired to go to Mississippi in 1964. Sweeney had been married briefly to Mary King, the SNCC worker who coauthored the position paper about the role of women.

J. Edgar Hoover died on May 5, 1972. Hubert Humphrey, again a senator from Minnesota, succumbed to cancer on January 13, 1978. Richard Burton, long divorced from Elizabeth Taylor, died in 1984; Andy Warhol died in 1987; and Timothy Leary, after days of characteristic self-promotion, died on May 31, 1996. Nelson A. Rockefeller, in the company of a young woman, died of a heart attack on January 26, 1979, and Barry Goldwater lived until May 29, 1998.

After four years of preparation, George Wallace was able to do in 1968 what he could not improvise quickly enough in 1964, and he ran an independent presidential candidacy, for a while attracting support from more than a quarter of the electorate in public opinion polls. On Election Day, though, he got but 13 percent, most of it in the South.

Four years later he tried again, running in the Democratic primaries this time, and while campaigning in Maryland he was shot and seriously wounded. He lived the rest of his life in pain and paralysis, but his political career did not end. He was elected governor of Alabama again, this time with the support of most of the state's black citizens, to whom Wallace apologized for his segregationist past. He died in 1998.

In 1968, just a few days before Martin Luther King was killed, Lyndon Johnson did what he had threatened to do four years earlier. Challenged by both Kennedy and Eugene McCarthy because of the Vietnam War, he announced that he would not accept his party's presidential nomination. He sat through Richard Nixon's inauguration as his successor, then went back to Texas.

Four years later, Nixon was inaugurated for his second term. The next day, on January 21, 1973, a Vietnam cease-fire was announced, and Nixon declared that he would take new steps to dismantle the Great Society.

The following afternoon, Lyndon Johnson died at his ranch.

NOTES

Complete bibliographic information can be found in the Bibliography.

All of President Johnson's telephone conversations are taken from the tapes at the Lyndon Johnson Presidential Library in Austin, Texas. I listened to all the conversations I used in the book, but in some cases I did check my transcriptions against those in Michael Beschloss's *Taking Charge*.

Chapter 1
Not Entirely Legitimate

1. William Manchester, *The Death of a President,* pp. 452–455. Also Arthur Schlesinger, *Robert Kennedy and His Times,* pp. 626–627. Also RFK Oral History, p. 316, John F. Kennedy Presidential Library (hereafter cited as JFK Library).
2. RFK Oral History, interview with Arthur Schlesinger, February 27, 1965, pp. 42–43, JFK Library.
3. Doris Kearns Goodwin, *Lyndon Johnson and the American Dream,* p. 176.
4. Merle Miller, *Lyndon: An Oral Biography,* p. 347.
5. Manchester, pp. 451–453.
6. Lady Bird Johnson, *A White House Diary,* p. 8.
7. Bradley Greenberg, ed., *The Kennedy Assassination and the American Public: Social Communication in Crisis,* pp. 153–166.
8. Harold Banks, "Some Cared Only a Bit," *Boston Record American,* November 26, 1963, p. 29.
9. Christopher H. Sterling, *Stay Tuned: A Concise History of American Broadcasting,* p. 409.
10. Anthony La Camera, "Emotions Get Terrific Test," *Boston Record American,* November 25, 1963, p. 15.
11. Carl Solberg, *Hubert Humphrey: A Biography,* p. 240.
12. Interview with Robert Goldwater.

13. Jay Stevens, *Storming Heaven*, p. 205.
14. Timothy Leary, *Flashbacks*, p. 192.
15. Andy Warhol, *POPism: The Warhol 60s*, pp. 55–58.
16. Interview with Jack Weinberg.

Chapter 2
"Let Us Continue"

1. Social Protest Collection, Bancroft Library, Berkeley, California, Carton 1, Folder 28.
2. Interview with William Rusher.
3. Loren Baritz, *Backfire*, p. 120.
4. RFK Oral History, p. 425, JFK Library.
5. *Time*, December 9, 1963, p. 19.
6. *Newsweek*, December 23, 1963, p. 23.
7. RFK Oral History, pp. 311–312, JFK Library.
8. Arthur Schlesinger, Jr., *Robert Kennedy and His Times*, pp. 606–607.

Chapter 3
Fathers and Sons

1. David Belin, *Final Disclosure*, p. 13.
2. LBJ tapes in Michael Beschloss, *Taking Charge*, pp. 59–61.
3. *Newsweek*, February 10, 1964, p. 77.
4. RFK Oral History, p. 316, JFK Library.
5. Martin Lee and Bruce Shlain, *Acid Dreams*, p. 97.
6. *Commentary*, January 1964, p. 24.
7. Cartha DeLoach, *Hoover's FBI*, pp. 378–379.
8. *Life*, December 6, 1963.

Chapter 4
Conservation

1. David Cort, "The Cities Downstream," *The Nation*, January 17, 1964, p. 97.
2. Interview with Robert Odle, Washington, DC, May 1997.
3. DeLoach, p. 380.
4. Kenneth O'Reilly, *Racial Matters*, p. 142.

Chapter 5
Happy New Year

1. *New York Times*, January 1, 1964, p. 18.
2. *Time*, January 10, 1964, p. 37.

3. Letter from Richard Flacks, Social Protest Collection, Bancroft Library, Berkeley, California, Box 16.
4. Todd Gitlin, *The Sixties,* p. 198.
5. James Miller, *Democracy Is in the Streets,* pp. 190ff.
6. Ibid.
7. Interview with Robert Goldwater.
8. Robert Alan Goldberg, *Barry Goldwater,* p. 39.
9. Joseph L. Schott, *No Left Turns,* pp. 204–205.

Chapter 6
The Business of America

1. David Farber, *The Age of Great Dreams: America in the Sixties,* p. 120.
2. *Encyclopedia Americana Yearbook, 1965,* p. 270.
3. *Look,* January 14, 1964, p. 120.
4. Eileen Shanahan, "Factory Wage $2.50 an Hour in December," *New York Times* News Service, in *Boston Sunday Herald,* January 19, 1964, p. 22.
5. White House Tapes WH6401.21, LBJ Library.
6. *Look,* January 14, 1964, p. 22.
7. *New York Times,* January 4, 1964, p. 47.
8. David J. Garrow, *Bearing the Cross,* p. 312.

Chapter 7
Rot in the Structure

1. Interview with George Wilson, October 24, 1997.
2. J. D. Harts, "The Creation of an American Political Movement: The Draft Goldwater Committee, 1960–1964" (master's thesis, Villanova University, 1995), pp. 40ff.
3. William Rusher, *The Rise of the Right,* p. 91.
4. William Vanden Heuvel and Milton Gwirtzman, *On His Own: RFK 1964–1968,* p. 13.
5. Hubert Humphrey, *Education of a Public Man,* p. 221.
6. Doris Kearns Goodwin, p. 101.

Chapter 8
Sober, Responsible Men

1. Joseph Persico, *The Imperial Rockefeller,* p. 26.
2. Ibid., pp. 27ff.
3. James Baughman, *The Republic of Mass Culture,* p. 100.
4. *Encyclopedia Americana Yearbook, 1965,* p. 78.
5. Baughman, p. 107.

6. Edward Jay Epstein, *Inquest,* p. 34.
7. Stanley Karnow, *Vietnam: A History,* p. 324.

Chapter 9
One Good War Deserves Another

1. Baritz, p. 123.
2. Ibid., pp. 123ff.
3. *Life,* May 29, 1964, p. 29.
4. Doris Kearns Goodwin, p. 197.
5. *Newsweek,* February 10, 1964, p. 27.
6. *Newsweek,* February 17, 1964, p. 19.
7. *Newsweek,* December 2, 1963, p. 92.
8. "Gift to the Utilities," editorial, *New York Times,* February 4, 1964, p. 32.
9. Interior Department Solicitor memorandum, March 3, 1964.
10. Interview with Mike Mansfield, March 12, 1998.

Chapter 10
A Civil War

1. Doris Kearns Goodwin, pp. 132–133.
2. Interview with Nicholas Katzenbach, February 15, 1998.
3. Schlesinger, pp. 651–652.
4. William Chafe, *The Unfinished Journey: America Since World War II,* p. 238.
5. Harris Wofford, *Of Kennedys and Kings,* p. 295.

Chapter 11
Invasions North and South

1. Curtis Wilkie, "Files to Show FBI as Civil Rights Foe," *Boston Globe,* July 30, 1997, p. A4.
2. Humphrey, pp. 216–217.
3. Walter Lippmann column, "Today and Tomorrow," March 17, 1964.
4. Commerce Department press release, April 1, 1964.
5. *Newsweek,* February 24, 1964, p. 58; March 3, 1964, p. 25.

Chapter 12
Local Politics

1. Charles Brereton, *First in the Nation,* p. 86.
2. Hilsman, in Jean Stein, *American Journey,* p. 204.
3. Michael Forrestal, in Stein, pp. 205–207.

4. Theodore S. White, *The Making of the President,* p. 132.
5. Letter to Kleindienst from Stephen Shadegg, March 3, 1964, Ashbrook Center Files, Ashland University, Box 26.
6. Richard Hansen, "Civil Rightists Close San Francisco Hotels," Associated Press story, in *New Hampshire Sunday News,* March 8, 1964.

Chapter 13
A Matter of Choice

1. Interview with Edward Zahniser.
2. Donald Spoto, *A Passion for Life,* pp. 213–214.
3. Merle Miller, pp. 374–375.

Chapter 14
Democratic Societies

1. Interview with Todd Gitlin.
2. Thomas A. Brooks, *Walls Come Tumbling Down,* pp. 242–243.

Chapter 15
Uprisings

1. *Statistical Abstract of the United States 1996,* p. 336, tables 471 and 472.
2. *Time,* June 10, 1964, p. 62.
3. *New York Times,* April 17, 1964, p. 25.
4. John Kenneth Galbraith, *The New Industrial State,* p. 11.
5. Frank N. Magill, ed., *Great Events From History II,* pp. 1224ff. Also interview with Thomas Kurtz, April 1, 1998.
6. *New York Times,* April 17, 1964, p. 25.
7. Farber, p. 21.
8. *Look,* March 10, 1964.
9. Thomas Hine, *Populuxe,* pp. 83–106.
10. *Newsweek,* February 17, 1964, p. 7.
11. *Time,* December 16, 1963, p. 63.
12. *World Almanac 1966,* p. 321.
13. Kleindienst memo to White, White Papers, Ashbrook Center Files, Ashland University, Box 26.
14. H. R. McMaster, *Dereliction of Duty,* p. 93.
15. RFK Oral History, pp. 639, 655ff, JFK Library.

Chapter 16
Middle-Class Life

1. Richard Schickel, *The Disney Version*, p. 335.
2. Len Holt, *The Summer That Didn't End*, p. 157.
3. Hugh Sidey, *A Very Personal President*, p. 56.
4. Douglas Cater, in *The Johnson Years*, ed. Robert A. Divine, pp. 21–22.

Chapter 17
A Great Society

1. Theodore S. White, p. 387.
2. Lewis Gould, *Lady Bird Johnson and the Environment*, p. 23.
3. Humphrey, p. 213.
4. Solberg, p. 226.
5. F. Clifton White, *Suite 3505*, p. 98.
6. Dan T. Carter, *The Politics of Rage*, p. 218.
7. Gerald Ford, *A Time to Heal*, p. 75.
8. *New York Times*, August 28, 1964, p. 38.
9. *Time*, July 19, 1964, p. 13.

Chapter 18
Our Freedom Year

1. Edward L. Schapsmeier, *Dirksen of Illinois*, p. 240.
2. *Time*, July 10, 1964, p. 20.
3. Lady Bird Johnson, pp. 166–167.

Chapter 19
A Simple Case of Murder

1. Doyle Barnette confession in FBI Mississippi Burning file, quoted in Seth Cagin and Philip Dray, *We Are Not Afraid*, p. 295.
2. James Jordan confession in FBI Mississippi Burning file, quoted in Cagin and Dray, p. 295.

Chapter 20
The Comedy Continues

1. Schlesinger, p. 637. Also RFK Oral History, Adam Walinsky interview, November 29, 1969, p. 31, JFK Library. Also Stein, pp. 277–278.

2. Robert Adelman, *The Art of Roy Lichtenstein,* p. 20.
3. Arthur Danto, "The Artworld," *Journal of Philosophy* 61, no. 19 (October 1964), pp. 571–584.
4. *Newsweek,* April 6, 1964, p. 52.
5. Rita Lang Kleinfelder, *When We Were Young,* p. 377.
6. Barry Goldwater on *NET Journal:* "That Was the Election That Was," September 18, 1967.
7. Theodore S. White, pp. 222–223.

Chapter 21
Security and Its Discontents

1. Thomas R. Brooks, p. 238.
2. *New York Times,* July 20, 1964.
3. F. Richard Ciccone, *Daley: Power and Presidential Politics,* pp. 182–183.
4. Thomas R. Brooks, p. 241.
5. Ed Guthman, *We Band of Brothers,* p. 280.
6. Lyndon B. Johnson, *The Vantage Point,* p. 576.
7. Interview with Robert Wolf.

Chapter 22
Another Sting

1. Haynes Johnson and Bernard Gwertzman, *Fulbright,* p. 195.
2. Interview with Gaylord Nelson.
3. Interview with Adam Yarmolinsky.
4. Interview with the Reverend Ed King.

Chapter 23
Breakdowns

1. Kenneth O'Reilly, *Racial Matters,* p. 178.
2. Sara Evans, *Personal Politics,* p. 80.

Chapter 24
Recovery

1. DeLoach, p. 10.
2. Garrow, p. 352.

Chapter 25
The Young and the Restless

1. Taylor Branch, *Pillar of Fire,* p. 578.
2. Evans, pp. 83–87. Also interview with Mary King.

Chapter 26
Victory and Other Defeats

1. Codebook of the American National Election Study of 1964. I am indebted to Professor Bill Mayer of Northeastern University for providing me with this document.

BIBLIOGRAPHY

Adelman, Robert. *The Art of Roy Lichtenstein: Mural with Brushstroke.* New York, Arcade, 1987.

Bailey, Beth. *From Front Porch to Back Seat: Courtship in Twentieth Century America.* Baltimore: Johns Hopkins University Press, 1989.

Baritz, Loren. *Backfire.* New York: Ballantine Books, 1985.

Baughman, James. *The Republic of Mass Culture.* Baltimore: Johns Hopkins University Press, 1970.

Belin, David. *Final Disclosure.* New York: Scribner, 1988.

Bernstein, Irving. *Promises Kept: John F. Kennedy's New Frontier.* New York: Oxford University Press, 1991.

Beschloss, Michael R. *Taking Charge: The Johnson White House Tapes, 1963–64.* New York: Simon & Schuster, 1997.

Blum, John Morton. *Years of Discord: American Politics and Society, 1961–1974.* New York: W. W. Norton, 1991.

Branch, Taylor. *Pillar of Fire: America in the King Years, 1963–65.* New York: Simon & Schuster, 1998.

Brereton, Charles. *First in the Nation.* Portsmouth, NH: Peter E. Randall, 1987.

Brooks, Thomas R. *Walls Come Tumbling Down: A History of the Civil Rights Movement, 1940–1970.* Englewood Cliffs, NJ: Prentice-Hall, 1974.

Brooks, Tim, and Earle March. *The Complete Directory to Prime Time Television Shows.* New York: Ballantine Books, 1988.

Cagin, Seth, and Philip Dray. *We Are Not Afraid.* New York: Macmillan, 1988.

Carter, Dan T. *The Politics of Rage: George Wallace, the Origins of the New Conservatism, and the Transformation of American Politics.* New York: Simon & Schuster, 1995.

Cepican, Robert. *Yesterday Came Suddenly.* New York: Arbor House, 1985.

Chafe, William. *The Unfinished Journey: America Since World War II.* New York: Oxford University Press, 1986.

Ciccone, F. Richard. *Daley: Power and Presidential Politics.* Chicago: Contemporary Books, 1996.

Cramer, Richard Ben. *What It Takes: The Way to the White House.* New York: Random House, 1992.

Danto, Arthur. *After the End of Art: Contemporary Art and the Pale of History*. Princeton, NJ: Princeton University Press, 1997.

DeLoach, Cartha. *Hoover's FBI*. Washington, DC: Regnery, 1995.

Divine, Robert A., ed. *The Johnson Years*. Lawrence, KS: University of Kansas Press, 1987.

Draper, Theodore. *Abuse of Power*. New York: Viking Press, 1966.

Dyke, Richard W., and Francis X. Gannon. *Chet Holifield: Master Legislator and Nuclear Statesman*. Lanham, MD: University Press of America, 1995.

Edwards, Lee. *Goldwater: The Man Who Made a Revolution*. Washington, DC: Regnery, 1995.

Epstein, Edward Jay. *Inquest: The Warren Commission and the Establishment of Truth*. New York: Viking Press, 1966.

Evans, Sara. *Personal Politics: The Roots of Women's Liberation in the Civil Rights Movement and the New Left*. New York: Knopf, 1979.

Farber, David. *The Age of Great Dreams: America in the Sixties*. New York: Hill & Wang, 1994.

Ford, Gerald. *A Time to Heal*. New York: Harper & Row, 1979.

Galbraith, John Kenneth. *The New Industrial State*. Boston: Houghton Mifflin, 1967.

Garrow, David J. *Bearing the Cross: Martin Luther King and the Southern Christian Leadership Conference*. New York: William Morrow, 1986.

Gibbons, William Conrad. *The US Government and the Vietnam War: Executive and Legislative Roles and Relationships*. Washington, DC: U.S. Government Printing Office, 1984.

Gitlin, Todd. *The Sixties: Years of Hope, Days of Rage*. New York: Bantam Books, 1987.

Goldberg, Robert Alan. *Barry Goldwater*. New Haven, CT: Yale University Press, 1995.

Goodwin, Doris Kearns. *Lyndon Johnson and the American Dream*. New York: Harper & Row, 1976.

Goodwin, Richard. *Remembering America*. Boston: Little, Brown, 1988.

Gould, Lewis. *Lady Bird Johnson and the Environment*. Lawrence, KS: University of Kansas Press, 1988.

Greenberg, Bradley, ed. *The Kennedy Assassination and the American Public: Social Communication in Crisis*. Stanford, CA: Stanford University Press, 1965.

Guthman, Ed. *We Band of Brothers*. New York: Harper & Row, 1971.

Hackett, Pat. *The Andy Warhol Diaries*. New York: Warner Books, 1991.

Hayden, Tom. *Reunion: A Memoir*. New York: Random House, 1988.

Heirich, Max. *The Beginning—Berkeley 1964*. New York: Columbia University Press, 1971.

Heymann, C. David. *A Woman Named Jackie*. Secaucus, NJ: Lyle Stuart, 1989.

Hine, Thomas. *Populuxe: The Look and Life of America in the 50s and 60s*. New York: Knopf, 1986.

Hirt, Paul. *Conspiracy of Optimism*. Lincoln, NB: University of Nebraska Press, 1994.

Holt, Len. *The Summer That Didn't End*. New York: William Morrow, 1965.

Humphrey, Hubert. *Education of a Public Man: My Life and Politics*. New York: Doubleday, 1976.

Johnson, Haynes, and Bernard Gwertzman. *Fulbright: The Dissenter*. New York: Doubleday, 1968.

Johnson, Lady Bird. *A White House Diary*. New York: Holt, Rinehart & Winston, 1970.

Johnson, Lyndon B. *The Vantage Point: Perspectives on the Presidency, 1963–1969*. New York: Holt, Rinehart & Winston, 1971.

Karnow, Stanley. *Vietnam: A History*. Rev. ed. New York: Penguin Books, 1997.

Katz, William Loren. *The Great Society to the Reagan Era*. Madison, NJ: Raintree/Steck Vaughn, 1993.

Kessel, John. *The Goldwater Coalition*. New York: Bobbs-Merrill, 1968.

King, Mary. *Freedom Song*. New York: William Morrow, 1987.

Kleinfelder, Rita Lang. *When We Were Young: A Baby Boomer Yearbook*. Englewood Cliffs, NJ: Prentice-Hall, 1993.

Leary, Timothy. *Flashbacks*. Los Angeles: Tarcher, 1983.

Lebergott, Stanley. *The American Economy*. Princeton, NJ: Princeton University Press, 1976.

Lee, Martin, and Bruce Shlain. *Acid Dreams*. New York: Grove Press, 1986.

Magill, Frank N., ed. *Great Events from History II: Business and Commerce Series*. Englewood Cliffs, NJ: Salem Press, 1994.

Manchester, William. *The Death of a President*. New York: Arbor House, 1967.

Mars, Florence. *Witness in Philadelphia*. Baton Rouge: Louisiana State University Press, 1989.

McMaster, H. R. *Dereliction of Duty*. New York: HarperCollins, 1997.

McQuaid, Kim. *Big Business and Presidential Power from FDR to Reagan*. New York, William Morrow, 1982.

———. *Uneasy Partners: Big Business in American Politics*. Baltimore: John Hopkins University Press, 1994.

Miller, James. *Democracy Is in the Streets*. New York: Simon & Schuster, 1987.

Miller, Merle. *Lyndon: An Oral Biography*. New York: Putnam, 1980.

Nite, Norm. *Rock On: The Illustrated Encyclopedia of Rock 'n' Roll*. New York: Harper & Row, 1982.

Noble, David F. *America by Design: Science, Technology, and the Rise of Corporate Capitalism*. New York: Knopf, 1977.

O'Grady, Terence. *The Beatles: A Musical Evolution*. Boston: Twayne, 1983.

O'Reilly, Kenneth. *Black Americans: The FBI Files*. New York: Carroll & Graf, 1994.

———. *Racial Matters: The FBI's Secret File on Black America 1960–72*. New York: Free Press, 1989.

Persico, Joseph. *The Imperial Rockefeller*. New York: Simon & Schuster, 1982.

Raines, Howell. *My Soul Is Rested*. New York: Putnam, 1977.

Reisner, Marc P. *Cadillac Desert: The American West and Its Disappearing Water*. New York: Penguin Books, 1993.

Rorabaugh, W. J. *Berkeley at War*. New York: Oxford University Press, 1989.

Rusher, William. *The Rise of the Right*. New York: William Morrow, 1984.

Schapsmeier, Edward L. *Everett L. Dirksen of Illinois: Senatorial Statesman*. Urbana: University of Illinois Press, 1985.

Schickel, Richard. *The Disney Version*. New York: Simon & Schuster, 1967.

Schlesinger, Arthur M., Jr. *Robert Kennedy and His Times*. Boston: Houghton Mifflin, 1978.

Schott, Joseph L. *No Left Turns.* New York: Praeger, 1975.

Sidey, Hugh. *A Very Personal President: Lyndon Johnson in the White House.* New York: Atheneum, 1968.

Smith, Richard Candida. *Utopia and Dissent: Art, Poetry, and Politics in California.* Berkeley: University of California Press, 1995.

Solberg, Carl. *Hubert Humphrey: A Biography.* New York: Norton, 1984.

Spoto, Donald. *A Passion for Life.* New York: HarperCollins, 1995.

Statistical Abstract of the United States 1966, 87th edition. Washington, DC: U.S. Commerce Department, 1966.

Stein, Jean. *American Journey: The Times of Robert F. Kennedy*, ed. George Plimpton. New York: Harcourt, Brace Jovanovich, 1970.

Sterling, Christopher. *Stay Tuned: A Concise History of American Broadcasting.* Belmont, CA: Wadsworth, 1978.

Stevens, Jay. *Storming Heaven.* New York: Atlantic Monthly Press, 1987.

Stockdale, James B. *A Vietnam Experience: Ten Years of Reflection.* Stanford, CA: Hoover Institution, 1984.

Stone, I. F. *In Time of Torment, 1961–1967: A Nonconformist History of Our Time.* New York: Random House, 1967.

Vanden Heuvel, William, and Milton Gwirtzman. *On His Own: RFK 1964–1968.* New York: Doubleday, 1970.

Warhol, Andy. *POPism: The Warhol 60s*, ed. Pat Hackett. New York: Harcourt Brace Jovanovich, 1980.

Welles, Christopher. *The Elusive Bonanza.* New York: Dutton, 1970.

White, F. Clifton, with William Gill. *Suite 3505.* New Rochelle, NY: Arlington House, 1967.

White, Theodore S. *The Making of the President, 1964.* New York: Atheneum, 1965.

Wiley, Peter, and Robert Gottlieb. *Empires in the Sun: The Rise of the New American West.* Tucson: University of Arizona Press, 1982.

Wofford, Harris. *Of Kennedys and Kings: Making Sense of the Sixties.* Pittsburgh: University of Pittsburgh Press, 1992.

Wollin, Sheldon S., and John H. Schaar. *The Berkeley Rebellion and Beyond: Essays on Politics and Education in the Technological Society.* New York: Vintage Books, 1970.

World Almanac 1966. New York: World-Telegram and Sun, 1966.

INDEX